Crucibles of Political Loyalty

This book investigates one of the oldest paradoxes in political science: why do mass political loyalties persist even amid prolonged social upheaval and disruptive economic development? Drawing on extensive archival research and an original database of election results, it explores the paradox of political persistence by examining Hungary's often tortuous path from pre- to postcommunism. Wittenberg reframes the theoretical debate and demonstrates how, despite the many depredations of Communism, the Roman Catholic and Calvinist Churches transmitted loyalties to parties of the Right. Contrary to conventional wisdom, Church resistance occurred not from above, but from below. Hemmed in and harassed by Communist Party cadres, parish priests and pastors employed a variety of ingenious tactics to ensure the continued survival of local church institutions. These institutions insulated their adherents from pressure to assimilate into the surrounding socialist milieu. Ultimately this led to political continuity between pre- and postcommunism.

Jason Wittenberg is assistant professor of political science at the University of California, Berkeley. He has published articles in the *American Journal of Political Science, Organization Science, Political Analysis, Slavic Review*, and the *System Dynamics Review*.

Cambridge Studies in Comparative Politics

General Editor
Margaret Levi   *University of Washington, Seattle*

Assistant General Editor
Stephen Hanson   *University of Washington, Seattle*

Associate Editors
Robert H. Bates   *Harvard University*
Peter Hall   *Harvard University*
Peter Lange   *Duke University*
Helen Milner   *Columbia University*
Frances Rosenbluth   *Yale University*
Susan Stokes   *University of Chicago*
Sidney Tarrow   *Cornell University*

Other Books in the Series

Continued after the Index

Dedicated to the memory of my grandmother Elsa,
and of her sisters Rose and Florence,
whose tales of Hungary inspired me.

Hiányoztok!

Crucibles of Political Loyalty

CHURCH INSTITUTIONS AND ELECTORAL CONTINUITY IN HUNGARY

JASON WITTENBERG

University of California, Berkeley

CAMBRIDGE
UNIVERSITY PRESS

CAMBRIDGE UNIVERSITY PRESS
Cambridge, New York, Melbourne, Madrid, Cape Town, Singapore, São Paulo

Cambridge University Press
40 West 20th Street, New York, NY 10011-4211, USA

www.cambridge.org
Information on this title: www.cambridge.org/9780521849128

First published 2006

Printed in the United States of America

A catalog record for this publication is available from the British Library.

Library of Congress Cataloging in Publication Data

Wittenberg, Jason, 1963–
Crucibles of political loyalty : church institutions and electoral continuity in Hungary /
Jason Wittenberg.
    p.   cm. – (Cambridge studies in comparative politics)
Includes bibliographical references and index.
ISBN 0-521-84912-8 (alk. paper)
1. Hungary – Church history – 20th century.   2. Church and state – Hungary –
History – 20th century.   3. Elections – Hungary – 20th century.
I. Title: Church institutions and electoral continuity in Hungary.
II. Title.   III. Series.
BR869.52.W58   2006
322′.1′094390904–dc22   2005051321

ISBN-13   978-0-521-84912-8 hardback
ISBN-10   0-521-84912-8 hardback

Contents

Contents

List of Figures

List of Tables

Acknowledgments

I have incurred many debts in the course of this project. I thank the Program for the Study of Germany and Europe, Harvard University; the International Research and Exchanges Board; the Harvard Academy for International and Area Studies, Harvard University; and the University of Wisconsin, Madison, for funds that made fieldwork possible. For assistance with research in Hungary I am grateful to the staffs of the Institute of Political History, the Central Statistical Office, the Hajdú-Bihar County Archive, the Szabolcs-Szatmár-Bereg County Archive, the Veszprém County Archive, the Zala County Archive, the Veszprém Episcopal Archive, the Reformed Church Archive in Debrecen, and the Hungarian National Archive. I am especially indebted to Gyula Benda, László Hubai, and Imre Kapiller for their kindness and assistance over the years.

Generous fellowships from the Helen Kellogg Institute for International Studies, University of Notre Dame, and the Harvard Academy for International and Area Studies, Harvard University, afforded me uninterrupted time to think and write. Living away from home is never easy. I am grateful to Ili Földényi, Cicó and Hédi Volosin, Roy "Boober" and William Howell, and Marcy and Sally Phillips for providing much needed hospitality and distractions during these periods.

Valerie Bunce, Kathie Hendley, David Laitin, Margaret Levi, Roger Petersen, and Anna Seleny deserve special thanks for critical readings of drafts of the entire manuscript. I received welcome feedback on different chapters from Jim Alt, Mark Beissinger, Barry Burden, Kanchan Chandra, Ellen Commisso, Charles Franklin, John Giles, Kenneth Goldstein, Michael Hechter, Jeff Kopstein, Melanie Manion, Eileen McDonagh, Mark Pollack, Ken Scheve, David Weimer, the participants in the Laboratory in Comparative Ethnic Processes, and seminars at the Central

European University, the Miami University of Ohio, the University of Pennsylvania, and the University of Washington. I also benefited from many conversations with Eileen McDonagh, Jon Pevehouse, Michael Schatzberg, Joe Soss, Katherine Cramer Walsh, and David Weimer. For able research assistance I thank Colin Stouffer Belby, Sandra Borda, Jennifer Brick, Alice Kang, Jeremy Menchik, James Menz, Zsuzsanna Nagy, Mark Schrad, Rajen Subramanian, and Laure "Voop" de Vulpillieres.

Finally, I thank Grzegorz Ekiert, Jim Snyder, and especially Suzanne Berger for their astute guidance of the dissertation from which this book originated.

Introduction

The Paradox of Political Persistence

One of the oldest paradoxes in the study of politics is why mass political loyalties persist long after the circumstances around which they arose have disappeared. This paradox has emerged in a variety of different forms across a wide range of countries and time periods, and has puzzled not just political scientists, but historians, sociologists, anthropologists, and many other observers of political life. Indeed, despite nearly a century of empirical research and theoretical development, we still do not fully understand why certain regions exhibit remarkable political stability even through dramatic and prolonged social upheaval. This book will show how to recognize, analyze, and explain political continuity by examining some particularly puzzling instances of it.

Perhaps the most remarkable example of persistence has occurred in France, where, at least since Siegfried (1913), scholars have attempted to decode the extraordinary longevity of political divisions that originated in much earlier periods of history. The French Revolution gave birth to our modern notions of "Left" and "Right" in politics, and these labels have continued to define French politics ever since. Since at least the middle of the nineteenth century, for example, large swathes of western France have consistently supported the Right, while parts of Mediterranean France have supported the Left.[1] This has remained true even through changes in political regime, wars, in- and out-migration, disruptive economic development, and dramatic organizational discontinuity in the political parties that have represented both the Left and the Right. As one analyst noted, decades

---

[1] Brustein (1988).

ago: "[P]olitical regimes follow one another, interrupted by revolutions or *coups d'état*: monarchy by divine right, revolutionary republic, charismatic empire, constitutional monarchy, liberal monarchy, presidential republic, plebiscitary empire, parliamentary republic, military occupation, multiparty republic, charismatic republic. But, in their passing, they leave layers of opinion, analogous to geological sediments. In the year 2000, there will still be Gaullists, as there were Orleanists, Legitimists, and Bonapartists in the 1880's."[2]

Others trace the Left–Right divide back to the French Revolution, which created two political camps. On one side stood the allies of the new antimonarchical, anticlerical republic, whose political descendants would later evince leftist loyalties. On the other side remained the supporters of the prerevolutionary order, whose descendants would eventually gravitate toward the Right. Indeed, there is an amazing similarity between the geographical distribution of Left–Right support in the legislative elections of 1981 and the results of assembly elections in the 1790s, just after the revolution. After nearly two centuries, "the division between a conservative north and a much more radical south seems almost 'traditional'."[3] For some, the roots of contemporary French cleavages stretch back even further into the past. Siegfried (1949: 57) ascribes political differences between French Catholics and Protestants to the Roman period: "If one realizes that the present area of Protestantism coincides with the old diocesan boundaries, themselves traced from the Roman *civitates* and the Gallic *pagi*, one cannot help feeling awed by the persistence of the millenary influence."[4]

The paradox also extends to the United States. For decades the Democratic Party's strength and later demise in the "Solid South" has been a central theme in the study of American politics. Key (1949: 76–7), for example, provides dramatic evidence of an "extraordinary durability of voting habits fixed by war and reconstruction" in his analysis of the evolution of voting behavior in Tennessee between 1861 and 1944. There is a remarkably high correlation across counties between the vote for or against seceding from the Union in 1861 and the presidential vote in 1944. Almost all antisecession counties continued to favor the Republican Party eighty-three years later. According to Key (1949: 79), "[T]he greenest carpetbagger, provided he had the Republican nomination, could win." The former slave-holding

[2] Dogan (1967: 182–3).
[3] Hunt (1984: 133).
[4] Cited in Dogan (1967: 183).

counties, on the other hand, still preferred the Democrats. Why is it that so many Southern Whites could not bring themselves to vote for the party of Abraham Lincoln nearly a century after the end of the Civil War?

The "standing decision by the community" for a particular political party extends beyond the Confederacy, though it may involve the remnants of confederate attitudes. Key and Munger (1959: 287) note for Indiana in the latter part of the nineteenth century "the long persistence of county patterns of party affiliation despite changes in 'interest' and the disappearance of issues that created the pattern." For them this persistence in party division, with Democrats in the southern counties and Republicans in the North, is a consequence of "a crystallization of attitudes at the time of the Civil War."[5] According to Levine (1976) a similar standing decision existed in Maryland between 1872 and 1924. There a "post-war 'political confessionalism' grew out of the Civil War loyalties and the regional-cultural differences they represented."[6] Maryland became split into stable Republican and Democratic bastions, each reinforced through energetic party competition. These areas of persistence would dissolve only as technological developments "destroyed the separateness and parochialism of the economic, social, and ideological life in the grass roots community."[7]

In Western Europe persistence is manifest in different ways. At the level of national party systems, its most famous expression comes in the form of Lipset and Rokkan's (1967: 50) "freezing hypothesis," which states that "the party systems of the 1960's reflect, with few but significant exceptions, the cleavage structures of the 1920's." Despite the Second World War, postwar prosperity, and the subsequent emergence of a bevy of new political issues, not just the same basic political tendencies (such as the Left and the Right) lived on, but in many cases the same party organizations. As Lipset and Rokkan (ibid.) note, many of these parties "are older than the majorities of the national electorates." The freezing hypothesis has spawned dozens if not hundreds of efforts to locate persistence and volatility in different European systems.[8]

The paradox is not limited merely to the structure of political cleavages. As in France and the United States, various Western European countries

---

[5] Key and Munger (1959: 283). More recent political continuities in Indiana are explored in Shaffer and Caputo (1972).

[6] Levine (1976: 301).

[7] Hays (1967: 158). Cited in Levine (1976: 324).

[8] The best of these is Bartolini and Mair (1990), which also includes an extensive review of the literature.

exhibited astonishing persistence in mass attachments to particular political groupings. For example, despite considerable economic development and frequent instability in support for individual parties, there has been persistent postwar support for leftist and confessional parties in Austria, Denmark, and the Netherlands.[9] In the Federal Republic of Germany the Social Democratic Party maintained a stable postwar electoral base, even as its constituents became increasingly affluent and socially mobile.[10] The same has been true for Sweden.[11] In Italy, rapid postwar modernization did not prevent both leftist and Christian democratic parties from enjoying decades of steady political support.[12]

Such continuity extends well beyond the stable, established democratic systems of Western Europe and North America. Even more surprisingly, it has also been observed in nations that have undergone redemocratization after a period of disruptive authoritarian rule, such as Austria after Naziism and war, post-Mussolini Italy, and post-Franco Spain.[13] Spain provides a fascinating example. Four decades of Francoist dictatorship separated the last free preauthoritarian election in 1936 and the first postauthoritarian election in 1977. Yet despite such a lengthy absence of democratic politics, significant economic development, severe political repression, and extensive disruption in the leaderships and organizations of anti-Franco political movements, there nonetheless emerged striking regional continuities in patterns of electoral support. Linz (1980) reports a significant correlation across provinces between support for the conservative Spanish Confederation of the Autonomous Right (CEDA) in the 1936 election and for the Union of the Democratic Center in 1977. Both he and Maravall (1982) document even stronger continuities in loyalties to the Socialist Party (PSOE), which competed in both pre- and post-Franco elections. Remarkably, loyalties to the PSOE remained after four decades even as the party itself was ruthlessly suppressed and most of its preauthoritarian supporters had passed away.

The paradox has also been observed in redemocratizing Latin America and takes its most striking form in Chile.[14] Until the advent of the

---

[9] For Netherlands and Denmark, see Mair (1990). For Austria and the Netherlands, see Houska (1985).

[10] Hoschka and Schunck (1978).

[11] Heclo and Madsen (1987).

[12] Sani (1976).

[13] On Austria, see Cotta (1996); for Italy, Golden (1988) and Sivini (1967).

[14] For Colombia and Honduras, see Remmer (1985); for other countries, Geddes (1995).

Pinochet dictatorship in the early 1970s, Chile featured the most stable democracy in South America and was characterized by persistence in what has been termed the "logic of the three thirds." This refers to the division of Chilean politics into "Left," "Center," and "Right" tendencies, each of which claimed between 25 percent and 40 percent of the electorate in the decades prior to the democratic collapse in 1973.[15] Chile's military regime may not have lasted as long as Francoism, but democratic politics were, nonetheless, forcibly terminated: Political parties of all stripes were banned and many opposition leaders were imprisoned or forced to flee. As Valenzuela and Valenzuela (1986) document, the preauthoritarian parties, faced with extinction, clandestinely struggled to maintain their ideological and organizational vitality in Chilean society.

Yet despite the hardships of authoritarianism in Chile, the preauthoritarian political divisions proved highly resistant to change. Indeed, all three tendencies survived the dictatorship and, with some deviation, managed to recoup much of their former strengths. In the 1992 municipal elections, parties of the Right won 29.9 percent of the vote versus an average of 30.1 percent between 1937 and 1973. Center parties won 29.4 percent, down from an average of 39.7 percent in the pre-authoritarian period. Leftists received 29.6 percent, up from an average of 24.2 percent before the dictatorship. There was some change to be sure, but less than might be expected given that roughly half of the postauthoritarian Chilean electorate had never voted before.[16] Moreover, some continuities extend to the local level. For example, across communes there is a high correlation between a vote for the leftist Salvador Allende in the 1970 presidential election and a "no" vote in the 1988 plebiscite on whether Pinochet should continue to wield power. This pattern carried over into the 1989 presidential election.[17]

Perhaps most puzzling of all, political continuities have been observed in countries that have suffered war and decades of disruptive communist rule. Many of the symbolic continuities between pre- and postcommunism are well known. Cities, streets, and squares assumed their old names, parties with precommunist names were launched, and new political elites used every opportunity to emphasize a "return to history." Yet the signs of persistence are more substantial than the symbolic rejection of communism.

---

[15] Siavelis (1999).
[16] Valenzuela and Scully (1997: 517–19).
[17] Ibid.: 521–2.

Throughout much of postcommunist Eastern Europe regional patterns of support on both the Left and the Right resemble those from precommunist elections. For Poland, Kowalski and Śleszyński (2000: 79) reveal in maps the resilience of center–Right political support between 1922 and 1997 in the regions surrounding the towns of Białystok, Warsaw, Krakow, and Rzeszów. This is astounding because between these two elections Poland suffered a right-wing dictatorship, German and Soviet invasion, the loss of a significant proportion of its population in war, massive territorial revision, and four decades of communism. In the Czech Republic the regional base of the Communist Party's success in the 1990 and 1992 national parliamentary elections is similar to the areas where its preauthoritarian predecessor party scored gains during the interwar and immediate postwar periods.[18] In Slovakia, there are few continuities at the level of individual party organizations, yet current regional support for populist and nationalist parties bears an uncanny similarity to the regional vote patterns of the prewar Slovak People's Party.[19]

Political Continuity in Hungary

This book investigates the paradox of political persistence through an in-depth study of Hungary's path from democracy to communism and back to democracy during the twentieth century. Hungary is a fascinating and unlikely case.[20] The reemergence of revived precommunist parties in the heady early days of the transition and the victory of the Right in the first postcommunist national parliamentary election in 1990 provoked immediate comparisons with Hungary's precommunist history of support for right-wing parties. József Antall, the new prime minister, triumphantly declared: "After having gone through the last 45 years, the Hungarian people have cast votes more or less the same way. This means that after several decades of dictatorship, their historical and political reflexes are not different. We are still alive."[21] Szelenyi and Szelenyi (1991: 123) interpreted the election result in even more dramatic terms: "Astonishingly, as the curtain was raised, the audience was confronted with a still life: the 'act' that was interrupted 40 years ago with the transition to socialism seemed

---

[18] Jehlička, Kostelecký, and Sykora (1993) and Kostelecký (1994).

[19] Buerkle (2003), Kostelecký (2002: 81–3) and Krivý (1997, 2003a, 2003b).

[20] For prior efforts to uncover continuities, see András (1996), Körösényi (1991), Wiener (1997), and Wittenberg (1999).

[21] Cited in Kostelecký (2002: 84).

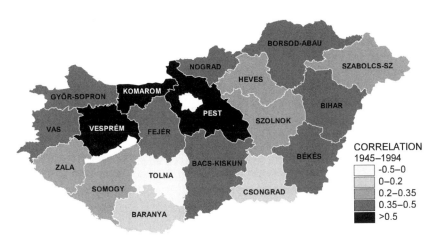

Figure I.1 Rightist Electoral Persistence in Hungary, 1945–1994

to have resumed, as if nothing had happened in between ... embedded in Hungarian political culture is a strong taste for Christian-national political rule."

Similarities between pre- and postcommunist politics are especially striking if we examine the 1994 election outcome in historical perspective. Figure I.1 displays a correlation map that compares the vote for right-wing parties in 1945 and 1994 across Hungarian settlements. The map is constructed by grouping settlements together according to which of Hungary's nineteen provinces ("counties") they currently belong, and then correlating, for each of those provinces, the right-wing vote share across municipalities in the two periods.[22] Each county is then shaded according to the magnitude of its correlation. Remarkably, the correlation between the votes exceeds 0.5 in three of Hungary's counties and is greater than 0.35 in eight more. To put this in perspective: In the United States, the most stable of democracies, the correlations across states between pairs of elections separated by an equal or lesser period sometimes dipped below 0.5.[23] The Hungarian correlations are huge in comparison with this figure.[24] Indeed,

[22] To do this it was necessary to construct geographic units that were constant between 1945 and 1994. I postpone discussion of this and other technical details until Chapter 2.

[23] Burnham (1968).

[24] That the U.S. correlations are computed using states as a unit makes the Hungarian result even more remarkable, because high levels of geographic aggregation tend to inflate correlation coefficients. I discuss this in more detail in Chapter 1.

someone who knew no history might gaze at the map and be amazed that Hungary endured a brutally repressive authoritarian regime between these two elections. Such a person would be flabbergasted to discover that in the interim state-socialism eviscerated the peasantry and created in its place an industrial working class; that it leveled gaping economic and social inequalities and broke the power of the bourgeoisie and the Churches; and that it implemented a vigorous program of reeducation and indoctrination in an attempt to create a "new socialist man."

Refining the Problem

Why should old patterns of political loyalties reemerge after such prolonged economic, social, and political disruption? How should such patterns be measured and by what means are they reproduced? These are the central questions for this book. They are certainly easier posed than answered. It is best to begin with a more precise definition of the outcome to be explained, as it is not possible to answer the "why" before I have established the "what." First, I focus on persistence in mass attachments rather than in political parties, party families, or party systems. Clearly, one cannot totally separate party elites from the masses who are their followers: parties (or party families) cannot survive without popular support. However, it is necessary to distinguish between the continuing existence of parties and the distribution of loyalties to them. What is most puzzling is not the longevity of the Democratic or Republican parties in the United States, but that they maintained stable constituencies for so long. Likewise, for redemocratizing regimes it is not the reemergence of the alternatives that is puzzling, but the uncanny similarities in their bases of support over time. Second, I use the continuing electoral preference for the same family of parties as an indicator of persistent mass partisan attachments. Some may quarrel with the equation of vote choice and partisan attachment given that voters are often motivated by factors other than partisan identification. However, in the case of the paradox of persistence, there is good cause to believe that vote choice does indicate a diffuse underlying partisanship.

First, even for U.S. politics, with its stable system of parties, *prolonged* persistence implies a partisan link. Bartels (1998: 306) expresses the conventional wisdom: "[T]o the extent that successive elections with different candidates, issues, and political conditions produce essentially similar voting patterns, it seems safe to infer that these patterns somehow reflect

8

the organizing force of partisanship."[25] This statement is even more germane for systems where there is volatility in individual party organizations. Indeed, this organizational volatility is part of what makes persistence so paradoxical and compels us to shift the locus of analysis from individual parties to party families. As Mair and Smith (1990: 179) note, "the greatest puzzle in understanding party system change is the need to explain how broader familial or bloc loyalties can persist *despite* the evident vulnerability of individual party organizations." Partisanship is thus even more resilient than individual political parties. Second, I focus exclusively on vote for parties on regional lists. According to Carey and Shugart (1995), closed list results are less apt to reflect personal reputations than the candidate-voting in single-member constituencies. This will further reduce any "candidate effects" contaminating the electoral results.

An added benefit of employing electoral behavior is empirical tractability. Long before the collapse of state-socialism, scholars noted the persistence of various precommunist political values within society. Paul (1985) and Skilling (1985), for example, identify "pluralism" as a continuing deeply held value in Communist Czechoslovakia. Schöpflin (1979) finds surviving "petit-bourgeois" and "peasant-traditional" mentalities in Hungary. Jowitt (1974) attempted to explain the continuing importance of bribery and "connections" in Communist Romania. There is a sizable literature on the continuities and discontinuities between Czarist and Communist political culture in the Soviet Union.[26] To begin studying continuity and discontinuity for a given value, belief, or behavior, one needs, at a minimum, directly comparable measures at two different points in time of the phenomenon of interest. While postcommunist political culture has been amply documented through surveys, we have no comparable data from the precommunist period. Indeed, one of the most trenchant criticisms of the literature on political culture under state-socialism is that it was based largely on impressionistic accounts of the political values within society.[27] Electoral results, by contrast, are available for both the pre- and postcommunist periods.

As a redemocratizing country, Hungary is an ideal place to study political continuity. First, the best-developed explanations of the phenomenon have focused largely on the open, democratic, stable, multiparty democracies in

---

[25] Bartels (1998).

[26] For a review, see Welch (1993).

[27] For an excellent review and critique of the methodological problems in studying political culture under communism, see McAuley (1985).

North America and Western Europe. As such, they rely on the existence of neatly archived electoral and survey data, regularly held free and fair multiparty elections, and freely operating civic and political institutions. Although great strides have been made in accounting for the startling electoral persistence observed in so many stable democratic states, such arguments fare poorly when the focus turns to countries where during the authoritarian period opposition parties were suppressed, elections were a sham, and civil society was either destroyed or co-opted by the regime. Yet, to understand the general roots of electoral persistence we should seek an explanation that can encompass the entire universe of cases, both stable democracies and redemocratizations. As we shall see, arguments developed for the stable democracies are either inapplicable to redemocratizing countries or, if they can be made applicable, are unlikely to be the principal source of persistence. Redemocratizing countries thus offer a means by which we can come to understand the sources of continuity in all countries that exhibit the phenomenon.

Second, there exists a smaller, less-developed set of explanations for continuity that has focused exclusively on (mostly right-wing) redemocratizing regimes. These accounts are tailored to accord with situations in which democracy is interrupted by a period of authoritarian rule. However, they suffer from a number of problems, including inadequate theorization of the links between the pre- and postauthoritarian periods and an overly aggregate level of analysis. Indeed, one of their central theoretical claims is that the less intrusive the authoritarian regime, the more likely there is to be partisan persistence between pre- and postauthoritarianism. Yet state-socialist countries endured an authoritarianism far more disruptive than that experienced by Chile, Spain, or, for that matter, any other country emerging from right-wing authoritarian rule, save perhaps Germany. Thus, if there should be discontinuity within redemocratizing regimes, it should be most visible in postcommunist countries, at least those that had experienced significant democratic politics before the communist period, such as in Czechoslovakia, Hungary, and Poland. The question of continuity cannot easily be posed for the former Soviet Union, where precommunist democratic politics were tenuous or nonexistent.

Finally, within redemocratizing Eastern Europe the peculiarities of Hungary render it an especially ironic case. Like the rest of the region, it suffered through the brutal imposition of Stalinist political rule, the painful reorganization of economy and society along socialist lines, and the repression of the Churches. As in Czechoslovakia and Poland, mass popular

10

uprisings were violently suppressed. But three features of Hungary make it the least likely place of all to find continuities. First, it entered communism less industrialized than Czechoslovakia. Well before the communists came to power, Czechoslovakia was by far the most industrialized country in Eastern Europe. In 1930 only 28 percent of its population engaged in agriculture, versus 51 percent in Hungary, 65 percent in Poland, and even higher in other countries.[28] This meant that the road to an industrialized socialist economy was less arduous for Czechoslovakia than for Hungary or Poland, where to a far greater extent industries had to be created *de novo*, with all the attendant social disruptions. This greater social disruption, particularly when it involved the proletarianization of the typically conservative rural peasantry, shrunk what after communism could have been a "natural" base of support for conservative parties, and increased the potential support for leftist and liberal parties.

Second, in contrast with Poland, Hungary was far more successful in reorganizing agriculture along socialist lines.[29] Agricultural collectivization was another strike at the precommunist Right's base of support among the small-holding strata. Socialized agriculture did not always produce leftist sympathies. Szelenyi (1988: 22) notes, for example, that some former small-holders returned "to old, familiar ways" when the opportunity arose once again to regain economic autonomy. But sometimes the shift to leftist sympathies appears striking: In 1945, rural Somogy county in southern Hungary was among the most rightward leaning counties, and gave roughly 80 percent of its vote to the Independent Smallholders Party; by 1994 it was the strongest supporter of the Hungarian Socialist Party.[30]

Finally, the Communist Party in Hungary enjoyed greater mass appeal than communist parties elsewhere in Eastern Europe. In contrast with Czechoslovakia, where but for a few years the Stalinists remained in control, or Poland, where repeated mass protests and the formation of the Solidarity trade union led ultimately to the introduction of martial law, in Hungary the Party came to follow a policy of relative accommodation with society in the years after the 1956 revolution. This led to the most humane regime in the communist world and earned Hungary the moniker

[28] Berend and Ránki (1974: 306). Cited in Janos (2000: 344).

[29] In 1970 12.7% of all farms in Poland were collective or state owned. In Hungary the corresponding figure is 82.9%. That same year the private sector (largely individual plots) in Poland covered 84.4% of all agricultural land, versus only 17% in Hungary. See Wädekin (1982: 85–6).

[30] Luca, Levendel, and Stumpf (1994: 565), and Vida (1986: 142–3).

"happiest barracks in the bloc." Although it would be an exaggeration to say that Party rule was popularly endorsed, there, nonetheless, did not exist the hostility that was evident in Czechoslovakia or Poland.[31] According to Blumstock (1981: 367), "[w]hat little politically relevant survey data we have suggests that there is widespread acceptance and perhaps respect – if not enthusiasm – for prevailing political and ideological tenets in Hungary." As a consequence, the Hungarian Party should have had greater success, relative to the other ruling parties, in attracting support from across the social spectrum. The greater this success, the greater the ultimate electoral discontinuity should have been once communism fell.

I focus on the survival of attachments to rightist parties. The persistence of rightist loyalties is perhaps the most paradoxical postcommunist outcome. First, communist resocialization efforts were aimed at creating leftists, not rightists. In retrospect, it is easy to dismiss attempts to create a "new socialist man" that would believe in Marxism–Leninism and accept the leading political role of the Communist Party. Yet, for roughly forty years the Hungarian and other Eastern European communist regimes enjoyed virtual monopoly control of the culture, education, and media instruments with which socialist attitudes could be inculcated. Radio, television, newspapers, magazines, books, schools, music, and organizational involvement were all harnessed, in varying degrees and at different times, toward this end.[32] It is true that these efforts were not always successful, but even failure could count as success: While only a small percentage of those exposed to socialist messages became committed Marxist–Leninists, a far greater number might at least have been induced to abandon their rightist sentiments. Second, as alluded in the preceding text, communist industrial policies targeted the Right's precommunist base in the rural peasantry. These policies both drew peasants out of the village into growing industrial towns and brought the industrial world to the villages. In both cases, the intended effect was to turn "peasants" into "proletarians," a class that in theory was supposed to harbor leftist, not rightist sympathies. Of course, things did not always go according to plan here either, but, as we will see, industrial and agricultural reorganization and the attendant infiltration by

---

[31] Kovrig (1979: 429–32) and Schöpflin (1993: 211–17).

[32] Many of the early studies of political socialization in communist Eastern Europe, written during the initial phases of the Cold War, exaggerated both the goals and the means of communist political socialization. See, for example, Juhász (1952). Volgyes (1975) provides a more balanced overview of political socialization methods throughout the region, though it was not possible at that time to gauge the success of the regime's efforts.

the Party of what had been before communism *terra incognita* in the villages exerted powerful pressures on the rightist constituency.

Anticipating the Argument

How did rightist partisan loyalties persist against such overwhelming odds? The answer, discussed more fully in Chapter 1, lies in the power of local institutions, even those under extreme duress, to act as focal points for mutual interaction. Persistence attachments to rightist parties emerged as an outgrowth of local church-based social networks that girded their members against pressures to succumb to the many incentives to assimilate into the surrounding socialist milieu. This process can be broken up into several discrete components. First, local church institutions had to survive as loci of mass attachment. Given concerted Communist Party efforts to enfeeble the Churches, this survival can by no means be taken for granted. With the Church hierarchies largely co-opted by the Party, preserving church community fell to the local clergy. In an incessant battle with Party cadres, and often their own ecclesiastical superiors, many local priests prevented the Party from severing ties between the Churches and society. This endeavor required extraordinary ingenuity. Successful clergymen walked a fine line between excessive opposition, which would invite the wrath of the Party and disrupt local church life, and insufficient activity, which would precipitate a decline in church community.

Second, the faithful who comprised this community were not merely passive objects of Party and Church manipulation, but active players in the battle between the Party and the Churches for mass loyalties. The decision to engage in public religious practice under conditions of oppression is a form of resistance. Like other forms of resistance to authoritarianism, its dynamics can be understood in terms of collective behavior. I interpret changes in aggregate levels of religious practice as a tipping process in which an individual's weighing of the rewards and risks of participation is influenced by his or her beliefs concerning others' behavior and expectations.[33] In this model, each individual has a threshold, the *tipping point*, at which he or she has obtained enough assurance of others' actions to trigger participation. The level of participation in a given community depends on the distribution of thresholds within that community.[34] For example,

---

[33] The literature here is substantial. Two excellent recent treatments, with extensive reviews, are Kuran and Sunstein (1999) and Petersen (2001).

[34] In game theoretic parlance these levels or outcomes are termed *equilibria*.

if everyone is so fearful that they would attend church only if they were sure everyone else were attending, then attendance would most likely be zero, as that level of coordination would be difficult to achieve. By contrast, if everyone believes that church attendance is the only ticket into heaven, and would attend regardless of the actions of others, then attendance would be 100 percent.[35]

Local cadres and clergymen play opposing roles in this dynamic. The former harassed priests and intimidated the faithful, all in an effort to increase the perceived risks of participation. The latter assumed the role of activists by standing up to the Party and mobilizing as many as possible to take part.[36] This assured the more fearful among the faithful that the risks would be worth taking. The cadres and the clergymen can be said to have engaged in an elaborate "cat and mouse" game, with each side engaging in ever more creative, ever more nuanced tactics of persuasion. Church community, understood as the aggregate adherence to religious rites and rituals, survived best where the priests succeeded in outfoxing the cadres. The Roman Catholic church community proved far more resilient against the depredations of communism than the Reformed (Calvinist) church community. This is due to both the differing structures of these Churches as institutions and theological developments in response to communism.

Finally, those church communities that did survive transmitted what would become support for the postcommunist Right by enabling their members to resist internalizing the socialist messages to which they were exposed. Local church institutions marked them off from the rest of society, and in particular from those within socialist milieux. Although these church groups were predominantly rightist in orientation at the advent of state-socialism in the late 1940s, no single mechanism can account for how future rightist preferences were reproduced through the long period of

---

[35] I use the term *Church* (in upper case) to refer to the macrolevel institution, encompassing all levels of administrative organization; *church* (in lower case) applies to the local level institution overseen by a priest or pastor. Local church institutions refer to the customs and practices associated with church life such as participation in festivals, church attendance, baptism, and so forth. The church community refers to those who take part in church life.

[36] Petersen (2001) refers to such activists as "first actors." I employ the term *cadre* to mean both ordinary Party members and low-level State functionaries who may not have been formally Party members, but nonetheless operated as foot soldiers in local battles against the Churches. The term *local clergy* is meant to encompass not just Catholic parish priests and Calvinist pastors, but also deacons, assistant pastors, and other local Church representatives.

14

state-socialism. In some ways, local church institutions operated in ways akin to the "intermediate organizations" that early modernization theorists posited as a palliative to the dangers of social atomization in the face of an overweening political authority. Deutsch (1961: 494) defined *social mobilization* as "the process in which major clusters of old social, economic, and psychological commitments are eroded or broken and people become available for new patterns of socialization and behavior." Although he was describing how traditional societies become modern, this characterization is equally germane to the first stage in the transition from bourgeois society, where property and Church are bedrock institutions, to socialist society, where faith would be in the Party alone. For those remaining within church networks, the common experience of hardship during communism fostered within-group cohesion and continually renewed attachments to the Churches. These attachments, and the social interaction emerging out of them, gave members of church communities both the means to exchange political views and the wherewithal to resist the many incentives the Party was offering them to leave the church orbit. Rooted in the remnants of precommunist rightist support, and sustained throughout state-socialism in opposition to the Party and its worldview, these groups provided a "natural" reservoir of support for rightist political parties after 1989.

Research Design and Methods

This book tackles one of the oldest empirical paradoxes in democratic politics by examining some very unlikely occurrences of it at the microlevel in one country. While every research design has its limitations, this particular approach confers two big advantages. First, expanding the universe of potential instances of political continuity to include both redemocratizing countries and stable democracies brings key inadequacies of received theory into high relief. Tailored for systems that feature regularly scheduled competitive elections and genuine multiparty politics, these explanations are inadequate when applied to countries where democratic politics gets usurped for lengthy periods. If political persistence can occur even after a regime as intrusive as state-socialism, then the theories adduced to explicate the phenomenon for stable democracies, while perhaps sufficient within the domain for which they were formulated, cannot serve as general explanations. A more general theory of persistence cannot presuppose background conditions that exist only in stable democracies.

15

Focusing on redemocratizing regimes, then, is not merely a matter of "increasing N," always a laudable goal, but of using unusual instances of political persistence to shed light on similar political dynamics within older democracies. Perhaps what happened in the East is also happening in the West.

Second, after nearly a century of research, we know far more about worldwide patterns of continuity and discontinuity than we do about the microlevel mechanisms of transmission underlying these patterns. To address this lacuna, I eschew cross-national breadth in favor of empirical depth and within-nation comparisons. My explanation is "causally deep" in that it extends over a period of nearly fifty years.[37] At the same time, it specifies in rich detail the empirical and theoretical links between pre- and postcommunism. Although the national focus of research is Hungary, the unit of analysis is the municipality and there are thousands of observations with widely varying degrees of persistence and volatility. I document and explain political continuity through a combination of large-N statistical methods and detailed historical and interpretive analysis of settlement samples.

Patterns of continuity and discontinuity must be established before they can be explained. A statistical analysis of municipality-level electoral outcomes thus precedes the historical argument. I assembled a unique database of electoral outcomes from the 1945, 1990, 1994, and 1998 national parliamentary elections for virtually all of Hungary's roughly 3,000 villages and towns, reconstructed so that there are constant units for comparison. The municipality is the smallest geographic unit for which matching pre- and postcommunist electoral results are available for Hungary, so these data yield the richest possible picture of the outcomes to be explained. They reveal both rightist and leftist continuity and discontinuity.

I illuminate the trajectories between the pre- and postcommunist periods through archival materials and a broad range of other sources, including ethnographic reports and memoirs. Scholars are fortunate that the Party considered the Churches a force to be reckoned with because their prolonged struggle left a rich documentary legacy. To reconstruct the ebb and flow of this struggle, the battles won and lost, I collected information on events in multiple provinces, across four decades, from previously closed Party and Church archives. These are not stale, factless descriptions of "counterrevolutionary activity," but provide detailed evidence of

---

[37] For a concise discussion of "deep" and "shallow" explanations, see Kitschelt (2003).

the quotidian tactics used by both local clergymen and local cadres in their efforts to secure mass loyalties. They reveal a war not just of words, but of deeds, and chronicle a myriad of triumphs and disappointments.

I focus, in particular, on events in Hajdú-Bihar and Zala counties. Situated at opposite ends of the country, they provide additional leverage due to differences between the Roman Catholic and Reformed Churches. Zala in the west is overwhelmingly Roman Catholic. Hajdú-Bihar in the east is predominantly Reformed (Calvinist) and Debrecen, the county seat, has been termed the "Calvinist Rome." These counties thus provide crucial variation in the nature of local church institutions. The choice of religious strongholds does not appear to bias the outcomes of interest one way or the other. Although clerical resistance and popular religiosity might have been more intense in these areas, so too were the Party's efforts to constrict church life. Moreover, the settlements in these counties exhibit a broad range of both church community and electoral volatility. As an extra precaution, however, I also examine documents relating to Győr-Moson, Szabolcs-Szatmár-Bereg, and Veszprém counties.[38]

One of the most important focal points of Church–Party conflict was religious instruction in the State schools. These classes were highly contested terrain, as the level of enrollment became a symbol of which side was winning the war for popular allegiance. The clergy did everything it could to elevate enrollment; the cadres went out of their way to reduce it. The authorities collected detailed data on the fraction of students in a given municipality enrolled in this instruction. I use this information, gleaned from archival material for hundreds of settlements across many years, as an indicator of the strength of church community. I distinguish in particular between municipalities where the fraction of students enrolled in religious instruction remained high throughout much of the communist period from those where it was high initially, but ultimately declined. The difference in levels of rightist persistence across these two trajectories, established through statistical analysis, is key evidence for the importance of clerical activities. I further validate the nexus between church community and rightist persistence with survey data. In particular, I document the church community's preference for rightist parties using International Social Survey Program surveys from 1991 and 1998.

---

[38] Reliance on materials created under Communist Party supervision raises larger questions about the truthfulness of the events and data described therein. I address these concerns in Appendix 5.

A Road Map

Chapter 1 revisits extant theories of political persistence to illustrate in greater detail why redemocratizing Hungary is such a difficult case for them to explain. It also remedies a number of conceptual and methodological flaws that have prevented a clear understanding of what counts as political continuity between pre- and postcommunism. These include the specification of a proper baseline against which the postcommunist period may be compared, the reemergence (and generally dismal electoral performance) of "historic" parties that existed during the precommunist period, and the criteria for identifying blocs of parties. Chapter 2 then establishes, with a large-N analysis, the overall pattern of electoral continuity and discontinuity. I measure outcomes in terms of party blocs, defined as "Left" and "Right" for the precommunist period, and "Left," "Liberal," and "Right" for the postcommunist period. Electoral evolution is conceptualized as occurring along six different trajectories, leading from one of the two precommunist blocs to any of the three postcommunist blocs.

Chapters 3 through 5 then move from statistical to interpretive analysis, reconstructing the struggle between Church and Party in state-socialist Hungary. Chapter 3 describes the deep roots the Churches had in Hungarian society and chronicles the dramatic decline in their influence in the years following World War II, as the Communist Party increasingly asserted its authority. Chapter 4 employs primary source materials to document how the battle for popular allegiance played out at the local level in the years leading up to the aborted 1956 revolution. It describes both Stalinist repression and the strategies the clergy used to maintain local church institutions. Using data from registration for religious instruction in the schools, it shows that while the Party had made inroads into the Churches, it could by no means declare victory. Chapter 5 chronicles the variegated strategies the clergy employed to sustain local churches in the years after 1956. Although the Party ceased employing its most repressive methods, its implementation of agricultural collectivization presented a new threat to the integrity of the church community. I document the many creative ways in which the clergy sought to overcome these new obstacles and illustrate how Catholic priests proved more adept at this task than Calvinist pastors. Employing data on both agricultural collectivization and registration for religious instruction in the schools, I provide evidence for the tipping dynamic underlying the evolution of the church community.

Chapter 6 shifts back to statistical analysis to illustrate the macropolitical consequences of communist-era clerical activities. Employing a variety of graphical and multivariate statistical methods across multiple datasets, it demonstrates both the influence of the precommunist past on postcommunist electoral outcomes and the correlation between high levels of church community during communism and the preservation of rightist electoral attachments. I reveal this correlation at the aggregate level – across settlements – with regression analysis on a sample of roughly 200 settlements from western Hungary for which there are extraordinarily rich data. While Catholic areas enjoyed higher levels of church community than Calvinist ones, for a given level of community there are few confessional differences in support of the Right as a whole. Such differences emerged only in the choice of parties within the rightist bloc. Also, I estimate the individual-level probabilities of a church affiliate supporting the Right, using both ecological inference and survey analysis methods.

Chapter 7 discusses the importance of these findings for understanding politics in other countries. After considering the implications for Hungary, it describes this study's contribution to our knowledge of state-socialism, resistance to authoritarian rule, and path dependence. My ultimate aim in this study is to understand the general roots of political persistence. The book thus concludes with suggestions for how the argument might be tailored to explain political continuity in both redemocratizing countries and stable democracies.

1

Explaining Political Persistence

1.1 Introduction

As discussed in the preceding chapter, current theory suffers from a number of inadequacies. The task in this chapter is to fully explicate and propose possible solutions to these problems and then formulate a different explanation for electoral continuity. First, I show how redemocratizing state-socialist countries in general, and Hungary in particular, challenge our understanding of the roots of political continuity. As we shall see, extant theories are either inapplicable to former state-socialist countries or, if they are applicable, cannot explain the remarkable levels of persistence we see in such deeply disrupted societies. Second, I identify and resolve a number of theoretical and empirical inconsistencies that have prevented the formulation of a theory that can apply to both stable democracies and redemocratizing countries. Finally, I advance a new view of persistence.

1.2 Theoretical Approaches

1.2.1 Two Views of Persistence

The literature on electoral persistence can be broadly divided into "instrumental" and "expressive" approaches.[1] The distinction between the two schools of thought is pithily summarized by Schuessler (2000) as one of "Doing" versus "Being." Instrumental approaches view the voter as

---

[1] These terms were used by Butler and Stokes (1969: 25) to distinguish among theories of why individuals turn out to vote. However, they may also be used to characterize the logic of choice. See Fiorina (1976: 390–415).

deciding among parties (or candidates) based on what parties *do*. Expressive approaches, by contrast, emphasize instead the importance of what parties *are*. This distinction is not meant to be essential, as one could argue that what parties are in the minds of the voters is ultimately a function of what they do (and vice versa). Moreover, in practice many explanations do not carefully distinguish between the two and in any given election both types of decision are surely taking place. However, each approach generates very different expectations about persistence, so it is useful to consider them separately.[2]

The predominant view is an expressive (Being) one and holds that electoral persistence is a consequence of an underlying set of stable partisan self-images within the electorate. The exact nature of this self-image has, however, been the subject of considerable debate. Within American politics, where the same two parties have dominated politics for well over a century, it is usually conceived of as party identification: people vote Democrat (or Republican) because they *identify* as Democrats (or Republicans). In countries where instability in individual party organizations prevents the formation of the kinds of party attachments documented in the United States (or the United Kingdom), these partisan self-images are more often conceived in terms of the voters' self-placement into more general partisan categories or families of parties, such as the Left, the Right, Christian democracy, or social democracy. As in the case of party identification, these more diffuse loyalties are thought to stabilize electoral behavior.[3]

There are two basic views of how this stabilization process works in the expressive (Being) approach. Converse (1969) has offered what might be termed a behavioral theory of stability. His model argues that partisanship, initially acquired through early political socialization, strengthens across an individual's life cycle as he or she repeatedly participates in the democratic political system. This occurs through the "progressive 'binding in' of popular loyalties to one or another of the traditionally competing political parties."[4] Within the electorate as a whole, this individual-level process is seen to result in a steadily increasing level of stable partisan

---

[2] Mair (1997: 20–4) lists conditions under which a party's historically derived identity is likely to coincide with contemporary political appeals.

[3] The preeminent example of a system exhibiting persistence despite organizational discontinuity is France. See Converse and Pierce (1986), Lewis-Beek (1984), and Pierce (1992).

[4] Converse (1969: 141).

identifiers. These partisans are considered "ballast" against lasting disruptions to the political system. Where particular issues, candidates, or parties do arise to shock the system, these mature partisan attachments are thought to bring electoral results quickly back to the old equilibrium.[5] Converse's model allows for the suspension (and subsequent resumption) of democratic politics, through the "forgetting function." During the authoritarian interlude normal mechanisms of parental transmission and partisan growth are taken to be disrupted. Individuals are assumed to gradually lose their partisan attachments and each new generation is less partisan than the previous one.

A second, organizational type of Being explanation of persistence grants political elites a far more powerful role in the shaping of partisan loyalties. Rooted in the social cleavages model popularized by Lipset and Rokkan (1967) and skillfully extended by Houska (1985) and Bartolini and Mair (1990), these explanations see elite-mass organizational linkages as the principal means through which stable mass electoral blocs are maintained. In this view, party elites organize a portion of the electorate by seeking party members or through affiliation with organizations, such as trade unions or religious associations, which do not compete in elections, but maintain affinities with particular parties. According to Houska (1985: 34–40) such a network of organizations, with a party at its apex, affects political behavior through two mechanisms: education and encapsulation. Organizational elites are thought to educate the rank and file by transmitting desirable values, beliefs, and attachments in the course of organizational participation and contact. This is said to lead to subcultural homogeneity and, in extreme cases, a "we–they" division of society. *Encapsulation* refers to the process by which organizations "insulate" a group from "contamination" by rival ideas or groups. The more the affiliates of a given organizational network interact only with other members of that network, the more they are said to be encapsulated. By blocking out pressures or incentives to stray from one's subcultural group, these networks are thought to foster homogeneous patterns of electoral behavior.[6]

Instrumental (Doing) approaches downplay the importance of partisan self-images of any kind and focus instead on the ways in which voters

---

[5] This equilibrium is equivalent to what Converse (1966) calls the "normal vote," a baseline division of partisan preferences. For a more recent application, see Nardulli (1994).

[6] For details, see Bartolini and Mair (1990), Houska (1985), Luther and Deschouwer (1999), and Panebianco (1988).

evaluate the policies and performance of parties (or candidates). In the classical statement, courtesy of Downs (1957), a voter chooses the party whose policy package most closely suits his or her desired policies. Most commonly, these arguments appear in models of economic voting, where voters are assumed to punish or reward parties based on their handling of the economy. Instrumental arguments are often invoked to explain electoral volatility rather than persistence,[7] but there are at least two ways in which they might account for persistence. The first is through underlying stability in the structure of economic interests or issues. Shively (1972: 1222), for example, argues that to explain persistence in the Weimar Republic, "a voter who is a member of a clear and distinct social and economic group, for which he feels that some party is the clear spokesman ... may not need a further guide to voting." In short, the argument goes, workers vote for workers' parties and farmers vote for farmers' parties – without the need to develop any form of partisan self-image. Where the structure of interests remains constant, according to this view, so too should voting behavior. The second instrumental mechanism for electoral persistence is through the ability of political parties to adapt to economic and social change within their constituencies. Even where parties have not encapsulated their voters, they do maintain links with them and may alter their programs to suit the electorate's evolving needs and demands. However, this is not an easy task. Party leaders must adopt the correct strategy in a timely manner and then sell this strategy to the rest of their party and to the electorate. Opportunities to fail abound.[8]

1.2.2 The Challenge of Redemocratization

Redemocratizing countries expand the venue for studying the paradox of electoral persistence because both instrumental and expressive explanations are either inapplicable under authoritarian conditions or, if they are applicable, unlikely to be the principal sources of persistence. Consider Converse's model. It is extremely parsimonious and elegant and predicts rates of partisan attachment consistent with empirically reported levels in the United States and United Kingdom. The issue here is not, however, how well the model accounts for persistence in stable democracies, but how well it

---

[7] See, for example, Dalton, Flanagan, and Beck (1984) and Roberts and Wibbels (1999).
[8] For a concise review of the difficulties of such adaptation in Latin America, see Levitsky (2003: 1–34).

predicts continuity after a resumption of democratic politics.[9] Although the model appears also to account for aggregate partisan patterns in redemocratized postwar Germany and Italy, it remains a poor guide to understanding persistence more generally in redemocratizing regimes. If the evolution of partisan loyalties under authoritarian regimes were truly represented by a simply model of decay, then there ought to have been no persistence at all after the resumption of democratic politics in post-Franco Spain or any of the redemocratizing postcommunist countries. To see why let us imagine an electorate at the time of democratic suspension that is fully partisan and that for each year of the authoritarian period 10 percent of that strength is lost. Let us further assume that those same people live to see the end of authoritarianism and are the only ones who vote in the first postauthoritarian election. This contrived example is clearly not realistic, but it creates a situation in which the model is most likely to predict continuity. If the authoritarian interlude lasts forty years, as it roughly did for Spain and Eastern Europe, then by the time of the first postauthoritarian elections partisan attachments would be only about 1 percent of their initial level. In other words, the electorate would be almost completely nonpartisan. This contradicts the findings of Maravall (1982) for the resurgence of the Left in Spain, Wittenberg (1999) for the reemergence of the Right in Hungary, and a number of studies on the Czech Republic and Slovakia.[10] Thus, even without decaying rates of parental socialization, which have been excluded from this simple calculation, Converse's model cannot account for persistence after lengthier periods of authoritarian rule.

The assumption that partisanship simply decays under authoritarianism is inadequate. It is necessary to specify more structure to the authoritarian period. Encapsulation arguments provide some structure in the form of organizational networks, but it is unclear how such an approach, which relies so fundamentally on the ability of organizational elites to build networks and educate constituents, could be applied in cases of redemocratization. Although the precise nature of authoritarianism may vary from country to country, such regimes are almost by definition hostile to opposition activity. Parties and independent civic organizations are co-opted, harassed, or forced to dissolve. Political leaders are imprisoned, killed, or compelled to

---

[9] Subsequent research has shown that the argument may in fact not hold for Britain, the United States, France, Switzerland, New Zealand, and Australia. See the reviews in Abramson (1992) and Leithner (1997).

[10] See Kostelecký (2002) for a review.

flee. Opposition activity is repressed, while the regime attempts to mobilize mass support for itself. The free flow of information is restricted and its content controlled. The situation was particularly extreme in communist Eastern Europe, where for the most part the Party was able to snuff out opposition with great success. Such conditions are hardly conducive to the development of autonomous organizational networks.[11]

Instrumental arguments do not suffer from the same theoretical problems when applied to redemocratization, but they are unlikely to be empirically plausible. Consider the first sociological correlate of electoral continuity: stability in the structure of occupational or social groups. What makes electoral persistence so puzzling is that it outlasts particular issues, candidates, and campaigns, often continuing even through wars, in- and out-migration, and disruptive economic development. That is, it exists despite demographic and social changes and in the face of presumably evolving preferences. Key and Munger (1959: 287) remark on how unlikely it was that stable "interests" could account for electoral persistence in Indiana between 1868 and 1900.[12] The latter half of the nineteenth century was undoubtedly a turbulent period for the American Midwest, but if stable interests were unlikely in the American heartland, how likely is it that patterns of interest in a postauthoritarian period match those of the preauthoritarian period outside the United States? Such congruence is particularly unlikely in redemocratizing communist countries. The communist regimes initiated and oversaw massive industrialization, urbanization, and social upheaval. Even a cursory comparison of social and economic indicators at each end of the communist era reveals dramatic differences.[13]

[11] This leaves out the regime's own networks, which presumably benefit favorably from government largesse. Such networks are important because the loyalties they engender reemerge in the postauthoritarian period and influence the partisan balance in society. This is abundantly clear in parts of postcommunist Eastern Europe, where socialist and social democratic parties enjoy stature and support they rarely enjoyed in precommunist times.

[12] Berelson, Lazarsfeld, and McPhee (1954: 74) also note that "[v]oting blocs are often perpetuated so long after group needs and political alternatives have changed that it is unrealistic to speak of 'interests' being involved in more than a few of the voting differences between groups...."

[13] Berend (1996: ch. 5) lists a number of comparative figures. For example, the percentage of the population working in agriculture dropped between the early fifties and the late eighties from 40% to 10–12% in Czechoslovakia, from 57% to 25% in Poland, and from 53% to 10–12% in Hungary. Between 1950 and 1987, per capita gross national product (GNP) more than tripled in Czechoslovakia, Hungary, and Poland, and nearly sextupled in Romania. Between 1937–8 and 1988 industry's share of gross domestic product (GDP)

Instrumental arguments also see electoral persistence resulting from the ability of parties to refine their strategies in response to the anticipated political consequences of prolonged economic and social transformation. Though such an explanation is consistent with the potential for massive underlying social change during the authoritarian period, it does not enjoy much *prima facie* validity. First, in Western Europe party adaptation required at least some mass elite linkages, so that parties could learn about and, if possible, accommodate the emerging concerns of the electorate. Such linkages required time and money to foster. In redemocratizing countries (and for that matter, in democratizing countries more generally), new political parties typically have neither the time nor the money, much less the expertise to develop strategies targeted for specific groups. In Eastern Europe in particular, the fall of communism was so sudden and unexpected, and the scheduling of free elections so early, that parties existed for only a few months before having to compete for votes. The reemergence and generally dismal postcommunist electoral performance of revived precommunist parties testify to the difficulty of anticipating the electoral consequences of the breathtaking transformations these societies had undergone. Second, a requisite for successful party adaptation is that parties should offer discernably distinct, competing policy packages. If voters are unable to distinguish among the parties on issues of policy, then it is unlikely their vote choices will be based on policy. Although there are significant national variations, in Hungary party-issue positions did not in fact figure highly as determinants of popular vote choice, at least in the initial phases of the transition.[14]

The reason the aforementioned accounts of persistence, be they instrumental or expressive, fare poorly when applied to redemocratizations lies in an impoverished conceptualization of authoritarianism and its impact on postauthoritarian electoral loyalties. If we are ever to understand why electoral congruences do exist even in the absence of democratic politics, we will need a richer understanding of authoritarianism and what happens to electoral loyalties under it than these models provide. The beginnings of such an explanation may be found in macrolevel comparisons of pre- and

increased in Hungary from 21% to 41%. In Poland the jump was from 19% to 48%. In Bulgaria in 1939 industry's share was less than 10% of GDP. By 1988 that had jumped to 58%. Perhaps the most telling statistic, from the viewpoint of individual lifestyles, pertains to passenger cars. Between 1955 and 1988 this number increased in Hungary from 10,000 to 1,790,000, and in Poland from 40,000 to 4,519,000.

[14] Kitschelt et al. (1999) and Tworzecki (2003).

postauthoritarian electoral patterns. Cotta (1996) and Remmer (1985), for example, find that electoral continuity between pre- and postauthoritarian regimes is positively correlated with the degree of institutionalization of the preauthoritarian system and negatively correlated with the duration of the authoritarian interlude, the severity of repression, and the mobilizational efforts of the authoritarian regime.[15] The basic logic here is clear and eminently reasonable. The more institutionalized the preauthoritarian system, the stronger the electoral loyalties and the more likely they are to survive the authoritarian period. The more severe and lengthy the period of authoritarian repression, the more the old party system and the social bases of its support are disrupted, and the less likely that postauthoritarian electoral patterns will match those of the preauthoritarian era. Likewise, the greater the authoritarian regime's success in mobilizing support, the more widespread the inculcation of new political loyalties, and the less congruence between pre- and postauthoritarian electoral patterns. Geddes (1995) emphasizes the importance of the authoritarian regime's success in creating new political channels for preauthoritarian political elites. Where these elites are co-opted by the authoritarian regime, preauthoritarian electoral patterns are unlikely to reemerge, even where repression is relatively light.

These and similar studies are fascinating, and highly suggestive, but they provide only the barest outline of what a theory of persistence might look like. There are at least three deficiencies. First, the level of analysis is too high. National-level averages of party support are excellent indicators of the aggregate partisan balance in society, but the causal forces underlying persistence operate at the subnational level and it is necessary to measure both explanatory factors and outcomes at the same level of analysis. This requires moving beyond national-level measures of such key concepts as repression and mobilization, and recognizing in analysis and rhetoric that these can vary across space (and over time). In short, microlevel explanation requires microlevel data. This has long been recognized in studies of North America and Western Europe.[16]

---

[15] Remmer studies cases from Latin America only. Cotta's analysis spans postcommunist Eastern Europe and postfascist Western and Southern Europe. For a similar analysis, see Bennett (1998).

[16] Siegfried (1913) worked with very disaggregated data, and the entire paradox of electoral persistence in France, the United States, and other countries is predicated on subnational

Second, they employ often inconsistent or inappropriate methods for establishing the congruence between any two elections.[17] For Geddes (1995) the more postauthoritarian electoral success a revived preauthoritarian party enjoys, the greater the continuity with the preauthoritarian period. This assumption mistakes success for persistence. It is one thing for large preauthoritarian parties to reemerge and regain their former popularity but if small ones reemerge with much larger popularity or large ones reemerge with lower popularity, then one cannot really speak of continuity. Other scholars are captive to an implicit "either/or" notion of continuity. Cotta (1996), for example, finds little persistence in postcommunist countries because "historic" parties failed to more or less reproduce their national-level precommunist results. It is true that persistence is ultimately a matter of replicating prior electoral outcomes: where an electoral result at time 2 is identical to that at time 1, we can speak of perfect persistence. But such an unrealistic situation never actually occurs, except in formal models. In reality, two successive outcomes are never identical, even in the stablest of democracies. Jehlička et al. (1993) and Körösényi (1991) emphasize regional rather than national continuities, but their discussions are framed in terms of party strongholds vis-à-vis the national average. Unfortunately, such a definition is consistent with a wide range of actual patterns of support, because any regional outcome above the national average is considered equivalent to any other. A better approach is exemplified in Kostelecký (1994), Krivý (1997), and Wittenberg (1999), where postcommunist results for parties and/or blocs are regressed on their precommunist counterparts. I discuss in greater detail in the next chapter the use of linear regression for quantifying different degrees of congruence between two elections.

Finally, even taken on their own terms, and allowing for the imprecision in measures of electoral congruence, these arguments make poor

geographical disaggregation. Some of the best works may be found in Allardt and Rokkan (1970), Dogan and Rokkan (1969), and Lipset and Rokkan (1967). For an excellent discussion of the merits of subnational comparisons, see Snyder (2001).

[17] It should be noted that even in studies of the stable democracies there are disagreements about how to identify political continuity. For inquiries into relatively recent electoral evolution, panel studies offer a glimpse into the dynamics of individual beliefs and behavior and how they change over time and across generations. Others tap into actual election results and employ concepts such as the "normal vote." There are lively debates concerning the appropriate measure of volatility and the relationship between aggregate and individual-level stability. See, for example, Box-Steffensmeier and Smith (1996) and DeBoef (2000).

predictions for Eastern Europe. Consider the aforementioned correlates of persistence: a strongly institutionalized preauthoritarian system, a short authoritarian period, mild levels of repression, and low mobilizational effort by the authoritarian regime. Each of these factors suggests lower persistence in Eastern Europe. First, only Czechoslovakia had what could be termed a well-institutionalized party system in the decades preceding the communist takeover, having enjoyed regularly scheduled free and fair multiparty elections throughout most of the interwar period. No other country in the region could boast such an unblemished democratic record. This factor would predict lower political continuity in Hungary.[18] Second, state-socialism lasted longer than authoritarian rule in other countries. Among redemocratizing countries only Spain endured an authoritarianism of approximately equal duration. Thus, the duration of state-socialism would predict greater discontinuity everywhere in Eastern Europe. Third, on average, communist regimes were more repressive, had greater capacity for social mobilization, and implemented far more ambitious plans for economic and social change than most other authoritarian regimes.[19] No program in authoritarian Latin America or Southern Europe can compare with the extensive, long-lasting effort in communist Eastern Europe to remake political identities and create a "new socialist man."[20] All these factors predict discontinuity for Eastern Europe. Thus, even if these aggregate-level theories successfully explain outcomes in the countries for which they were formulated, they fail when the empirical scope is expanded to include redemocratizing communist countries.

Scholars of long-run political continuities in Eastern Europe face two other knotty problems that almost never arise in studies of stable democracies. I list them briefly here and then elaborate on both at some length in the following text. First, the depth and durability of the social, economic, and political disruption under communism have created misapprehension about how to reconcile the unique and historically unprecedented character of the transition from communism with what might be deeper underlying political continuities with the precommunist past. The issue here is not the

---

[18] Both Hungary and Poland experienced authoritarian rule at various times during the interwar and immediate postwar periods, though each had at least one multiparty election in which it was possible to express a range of partisan preferences. See Rothschild (1993).

[19] Linz (2000) and Linz and Stepan (1996: ch. 3).

[20] The Nazi regime in Germany had aspirations equally as radical, but lacked the time to fully implement the creation of a "new German." As evil and deadly as that regime was, it lasted only twelve years, versus roughly forty years for Eastern European communism.

mechanics of correlating election results, but the prior decision of which parties or blocs should be compared with one another. Second, there is a dearth of reliable data from the communist period that can serve as a valid empirical link between the pre- and the postcommunist polities. If we are ever to uncover the causal mechanisms that lead from pre- to postauthoritarian partisan attachments, both of these problems must be resolved.

1.3 What Counts as Continuity?

1.3.1 Symbolic Continuity

In the immediate aftermath of communism's fall there was a tendency to see in the revival of parliamentary politics a reassertion of traditions and practices that had so long ago been forcibly expunged. Among the most visually stunning spectacles of late 1989 were flags waving, their communist insignias cut out. Throughout Eastern Europe, cities, streets, and squares regained their precommunist names. The new republics were launched with great fanfare and national symbolism. The formal return of parliamentary democracy and the resurrection of old political roles made historical comparisons virtually inevitable. In Poland, Lech Wałęsa was compared to the much revered interwar commander and Head of State Marshal Piłsudski. In Czechoslovakia, Václav Havel was likened to the interwar philosopher and Czechoslovak president Tomaš Masaryk. József Antall, the new prime minister of Hungary, was seen by some as continuing the legacy of Ferenc Deák, hero of 1848. Others felt he personified István Bethlen, the liberal-conservative prime minister of the early interwar period.[21] Negating communism was indeed the order of the day. Lech Wałęsa received his presidential insignia not from the president of the Polish People's Republic, but from a representatives of the so-called "London" Poles, who had formed a free Polish government in exile after the Nazi invasion and considered themselves the legitimate representatives of Poland long after the Polish communists had become entrenched.[22] In Czechoslovakia, the new parliament declared the communist regime "illegal."[23] Some Hungarian legislators went to the first meeting of the National Assembly from St. Stephen's Basilica, thus reviving a tradition of attending Mass before a

[21] Lányi (1993: 170).
[22] Rothschild (1993: 234).
[23] Bartosek (1993: 12).

legislative session.[24] All of this underscored the break with communism
that these new regimes were attempting to represent. Communism was
portrayed as alien to national traditions and cultures, an unwelcome detour
from normal political development.

1.3.2 *"Historic" Parties*

Another feature of this "return" to the past has been the emergence of
political parties that claim roots in the precommunist period. Many parties
attempted to use the names, slogans, symbols, and rhetoric of important
precommunist parties in a bid to gain votes in an electoral market in which
few parties other than the communist and former communist parties were
well known. Some of these, such as the Polish Peasant Party, the Czechoslovak People's Party, and the Czechoslovak Socialist Party, had enjoyed a shell
existence during the communist period as part of a communist-dominated
ruling bloc. Others, however, were completely repressed during the
communist period, enjoying neither organizational nor, for the most part,
leadership continuity with the designated precommunist predecessor party.
Better known examples of these "historic" parties include Czechoslovak
Social Democracy in the former Czechoslovakia (Jehlička et al. 1993); the
Christian Democratic People's Party, Independent Smallholders Party, and
Hungarian Social Democratic Party in Hungary (Körösényi 1991); and the
National Liberal and National Peasant Parties in Romania (Cotta 1996).[25]

Some parties did not adopt the name of precommunist parties, but
nonetheless are portrayed by some elites as inheritors of precommunist
traditions. Thus, for example, both the Slovak National Party and the
Movement for a Democratic Slovakia are seen as carrying on the "pro-
Slovak" traditions of Hlinka's interwar Slovak People's Party.[26] In the early
years of the transition, some maintained that the intellectual origins of the
Hungarian Democratic Forum and the Alliance of Free Democrats, the former rightist and the latter liberal, lay in interwar divisions among Hungarian

---

[24] Barany (1990: 26).

[25] This list is by no means comprehensive. For example, a Hungarian Independence Party,
Independent Hungarian Democratic Party, and National Smallholders Party (purported
precommunist revivals all) had regional lists in the 1990 election (Szoboszlai 1990: 16).
Waller (1996: 37) lists the Bulgarian Agrarian National Union and Czech Agrarian Party
(the latter having merged with other parties to form the Liberal Democratic Union in
1991).

[26] Jehlička et al. (1993), Kostelecký (2002: 82–3), and Krivý (1997).

intellectuals between "populists," who stressed a "Third Road" between communism and capitalism, and cosmopolitan "urbanists."[27] In Poland the Non-Party Bloc for the Support of Reforms had a Polish acronym, BBWR, that was intentionally identical to the interwar political movement established by Marshal Piłsudski one year after having engineered a coup d'etat.[28] One observer concluded that, "...in Poland, Hungary, Czechoslovakia, Romania, and Bulgaria, where state-socialist society and politics came into existence not through indigenous revolution but as a consequence of war and the entry of the Red Army, the abolition of people's democracies [i.e., socialist systems] took place in the symbolism of a reconnection to prewar political traditions and party structures."[29]

The leitmotiv of most scholarship on "return" has emphasized the radical break with the precommunist past that postcommunist politics represents. These arguments come in two flavors. The first rejects the very idea of comparing pre- and postcommunist parties because they are seen as too different from one another to provide a valid basis of comparison. The second acknowledges that the comparison might prove fruitful, but finds little empirical evidence for persistence. I shall argue that although these arguments make many valid points, they employ an overly narrow view of party identity and the empirical requisites of persistence. Let us consider first the argument that rejects the comparison altogether. At the level of individual parties, this view sees "historic" parties as too different from their precommunist predecessors to warrant being considered the same party. Sukosd (1992), for example, points out that the early postcommunist Independent Smallholders Party (FKgP) was quite different from its precommunist counterpart. The postcommunist FKgP sprang up as a one-issue party concerned with the reprivatization of land seized by the communists and later evolved into a magnet for the disaffected that flirted with the extreme Right. The precommunist FKgP, by contrast, represented not only small farmers, but portions of the middle class and intellectuals in a broad center-Right coalition opposed to the Left. Likewise, Waller (1996) notes how the Czech Agrarians went from having defended farmers against nationalization in the precommunist period to protecting cooperatives faced with privatization after communism. In these and other cases, the symbolism of the precommunist party is seen as little more than a calculated elite

[27] Körösényi (1991).
[28] Kostelecký (2002: 87).
[29] Habermas (1990: 214–15).

strategy to mimic traditions that they see as providing ready-made, easily recognizable identities that can resonate within the population.[30]

The problem with such arguments denying the authenticity of "historic" parties is that they equate persistence with stasis. Conceived of as a literal return to some precommunist status quo ante it is easy to dismiss the idea of persistence as a fancy of romantic historians and aspiring demagogues, or the nightmare of fearful liberals. First, which past would be returned to? The precommunist period is not unitary and politically homogeneous. In Hungary, for example, enormous differences separated the coalition of the immediate postwar years, the quasi-authoritarian interwar period, and the era of liberal dominance in the waning years of the Hapsburg empire.[31] Second, even if such a reference point could be established, the exact status quo ante is not a reasonable baseline against which to judge the identity of a postcommunist party. If revived parties have different policies or target different constituencies than their precommunist counterparts, it is because the economic and social conditions they face are radically different from those a half century ago. Thus, some changes in policy were a requisite for party survival.

If some change was necessary, then when is there enough change in a party to warrant calling that party "new"? Put another way, how different can revived parties be from their predecessors before they are considered "different" parties? This is a tough question. Sartori's distinction between a party's "historically derived identity" and its "contemporary political appeals" seems particularly apt here. The former is based on symbols, folklore, and historical experience; the latter on programmatic issues and strategic requirements of party survival in competitive electoral markets.[32] In practice, it seems that if a party maintains organizational continuity, then quite a lot of programmatic and other changes may occur without that party being perceived as an essentially different party. Mair (1997: 50–51) notes the dramatic evolution of the British Labour party between 1945 and 1987, from a socialist party of the working class to a moderate bourgeois party for all classes. An even starker example is the U.S. Republican Party, which along many dimensions today, most especially its electoral strongholds, bears only faint resemblance to the party of Lincoln. More dramatic still are the former communist parties in Eastern (and Western) Europe. With the fall

---

[30] Gyáni (1993) and Kende (1992).
[31] Kende (1992).
[32] Sartori (1976: 171). Cited in Waller (1996: 23).

of state-socialism they changed their names, their symbols, and their core ideologies. Yet like the British Labour party and the U.S. Republican Party, they are not conceived of as "different" parties, at least in the sense of being incomparable with themselves at an earlier period.

Absence of organizational continuity might be compensated for where old party elites are around to christen and legitimize the refounding of parties. This appears to have happened following the Second World War in Germany. Despite violent Nazi repression and destructive war, leading members of the Weimar communist, social democratic, liberal, and conservative movements survived to restore their political traditions in postwar Germany. The case of the conservative tradition is particularly interesting because the postwar version represented a significant discontinuity with its pre-Nazi predecessor. Herf (1993) notes how Konrad Adenauer, a leading politician of the Weimar-era Catholic Center party, helped restore West German conservatism, but without its prior anti-Western tilt or the formerly bitter confessional divide between Catholics and Protestants. Yet despite this fundamental change in identity, the newly formed Christian Democratic Union, led and staffed by many Weimar-era party activists, is seen as a legitimate descendant of the Catholic Center Party (Loewenberg 1968). Neither programmatic, ideological, nor organizational continuity appear to be essential features of party identity. I apply the same logic to revived precommunist parties.

1.3.3 From Parties to Blocs

As we move from the level of individual parties to that of more underlying party families or blocs, similar issues of "identity" emerge. In this case, it is not about establishing whether a given postcommunist party is the same party as its putative precommunist counterpart, but rather determining the extent to which there are identifiable party families that include both pre- and postcommunist parties. Such families may, of course, include both "historic" and "new" parties. If they can be identified, then electoral persistence may be understood with reference to continuing support for them rather than for individual party organizations. Scholars have understood partisan continuities in France, where individual parties have risen and fallen with great frequency, in precisely this manner.[33] The notion of a party family has been a staple of comparative party and electoral research.

---

[33] Brustein (1988) ably reviews this literature.

However, as Mair and Mudde (1998) demonstrate, researchers do not typically provide theoretical justification for the family groupings they employ, preferring instead to treat them as "self-evident categories, requiring neither justification nor specification."[34] Though perhaps unsettling in a discipline that prides itself on rigor, the apparently impressionistic use of party families does not pose a particularly troublesome problem for research on stable democracies. For all the changes that Western European party systems have undergone, including the emergence of Green and other "new politics" parties, older categories, such as Left and Right, social democrat and Christian democrat, and liberal and conservative, continue to structure politics in most places.

Most scholars of political continuity in Eastern Europe, like their colleagues studying stable democracies, proceed inductively, as if their chosen party families were self-evident. Perhaps the most common objection to this practice is the alleged conflation of the party's name or moniker with the party family to which the party is assigned. In this view, most postcommunist socialist parties, for example, are not "truly" socialist because they have neglected the workers, or accept the necessity of privatization, or have otherwise abandoned the traditional policies and goals of the socialist movement. At root, these objections are no different from those put forth against "historic" parties: "social democracy" or "Christian democracy" has evolved in response to the changing demands of the electorate no less than any individual party. Nonetheless, it is important to more rigorously specify the conditions under which precommunist and postcommunist parties may be considered members of a common family.

Mair and Mudde (1998: 223) recommend, for studies of the long-term development of political parties, a "genetic" view of party identity. In this approach, parties that emerge out of the same social movement (e.g., workers, farmers, or Catholics) or originally mobilized on the same side of a political divide (e.g., capital–labor or clerical–secular) constitute a distinct party family, regardless of subsequent changes in ideology, party program, targeted constituency, or other contingent party characteristics. As they note, "[a] socialist party is a socialist party is a socialist party." This approach has much to recommend it inasmuch as it loosens the connection between the identity of a party family and the self-presentation and actions of parties within it. However, as we saw in the preceding discussion

---

[34] Mair and Mudde (1998: 214).

of "historic" parties, it is the genetic provenance of most postcommunist parties, having emerged *de novo*, that is the central issue of contention. An impressive body of research has shown that, as a result of a combination of communist legacies and the necessity to cope with the "triple transition" of democratization, marketization, and state-building,[35] political parties and party systems in postcommunism operate in very different ways, at least in the early transition period, from parties and party systems that emerged in other transitions to democracy. If this is true, and all evidence from the early period of transition suggests that it is, then postcommunist Christian democratic parties, for example, would not share the same genetic origin as precommunist Christian democratic parties, even when those parties all emerge within the same national setting. Nor would socialist or conservative parties from the two periods share the same origins.[36]

A solution to this conundrum is to tie the family identities of parties not to the circumstances of their birth, but to the relationship between a party and rival political parties. Like Mair and Mudde's genetic view, this approach loosens the coupling between a family identity and the ways in which parties present themselves and act in their efforts to garner votes. Parties are free to change as they see fit, but their family identity is determined by their evolving location in political space relative to competing political parties. Bartels (1998: 317), for example, notes how in the United States, the Republicans exist to oppose the Democrats, and the Democrats to oppose the Republicans, even as each sheds old ideologies and competes in new areas. Party families may be construed in similar ways. Thus, the "Left" opposes the "Right," and the "Right" the "Left," even as the content of these labels and their sets of prescriptions for economy and society vary over time. What matters for the identification of blocs is not the absolute position of a cluster of parties in some political space, but the position of blocs relative to one another. That is, one cluster of parties should maintain a similar opposing position over time relative to a competing cluster.

Identifying which parties belong in which blocs proceeds first by recognizing that in redemocratizing Eastern Europe the identities of "leftist"

---

[35] The notion of "triple transition" is due to Offe (2004).

[36] The literature on postcommunist parties and party systems grows by the day, but few scholars undertake to make explicit comparisons between postcommunist systems and older party systems. One of the clearest expositions and summaries of research is Mair (1997). See also Kitschelt (1992) and Kitschelt et al. (1999).

parties are not, in general, subject to the same sorts of uncertainties as either "historical" or "new" parties. This is because the former communist parties and their various offshoots, which for better or worse are the standard bearers of the "Left" in contemporary Eastern Europe, share an organizational continuity with their precommunist forebears. Through all the name changes, mergers, fissures, and twists and turns of policy for any given country, one can draw a direct, largely uninterrupted line from the contemporary party back to the precommunist period. The notion of "Left" may have changed dramatically in the meantime, but these parties have been, nonetheless, the organizational manifestations of that party family.[37] Other families may then be identified by noting their oppositional position vis-à-vis the "Left." The preeminent family is, unsurprisingly, the "Right." What postcommunist "rightist" parties share with the precommunist Right is not necessarily ideology or a common approach to politics (though in almost all cases some such similarities can be identified), but being the principal opposition to their "leftist" opponents. More generally, precommunist "rightist" parties can be considered in the same category as postcommunist "rightist" parties even though the latter are palpably more secular on their vision of Church-State relations and, in many cases, less accepting of free-market capitalism than the former. They bear an affinity for one another as a result of occupying a similar oppositional position relative to the "Left." The task is complicated somewhat where more than one party family opposes the "Left," but not all contemporary party families necessarily must include members from the precommunist period. Secular, free-market "liberal" parties have played prominent roles in a number of postcommunist states. Although such parties enjoyed prominence before many Eastern European states achieved independence after World War I, they were not major players during the 1920s and 1930s in Czechoslovakia, Hungary, or Poland. For the postcommunist period I include them in their own bloc, separate from the "Left" or the "Right."[38]

[37] Lewis (2000: 79–80) discusses the contrast between leftist organizational continuity and ideological discontinuity.

[38] The situation is complicated for Hungary due to the gradual assimilation of the post-communist liberal parties into the "Left" and "Right" blocs. I discuss this in Chapter 2. I have been denoting all party family names in quotes to emphasize that they designate conventional labels for clusters of parties rather than concrete policy prescriptions or even ideological orientations. From here on I drop the quotation marks surrounding references to the Left and Right, it being understood that the labels refer to party groups.

1.4 Illuminating the Trajectory

1.4.1 Methodological Concerns

In the end, the mechanics of comparing two elections separated by forty years of communism is (or at least ought to be) no different from comparing two elections separated by an equal period in stable democracies. Electoral persistence may be understood either with respect to continuing support for individual parties, in cases where a post- and precommunist party can be identified as the same party, or with respect to reemergent blocs of parties. Having specified the means for identifying the starting and ending points of the trajectory, we can now address the issue of delineating the empirical links for the communist period.

Uncovering what happened during communism that led from the "pre" to the "post" cannot proceed as in Western Europe or North America, where regularly scheduled elections and, after World War II, recurrent public opinion polling mean that never more than a few years go by without an "update" of electoral preferences. These rich data discipline research because they illuminate long-run electoral trajectories, providing much needed intermediate data points that chart the slow evolution (or not) of partisan preferences. The search for electoral trajectories through communism does not benefit from such copious intermediate snapshots. Imposed against the will of the bulk of their populations, the communist regimes were not keen to risk revealing their unpopularity by tapping and publicizing party or other partisan preferences.

The elections held by some communist regimes are interesting as attempts to garner some sort of legitimacy. But, they were not a forum in which the electorate could express genuine partisan preferences. First, the regime screened all candidates, so that even "competitive" elections with more than one candidate offered no real choice.[39] Some countries, such as East Germany and Poland, maintained "bloc" parties (e.g., the Peasant Party in Poland or the People's Party in Czechoslovakia) that had phantom status as junior partners in a "coalition" led by the communists. Yet, even there votes were cast for the entire coalition, not for individual parties within the bloc. Thus, it was not possible to gauge popular support (or the

---

[39] One exception to this is the 1985 parliamentary elections in Hungary, which featured both official candidates and others who were approved, but not officially endorsed, by the Party. Vote for these other candidates may be interpretable as a vote against the Party.

lack thereof) for the Party. Second, the uncertain consequences of voting against the Party, combined with electoral manipulation, meant that regardless of the true underlying popular preferences the communists routinely gave themselves well over 90 percent of the vote.[40]

There were also numerous public opinion surveys conducted under communism. For obvious reasons, ideological and political questions that might have challenged the legitimacy of the regime did not dominate, but they did occur and provide at least a rough barometer of mass political attitudes. Kuran (1995: 211–13), for example, reviews formerly confidential survey results, apparently from studies guaranteeing the respondents' anonymity, showing that through the mid-1980s there remained significant support for "socialism" in Czechoslovakia, East Germany, Hungary, and Poland, and that in East Germany and Hungary there was significant confidence in the regime (as opposed to socialism more generally). Faith in both "socialism" and the regime began to drop in all countries after around 1985. A survey conducted in Czechoslovakia during the Prague Spring in 1968 asked respondents their voting intentions in hypothetical elections. Between 39 and 43 percent of those polled would have voted for the (then-reforming) Communist Party.[41] This finding of Czechoslovak "social-democratism" is interesting in light of the 40 percent support given to the Communist Party in the last free elections in 1946.[42] Support for "socialism," though not necessarily the ruling Party, is also reflected in surveys of Hungarian, Czechoslovak, and Polish travelers to Western countries in the late 1970s. They indicate a preference (roughly 40–45 percent) for a "Democratic Socialist" party over a "Communist" party (<10 percent) or a "Christian Democratic" party in hypothetical multiparty elections.[43]

These survey outcomes can be challenged in any number of ways. Consider first the surveys conducted within Eastern Europe. As Henn (1998) demonstrates, a commonly held view under communism was that polls were used to monitor mass loyalties. Many people feared official retribution if they provided any information that could be interpreted as critical of the regime. Kuran (1995) notes the ubiquity of "preference falsification" in

---

[40] The most comprehensive treatment of communist elections remains Furtak (1990).
[41] Brown and Wightman (1979: 181).
[42] Jehlička et al. (1993: 238).
[43] See Hart (1983), cited in Kuran (1995: 212). Many other results may be found in Connor and Gitelman (1977) and Welsh (1981).

communist regimes, suggesting that many respondents were only feigning support for the socialist system. Even if the official survey results were valid, it is often not clear how they would translate into support for alternative political parties. Lack of support for the regime does not necessarily imply Christian democratic, liberal, or any other sentiment. This is not a problem for the surveys of travelers to the West, which might be seen as a rough gauge of support for leftist and rightist party families, but those outcomes may not be representative of the distribution of preferences within the home countries. Those permitted to travel are likely to have (or least pretend to have) more "socialist" sympathies than the population at large.[44] For purposes of "filling in the blanks" of state-socialism, the biggest problem with these and similar studies of communist-era public opinion is not their potential methodological flaws, but that there is a mismatch between their results and the electoral outcomes from either the pre- or postcommunist period. Except in the case where we are interested only in national-level outcomes, the units for which there are survey data from the communist period do not match the subnational units for which there are pre- and postcommunist electoral data. Consequently, while these data may be informative on the overall national mood, they cannot illuminate the partisan trajectories for which the electoral data serve as the start and end points.

1.4.2 The Churches under Communism

In Hungary, the Churches provide both the theoretical and empirical links between pre- and postcommunist rightist partisan attachments. The reasons for this are rooted ultimately in the multifaceted interaction among Christianity, Marxism, the Churches, and state-socialist regimes. Marxism and Christianity were rivals long before the communists took over Eastern Europe. Marx famously dismissed religion as "the groan of the downtrodden creature ... the opium of the people."[45] Lenin referred to it as "a sort of spiritual moonshine ... in which the slaves of capital drown their human figure, their demands for any sort of worthy human life."[46] Marxism was, for Lenin, "absolutely atheistic and resolutely hostile to all religion."[47] The

---

[44] Connor and Gitelman (1977) provide a detailed discussion of the pitfalls of public opinion research in socialist regimes.

[45] Quoted in Tobias (1956: 10).

[46] See *Socialism and Religion*, vol. VIII, quoted in Tobias (1956: 10, fn. 2).

[47] Lenin (1943: 666). Quoted in Tobias (1956: 10).

Roman Catholic Church, in particular, was seen as the center of religious power. In 1925, Soviet diplomat Georgi Chicherin is reputed to have told a representative of the Vatican that "[i]f Rome did not exist, we could deal with the various brands of Christianity. All would finally capitulate before us. Without Rome, religion would die."[48] For its part, the Catholic Church made no secret of its distaste for communism. As early as 1846, Pope Pius IX warned that it would "completely destroy men's rights, their property and fortune, even human society itself."[49] In the 1931 Papal encyclical *Quadragesimo Anno*, Pius XI proclaimed socialism "irreconcilable with true Christianity" and that "no one can be at the same time a good Catholic and a true socialist." In 1937, he urged a campaign to thwart communism's "counterfeit mysticism" and "monstrous and hateful blasphemies." According to the Pope, communism was "intrinsically evil, and therefore no one who desires to save Christian civilization from extinction should render it assistance in any enterprise whatsoever."[50] His successor, Pius XII, excommunicated all communists in 1949.

As Michel (1991: 22) notes, "the very presence of a Church constitutes a breach of the uniformity on which Soviet-type regimes are based." This breach was multidimensional. First, as purveyors of Christianity, a worldview that is at root incompatible with the basic tenets of Marxism, the Churches could serve as a pole of potential opposition. Second, at a more symbolic level, the cross enjoyed far greater iconic status for the masses than the hammer and sickle or the red star. Church buildings, their ornate and beautiful designs a testament to both a devotion to God and the power of the Churches, offered a constant reminder that there existed an alternative to the Party and Marxism-Leninism. They offered a world of creativity and beauty that stood in dramatic contrast with the drab, distinctively "this-worldly" socialist architecture to which most people had been consigned. Finally, these physical spaces, together with devoted clergymen and lay people, had the potential to provide both space and succor for alternative views to develop and be nurtured while shielded from incessant Party scrutiny. Thus, the Churches could pose real obstacles to the remaking of society along socialist lines.

It would be a mistake, however, to view relations between the Churches and communist governments merely through a prism of mutual

---

[48] Quoted in Luxmoore and Babiuch (1999: 11).
[49] Quoted in ibid.: 2.
[50] Quoted in ibid.: 21–2.

antipathy. Their interaction was informed by both pragmatic and doctrinal considerations:

> The aim of the Party is finally to destroy the ties between the exploiting classes and the organization of religious propaganda, at the same time helping the toiling masses actually to liberate their minds from religious superstitions, and organizing on a wide scale scientific-educational and anti-religious propaganda. . . . It is, however, necessary to avoid offending the religious sensibilities of believers which leads only to the strengthening of religious propaganda.[51]

According to Stalin, "To close churches is easy, but the peasants build churches in their souls."[52]

These quotations are emblematic of the attitude of state-socialist regimes toward religion and the Churches. Although the details of Party strategy varied from country to country, the broad contours were similar: cripple, infiltrate, and co-opt the Churches; harass, intimidate, and imprison recalcitrant clergymen; erect formal and informal barriers to religious practice; proselytize and educate against the religious worldview; and employ naked force and terror where "persuasion" is insufficient. In short, religion was to be eradicated (eventually) and the Churches were to be used to legitimate communist rule.[53] The lion's share of research describes, often in harrowing detail, the many indignities the Churches and ordinary believers suffered at the hands of the communists.[54]

1.5 An Institutional Explanation

1.5.1 Clerical Resistance and the Survival of Church Community

Much of what we know about the Hungarian Churches' experiences under state-socialism suggests they should be unlikely loci for the transmission of rightist partisan attachments. It is true that at one time Cardinal

---

[51] VIII Congress of the Soviet Communist Party, March 18–23, 1919, quoted in Tobias (1956: 16).

[52] Attributed to Joseph Stalin, in an address to the Central Executive of the League of Militant Atheists. Quoted in Tobias (1956: 20).

[53] Michel (1991: 24).

[54] One of the best early works on Church-State relations in the communist world remains Tobias (1956). See also Bociurkiw and Strong (1975), Gsovski (1973), Michel (1991), and Ramet (1987, 1990, and 1992). Works related specifically to Hungary include András and Morel (1969, 1983a, and 1983b), Gergely (1985), Hainbuch (1982), Havasy (1990), Nagy Péter (2000b), Tibori (1996, 1998, and 2000), and Turányi (1988).

Mindszenty, leader of the Catholic Church in Hungary and inveterate foe of the communists, was the preeminent symbol of resistance to communism. Imprisoned in the early 1950s and released during the 1956 revolution, he subsequently took refuge in the U.S. embassy, where he resided before finally being allowed to leave the country in 1971.[55] But Mindszenty and many other less dramatic cases proved to be the exception rather than the rule. As detailed in chapters to follow, the communist regime succeeded in co-opting the Church leaderships and a portion of the local priesthood. Referring to the Catholic Church in the late 1970s, one analyst bemoaned that "[t]he Church has been humiliated, decapitated. It is a living organism without a head, marked more by mediocrity than cowardice."[56] Others have referred to the Church as "subservient"[57] and "servile."[58] One Calvinist minister called the Protestant Churches, and especially the Calvinist Church, "the last and most loyal satellites of Bolshevism in Hungary."[59] In 1980, Hungarian Party leader János Kádár acknowledged that the Churches were "without exception loyal to our regime."[60]

What has yet to be recognized is that the real locus of Church power lay not in Budapest, where Party and Church elites haggled over the contours of Church-State relations, but in the provinces, where the local clergy and the cadres struggled to undermine each other's influence. These battles took place "beneath" what appeared to be harmonious relations between Church and State at the national level and were by no means a one-sided contest, with the agents of a totalizing State ineluctably chipping away at an ever-diminishing range of clerical influence. To be sure, the conditions under which Churches had to operate placed them in a fundamentally defensive position: the Party-State controlled the schools, the media, mass organizations, and virtually all other means through which the Churches might have reached out to society. Moreover, although the Communist-imposed 1949 constitution separated Church and State and recognized freedom of religious activity, in practice the Party interfered with Church affairs and employed numerous informal methods to ensure that as few individuals as possible would take advantage of their religious freedom. These included

---

[55] These and related events are discussed in Chapters 4 and 5.

[56] Woodrow (1979). Cited in Michel (1991: 118).

[57] Michel (1991: 27).

[58] Wildmann (1986: 166).

[59] Majsai (1991: 58). There is some debate about whether the Churches ceded more than was actually necessary. Regarding the Lutheran Church, see Terray (1997).

[60] Cited in Ramet (1987: 187).

not just the familiar tactics of intimidation and incarceration, but the creative use of laws, decrees, administrative rules, and red tape, all designed to constrict the Churches and limit contact between the clergy and society. It sometimes took little to drive someone away from the Church. One woman remembers:

I grew up in a Catholic family, and as a child I had to go to church. When I was fourteen, I went to school in a town, and I lived at the school and I went to the church. One day somebody told me, 'You shouldn't go to church and you shouldn't wear a crucifix.' And somehow, now I don't go because I'm lazy or because I lost my religion.[61]

However, some clergymen fought back, exploiting to the fullest every opportunity to increase their influence. These clerical struggles bear some resemblance to the "everyday forms of resistance," defined by Scott (1989: 23) as "a stratagem deployed by a weaker party in thwarting the claims of an institutional or class opponent who dominates the public exercise of power." Similar to the tenants Scott describes in rural Indonesia, the lower clergy engaged in a "never-ending attempt to seize each small advantage and press it home, to probe the limits of the existing relationships, to see precisely what can be gotten away with at the margin...."[62] By citing the law in defense of their activities, for example, priests and pastors put the regime in the position of having to appear before the public as if it were reneging on its promise to respect religious freedom. Other strategies included efforts to couch requests within the language of the prevailing Marxist discourse, willful misinterpretation of rules designed for other purposes, feigning loyalty to socialism, and temporarily disavowing explicitly religious objectives. As in subaltern struggles elsewhere, these activities were "conducted just beneath the surface of a public realm of deference, compliance, and loyalty" and were "finely tuned to the opposition they encounter."[63] Like de Certeau's (1984) Latin American rural dwellers, who "subvert the fatality of the established order," some clergymen, having had the communist system foisted upon them, invented clever ways of beating the communists at their own game.[64] That this could occur even with coopted Church hierarchies illustrates what Osa (1989: 296–99), in reference

[61] Quoted in Bergquist and Weiss (1994: 91).
[62] Scott (1985: 255).
[63] Scott (1989: 23–4).
[64] de Certeau (1984: 17–18). Such strategies have a long pedigree. In the immediate aftermath of the French Revolution, for example, there was a law requiring Catholics to declare if they

44

to communist-era Poland, identifies as a "loose coupling" between a formal structure at the higher level and an informal organization at the lower level. Osa describes how this flexible model of Church organization permitted the Roman Catholic Church in state-socialist Poland to support collectivization of agriculture at the higher levels, but to turn a blind eye toward the political activities of the lower clergy. Likewise in Hungary, such a loose coupling permitted members of the lower clergy to improvise new strategies for maintaining church affiliation while the upper clergy professed fealty to socialism.[65]

The image of "disguised, low profile, undisclosed"[66] resistance from below provides a potent, but ultimately inapt metaphor for Church-based collective defiance. The clergy's success in maintaining church community lay in the very public nature of its battles with the regime. In this respect, clerical resistance to state-socialism resembled more canonical forms of open, contentious politics. The Churches had deep roots in society, nourished not only through religious belief, but also through mass religious practice: religious instruction in the schools; Easter, Christmas, and other festivals; and baptisms, weddings, and funerals. The Party realized early on that the religious worldview would not disappear overnight, but it hoped for a quicker victory in its efforts to confine religion to the inside first of churches, and eventually of homes. "Naming ceremonies" were offered in lieu of baptisms, "farewells" in lieu of funerals, and civil ceremonies instead of church weddings. The clerical struggle to preserve the public face of religion resembles Kertzer's (1980) description of the battle for popular allegiance fought in the Italian village of Albora between the Roman Catholic Church and the Italian Communist Party. In Italy, according to Kertzer, as in Hungary, there was a public struggle for "ritual supremacy," with the Church and the Party each promoting competing rites, rituals, and symbolic attachments.

As noted in the Introduction, the ebb and flow of individual church communities over time can be understood in terms of tipping behavior, where the decision to take part (or not) in religious practice is predicated on how others act or are likely to act, which influences the perceived risk of participation. Individuals will take part only if the rewards are seen to

---

intended to use their parish church. Some Catholics, however, acted as if the law *required* them to use their church. See Desan (1990: 141).

[65] For more on "loose coupling" in complex organizations, see Vaughan (1992: 186–7).

[66] Scott (1990: 198–201).

outweigh the risks. Each person has an internal tipping point, a threshold at which he or she receives enough assurance of others' actions such that the rewards of taking part outweigh the risks, thus triggering participation. If the distribution of thresholds is heterogeneous within a community, as it is in real communities, then religious practice should exhibit "cascade" or "snowball" behavior: the first few who participate trigger the participation of others, which induces still others, until only those with high-risk thresholds remain at home. We might then observe communities with either no or low religious practice, where only the truest of believers attend, and high levels of religious practice, where a participation cascade occurred.

The repeated clashes between the clergy and the cadres represented a multifaceted effort to manipulate how the population perceived the risks and rewards of engaging in public religious practice. Consider an individual deciding whether or not to go to church under conditions in which the State discourages it. Perhaps the largest risk in attending was being permanently labeled by the authorities as a believer. Given the regime's hostility toward religion and the Churches, it would have been reasonable to fear harassment or educational and professional discrimination. This fear would be weighed against countervailing factors, such as the satisfaction of interacting with fellow believers, and the belief that if enough people attended, the chances of being singled out would be slim.[67] The cadres sought to minimize the perceived benefits and maximize the perceived risk of participation. The clergy fought to maximize the perceived reward and minimize the risk. The fate of local church communities, and ultimately of rightist persistence, is a residue of which side ultimately triumphed.

To see how this works in practice, consider enrollment in religious instruction in the schools, my principal indicator of church community across localities. For those parents who desired it for their children, registration was statutorily public, mandatory, and required at least one signature. These rules in themselves raised the perceived risk of registration, as they required a public and written parental declaration. The local clergy could do little to evade a legal statute, but there were several other intervention

---

[67] Many "threshold" approaches to collective behavior view individual perception of risk and reward as a function solely of the proportion of others from the community who are expected to participate. See Lohmann (1994) and Petersen (2001) for excellent discussions of the relevant literature.

points in the registration process where it could counter the Party's actions.[68] One was communicating the location, date, and time of registration. If no one knows where and when registration is to take place, and everyone knows no one knows, then this will depress expected turnout and hence raise the perceived risk. The Party discouraged the announcement or posting of this information and monitored efforts to inform the rest of the community. The clergy nonetheless often broadcast it from the pulpit and enlisted the help of the laity to spread the word, often door-to-door.

Another intervention point was the period immediately preceding registration. As detailed in forthcoming chapters, the Party organized elaborate "persuasion" campaigns that included lectures extolling materialism and home visits. The Party simultaneously tried to lower the expected reward (by denigrating religion, which happened in the schools anyway) and to raise the perceived risk (through subtle and often not-so-subtle intimidation). The clergy responded with visits of its own, which often emphasized the public's legal right to religious instruction and the importance of such instruction for imbuing moral sentiments. The reference to the law was meant to assuage fears that registration could lead to prison, while the emphasis on morals dangled the promise of raising a better child as a reward. Some clergymen are alleged to have threatened to withhold Holy Communion from those who failed to register their children, thus threatening the ultimate penalty: denial of heaven. For the most pious, this must have seemed far worse than any punishment the Party could muster.

A third flash point occurred on the day of registration. As a last resort, the local cadres might try to intercept the parents on their way to register or cancel the process altogether by claiming "administrative irregularities." To prevent this, the clergy often arranged for the more fearful among the faithful to be accompanied to the registration by someone prepared to fend the cadres off and ensure that all could exercise their right to religious instruction. In some cases, the cadres themselves were persuaded to register their children. This was a particularly effective strategy at assuaging popular fears, as it telegraphed to others not only that the Party could be thwarted, but that it actually approved of the instruction.

---

[68] The Churches were, however, well aware of the deleterious effect of the procedures for registration. As I describe in Chapters 3 through 5, they were periodically brought up in discussions with the Party.

Registration for religious instruction in the schools, church attendance, and similar activities are important not just as acts of commitment under trying circumstances, but as indicators of the formation and maintenance of social networks. These networks, forged initially in the context of church life, were maintained even in the absence of a specifically religious context. A favorite clerical strategy was to organize activities, such as hikes, sporting events, movie showings, book discussions, and other social endeavors. While perhaps overseen by a clergyman or other trusted individual, these endeavors were not intended or used to directly foster religious belief. Rather, the clergy sought to maintain contact between Church and society, thereby preventing the Party's mass organizations from totally monopolizing the laity's time. The hope, of course, was that this would prevent or at least slow down the erosion of loyalty to the Churches. Naturally, the interactions emerging out of these formally organized activities often led to informal meetings elsewhere and at other times.

The degree to which church communities survived differed across Christian confessions. The two largest denominations are Roman Catholicism, claiming approximately two-thirds of the population, and the Hungarian Reformed (Calvinist) Church, with about one-quarter. Although these Churches suffered similar types of repression under communism, their responses to this repression were quite different. Catholic priests were, on average, more active and successful than Calvinist pastors in preserving church community. Following Laitin (1986), I distinguish between theological doctrine as enunciated by Church founders and the way in which that doctrine is lived in practice.[69] The focus here is on how doctrine and rules shape expectations and behavior. The reasons for the Catholic–Calvinist disparity lie partly in accidents of geography and partly in how doctrinal and organizational differences conferred advantages to Catholics in a communist context. First, the center of the Roman Catholic Church lay outside the communist world. Although the Hungarian episcopate had been forced to make unpleasant compromises in its dealing with the Party, the Church remained resolutely anticommunist. Thus, the priesthood knew where the Church stood on the matter of state-socialism, even if the bishops were compelled to collaborate. The central leadership of the Hungarian Reformed Church, by contrast, remained in Hungary and thus

[69] Laitin refers to the latter as the "practical religion of the converted."

vulnerable to communist pressure. As detailed in Chapters 3 through 5, the Church ultimately modified its theology to fit its new socialist circumstances. It saw communism as a punishment for past sins, in particular its collusion with fascism, and redefined its role as subordinate to communist authority. Thus, although some Reformed clergymen bravely continued to fight for their local churches, changes in Reformed theology legitimated clerical cooperation in a way not available to Catholic priests.

Second, doctrinally the Roman Catholic Church imposes greater obligation toward communal worship than the Reformed. Catholic Canon Law dictates that the faithful go to Mass on Sundays and select holy days.[70] On the Reformed side, by contrast, the Second Helvetic Confession states only that "it is very needful that there should be holy meetings and ecclesiastical assemblies."[71] For Catholics, sacraments, such as the Eucharist and penance, convey God's grace, rendering them indispensable for entry into heaven. In the Reformed view the sacraments confirm and aid, but do not create faith.[72] Because the bread and wine that symbolize Christ's body and blood are distributed during services, Catholics have an extra incentive to attend.

Third, the relations of authority between the clergy and the laity are quite different for the two Churches. In Catholicism, the lower clergy is appointed by the Church leadership. The priesthood is considered to be part of a divinely inspired hierarchy that mediates between God and humanity, arrogating to itself the right to interpret scripture. Calvinist pastors, by contrast, are elected and possess no such divine sanction. The authority to forgive sins confers a power to Catholic priests that no Calvinist pastor enjoys. As Carey (1985: 107) puts it, "[t]he 'Catholic' God is immanent in the world, accessible through his chosen priests and channels. The 'Protestant' God is transcendent, out there, sovereign, revealing himself to whomever he wishes." Ultimately, for Catholics there is no salvation outside

---

[70] Canon 1247, reprinted in Beal, Coriden, and Green (2000: 1445). Canon Law has evolved over time, in particular as a consequence of Vatican II, which occurred during the middle of the communist period. Unless specifically noted, all doctrine discussed here remained in force both before and after Vatican II.

[71] Cited in Leith (1963: 176). The Hungarian Reformed Church accepts the authority of both the Heidelberg Catechism and the Second Helvetic Confession. See Magyarországi Református Egyház (1967: 3).

[72] For the Catholic view, see Campbell (1996: 102–12); for the Reformed, see Niesel (1962: 262–5). Calvinists do not recognize penance (confession) as a sacrament, and refer to the Eucharist as the Lord's Supper.

the Church, whereas faith in God (and Jesus) is sufficient for Calvinist sin to be forgiven.[73] In short, Catholics had far greater incentives to participate in church life than Calvinists.

Most Catholics and Calvinists in Hungary did not attend services every week, and among those who did it is unlikely that many could convey with much precision their Church's doctrines of faith and salvation. However, this would not have precluded them from developing an informal picture of the stakes involved in religious practice. For Catholics, the choice was not merely between the Church and communism, but between heaven and eternal damnation. Any believer would think twice before leaving the church community, a fact that the clergy exploited on more than one occasion. Calvinists, by contrast, enjoyed much greater autonomy. Faced with a theology that appeared to reconcile communism and Christianity and with pastors who enjoyed no real authority over their parishioners, it was "easier" for them to leave the church fold.

1.5.2 Churches as Contexts

It is remarkable that surviving local church institutions managed to transmit what would become rightist electoral loyalties after communism, for if one lived under state-socialism it was not easy to escape the socialist message. The regime employed every tool in its arsenal to present its image of the world, from the schools to the workplace and leisure venues. Even in Hungary, with the most liberal and tolerant regime in the bloc, these efforts continued long after the end of Stalinism. As Party Secretary Kádár noted in 1970, well into Hungary's reform period, "[l]et us educate our youth that they will select socialism and will have a socialist worldview."[74] It is tempting to view the Churches as "shielding" their members against these corrosive views, but as discussed previously in this chapter, they could not provide even a semblance of such social seclusion. There was no "red" world and "white" world, each existing side-by-side in a "Siamese-twin" society, as Morin (1970) so eloquently described the situation in France. On the contrary, church networks in Hungary were permeated by cross-cutting pressures emanating from all sectors of socialist society. Church members belonged to communist mass organizations and unions and worked in factories and on collective farms with other members

---

[73] Campbell (1996: 158–9).
[74] Quoted in Medyesy (1975: 56).

of society. They served in government and were sometimes even Party members.

Moreover, the churches were made to serve as conduits for spreading socialist views. The Party succeeded not only in co-opting the higher clergy, but in introducing a fifth column of "patriotic" priests at the lower level. Known as "peace priests" for their support of the Soviet-sponsored peace movement, they were sympathetic to the regime and used the pulpit to justify Party policies and actions in Christian terms. Not all of the local clergy allied themselves with the regime. Some "reactionary" priests were courageous enough to openly exhibit their disdain for the communist regime, but they were in a distinct minority and usually received the least favorable assignments. Others attempted to avoid politics altogether, preferring the security of the gospel to the perils of entanglement with the whims of the Party line. In the end, whatever explicitly political messages were communicated within the churches were biased in favor of socialism.

How then did those local church institutions that survived transmit what would become rightist electoral loyalties after communism? The answer lies in their role as social contexts. Contextual arguments model beliefs (or behavior) as a function of both individual characteristics and the characteristics of the social environment.[75] My central claim is that being nominally Roman Catholic (or Calvinist) mattered less for the transmission of rightist attachments than being around other Catholics (or Calvinists) in a church community. Researchers have identified two broad paths through which social context operates: by maintaining a social identity that serves as a source of loyalty and by facilitating repeated social interaction that permits the formation and preservation of a political consensus. In the "identity" view a sense of shared fate predisposes group members to view their distinctiveness as a basis for common political beliefs. The "interaction" approach emphasizes social solidarity and the role of interpersonal communication in creating consensus, independent of any underlying sense of "groupness."[76]

Although it is difficult to disentangle the two mechanisms in the Hungarian context, the Churches' more important role was in fostering social

---

[75] For an extended introduction and review of the literature, see Books and Prysby (1991).

[76] For recent applications and relevant citations, see Huckfeldt, Plutzer, and Sprague (1993), Huckfeldt and Sprague (1995), and Walsh (2004). For excellent analyses focusing just on churches see Wald (1983), Wald et al. (1988), and Wald et al. (1990). An early statement of the importance of social contact for electoral persistence can be found in Berelson et al. (1954: 74–5).

interaction independent of the Party's supervision. The Party's battle against religion certainly fostered a bond between the Churches and their adherents, as both clergymen and ordinary believers were stigmatized as backward and relegated to the margins of society. The Churches were not just another organization that people belonged to, alongside a trade union or other communist mass organizations, but a focus of allegiance that existed in opposition to official loyalties. Yet, adherents interpreted and reinterpreted their political beliefs through prolonged and repeated interaction. This is why what emerged after communism was not some anachronistic constituency, wedded to outdated visions of an idealized past, but a community prepared to engage in contemporary politics. Ironically, this reformulation and preservation of rightist beliefs occurred even as some clergymen espoused socialism from the pulpit. In a study of Protestant congregations in the United States, Wald, Owen, and Hill (1988: 533) note that the respect accorded churches meant that "any political messages transmitted by church authorities are likely at least to receive a respectful hearing, to enjoy substantial credibility, and potentially to alter opinions initially in conformity with the prevailing views." Similarly, Harris (1999: 92–5) attributes the political quiescence of many Southern Black churches before the U.S. civil rights movement in comparison with their activist brethren in the North directly to differences in the activities of the resident pastors. Under statesocialism, however, congregants were aware of the pressures being put on the clergy and distinguished between the Churches as institutions and the political messages being broadcast on their behalf. Lutheran Bishop Zoltán Káldy acknowledged this in noting the popular habit of calling a pastor who attempted to link socialist politics with the Bible as "uncharitable, politician, peace pastor."[77] In its zeal to marginalize the Churches, the Party created the conditions under which alternative loyalties could thrive.

Church community provided a "natural" constituency for rightist parties once communism fell. Given the antagonism between Church and Party, rightist electoral continuity might appear to be a natural outgrowth of a desire to punish the Party's postcommunist successor for sins committed during the communist period. However, such an explanation cannot account for some anomalous facts. While anticommunist sentiment certainly accounted for the Left's stinging defeat in the first postcommunist election, it cannot so easily explain why the bulk of the church community vote went

---

[77] See "Pastors and Politics," *Lutheran Life*, May 10, 1959, translated and appearing in Juhász (1965: 241).

to parties of the Right rather than to liberal parties, which were also quite popular and equally against the communists and their successors. Moreover, the church community's preference for rightist over liberal parties is not due solely to liberal issue positions inimical to some Church doctrines. As we shall see in Chapter 6, members of the church community favor the Right even when they disagree with the Churches on matters such as abortion.

The existence of rightist electoral continuity beyond the first postcommunist election suggests that what survived during communism was not just a negative partisanship, against the communists, but a latent positive one that rightist parties found easy to tap after the fall of state-socialism. Because there were neither multiparty elections nor much relevant public opinion polling during communism, any details about the nature of this partisanship must remain tentative. However, in the early years of state-socialism, when precommunist memories were still vivid, rightist loyalties were centered within the Churches. Local church institutions prevented these attachments from withering away, even as the organizational manifestations of the Right, such as FKgP, disappeared from the political stage. These institutions operated not in lieu of family socialization, but as a necessary complement to it. If family socialization by itself had been sufficient to transmit partisan loyalties, we would see more electoral continuity than we actually do. The inroads made by the postcommunist Left into formerly rightist territory could not have occurred if rightist parents had been able to successfully pass their political attachments to their children without the assistance of other institutions. Local church institutions girded individuals against pressures to assimilate into the surrounding socialist milieu. Once communism fell, the latent partisanship shared among church adherents oriented them toward their "natural" place in the new political firmament.

1.6 Conclusion

This chapter has performed three tasks. First, it has shown that redemocratizing state-socialist countries in general, and Hungary in particular, challenge theories that purport to explain long-run political persistence. Extant theories are either inapplicable to former state-socialist countries or, if they are applicable, cannot explain the remarkable resilience of partisan attachments in such deeply disrupted societies. Second, it has identified and proposed solutions to a number of misinterpretations and inconsistencies that have prevented the formulation of a theory that takes into account the special features of redemocratizing countries. Third, it has advanced a new view of electoral continuity that relies on institutions as contexts for main-taining social interaction. As we shall see in the concluding chapter, al-though the explanation is couched in terms of Hungarian politics, it can readily be extended to other national systems where the relevant institu-tions may not be Churches and the transmitted partisan attachments may not be rightist. The immediate task, however, is to establish the pattern of electoral continuity and discontinuity between the pre- and postcommunist periods.

2

Electoral Persistence and Volatility in Hungary

2.1 Introduction

This chapter explores trends in Hungarian electoral behavior between 1945 and 1998. Its purpose is to "pin down the numbers" on Hungarian continuity and discontinuity.[1] The highly disaggregated database I have constructed permits a far more detailed examination of the many paths between pre- and postcommunist partisan attachments than has ever been possible. We will discover significant continuities in support for the Right, but also see how the postcommunist liberal bloc fashioned its support out of fragments of the old leftist and rightist constituencies. Section 2.2 provides a brief introduction to democratic politics in Hungary before communism and identifies the political blocs that will form the basis of analysis. Section 2.3 introduces postcommunist blocs, explains the shift from a three-bloc to a two-bloc system between the 1994 and 1998 national parliamentary elections, and discusses aggregate-level electoral results for all blocs between 1945 and 1998. Section 2.4 briefly reviews existing methods for comparing the results of two elections and proposes a new one that is tailored for elections that are far apart in time.

2.2 Precommunist Blocs and Elections

Although electoral politics in Hungary go back well into the nineteenth century, the most reliable, detailed snapshot we have of precommunist partisan preferences within the electorate comes from the mid-1940s, just after

---

[1] The quotation, from Stein Rokkan, appears in Bartolini and Mair (1990: 5).

World War II and before the advent of state-socialism.[2] Hungary had two national parliamentary elections, in November 1945 and August 1947, between the time Hungary was liberated in early 1945 and the formal abolition of democratic politics in 1949. The 1945 election was generally fair, but not entirely free. Held under the supervision of the Allied Control Commission, only "democratic" parties were permitted to participate. In practice this meant the exclusion of most of the prewar right-wing parties and those parties that did not participate in the Hungarian National Independence Front, an alliance that opposed fascism during the war. Six parties competed in total: the Independent Smallholders Party (FKgP), the Hungarian Communist Party (MKP), the Social Democratic Party (SZDP), the National Peasant Party (NPP), the Hungarian Radical Party (MRP), and the Civic Democratic Party (PDP).

The 1947 election was more free, because four more parties participated: the Democratic People's Party (DNP), the Hungarian Independence Party (MFP), the Independent Hungarian Democratic Party (FMDP), and the Christian Women's Camp (KNT). Only fascist parties were still prohibited. But the election was not fair. The MKP had been attempting to weaken FKgP and other parties in the years since the end of the war and encouraged the fragmentation of FKgP into smaller parties. As a consequence of the communists' well-known "salami tactics," many noncommunist party leaders fled into exile; others were arrested and deported. The period leading up to the election was marred by communist intimidation, and the results

[2] During the period of the Dual Monarchy the franchise never reached more than 7% of the population, and the secret ballot was not universal. The results thus provide little basis on which to infer whatever political attachments most people might have held. By 1920, a more liberal electoral law removed property qualifications, included women, and introduced a secret ballot. Unfortunately, although roughly 40% of the population became eligible to vote, the electoral results provide a skewed view of popular preferences. Under pressure from the government in the aftermath of the brief and unsuccessful communist "Councils Republic," the Hungarian Social Democratic Party, the standard bearer of the Left, decided to boycott the election. (The Communist Party was outlawed.) Beginning in 1922, open balloting was reintroduced into the countryside, rendering impossible an interpretation of the electoral results as a mirror of partisan preferences. The larger towns did retain secret balloting, and there the Social Democrats succeeded in winning roughly 30% of the electorate throughout the 1920s and 1930s. But there is no way of knowing what support that Left might have received in rural areas, where the party was forbidden from organizing. A secret ballot was reintroduced in 1938, but the 1939 election, conducted under the auspices of an authoritarian regime and with the leftist opposition still disadvantaged vis-à-vis government supported and extreme right-wing parties, does not provide as reliable a guide to the genuine preferences of the electorate as the 1945 outcome. See Földes and Hubai (1999), Janos (1982: *passim*), Romsics (1999: 181–91), and Ruszkai (1959).

2.2 Precommunist Blocs and Elections

Table 2.1 *Published Results of the 1945 and 1947 Elections.*

Party	1945		1947	
	Vote	(%)	Vote	(%)
FKgP (R)	2,697,503	57.0	769,763	15.4
SZDP (L)	823,314	17.4	744,641	14.9
MKP (L)	802,122	16.9	1,113,050	22.3
NPP (L)	325,284	6.9	415,465	8.3
PDP	76,424	1.6	50,294	1.0
MRP	5,762	0.2	84,169	1.7
DNP (R)			820,453	16.4
MFP (R)			670,547	13.4
FMDP (R)			260,420	5.2
KNT (R)			69,536	1.4
Left	1,950,720	41.2	2,273,156	45.5
Right	2,697,503	57.0	2,590,719	51.8

Note: The "R" and "L" indicate membership in the Right and Left bloc, respectively. The meanings of the abbreviations are given in Appendix 2.
Source: Vida (1986: 280).

are biased by the fraudulent votes known to have been cast for MKP and doubts about whether the votes were counted properly. Estimates of the number of such votes range as high as just over 200,000 out of roughly 5,000,000 valid votes cast.[3]

The results of both elections are displayed in Table 2.1, with the "L" and "R" labels denoting whether a party is classified as leftist or rightist. Both the 1945 and 1947 outcomes provide evidence of a preference for rightist parties.[4] The FKgP received the vote of Christian, nationalist, and other conservative elements to take an absolute majority of 57 percent. The workers parties MKP and SZDP together took 34 percent, and their ally NPP an additional 7 percent. As noted, the 1947 election was tainted by fraud and intimidation. Although this renders it inappropriate for further statistical analysis, the aggregate results in the table nonetheless provide further evidence that the 1945 result, which will serve as the baseline against which postcommunist results are compared, was not unrepresentative of partisan divisions between Left and Right in society. Even the reported 1947 result, which overestimates MKP support, shows rightist parties together

---

[3] For a more detailed discussion, see Szerencsés (1992).

[4] Both elections featured regional lists only. Single-member constituencies would not return until the first postcommunist election in 1990.

getting nearly 52 percent of the vote, only five percentage points lower than it had been in 1945.[5]

I designate FKgP as rightist because on the political palette of the 1945 election it was the most "bourgeois" of the parties. It is true that this party represented something of a leftist opposition to the prewar rightist authoritarian government, and that it made common cause with communists, social democrats, and others in the struggle against fascism. But as I argued in the previous chapter, what matters is less a party's absolute position with respect to one or another issue than its location relative to other parties in the system. Fascism, war, and the presence of Soviet troops shifted Hungary's entire political discourse to the left. When the exigencies of war ended, FKgP assumed a position decidedly to the right of the worker-based MKP and SZDP and their peasant allies in the NPP. The party's motto was "God, Family, and Home," and its leaders emphasized the party's respect for national and religious tradition. Some of its leaders were prominent members of the Calvinist Church, an unmistakable mark of difference with the two workers parties. Significantly, the Roman Catholic Church came out in favor of FKgP a month before the election. This probably sealed a Smallholders victory and certainly ensured the animosity of MKP. The NPP advocated a form of agrarian populism and its most important issue was land reform. Although the party contained both leftist and rightist elements (as the terms are used broadly here), it is, nonetheless, widely considered to have been an ally of the workers parties. Certainly some of its leaders cooperated with MKP, given their shared goal of radical land reform. Indeed, NPP's support for the poorest peasants made it a natural rural ally of the workers parties, which had never made much headway in the countryside.[6]

---

[5] The two results appear even closer if we examine raw votes rather than percentages. If the communists cheated by depositing more votes for themselves, then this would affect the proportions for each party, but the raw numbers only of their own party. Thus by comparing the raw totals we can "remove" the effect of additional MKP ballots. Rightist parties obtained 2,590,719 votes in 1947, 96% of their success in 1945.

[6] For information on the campaign leading up to election, see Balogh (1999). Gati (1986: 67–72) argues that the 1945 election was ultimately about a preference for evolutionary versus revolutionary change in Hungary. He speculates that the bulk of FKgP's supporters favored a "bourgeois-democratic" future, whereas MKP's, NPP's, and half of SDP's electorate preferred revolutionary transformation. This finding for the SDP is in accord with Felak (2000), who finds that the "right-wing" Social Democrats preferred the Smallholders to the Communists, whom it already suspected of wanting absolute power. For information on the 1947 election campaign, including evidence for why the new additions to the party system are labeled rightist, see Izsák (1999: 235–58).

2.3 Postcommunist Blocs and Elections

2.3.1 Blocs

The transition from communism to postcommunism represented a fundamental transformation of the ideological and issue space within which parties compete. Private property, multiparty democracy, respect for human rights, and many other concepts either condemned or at best minimally tolerated under communism became largely inviolable principles of postcommunist politics. All parties that hope to survive have been compelled to adopt what during the dictatorship would have been considered "bourgeois" stances regarding the free market, political pluralism, and tolerance for social diversity. In a sense the postcommunist political palette represents a wholesale shift to the right in comparison with the communist period.

Empirical studies of postcommunist parties and their constituencies, in Hungary and elsewhere, demonstrate the existence of an underlying bloc structure beneath the welter of new parties, ever-shifting political coalitions amid the exigencies of everyday politics, and uncertainty and political ignorance within the electorate. These bloc divisions characterize both the political elite and the mass public. Kitschelt et al. (1999: 238) employ factor analysis of midlevel party elites' survey responses to identify three distinct party groupings in Hungary through the second postcommunist election in 1994, labeled "postcommunists" (former communist parties), "liberals," and "Christian nationalists." Körösényi (1999), in a study of members of parliament, finds the same three groupings.[7] I will usually refer to "leftists" rather than "postcommunists" for the postcommunist Left. I will employ "rightist," "Christian national," and "conservative" interchangeably to refer to the grouping of parties on the right of the political spectrum.

The identities of the parties in these three blocs would surprise no one with even a cursory familiarity with contemporary Hungarian politics. In the leftist category we find, among the larger parties, the Hungarian Socialist Party (MSZP). The MSZP is an organizational successor to the old ruling MSZMP. In October 1989, the Party had split into a large moderate faction, MSZP, and the Hungarian Socialist Workers Party (MSZMP), later

---

[7] See in particular Körösényi's Chapter 5, Table 9, in which the ideological self-placement of deputies is summarized.

renamed the Workers Party. The liberal bloc features, for at least the early postcommunist period, the Alliance of Free Democrats (SZDSZ) and the Alliance of Young Democrats (Fidesz). The SZDSZ emerged from out of democratic opposition circles that, beginning in the 1970s, had criticized the regime's human rights record. Formally launched in 1988, it advocated radical regime change rather than a measured transition from communism. Over time it would gravitate more and more into the leftist camp. Fidesz was founded as a radical anticommunist youth party. Although initially identified as a liberal party, it would later undergo a dramatic shift to the right in its quest for power. I address the virtual disappearance of the liberal bloc in the following text.

The rightist camp initially comprised the Hungarian Democratic Forum (MDF), FKgP, and the Christian Democratic People's Party (KDNP). The MDF was founded by a diverse array of intellectuals in 1987 as a forum for discussions on the necessity for reform within the communist system. Initially associated with reformist circles in the ruling Party, it adopted a more anticommunist tone as the first election approached. The FKgP fashioned itself as a "historic" party, heir to the precommunist Smallholders Party that had struggled so valiantly against fascism and then communism. Relaunched in late 1988, its most important issue early on was the return of agricultural land to its former owners. The KDNP was formed in early 1989 by politicians who had been active in DNP between 1945 and 1948. The party defined itself in Christian terms. While it attempted to appeal to both Protestants and Catholics, its leaders were Catholic and the party maintained many informal ties with Catholic organizations.[8] Several smaller parties are also included included as members of particular blocs. A complete listing can be found in Appendix 3.

These bloc groupings also appear within the mass public. This is important, because it provides direct evidence for the existence of more general underlying partisan loyalties. As I have argued, what survived communism was not, in general, identification with a specific party, but rather a more diffuse attachment to larger party families.[9] Remarkably, given the decades-long absence of democratic politics and the very different meanings attributed to left and right under communism, voters in Hungary (and elsewhere) proved remarkably adept at placing parties on a left–right scale

---

[8] Enyedi (1996).

[9] In some cases, such as MSZP and FKgP, party loyalties did play a role in popular support. See Bruszt and Simon (1991: 627).

in ways consistent with the three-bloc system described in the preceding text.[10] That is, leftist parties would be placed on the left side of the spectrum, liberal parties in the middle, and rightist parties on the right end. Over time, of course, we should expect elite and mass conceptualizations to converge, because parties continually articulate their identities through political campaigns, policy choices, legislative activity, and coalition behavior. Voters eventually learn what the parties (and they themselves) are about.

Yet, even before the firstpostcommunist election, voters were beginning to sort things out. Given the rapidity of the transition from communism, it is clear that the public cannot have known much of substance about the many parties that were competing for their attention. The old ruling MSZMP had dissolved in October 1989, the same month a new electoral law set the stage for elections to be held at the beginning of March 1990. Although many embryonic parties were already in existence by late 1989, most were unknown, except perhaps for their names, and whirlwind electoral campaigns could at best communicate broad party profiles. Nonetheless, in a February 1990 poll a plurality of respondents placed both FKgP and KDNP on the right and MSZP on the left. At this time, the MDF was seen primarily as a center party, no doubt as a consequence of its association with reformist circles in the Communist Party. Only in the final weeks of the campaign, as parties attempted to appeal to uncertain voters, did divisions between liberal and rightist opposition parties emerge more sharply into public view.[11]

By November 1990, voters were already placing the six major parliamentary parties on the left–right scale in the following order: MSZP as the most leftist; Fidesz and SZDSZ as middling; and MDF, KDNP, and FKgP as most right-wing. This relative ordering, which is also perfectly consistent with the elite characterizations, remained through late 1993.[12] Voter self-placements on left–right scales can be difficult to interpret when the scales have an odd number of categories due to a tendency for respondents to choose the midpoint. Yet, even given limited response variance, we see the expected patterns. By late 1992, those who preferred FKgP, MDF, or KDNP saw themselves as more right-wing than voters

[10] Kitschelt et al. (1999: 282–3) provide a concise discussion of the complexities of left–right semantics in Eastern Europe.

[11] Tóka (1993: 334–5).

[12] Bruszt and Simon (1994: 782).

for other parties. Likewise, MSZP sympathizers were the most left-wing, and SZDSZ and Fidesz sympathizers placed themselves in the middle.[13] Employing different data and methods, Tworzecki (2003: 109) also finds that in 1992 MDF, FKgP, and KDNP supporters were more rightist than the supporters of other parties. The three-bloc configuration thus emerges robustly across several studies.

After 1994, the three-bloc system evolved into a two-bloc system, with SZDSZ becoming more closely identified with the Left and Fidesz emerging as the standard bearer of the Right. The SZDSZ's transformation was gradual. Too unpopular to rule on its own, it agreed to serve in coalition with MSZP after the latter's stunning victory in the 1994 parliamentary elections. It then joined MSZP in opposition after Fidesz's victory in the 1998 election. The fascinating details of Fidesz's transformation, engineered by the party leadership in the hope of uniting a fragmented Right and including a name change to Alliance of Young Democrats-Hungarian Civic Party (Fidesz-MPP), have been related elsewhere.[14] What is clear is that the disappearance of the liberal bloc is also reflected in mass opinion. By 1995, 60 percent of MSZP and 30 percent of SZDSZ voters classify themselves as "left-wing," whereas only 14 percent of Fidesz voters, 13 percent of MDF voters, and even fewer voters for the other rightist parties do. Likewise, whereas 26 percent of Fidesz voters and 34 percent of MDF voters label themselves "right-wing," only 12 percent of SZDSZ and 3 percent of MSZP voters do.[15] Tworzecki (2003: 109) similarly finds that by 1995 Fidesz voters had moved into the rightist camp. The two-bloc system is also evident in the evolution of electoral constituencies' sympathies for competing parties. Among SZDSZ voters, the percentage with a positive evaluation of MSZP increased from thirty-one in May 1991 to sixty-four in October 1998. During the same period such evaluations of Fidesz dropped from 91 to 51 percent. For Fidesz supporters the shift to the right appears as increasing sympathy for FKgP, which grew from 23 to 57 percent during these years. Fidesz sympathy for SZDSZ dropped from 64 to 22 percent of supporters.[16]

---

[13] Gazsó and Gazsó (1994: 143). Late 1992 was a period of tremendous and ultimately temporary Fidesz popularity, which drew from all parts of the political spectrum. All surveys from this period illustrate this lopsided support.

[14] See, for example, Kiss (2003).

[15] Körösényi (1999: 114).

[16] Angelusz and Tardos (1999b: 631).

2.3 Postcommunist Blocs and Elections

Table 2.2 *Nationwide Party List Electoral Results, 1990–1998.*

Parties	1990	1994	1998
MSZP (L)	10.89%	32.99%	32.92%
SZDSZ (Li)	21.39	19.74	7.60(L)
MDF (R)	24.73	11.74	2.80
FKgP (R)	11.73	8.82	13.15
KDNP (R)	6.46	7.03	2.31
Fidesz (Li)	8.95	7.02	29.48(R)
MIÉP (R)	–	1.59	5.47
MSZMP/MP (L)	3.68	3.19	3.95
MDNP (R)	–	–	1.34

Note: Fidesz switches from the liberal to the rightist bloc, and SZDSZ from the liberal to the leftist bloc, by 1998. The dash indicates the party did not exist at the time of the indicated election.

Source: Adapted from Körösényi (1999: 121), with added labels for Leftist, Liberal, and Rightist parties.

2.3.2 Elections

Postcommunist Hungary has a complex two-round electoral system that mixes regional party lists (one for each of nineteen provinces and one for Budapest) with single-member districts. Parliamentary seats are assigned through proportional representation with the lists, while individual candidates can be elected with merely a plurality of the vote in the districts. Analysts have termed Hungary's electoral system "uniquely complicated,"[17] and "fabulously incomprehensible,"[18] but fortunately the most difficult details need not be of concern.[19] As noted in the introductory chapter, regional party list results provide a better indicator of underlying partisan orientations than support for individual candidates. Therefore, while I will reference a party's parliamentary strength, the discussion focuses primarily on party (and bloc) popularity as measured in the regional list results from the first round. The list results for the most important parties in 1990, 1994, and 1998 are listed in Table 2.2.[20]

The 1990 election was primarily a referendum on communism. Yet unlike in Czechoslovakia or Poland, where the former communists faced a

---

[17] Benoit (1999: 12).

[18] Tóka (1995b: 44).

[19] For an excellent nontechnical overview of the electoral system, see Körösényi (1999: ch. 7).

[20] For a full list of parties and results, see Szoboszlai (1990: 596–7).

united opposition in the "founding election," in Hungary they faced a welter of different anticommunist parties. Nineteen political parties fielded a list in at least one region in the first round of the 1990 election, but only six gained the minimum popular support necessary to gain entry into parliament: MDF, SZDSZ, FKgP, MSZP, Fidesz, and KDNP. The MDF ultimately headed a rightist coalition government that included FKgP and KDNP. The SZDSZ and MSZP went into opposition.

Enormous disappointment, bitterness, anger, and resentment arose after 1990 in the course of Hungary's often painful transition to free markets and liberal democracy. As a consequence, in 1994 Hungarian voters followed their counterparts in Lithuania and Poland and voted MSZP, the former communists, back into power. The victory of MSZP was impressive. It roughly tripled its share of the popular vote and the success of its candidates in single member constituencies catapulted the party into an absolute majority in parliament. Stunned by the magnitude of its triumph, and not wanting to bear sole responsibility for painful decisions yet to be made, MSZP formed a center-Left coalition with the liberal SZDSZ. The parties of the Right, victors in the first postcommunist election, suffered a crushing defeat. The MDF bore the brunt of popular disillusionment. Battered by the defection of its extreme right-wing, which formed the Hungarian Justice and Life Party (MIÉP), it hemorrhaged support, dropping from nearly 25 percent to under 12 percent.[21] Remarkably, however, despite vicious infighting within and between parties, the formation of new parties, enormous swings in party preferences, and fears of an extremist resurgence, the six incumbent parliamentary parties were the only ones to reenter parliament through the regional lists in 1994.[22]

The Right's defeat in 1994 led to further fragmentation and political dissension. Struggles between conservatives and centrists within MDF led to the departure of the latter and the formation of the Hungarian Democratic Peoples Party (MDNP) in 1996. Leadership squabbles within KDNP over whether to take the party further to the right led in 1997 to the departure of moderates and the creation of the Hungarian Christian Democratic Alliance (MKDSZ).[23] The biggest beneficiary of these fissures on the Right

[21] For an analysis of this dramatic turn of events, see Kovács (1996).
[22] For detailed results of 1994 election, see Luca et al. (1994). Regional list outcomes are listed on p. 574.
[23] Körösényi (1999: ch. 2) provides concise descriptions of the evolution of the main parties up through 1998.

2.4 Electoral Evolution, 1945–1998

Table 2.3 *Nationwide Bloc Electoral Results, 1945–1998.*

Bloc	1945	1990	1994	1998
Left	41%	18%	37%	44%
Liberal	–	32	30	–
Right	57	43	30	53

Note: Numbers do not add up to 100 percent because some parties could not be reliably placed in any of the blocs.

Source: Author's computation based on official electoral results for regional lists, and rounded to the nearest percentage. Bloc memberships are listed in Appendix 3.

was Fidesz-MPP, whose rise in popularity coincided with a catastrophic decline in MDF's and KDNP's fortunes and also the waning of its former sister party, SZDSZ. In 1998, neither MDF nor KDNP obtained enough votes on regional lists to enter parliament on their own and succeeded only in gaining representation in single-member constituencies or in alliance with other parties. While the moderate wings of the MDF and KDNP gravitated toward Fidesz-MPP, the more extreme elements joined forces with FKgP and MIÉP, both of which saw their support rise in 1998. Although Fidesz-MPP was slightly less popular than MSZP in the regional list voting, its victories in single-member constituencies brought it into government as the leader of a rightist coalition.[24]

2.4 Electoral Evolution, 1945–1998

Table 2.3 illustrates the evolution in support for political blocs at the national level between 1945 and 1998. There are two points to be noted. First, when viewed from the perspective of the 1945, 1994, and 1998 outcomes, it is clear that the 1990 result is historically anomalous. For all the hoopla about the return of Christian national rule and mass preferences for conservative parties, the Left had and continues to have a substantial support base. Only in the critical "founding election" of 1990, when even many leftist voters tried something new, did these preferences recede. Second, the dissolution of the liberal bloc after 1994 benefited the Right far more than the Left. In aggregate terms, the 1998 outcome resembled

---

[24] Detailed electoral results, public opinion studies, and other information relating to the 1998 election may be found in Bőhm et al. (2000) and Kurtán, Sandor, and Vass (1999).

the 1945 outcome to a far greater degree than either the 1990 or 1994 results.[25]

The truly interesting patterns of persistence and volatility, however, do not become visible until we move to the subnational level. Previous attempts at uncovering subnational continuities have foundered due to either too few observations or from comparing dissimilar geographic units. Körösényi (1991), for example, compared the results of individual parties between 1947 and 1990 across five large regions. Even assuming that the 1947 results are reliable, and that the borders of these regions were more or less stable over time, increasing the number of observations from one to five does not yield much extra traction. Wiener (1997) describes in more impressionistic terms the reemergence of historical political loyalties across nineteen provinces and Budapest, but ignores border changes. This severely limits the usefulness of his analysis, because these modifications were not trivial. In 1945, Hungary was divided into twenty-five provinces ("counties") and the capital Budapest. In 1949 and 1950, a series of decrees simplified this system, reducing the number of counties to nineteen and substantially changing most of the county boundaries.[26] At the county level pre- and postcommunist results are thus not directly comparable. Until the 1970s, there existed an administrative unit between the settlement and the county. These districts (*járások*) numbered 150 in 1945. Unfortunately, their borders were frequently modified and they were abolished entirely in the 1970s. Postcommunist electoral data are available at the precinct, settlement, electoral district, and county levels. Of these, only the settlement is in principle matchable with data from the precommunist period.

The procedure for matching settlements over time involved tracking the evolution of the settlement network between 1945 and 1990. Communities often changed names, were merged together with other municipalities to form new settlements, or were absorbed by neighboring cities. More rarely they were split into smaller villages. Fortunately, the Hungarian Central Statistical Office recorded and published these transformations in a series of gazetteers.[27] I used this information to create geographic units that are

---

[25] Leftist support would rise to 50% in 2002, while the rightist vote would drop below 50%. Clearly there are many voters who are switching blocs. For other discussions of electoral evolution between pre- and postcommunism, see Hubai (2002), Kovács (1995), and Wiener (1997).

[26] Siegel (1958).

[27] See KSH (1973), (1985), (1987), and (1990).

2.4 Electoral Evolution, 1945–1998

Table 2.4 *Correlations Across Elections at the Settlement Level, 1945–1998.*

Elections Correlated	Rightist	Leftist
1998 and 1945	.37	.37
1994 and 1945	.39	.35
1990 and 1945	.25	.25

Note: The quantities in the table represent the correlations, across all settlements ($N = 2,534$), between pre- and postcommunist support for the Left and the Right.

constant between 1945 and 1990. In virtually all cases this involved aggregating villages together. To see how this works consider the capital city, Budapest. The sprawling metropolis of today was created during the 1950 reorganization, when twenty-three previously separate communities were absorbed into the city. In the dataset Budapest remains one point and its precommunist data are aggregated together to reflect the contemporary structure. Out of 3,420 observations in the data, 281 represent such aggregated constant units.[28]

How congruent are the pre- and postcommunist electoral results when viewed from the settlement level? As a first cut consider Table 2.4, which reports the grand correlation between the two periods, for both the Left and the Right, across all settlements for which there are data. There are a number of important lessons to be drawn from this table. First, because the magnitudes do not exceed 0.4, it is clear that Hungary is characterized by a mixture of persistence *and* volatility, and thus ascribing either label alone does not do justice to the variegated pathways settlements underwent between pre- and postcommunism. Second, these magnitudes are not epiphenomenal of the comparison of the three-bloc postcommunist system with the two-bloc precommunist system. The 1998 result, which featured mainly leftist and rightist parties, is not more correlated with

[28] Hereafter I employ interchangeably the terms *municipality*, *settlement*, and *village*, it being understood that in some cases the unit being referred to is an aggregated entity. The number of observations exceeds the contemporary number of registered municipalities (3,020 in 1990) because the data include villages that no longer existed in 1990. The 1945 electoral data were generously provided by the Institute for Political History, and subsequently published in Hubai (2001). The 1990–8 data are available in machine-readable format from the National Election Bureau of the Ministry of the Interior. Census data are available in KSH (1993).

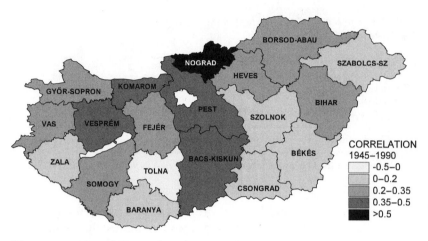

Figure 2.1 Map of Electoral Continuity and Discontinuity, 1945–1990

the precommunist outcome than the 1994 result.[29] Third, reading down each of these columns, we see that the 1994 outcome is significantly more correlated with the 1945 than the 1990 result for both the Left and the Right. Thus, for example, the correlation is 0.39 for the Right between 1945 and 1994, but only 0.25 between 1945 and 1990. This finding for the Right is robust even when the correlations are run separately for each province. The 1994 Right exhibits more continuity with the precommunist Right in sixteen out of nineteen provinces.[30] Thus, far from representing a radical departure from tradition, the 1994 election, Socialist landslide and all, was actually more continuous with the past than the 1990 election. It is the 1990 outcome, which so many hailed as a natural continuation of Hungary's conservative traditions, that was the historical anomaly.

The provincial correlations in rightist support, which vary widely, can be seen best on a map. Figures 2.1 through 2.3 illustrate continuities in support for the Right in 1990, 1994, and 1998, for all nineteen provinces. Each county's coefficient is computed by correlating the vote fractions for all the

[29] The two-bloc system is also why the correlations are the same for the Left and the Right in 1998.

[30] The exceptions are Csongrád, Nógrád, and Tolna counties. See Appendix 4 for the detailed provincial results. For the 1994 Left, ten out of nineteen provinces follow this pattern.

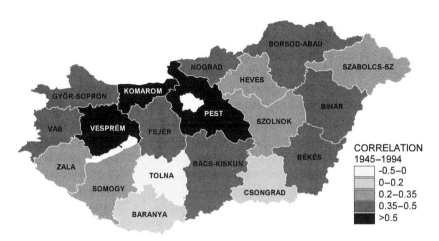

Figure 2.2 Map of Electoral Continuity and Discontinuity, 1945–1994

settlements in that county.[31] The remarkable rightist persistence between 1945 and 1994 is illustrated in Figure 2.2, with the correlation in three counties exceeding 0.5 and many more between 0.35 and 0.5. Comparing these correlations with similar ones computed for other political systems can be tricky because high levels of geographic aggregation (i.e., fewer observations) tend to inflate the size of correlation coefficients.[32] Fortunately, the data under analysis here are at a lower level of aggregation than the units often employed in other studies, so if the Hungarian numbers are equal or close to those from studies where larger units are employed, we have even more evidence for persistence. As noted in the Introduction, the Hungarian magnitudes are huge· in comparison with similar correlations across counties for presidential elections in the United States. The same is true in comparison with the United Kingdom. Miller (1977: 135) reports a correlation of 0.67 between the 1924 and October 1974 Conservative Party vote shares for 161 English constant units. Even with such highly aggregated areas, and under conditions as favorable as those in Britain, which did not experience a disruption in its party system during the entire period, the correlations are not that much higher than in the most persistent regions in

---

[31] The small white unit within Pest county is the capital, Budapest. Because it represents one observation in the data, it has no associated correlation coefficient.

[32] See Blalock (1964). The logic is most easily illustrated by imagining a country with two provinces, where the rightist vote is being correlated between two elections. Because two points define a line, the correlation between the two elections will always be one.

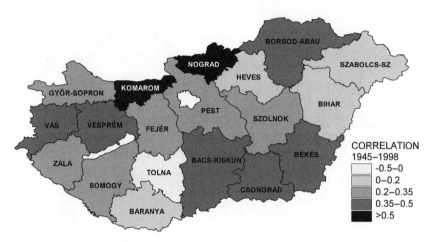

Figure 2.3 Map of Electoral Continuity and Discontinuity, 1945–1998

Hungary. Given all that Hungary endured during the communist period, the degree of continuity is remarkable.[33]

As seen in Figure 2.3, only some parts of Hungary maintained their historical preferences with the shift to the two-bloc system in 1998. This is not unexpected. In many ways, the liberal parties represented a way station between the Left and the Right, with part of their support coming from former leftist areas and part from former rightist areas. In 1994, the liberals received an average of 27 percent of the vote in 361 settlements that gave greater than 90 percent of their vote to the Right in 1945.[34] Likewise, they received an average of 27 percent in the forty-nine settlements where the Left vote was greater than 80 percent in 1945.[35] Thus, it appears as though both the former leftist and former rightist political camps "donated" significant support to the liberal bloc.

If we examine postcommunist liberal strongholds and project back to see how they voted in 1945, we see that the liberals had somewhat better luck in formerly rightist than in formerly leftist areas. Across 104 settlements where the liberal bloc received at least 40 percent of the vote in 1990 and

---

[33] All correlations have been computed using contemporary county borders. Rerunning the analysis using the 1945 borders does not significantly alter the magnitudes.

[34] The eight settlements that are listed as voting 100% for the Right are excluded, to guard against the possibility that there was coercion in these places.

[35] Leftist support was largely urban in 1945, whereas the Right won over most of the villages. Hence, there are many more places with a high rightist vote than a high leftist vote.

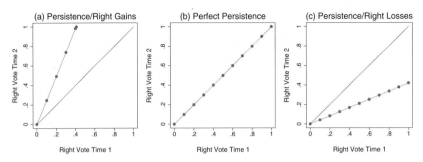

Figure 2.4 Perfect Correlation, Imperfect Persistence

1994, the average vote for the Right was 67 percent in 1945, roughly ten percentage points above the national average at the time. That the liberal constituency comprised many formerly rightist areas, however, does not guarantee that, once dissolved, the remnants of that liberal constituency will return to their precommunist preferences. The very existence of the liberal bloc through 1994 is evidence that many had neither firm leftist nor firm rightist loyalties. Moreover, much political learning had taken place by 1998. As Kitschelt et al. (1999: 384) note, the political institutions in place since the fall of communism begin to have an independent effect on the distribution of partisan attitudes. Where these effects operate in ways contrary to historical patterns, it is likely that those patterns will inevitably give way to new configurations. We will see further evidence of this in Chapter 6.

Correlation coefficients offer an intuitive illustration of political continuities, but we will need a better metric for evaluating the congruence between two electoral results. This is because even a perfect correlation between two outcomes is consistent with a wide range of actual votes in the two periods. To see this, consider Figure 2.4, which consists of three panels, each of which describes a scatterplot of results from two hypothetical elections. In each panel the dots represent imaginary geographic units, plotted according to the vote share received by the Right at two different points in time. In addition to plotting the Ordinary Least Squares (OLS) regression line in each panel, I also include the 45-degree line, seen in panels (a) and (c) without dots. The key feature of this figure is that in all three panels there is a perfect correlation in rightist support between election 1 (the horizontal axis) and election 2 (the vertical axis), even though each panel quite clearly presents a different relationship between the two elections.

71

There is perfect persistence only in panel (b), where the regression and 45-degree lines coincide: in each geographic unit, the Right receives exactly the same share of the vote in each election. Clearly, such a situation is inconceivable in a real political system because even in a world of perfectly effective parties, random shocks at time 2 are likely to move at least some units off the 45-degree line. If panel (b) has a utility it is as a theoretical baseline against which actual results can be measured. Indeed, one could construct a crude index of congruence based on the extent to which units deviate from the 45-degree line. Analogous to OLS, one could construct a sum of squared deviations from the 45-degree line and divide by the number of units to generate an average deviation. If we subtracted the entire quantity from one, the index would range in value from zero, where all points are the maximum distance from the line (which would place them all either at the [0,1] or [1,0] locations on the plot), to one, where all points fall on the 45-degree line.[36]

Panels (a) and (c) also represent forms of persistence, one in which the Right gains support (panel [a]), and one in which the Right loses support (panel [c]). For illustration purposes the regression lines are drawn with an intercept of zero, but that is incidental. The logic would work just as well if the intercepts were also varied in addition to the slopes. What matters is that in each panel we can predict the outcome at the second election by knowing the outcome of the first election. Again, in any real electoral comparison there will be variance about the regression line. However, the degree to which one outcome predicts the other is another form of stability. As Hoschka and Schunck (1978: 33–4) argue, by comparing the slopes, intercepts, and reduction of variance (R^2) to the theoretical baseline in panel (b), we can assess deviation from perfect continuity. That is, the closer the slopes are to one, the intercepts are to zero, and R^2s are to one, the greater the persistence.

As one final indicator of stability between two elections I consider the results of bivariate OLS regression of the latter outcome on the former. The results of these regressions should be interpreted in descriptive rather than causal terms. The precommunist vote does not directly cause the post-communist vote, but it is a factor further back in the causal chain. Bivariate regression does, however, describe the basic relationship between the post- and precommunist results. That is, it illustrates the variance between the

---

[36] This index is clearly sensitive to the number of major parties (or blocs) in the system. I leave the details for future research.

two votes that the postulated mechanisms of transmission (or their absence) should ultimately reduce. These mechanisms, described in Chapters 4 and 5, act as the intervening causal factors between the pre- and postcommunist periods. Ultimately, they will be included in a multivariate model of the postcommunist vote described in Chapter 6.

Detailed regression results for all counties and postcommunist elections are relegated to Appendix 4. Here I illustrate the regressions graphically, for select counties and Hungary as a whole. Following Bartels (1998), I define the rightist vote margin as the difference between the rightist and leftist vote proportions in each settlement in each election year. Thus, in 1998, for example, *Right Margin* 1998 = *Right Vote* 1998 − *Left Vote* 1998. Similar transformations are effected for 1945, 1990, and 1994. Working with vote margins dampens the depressive effect of the liberal bloc on rightist support, rendering vote fractions in the two-bloc precommunist period more comparable with fractions in the three-bloc postcommunist period. Figure 2.5 displays a matrix of scatterplots for Hajdú-Bihar, Veszprém, and Zala counties, and the entire country. The three counties are chosen because they will feature prominently in the historical analysis in Chapters 4 and 5 and the multivariate statistical analysis in Chapter 6. Each "cell" of this scatter matrix features a comparison of the 1945 and postcommunist rightist vote, defined as a vote margin.[37] Superimposed on each scatterplot are a solid 45-degree line and a dashed regression line. Each dot represents a settlement.

There are several interesting features of this scatter figure. First, examining the position of the points with respect to the horizontal axis, Right Margin 1945, we see that Hajdú-Bihar was more leftist before communism (due to support for NPP in 1945) than either Veszprém or Zala. That is, there are more points to the left of zero in Hajdú-Bihar than in the other two counties. Zala's conservatism really pops out in the third row of the matrix, with only a few leftist places and many more that were overwhelmingly rightist (close to 1 on the horizontal axis). Second, in most cases the slope of the mass of points is positive, though less than one (the 45-degree line). This is evidence of the success with which the Communist Party was able to "open up" the villages and make them available as a source of support for the postcommunist Left. Points that fall below the 45-degree line

---

[37] Hence, the axes range from −1 through 1. A margin close to 1 indicates a massively rightist settlement; −1 a leftist settlement. Evenly divided municipalities will have a margin close to 0. I discuss this in greater detail in Chapter 6.

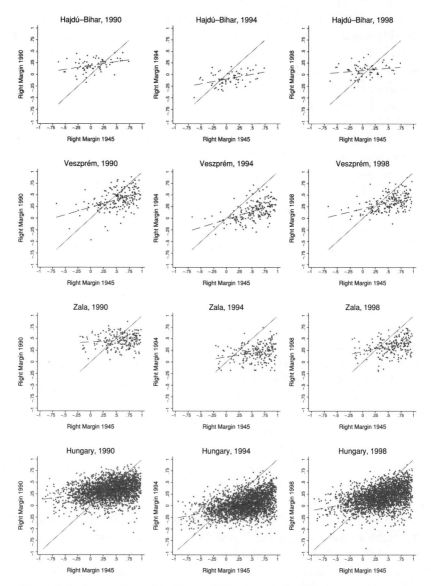

Figure 2.5 Scatterplots of the Pre- and Postcommunist Vote

experienced a net loss of support for the Right between pre- and postcommunism; points above the 45-degree line are more rightist today than in 1945. Glancing through the plots, we see that while the Left succeeded in permeating many formerly rightist areas, there remain substantial continuities. With the exception of Zala in 1990 (third row, first column of the matrix), on average the more rightist areas before communism remain more rightist after communism. Finally, this figure reminds us that persistence is ultimately a feature of individual localities, not aggregations of localities. That is, what is of greatest interest is why some points fall closer to the 45-degree line, whereas others lie further away. This remains true even if the "universe" of points shows no overall trend, as in Zala county in 1990. In Chapter 6 we will see that the presence of local church institutions is an important factor in determining the degree to which a locality preserved its rightist partisan attachments.

2.5 *Conclusion*

This chapter performed three tasks. First, it demonstrated the bloc structure of party politics at both the elite and mass levels. Far from being a "tabula rasa," diffuse partisan loyalties for political tendencies existed even early in the transition period. Second, it discussed multiple ways of conceptualizing electoral persistence, and illustrated extraordinary continuities in support for rightist parties despite nearly a half century of disruptive communist rule. Thus, not only did partisan loyalties for the Right exist, but their roots lay in the precommunist period. Third, it overturned the conventional wisdom regarding the historical interpretation of the 1990 and 1994 elections. The Socialist landslide in 1994, far from being a radical break with history, in electoral terms was far more continuous with the past than the rightist victory in 1990, touted by all as a return to the "natural" state of affairs.

Yet, while these comparative statics may depict the beginning and endpoints of the multiple pathways between pre- and postcommunism, they offer no illumination of the trajectory. It remains to uncover the mechanisms by which partisan attachments were transmitted through the communist period. Ultimately, this will take us deep into village life, but first we begin by describing the initial, fateful encounters between the communists and the Hungarian Churches. Chapter 3 shows how the Communist Party drastically curtailed the Churches' economic and organizational life.

3

The Churches First Confront Communism

3.1 Introduction

We now explore the Churches' role in providing an arena for resisting the Party's efforts to remake partisanship in society. Any retelling of the battle between Church and State under state-socialism should begin with a picture of the reservoir of support and tools each could call upon as the struggle began. Chapter 2 briefly discussed the communist movement; here we begin by summarizing the cultural, economic, political, and spiritual influence of the Churches in society in the years preceding the communist takeover. The purpose is not to provide a comprehensive account of Church-State relations, but rather to highlight the deep roots the Churches had in Hungarian society. The chapter then chronicles the dramatic diminution of the Churches' institutional presence between the end of World War II and the early years of the Stalinist regime. I focus in particular on the strategies the regime employed both to shrink the Churches and to harness what remained to the service of socialism. The Party's newly erected institutions of surveillance and control will serve as the backdrop for the discussion of the local struggles for mass loyalty in Chapters 4 and 5.

3.2 The Churches before State-Socialism

Roman Catholicism became the official religion of Hungary in 1000 A.D., when King Stephen received his crown from Pope Sylvester II. For nearly six centuries, Catholicism reigned supreme, enjoying economic, educational, spiritual, and legal predominance. Calvinism began to spread in Hungary beginning in the sixteenth century and the Reformed faith enjoyed legal protection beginning with the Diet of Torda in 1557. At one point up to 90 percent of the population had become Protestant, but with the support of the Hapsburgs the Church effected a successful counter-Reformation, re-Catholicizing a majority of the ethnic Hungarians in the empire.[1] Although the Hungarian half of the Austro-Hungarian monarchy contained a multitude of confessions, with the dissolution of the Hapsburg empire the Roman Catholic and Reformed (Calvinist) Churches became the dominant confessions in Hungary. By 1920 roughly 64 percent of Hungary's population was Roman Catholic and 21 percent was Reformed.[2] Jews and Lutherans each comprised roughly 6 percent of the population and Greek Catholics made up about 2 percent.[3]

The Churches were major landholders during the interwar period. According to a 1935 survey, of the 16,081,844 cadastral hold (about 183 million acres) that comprised the territory of the country, the Roman Catholic Church owned 862,704.[4] Of this, 736,593, or roughly 85 percent, was in the form of landed estates.[5] Although these estates were split up among many different bishoprics and monasteries, the Church as a whole was the largest landowner in a country where 0.15 percent of estates occupied one third of the holdings, and roughly three quarters of the dwarfholdings were five hold or less.[6] The Church's property made it a serious economic force, both as an employer and producer. The Reformed Church possessed 102,755 hold in 1935.[7] For both Churches the income derived from their agricultural holdings helped pay for the educational, charity, and other services they provided society.[8]

Both the Reformed and Roman Catholic Churches benefitted from a network of lay social and cultural associations. The most important

[1] Pungur (1992: 107).
[2] According to the 1910 census, which would have covered pre-Trianon Hungary, roughly 52% of the country was Roman Catholic, 15% Greek Orthodox, 13% Calvinist, 10% Greek Catholic, 6% Lutheran, and 4% Jewish. See Bangha (1931–3: vol. III, 244).
[3] András and Morel (1969: 97).
[4] A hold is an archaic measurement unit. 1 cadastral hold = 11.422 acres = 0.576 hectares.
[5] Gergely (1997: 297) and Laszlo (1973: 294, 303).
[6] Laszlo (ibid.: 294).
[7] Gergely (1997: 318).
[8] The land question remained one of the most pressing problems facing the country during the interwar period, yet land reform efforts proved modest in execution. The 1920 reform distributed a total of 1,275,548 hold, amounting to merely 8.5% of the arable land in the country. The 412,000 landless and dwarfholders who benefitted received on average only about 1.5 hold. Most of the new landowners still owned less than the 8–12 hold experts considered necessary for subsistence. See Laszlo (1973: 292–3). No significant land reforms were enacted until 1945.

organizations for the Reformed were the Kálvin Association, the Soli Deo Gloria student alliance (SDG), the Protestant Literary Society, the Gábor Bethlen Association, and the Christian Youth Association (KIE).[9] The general purpose of such organizations was to imbue society with a Christian spirit, though they often had more concrete educational, charity, and other missions as well. The SDG movement, for example, served to educate about the fate of the Hungarians in the aftermath of the peace treaty, land reform, the role of faith in modern society, and other topics of concern to the Church. Others performed missionary work among the youth and young adults, fostered Protestant cooperation, encouraged a religious worldview, or performed service for the poor and orphaned.[10]

The Catholic Church enjoyed a far broader and denser network of lay organizations than the Reformed Church. Though there is disagreement on the precise membership figures, it is clear that there was virtually no section of society that did not have its own organization. According to one estimate, by the end of World War II there were no fewer than 7,522 devotional groups alone, with a combined membership of over 700,000 people, representing over 10 percent of the Catholic population of the country.[11] The following, incomplete list of lay associations exemplifies some of the ways in which society had been organized:[12]

Szívgárda: An association of elementary school children, intended to strengthen the children's spiritual outlook. There were approximately 2,500 groups with 250,000 to 300,000 members.

[9] Bolyki and Ladányi (1987: 89–90).
[10] For a detailed description of the origin and activities of Protestant lay organizations through World War II, see Laszlo (1973: 263–313). Unfortunately, there appears to be little information regarding the membership sizes of these associations.
[11] Gergely (1985: 229).
[12] Unless otherwise noted, figures are taken from Póka (1988: 285–8). The numbers refer to the situation as of 1942, and thus reflect the territories gained from Romania and Slovakia before and during World War II. See also Adriányi (1974: 79–80), András and Morel (1969: 135–6), Galter (1957: 198), Gergely (1997: 206–10), and Laszlo (1973: 276–81). For a more comprehensive list of organizations, see Bangha (1931–3: vol. II, 524–5). Póka (1988: 283–8) is less comprehensive, but provides some membership figures. Catholic organizational strength was made even more effective through the formation in Hungary of Catholic Action, a movement launched in 1922 by the Holy See to help counter the rising organizational power of anticlerical groups. Established in 1933 in Hungary, it operated as a "peak organization" to coordinate the activities of all Catholic associations and movements. According to Galter (1957: 197) there were 5,000 Catholic Action groups operating in Hungary by 1945. For details on Catholic Action's activities during this period, see Gergely (1997: 152–5) and Póka (1988: 278–82).

Mária-kongregáció: An association of middle-school students whose goal was to encourage people to perform their tasks conscientiously and to deepen their spiritual identification with the Church. There were approximately 500 such groups with 23,000 members.

Credo: Intended for adult males, this organization deepened religious life and prepared its membership to proselytize. There were approximately 352 groups with 60,000 members.

Élő Rózsafüzér Egyesület: Similar to Credo, but composed primarily of women, this association had approximately a half million members across 1,500 congregations.

KIOE: The National Association of Catholic Workers had ninety groups and approximately 5,000 members.

KLOSz: Young Women's Catholic Association had seventy-six groups, each with twenty to sixty members.

KALOT/KALÁSZ: Peasant youth movements for men and women, respectively. By 1940, KALOT existed in roughly 2,500 villages, with membership of almost 300,000.[13] By 1942, membership had risen to a half million.[14] In 1939, KALÁSZ had 1,400 local associations with 60,000 members.[15]

EMERICANA: A university youth union with forty-seven groups, thirteen provincial sections, and approximately 10,000 members in 1945.[16]

The Catholic Church had religious orders as well as lay organizations. In 1909 the Jesuits started an independent Hungarian order, which grew by 1931 to seven cloisters and 264 members.[17] The Lazarists arrived in 1898 and by 1926 had established four cloisters with sixty-eight friars. The Salesians, resident in Hungary since 1900, had by 1933 established nine branches with 140 members. According to 1950 figures, there were a total of twenty-three male orders, with 182 monasteries and 2,582 members. The number of female religious was equally impressive. Between 1919 and 1935, the number of houses grew from 231 to 409, with an increase in membership

---

[13] Farkas (1988: 298).
[14] Adriányi (1974: 79).
[15] Stettner (1988: 314).
[16] András and Morel (1969: 136) and Galter (1957: 198).
[17] Unless otherwise noted, all figures on the size of orders are drawn from Adriányi (1974: 77–8).

from 3,290 to 6,676.[18] In 1950, there were thirty-nine orders with 11,538 members. The primary task of these orders was devotion to prayer and the dissemination of Christianity, but they also provided a range of social services. Some orders ran their own hospitals and schools, and many religious worked in other hospitals, schools, orphanages, homes for the needy, and other charitable organizations.[19]

The Churches had a commanding position in education. Roughly 69 percent of all elementary schools in 1930 were denominational and educated 70 percent of the eligible population. Of the Church schools, 61 percent were Roman Catholic and 24 percent were Reformed. Church presence was considerably less in the middle schools. Only 28 percent of these schools were denominational, and of these 76 percent were Roman Catholic and 13 percent were Reformed. The Roman Catholic Church ran 52 percent and the Reformed Church one-eighth of forty-eight teacher training schools. The State maintained 37 percent of all secondary schools versus 52 percent by the Churches or Church educational funds. Of the eighty-one denominational secondary schools, 46 percent were Roman Catholic and 28 percent were Reformed.[20]

The Churches' eminence in interwar society was even greater than that indicated by the human and material resources it formally commanded. During the era of liberal government prior to the collapse of Austria-Hungary, the relationship between the State and the Catholic Church had often been conflictual, with the Church struggling, ultimately unsuccessfully, against the introduction of civil marriage, the legalization of divorce, a law on freedom of conscience permitting people to be nonbelievers, and other laws challenging the Church's traditional prerogatives.[21] The

---

[18] Gergely (1997: 179) lists 6,677 female religious in 1935.

[19] For details on female religious orders during this period, see András and Morel (1969: 190–210). For both male and female orders, see Gergely (1997: 177–205) and Hervay (1988: 157–321).

[20] Kornis (1932: 277–84). Elementary school (*népiskola* or *általános iskola*) lasted from grades 1–4. Those planning to attend vocational schools would first attend a middle school (*polgári iskola*) from grades 5–8. Otherwise the secondary school (*gymnázium*) would last from grades 5–12. See ibid.: 289. A comprehensive breakdown of the number of different types of schools and their overall enrollment by confession for the 1928/29 school year may be found in Bangha (1931–3: vol. II, 375–6).

[21] The Hungarian *Kulturkampf* took place in the 1890s with the full support of the Protestant Churches, who saw liberal reforms as ameliorating their own inferior position vis-à-vis the Catholic Church. This Catholic defeat was a major factor behind the Church's renewed organizational vigor in the interwar period. See Laszlo (1973: 49–52).

interwar State, while not abrogating the gains that had been made, abandoned laicization efforts. Following the failed leftist revolution after World War I, it embarked on a distinctly "Christian" course. The rule of the new regent, Admiral Miklós Horthy, was conservative, intending to "restore traditional values, institutions, and authorities, belief in the God of the Churches, in the army of the crown, in the sanctity of family ties and of private property."[22] In a letter to the Archbishop of Esztergom after his election as regent, Horthy, a Protestant, declared that "the religious and moral basis which the Church led by Your Eminence has always faithfully fostered is the sole foundation of the reconstruction of our country...."[23]

The Christian course was particularly vivid regarding education. The State effectively ceased to compete in this area with the Catholic Church. There was an implicit understanding that the State would not establish schools in Catholic villages and would alter the curriculum of preexisting schools so as not to compete directly with Catholic institutions. The State also agreed to appoint a Minister of Education that was acceptable to the Church hierarchy.[24] Moreover, the government continued its earlier practice of subsidizing denominational schools and also permitted education in nondenominational schools to assume a religious hue. According to Act XII of 1927, the purpose of the middle schools was to imbue "the pupils in a religious, moral, and national spirit."[25] A similar act in 1934 charged high schools "to rear the pupils to be moral citizens on a religious basis."[26]

The social and political importance of the Churches can best be summed up in Prime Minister István Bethlen's explanation for why the State was reserving seats for Church dignitaries in the Upper House, reconstituted in 1926:

The Christian Churches in Hungary have always been important factors in the maintenance of the State, and when we now wish to organize the Upper House so as to provide participation for all the significant elements of Hungarian society, it is impossible to disregard the chosen leaders of these Churches and it is impossible to abrogate their historic privileges when these historic privileges still represent significant authority and an important asset in Hungarian society. The Christian Churches participated only recently with united effort in the work of rebuilding the Hungarian State and the relationship of the Hungarian State to them

---

[22] Ignotus (1972: 152–3).
[23] Cited in Laszlo (1973: 192).
[24] Janos (1982: 231).
[25] Cited in Laszlo (1973: 217).
[26] Ibid.

has, following the anti-religious strivings of the revolutions, become perhaps even more intimate than it had ever been during the era preceding the revolutions. It is impossible that the overwhelming majority of Hungarian society should wish to sever this connection which represents a valuable asset for the Hungarian State also; on the contrary, the majority of Hungarian society no doubt wishes to cultivate and develop it.[27]

3.3 Enfeeblement

Between 1944 and 1950 the Churches' imposing institutional presence was largely expunged from Hungarian society. This dramatic change was bound up with the country's transformation into a communist dictatorship during the same period, and indeed formed a crucial component of that transition. Details of the actions and events by which the pillars of Church power were progressively eliminated in the aftermath of World War II have been well described elsewhere.[28] However, it is necessary to describe some of the important early clashes between Church and State because they set the stage for the framework the Communist Party would later erect to regulate the Churches' activities during the state-socialist period. If the narrative emphasizes Catholic travails over the Reformed, it is not because the Reformed Church suffered any less. The Catholic Church was a far larger and more formidable opponent for the communists and resisted communist encroachment more vociferously and for a longer period than the Reformed Church, even if in the end both Churches would be placed in a position of dependence.

Among the first challenges to the Churches was land reform. In late 1944, the Soviet Union set up a provisional Hungarian government with representatives from the Communist Party, the Social Democratic Party, the Smallholders Party, and the National Peasant Party. On March 15, 1945 this government announced a massive land reform. The decree called for all estates "belonging to traitors, Arrowcross members, National Socialist and other fascist leaders" to be confiscated in their entirety. Estates larger than 1,000 hold were also to be confiscated, with the exception of those belonging to local governments, communities, and Churches, which could retain 100 hold. Due compensation was promised. Those "who gained extraordinary merit in the national resistance and the anti-German freedom fight" would

---

[27] Cited in Laszlo (1973: 214).

[28] See, for example, Annabring (1953), Barron and Waddams (1950), Beeson (1982), Galter (1957), Gsovski (1973), Hutten (1967), MacEoin (1951), and Tobias (1956).

be allowed to retain 300 hold.[29] In the end, roughly 39 percent of all arable land would be expropriated. About 42 percent of this would be retained by the State with the rest being distributed to over 640,000 people.[30]

The reform had a decisive impact on the Catholic Church. Of the Church's 862,704 hold, the State expropriated 765,864, or 89 percent. Archdioceses, bishoprics, religious orders, and other institutional entities were permitted to retain 100 hold each.[31] The reform effectively removed the economic means by which the Church had financed its vast ecclesiastical, organizational, and educational network. According to one estimate, the Church was responsible for approximately 6,000 Church personnel, 12,000 teaching staff, 3,000 churches, 1,500 parishes, 200 Catholic social institutions, 2,000 retirees, and several thousand lay employees.[32] The danger was clear to the bishops, who feared that that decree threatened "the very existence of ecclesiastical institutions by depriving them of their material foundations."[33] The Church protested the "hateful spirit of vengeance" of the reform provisions and "the lack of consideration and dignity" with which the reform was being implemented, but did not offer much resistance.[34] The Church never received compensation adequate to cover its expenses.

The Reformed Church also suffered as a consequence of the land reform, though its losses were proportionally less than that of the Catholic Church. There were fewer large estates in the Reformed areas of eastern Hungary and the Church owned only about 12 percent as much land as the Catholic Church. It retained about 60 percent of its holdings.[35] As with the Catholics, there was concern in Church circles that the Church would be left with insufficient means to support its network of schools and other

---

[29] Ministerial decree n. 600/1945. Excerpts in English may be found in Juhász (1965: 13–14). Quotes are from p. 13.

[30] Figures are from Hoensch (1996: 171–2).

[31] Gergely (1985: 24–5).

[32] Gergely (1977: 238).

[33] Pastoral letter of May 24, 1945, reprinted in Mindszenty (1949a: 11–21). Citation is from p. 16.

[34] See Mindszenty's first pastoral letter as Cardinal, in October 1945, reprinted in Mindszenty (ibid.: 26–34). Quotes are from p. 31. The Church later defended itself against accusations that it opposed the land reform. See the statement on the Church and agrarian reform, published in the Catholic publication *Új Ember*, November 18, 1945, reprinted in Mindszenty (ibid.: 41–5). For a concise overview of the reform and the Catholic reaction, see Hainbuch (1982: 8–11).

[35] Kádár (1958: 96).

organizations.[36] However, the "Free Council of the Reformed Church," an unofficial movement within the Reformed Church that would later assume leadership of the Church, fully approved of the land reform.[37]

An early challenge to associational life occurred in July 1945 with a decree requiring all associations to submit reports to the Interior Ministry detailing their political activities since January 1, 1939, including what stand they took, if any, toward the war, and the names and functions of all officers.[38] With this act the government succeeded in collecting invaluable information on the numbers and types of civic associations. In June 1946, the government issued a decree placing all social organizations under the authority of the Ministry of the Interior.[39] This decree was meant to modify and fulfill a 1938 ordinance that empowered the government to dissolve an association that continued "clandestinely an activity which deviates from the statutes."[40] In practice this put the Interior Minister, a communist, in a position of absolute authority over religious and other associations. In July 1946, in response to the murder of a Russian soldier, the government began disbanding the most important youth social organizations, including the Catholic KALOT and KALÁSZ. According to one estimate, within a short time about 4,000 local Catholic organizations were suppressed.[41] Although purely religious associations, such as Credo, Mária-kongregáció, and Élő Rózsafüzér Egyesület, were not immediately dissolved, proscriptions on assembly rendered their effective operation impossible.[42]

The decree also touched Reformed associations, though they were far smaller and less numerous than the Catholic. Many had ceased any real

---

[36] This was expressed in various Protestant circles. See Tobias (1956: 433).

[37] Kádár (1958: 102). In the end, all Churches "voluntarily" gave up most of the land that remained in their possession in connection with the establishment of a Church fund (regulation 170/1951 of the Council of Ministers). The fund's purpose was "[t]o provide the material security necessary for the performance of Church-related activities and tasks." See András and Morel (1983b: 174) and Hainbuch (1982: 56–7).

[38] Decree Nr. 20.165/1945 B.M.I. See Gsovksi (1973: 89) and Hainbuch (1982: 130–1).

[39] Decree Nr. 7330/1946 M.E. may be found in Hainbuch (1982: 131).

[40] Cited in Barron and Waddams (1950: 62).

[41] Galter (1957: 206–7). The Church hierarchy immediately voiced concern that associations would be dissolved without concrete evidence that they were engaging in unlawful activity, and requested that the investigations be conducted lawfully. See Mindszenty's letter of protest to the Prime Minister, in Mindszenty (1949a: 65–7).

[42] Káldi (1956: 64). Gergely (1977: 251–7) summarizes the postwar reorganization of Catholic associations and their subsequent suppression. One organization that was not liquidated was Catholic Action, which continued to exist at least formally even during the height of Stalinism in the early 1950s. See Szeghalmi (2000: 10).

operations by the end of World War II or had merged with communist-dominated organizations. For example, even before the end of the war SDG was merged with the Hungarian Youth Freedom Front (*Magyar Ifjúság Szabadságfront*), which was directed by the Communist Youth Alliance (*Kommunista Ifjúsági Szövetség*).[43] Others altered their membership and leadership after the war to be more sympathetic to the communists, in anticipation of police interference. This happened with the KIE. KIE and other organizations were suppressed by 1950.[44]

Education reform led to the virtual elimination of Church influence in the schools. The exclusion of the Churches took place in several stages. In August 1945, the government implemented a rationalization of the school system that had been planned since 1940. The gist of the reform was that the four-grade *népiskola* would be combined with the four-grade *polgári iskola* or the lower four grades of the *gimnázium* into a new eight-grade general school (*általános iskola*). The *gimnázium* would then become four-grade. The problem for the Churches, which still dominated the education system, was that the reform would result in a reduction in the number of schools and entailed merging the schools of one confession with those of another or with State schools. This would clearly dilute their confessional character. The problem was especially acute for the Catholic Church because it predominated in the smaller villages of the North and West and schools in such villages were the most vulnerable. In a communication to the prime minister in early October, 1945, Cardinal Mindszenty strongly protested against the introduction of the new system, claiming that it infringed upon the Church's right to maintain autonomous schools.[45] The Reformed Church also saw the danger. Bishop László Ravasz agreed with the basic principle of providing equal access and uniform quality across all schools, but noted that the reform was "crippling" the Church's best schools.[46]

In January 1946, the government assumed financial responsibility for many of the confessional schools because the land reform had rendered the Churches unable to finance them. A decree later in 1946 ordered a reduction in the number of employees in confessional schools "in the interest

---

[43] László (1987: 296).
[44] Ibid.: 263–306.
[45] Gergely (1985: 34–5). Earlier the Bench of Bishops is said to have referred to the new eight-grade school as the "idol of the new world" [*új világ bálványa*]. Cited in Orbán (1962: 93).
[46] Cited in a declaration from November, 1946. See Ravasz (1988: 98–9).

of balancing the State budget."[47] The State had also been planning to assume sole responsibility for the content of textbooks used in denominational schools. The National Association of Catholic Parents responded by terming the proposal "dictatorial and a reminder of the dictatorship which has just ended."[48] The Reformed Church also demurred. Articles appeared in the Church press defending the Church's right to its schools given their historical importance in the nation's cultural development.[49]

These and other restrictions were merely a prologue to the nationalization of the confessional schools. In anticipation of such State action, both the Catholic and Reformed Churches voiced their strong commitment to retaining educational control. Reformed Bishop Ravasz ranked the schools equal in importance to the sacraments and spreading the Word for the life of the Church.[50] In essence, an attack on the schools was an attack on the Christian faith. In the words of one Church official, "[j]ust as the Church cannot give up its churches, so it cannot relinquish its other great missionary field, the schools."[51] Only with Bishop Ravasz's retirement and the ascension to power of Bishop Albert Bereczky and others more favorable to the socialist project did the Church officially "take cognizance of" the nationalization of schools, though with the proviso that religious instruction remain mandatory. The faithful remained undaunted by changes in the hierarchy. In meetings throughout Reformed church communities on the eve of the nationalization, a decisive majority of the presbyteries believed the schools should remain in Church hands.[52]

Catholic reaction to a potential nationalization of schools was equally if not more ferocious. In May and June 1948, Cardinal Mindszenty issued

---

[47] Decree No. 8230/1946 M. E. See Hainbuch (1982: 24–5).

[48] See "Textbook Monopoly," *Magyar Kurír*, November 6, 1946, reprinted in Mindszenty (1949b: 110–11). Catholic angst was heightened by press accusations throughout 1946 that the Catholic schools were antidemocratic, anti-Russian, and anticommunist. In a pastoral letter of May, 1946, Cardinal Mindszenty strongly defended the conduct of the Church schools and the quality of the education received. He insisted that it was a parent's right, not the State's right, to determine the education a child receives. See Mindszenty (1949a: 54–65).

[49] Bolyki and Ladányi (1987: 101).

[50] Ravasz (1988: 97).

[51] See the editorial of Gyula Muraközy, *Élet és Jövő*, January 17, 1947. Cited in Kádár (1958: 113–14).

[52] Bolyki and Ladányi (1987: 102). Theological changes within the Reformed Church resulting from the coming to power of Albert Bereczky are discussed in later chapters. The school nationalization would later be enshrined in the agreement signed between the Church and the State in October 1948.

four pastoral letters, read aloud in every Church in Hungary, strongly condemning such an action. If the Episcopate's view of these matters was not already clear to the faithful, then these letters would allay any lingering doubts: "[P]riceless spiritual treasures are at stake when sacrilegious hands are laid upon the immortal souls of children by depriving them of their Catholic schools."[53] There were warnings of retaliation: "In the stormy debates over the question of the nationalization of schools we have not used and will not resort to threats, unless we are compelled to do so by the forcible carrying out of this plan."[54] So grave was the fear that the authorities would intimidate the clergy or the faithful into supporting nationalization that Mindszenty hastened to inform them that such an act could result in excommunication from the Church.[55]

Parliament approved the nationalization of all confessional and private schools on June 16, 1948.[56] The law was truly sweeping in its scope. The State assumed ownership of all land, buildings, and equipment associated with the schools. All instructors and other employees of the schools immediately became State civil servants. Certain exceptions were made for institutions devoted entirely to Church affairs: theology schools, priest training schools, religious instructor training schools, and certain orphanages and other institutions. However, these constituted but a small portion of the Churches' educational activities. Even with mandatory religious instruction the Churches would lose their ability to educate children in a Christian spirit.[57] Cardinal Mindszenty was unequivocal in his condemnation of the new schools, declaring that they had "nothing in common with revelation, with our lord Jesus Christ, with the Catholic family, with our Holy King Stephen, and also nothing with our deceased forefathers."[58]

Mindszenty remained defiant, condemning increasingly frequent attacks against him in the press, on the radio, and in public speeches during the latter part of 1948. He accused the government of silencing all opposition:

---

[53] Pastoral letter of May 23, 1948, in Mindszenty (1949a: 141).

[54] Ibid.: 143.

[55] Mindszenty ordered that the relevant piece of Canon Law be read, in Hungarian translation, before the faithful. See "Warning of Excommunication" in ibid.: 153–4. The warning would also apply to Catholic members of parliament who would vote on such a bill.

[56] Law number XXXIII tc./1948, reprinted in Hainbuch (1982: 136).

[57] Details regarding implementation of the law may be found in Decree number 8.000/1948 V.K.M., from the Ministry of Religion and Education. See András and Morel (1969: 64–71), András and Morel (1983b: 145–56), and Hainbuch (1982: 136–7). Mandatory religious instruction would later be abolished.

[58] Cited in Vecsey and Schwendemann (1957: 146).

"The country is condemned to silence and public opinion is made a mere frivolous jest. Democratic 'freedom of speech' means that any opinion that differs from the official one is silenced."[59] To subdue him and the Church, the authorities arrested him on December 27, 1948, on fabricated charges of treason, espionage, and black marketeering. Tried before a "People's Court," he was sentenced to life imprisonment on February 6, 1949. That same month Pope Pius XII excommunicated all Catholics whose "sacreligious hands" had been involved in his incarceration.[60]

3.4 Institutions of Surveillance and Control

By 1949, the battle between Church and State was well under way. Church personnel had been intimidated, arrested, and imprisoned. Church lands had been expropriated, their schools had been nationalized, and their presses had been silenced. In February, 1949 the Hungarian Independent People's Front (MFNF) was founded as an umbrella party organization of the Communist Party and the remnants of other once-independent parties. All Front parties would compete in the May 1949 national parliamentary elections with a common program and candidate list. The Party was eager to obtain much support as possible for the Front, and enlisted the priesthood in this task. Some clergy signed declarations that stated:

I am a Catholic priest, and from my appointment onward I always worked in the people's interest. I consider it my duty even now to say: the politics that the Hungarian Independent People's Front is following serves the interests of the Hungarian people, so I support it.

For the good of Hungarian working people I hope that the goals of the Five-Year plan are realized as soon as possible. I agree that Catholic believers should line up behind those struggling for world peace. As a Catholic priest I consider it desirable for as many of our believers as possible to support the People's Front in the May 15 elections.[61]

According to government reports, 95.6 percent of the voters supported the MFNF in the May elections.[62]

---

[59] See "The Last Pastoral Letter," reprinted in Mindszenty (1949a: 182–4).

[60] Cited in Barron and Waddams (1950: 68). In January 1949 the bishops had already promised to uphold Roman Catholic Church laws. See Tobias (1956: 448).

[61] Z3/1949. To reduce citation complexity all primary sources have been indexed. In the text I refer only to the index number. The full citation is listed in the bibliography.

[62] Balogh et al. (1978: 160–1).

On August 18, 1949, the now utterly Communist-dominated parliament approved a constitution for a new Hungarian People's Republic. As elsewhere in the newly emergent Soviet bloc, the new constitution explicitly recognized freedom of religion. According to §54, section 1: "The Hungarian People's Republic guarantees its citizens liberty of conscience and the right to the free exercise of religion."[63] Such freedom included, of course, the right to choose to have no religion at all. Church and State were also juridically separated. According to §54, section 2: "In the interests of liberty of conscience the Hungarian People's Republic separates Church and State."[64] The irony of these clauses is that in practice the exercise of religion would not be free and the Church would not at all be separate from the State. As András and Morel (1983a: 105) put it, "cultic acts are thus allowed, but not the development of Church institutions." In other words, religion would be a private rather than a public matter. The State could continue whittling away at the institutional bases of the Churches' authority. For the Party, separation of Church and State meant that the Churches would no longer intervene in politics, while the State was free to meddle in the affairs of the Churches. As Péter (1995: 17) notes, the State was separated from the Church, but not vice versa.

The new regime set up an imposing institutional framework to limit the Churches' access to society and channel clerical energies toward supporting socialism. This framework consisted of numerous laws and decrees aimed at weakening the Churches' authority, encouraging a "patriotic" priesthood, forming official agreements between the Churches and the State detailing the rights and responsibilities of each toward the other, and creating a State Office for Church Affairs to oversee all Church activities.

3.4.1 Laws and Ministerial Decrees

The use of laws and ministerial decrees against the Churches accelerated in the period after the introduction of the People's Republic. They were designed to diminish the institutional presence of the Churches as much as possible, to compromise what remained and place it a position of complete dependence on the State, and to prevent as little unsupervised contact as possible between Church and society. Among the most important of these actions were abolition of obligatory religious instruction, introduction

---

[63] Cited in Galter (1957: 231).
[64] Ibid.

of a loyalty oath to the State, disbanding of religious orders, and affirming state control over appointments to Church positions.

Optional religious instruction in the schools was introduced less than one month after the promulgation of the People's Republic. Parents now had to request that their child receive such instruction. The regulations implementing this edict were designed to intimidate and prevent parents from enrolling their children, make the teaching of religion in schools as undesirable a job as possible, and minimize the effectiveness of the instruction. For example, parents were required to inform the school either orally or in writing of their intention to enroll their children. This prevented believing parents from remaining anonymous and opened them up to ridicule by the authorities. In municipalities where there was enough demand for religious instruction, that instruction was to be given by special religion teachers, who were not permitted to perform other jobs to supplement their incomes. This made the job financially undesirable. Provincial councils were responsible for choosing religious instructors, thus ensuring that they would be ideologically acceptable to the State. These councils could also remove any religion teacher who "took an inimical stance toward the People's Democracy or its enactments."

The authority of the State did not stop with the registration and choice of instructor; it also extended into the instruction itself, and attempted to limit contact between teacher and pupil. Instruction could be offered only after the last regular school hour was finished and had to be held in the schools. The intention was to make attendance as low as possible. The rules also forbade the teacher from bringing those students together for any other purposes, thus ensuring that contact between teacher and pupil could take place at the school only at the prescribed time. Although the religion teacher was free to draw up his or her lesson plans, they were subject to approval by the Ministry of Public Worship and Education. The educational authorities, and not the Churches, were charged with supervising the teachers' work. No grade could be given for that course and no disciplinary actions could be taken against students who missed class. Thus, even those students who were willing to stay after class could opt out without fear of penalty from the instructor.[65]

---

[65] See Decrees No. 1101/1-1949 (184) of the Ministry of Public Worship and Instruction (V.K.M.) and No. 1101-11-1/1950 (IX.15) V.K.M.. Original Hungarian texts of both decrees may be found in Hainbuch (1982: 137–8). For an English translation, see András and Morel (1983b: 156–9). The decrees are also discussed in Galter (1957: 251–2) and Gsovski (1973: 94–6).

A decree in October 1949 required civil servants, members of the armed forces, and anyone who received income from the State Treasury to take a loyalty oath to the new regime. Because Church personnel had been made State employees, they were also required to take the oath. The oath reads: "I . . . swear loyalty to the Hungarian People's Republic, its people, and its constitution; I shall keep official state secrets; in exercising my duties I shall act in the interests of the people and to see to it with all my endeavors that my activities promote the strengthening and development of the Hungarian People's Republic."[66] Such an oath posed several problems for the clergy, both Catholic and Protestant. The decree stipulated that failure to take it within a certain period of time would result in a loss of the State income supplement. Because the Churches had already been deprived of their land and other means of making money, not signing meant considerable financial hardship. But the stakes were far greater than financial. What if loyalty to the State and its constitution put the clergy in conflict with loyalty to Christianity and God? The Reformed and Lutheran Church leaders issued a common statement to Church personnel in December 1949 indicating that they found the oath "unobjectionable."[67] Nonetheless, some Reformed theology students found it problematic enough that they they chose not to become pastors to avoid having to take the pledge.[68]

For Catholic clergymen and other Church employees the situation posed great risks. Catholic clergymen throughout Eastern Europe had been under great pressure to break with Rome and establish "national" Catholic Churches. To prevent the breakup of the Church, Pope Pius XII attempted to reinforce discipline. In July 1949, he took the dramatic step of excommunicating any Catholic "who knowingly and freely defends or spreads the materialist and anti-Christian doctrine of Communism."[69] There followed another decree requiring special permission for priests to officiate at weddings between Catholics and communists and another forbidding children in communist youth groups from receiving the sacraments.[70] Although the

---

[66] The English text appears in Gsovski (1973: 96–7) and Galter (1957: 248); for the Hungarian, see Hainbuch (1982: 142).

[67] "The contents of the oath formula for church employees are according to the Christian conscience unobjectionable. No word is contained in it which a faithful servant of the Church of Jesus Christ cannot accept with a free and good conscience." See Tobias (1956: 453, 479).

[68] Takacs (1960: 301).

[69] Cited in Dunn (1977: 171). For a full text of the decree, see Luxmoore and Babiuch (2000: 65).

[70] Ibid.: 66.

decrees appear stark, there were hidden nuances: "freely," "defends," and "spreads" were all terms subject to varying interpretations.[71] Yet the intent was clear enough: willing cooperation with the communists meant losing God's grace and being denied entry into heaven.

In December 1949, the minister of religion and education sent a letter to the Hungarian Bench of Bishops expressing the State's expectation that the oath would be taken. The bishops had few desirable choices. If they refused outright, they would likely be martyred and replaced with others more willing to do the State's bidding. This would result in a complete split with Rome, if not destruction of the Church. If they accepted, they would compromise themselves, but at least might preserve some of the Church. In the end, the bench gave parish priests receiving State supplements permission to take the oath, but refused to take it themselves without special permission from the Holy See. The permission never arrived. It was only after the sentencing of Archbishop Grősz, Mindszenty's successor, and further threats against the bishops, that the last holdouts took the oath.[72]

In July 1951, the State introduced a regulation concerning appointments to Church positions. The regulation stated that "archbishops, titular bishops, bishops, auxiliary bishops, archabbots, abbots, and provincials of religious orders can be appointed to serve on Hungarian territory only after approval has been obtained from the Presidential Council of the Hungarian People's Republic."[73] The government had not refrained from harassing and arresting Church leaders it found undesirable, but that was time consuming and generated much bad publicity. This regulation gave the State the legal authority to veto any unsympathetic potential prelates, thus ensuring cooperative Church hierarchies. For the Reformed Church, where congregants elected their Church leaders, this meant ceding the freedom to choose their leadership.[74] This loss of freedom was also extended to the parish level. Calvinist tradition and Reformed Church law had protected

---

[71] Ibid.: 65.

[72] Gergely (1985: 85–6) and Hainbuch (1982: 5). Until 1918 only bishops appointed by the king under the right of supreme patronage were required to take oaths to the crown. Parish priests had always been exempted. See Gsovski (1973: 96–7).

[73] Cited in András and Morel (1983b: 175). For the Hungarian text, see Hainbuch (1982: 146).

[74] In practice elections to high-ranking posts were already less than free. For example, when Roland Kiss, who was supported by the regime, ran in 1949 against two other Church members for Chief Curator and lost, the State refused to recognize the results. Only after the third election, in which he was the sole nominee, did he win the election. See Takacs (1960: 284).

pastors from removal unless there was just cause as determined by a Church court. In 1951, the Reformed General Synod passed a law giving the hierarchy the authority to remove a pastor when it was in the "public interest." Another law in 1953 gave the bishops the power to fill these vacated posts through appointments rather than by election. Pastors were now vulnerable to removal if they did not tow the line.[75]

For the Catholic Church this regulation represented an arrogation by the regime of the "Right of Supreme Patronage" that the kings of Hungary had exercised over the Church. This right, which extended back to the foundation of the Hungarian State, gave the king the authority to nominate all prelates in the realm. Though the Holy See often disputed that right, in practice its role became limited to confirming the royal appointments.[76] After the First World War there was a struggle between the Vatican and the regime of Miklós Horthy over whether he, as regent, should inherit the right of patronage enjoyed by the kings of Hungary. The dispute was finally resolved in 1927: the government in consultation with the Vatican would compose a list of potential names, and the Vatican would choose among them; if the Vatican chose someone else, it made sure that the candidate was acceptable to the government.[77] As long as the government was sympathetic to the Church there was no fear that the right of patronage would be misused. In the hands of the communists, however, it presented an effective method for installing cooperative clergymen and driving wedges between the Hungarian Church and the Holy See. Since 1946 the Holy See had been making appointments without the approval of the Hungarian government. The regulation was thus made retroactive to January 1, 1946, so that these personnel would also be vulnerable to removal.[78]

3.4.2 Patriotic Priests

Laws and decrees could hem the Churches in, and even ensure that the Church hierarchies were cleansed of openly anticommunist elements. But, they could not easily neutralize the Churches' moral authority and influence, much less win them over to the cause of socialism. If the Churches had

[75] Gombos (1960: 53–4).
[76] Laszlo (1973: 33, fn. 37).
[77] Orbán (1996: 67–8). For a more comprehensive discussion of this agreement, see Csizmadia (1971: 127–38).
[78] András and Morel (1983b: 175).

to continue existing, then from the Party's perspective they at least ought to be loyal allies of the Party. In a further effort to isolate "reactionary" elements within the Churches the Party actively supported and elevated "progressive" clergymen. As with so many other Party tactics aimed at consolidating absolute power, this attempt to create "patriotic" movements within the Churches had been attempted in the Soviet Union during the 1920s. With the help of the Soviet secret police, a group of left-leaning Orthodox clergymen staged a revolt within the Orthodox Church in 1922. Calling themselves Renovationists, these priests sought, in addition to many modernizing reforms, an accommodation with the Soviet regime. In exchange for professing their support for the Soviet government and the principle of socialist revolution, they hoped to prevent the liquidation of the Orthodox Church. The Soviet government did not relish the idea of a strong "socialist" Orthodox faith, but initially encouraged the schism in the hope that internal battles might fatally weaken the Church.[79]

The Soviet-sponsored peace movement, formally launched at an international congress in Wrocław, Poland in August 1948, would provide the Hungarian regime with an effective tool for bringing a portion of the clergy into the communist orbit. The idea behind the peace movement was to rally world opinion against the alleged war plans of the Western powers and in particular those of the United States, which at the time enjoyed a monopoly in atomic weapons and was the principal barrier to Soviet influence in Western Europe. Whether or not the Soviet Union really feared a war with the West is beside the point. In a series of conferences, prominent politicians, intellectuals, and other public figures the world over came together in what evolved into a sustained denunciation of United States and allied "aggression" and "warmongering."[80]

The meetings were grand in scope and histrionic in tone. According to organizers, the Paris and Prague gatherings of April 1949 represented 600 million people in seventy-two countries. Exaggeration or not, participation was widespread and distinctly pro-Soviet. French scientist Frédéric Joliot-Curie, one of the movement's founders, opened the meeting with a warning to North Atlantic Treaty Organization (NATO) signatories that

[79] Luukkanen (1994: 133–5) and Young (1997: 149–50). The Renovationist movement ultimately failed to gain control of the Church, in part because it never really took hold among the faithful. See Young (1997: 150–3).
[80] For a detailed discussion of this movement and its precursors, see Wittner (1993: 171–90).

the war they were preparing would be met with "a revolt of the peoples."[81] The French writer Jean Genêt considered the Paris meeting "the most concentrated inflammatory anti-American propaganda effort in this part of Europe since the beginning of the cold war."[82] Soviet papers were ebullient. *Izvestia* referred to it as a "demonstration of solidarity with the bulwark of international peace, the Soviet Union. . . ."[83] The *New Times* boasted of "the rise of an unprecedented movement of the peoples" and the "hundreds of millions in all parts of the world" that have "united their efforts to foil the plans of the warmongers."[84] By the end of 1949, the Cominform adopted a resolution put forward by Mikhail Suslov, the Soviet official directing international communist affairs, that called on communist parties throughout the world to organize the forces of peace against the forces of war and, in particular, to "[draw] . . . trade unions, women's, youth, co-operative, sports, cultural, educational, religious and other organizations" into the struggle for peace.[85] With this, the Cominform clearly hoped to harness the peace movement to advance socialism.

For this to happen required a particular understanding of the relationship between peace and socialism. In their rhetoric, communist leaders equated socialism and the people's democracies with peace, and capitalism and bourgeois democracy with war. In this equation the struggle for socialism became the struggle for peace. By "peace," however, the communists had something very specific in mind. "Marxism is not Pacifism," Lenin wrote in *Socialism and War*.[86] Indeed, for doctrinaire Marxists there could be real peace only after the final struggle between socialism and capitalism. Anything else, Lenin insisted, would be a "bourgeois Utopia." So, by definition socialism would bring about peace.

Communist leaders also maintained that the struggle for peace was the struggle for socialism, reversing the order of "peace" and "socialism." The subtle difference in phrasing belies deep and consequential differences in meaning, for if the struggle for peace is the struggle for socialism, then to be against peace is to be against socialism. The peace movement would then be another tool with which the Churches and others could be brought into

---

[81] Cited in ibid.: 178.
[82] Cited in ibid.: 179.
[83] Cited in ibid.: 179.
[84] Cited in ibid.: 180.
[85] Cited in ibid.: 181.
[86] Cited in Orbán (1996: 151).

the socialist project. To equate peace and socialism in this way, however, required further elaboration. Communist rhetoric was clear that the struggle
for peace meant the struggle against the United States and its allies. However, the United States was accused not merely of "warmongering," but of
abetting fascism as well. The final resolution of the Wrocław conference
proclaimed that "a new fascism" was preparing for war.[87] The prominent
British communist scientist J. D. Bernal summed up the conference by noting that "nothing in the old panoply of Fascism is lacking" in the U.S. plan
for world domination.[88]

The United States was linked not only to international fascism, but to
domestic forces opposing socialism. In Hungary, this enhanced version of
the U.S. threat appeared in the Hungarian Workers Party's 1948 program.
"[P]eople's democracies and all believers in peace, national independence,
and social progress in the capitalist countries, colonies, and dependent
states" belong to the "anti-imperialist, democratic camp, led by the Soviet
Union." By contrast, the "imperialist, anti-democratic camp led by American imperialism" supports "anti-democratic, reactionary social strata and
political groups everywhere, revives and helps fascist forces, and interferes
in sovereign states' internal affairs"[89] The possibility of U.S. interference in
internal socialist affairs was important, because it justified enhanced domestic vigilance and efforts at increasing enthusiasm for the peace movement.
In a 1949 article in the Hungarian newspaper *Szabad Nép*, Mátyás Rákosi,
General Secretary of the Communist Party, reaffirmed that the world was
split into two camps, "one the camp of the defenders of peace, democracy,
and socialism, and the other the imperialists, the camp of the warmongers."
But he also cautioned that the peace issue was "collective and indivisible,"
and that it was necessary to struggle against any view that diminished the
importance of peace work in the people's democracies.[90] Ultimately, all
those who sided with Soviet peace plans (and hence also socialism) would
be termed "democratic" (*demokratikus*) or "progressive" (*haladó*), whereas
all others were labeled "reactionary" (*reakciós*).

The Churches were already vulnerable to accusations of collaboration with fascism, and by resisting the peace movement would be opening

[87] Cited in Wittner (1993: 176).
[88] Ibid.: 177.
[89] See "A Magyar Dologzók Pártjának Programnyilatkozata," in Habuda et al. (1998: 15–32).
Quotations are from p. 18.
[90] December 13, 1949. The article is reprinted in Rákosi (1951: 207–14). Quotation is from
p. 211.

themselves up to charges of aligning with the Western powers and domestic antisocialist forces. This would give the Party an ideal pretext for denying the Churches what remaining privileges they had. The Catholic and Reformed Churches responded very differently to these pressures. As we will see, the Catholic Bench of Bishops chose to resist the Party's embrace and, as a consequence, the priesthood was organized into the peace movement without the bishops' consent. The Reformed Church, by contrast, adjusted its theology to accommodate the advent of socialism.

The Catholic Church and the Peace Movement. The Catholic Church was particularly vulnerable to the charge of being antisocialist. The pope had called for outlawing the bomb in early 1948, and had lent support to the PAX Christi movement that had formed in Western Europe after the war, but fierce anticommunism prevented the Vatican from joining forces with the Soviet peace movement. Moreover, as detailed in the preceding text, Hungarian Catholic and communist leaders had already fought battles over land reform, the Church press, school textbooks, school nationalization, the suppression of religious associations, and many other issues. This earned vilifcation from communist leaders. In January 1948, General Secretary of the MKP Mátyás Rákosi, speaking to Party functionaries, declared that the "task of our Party this year is to settle the relationship between the Church and the Republic. It cannot be tolerated that the majority of the enemies of the people should hide in the shadow of the Churches, especially the Catholic Church."[91] In June of the same year he chided the "the majority of the leaders of the Catholic Church – above all Cardinal Mindszenty" for refusing to recognize government decrees concerning land reform and nationalization. He accused them of "dreaming, even today, of overthrowing the Republic with the help of external and internal [forces of] reaction. . . . "[92]

Mindszenty clearly recognized the dangers of communist peace efforts. In a February 1948 speech he attacked communist peace plans without mentioning them by name, asserting that their peace is not the peace intended by the Holy Father. "Peace does not utilize the acts of war, peace does not yield the fruits of war."[93] At a bishops conference in April 1948, the Hungarian Episcopate reaffirmed its own commitment to peace, but

[91] Quoted in Tobias (1956: 438). The original may be found in Rákosi (1955: 180).
[92] Rákosi (1952: 23–4).
[93] Cited in Vecsey and Schwendemann (1957: 81).

in Christian terms, declaring that "we as disciples of Christ condemn all weapons of death; weapons that strike not only the attacking enemy, but also the innocent."[94] The bishops made clear that they were speaking not only for themselves, but also for all organs of the Church, including the lower clergy. This was intended to prevent parish priests from making separate declarations of fealty to the peace movement.[95]

The Episcopate's fear that the communist authorities would attempt to organize a peace movement among the lower clergy turned out to be well-founded. In late 1948, the regime began identifying priests who might initiate a "peace priest" movement. It was rough going in the beginning. The first candidate, Zoltán Nyisztor, was "convinced" to take the job after a brief term in secret policy custody. He ultimately escaped to the West before having to assume his duties. The second candidate, Ferenc Varga, also attempted to escape to the West, but failed, and was sentenced to life in prison.[96] It is not surprising that the lower clergy was loathe to defy the Church hierarchy. The Episcopate and the government still had not reached an agreement regulating relations between Church and State and the bishops stood resolutely behind the embattled Mindszenty:

> If the bishops of Hungary raise their voices in strong protest in the name of justice, truth and freedom, they do so also to testify to his Eminence their confidence, their sympathy and the resolution to stand by him in his great work for Church, motherland and people, and to identify themselves with him completely.[97]

Given the bishops' stance and the uncertainty about whether the Church would win its battle against the State, clerical loyalty to the Church hierarchy was still eminently reasonable.

However, conditions would deteriorate dramatically between the end of 1948 and the founding of the Catholic peace priest movement in August 1950. The bishops attempted to negotiate a path between the Vatican and the regime even through Cardinal Mindszenty's arrest in December 1948 and condemnation in early 1949, the formal declaration of a People's Republic in August 1949, the liquidation of all remaining political opposition, and tensions over the loyalty oath and other matters. Canon law dictated that they could not participate in an international movement without

[94] Cited in Orbán (1996: 154).
[95] Ibid.
[96] Orbán (1996: 160).
[97] See "Testimony of the Bishops on Behalf of Cardinal Mindszenty," *Magyar Kurír*, November 5, 1948, reprinted in Mindszenty (1949b: 206–7).

the Vatican's approval, so they refused to bring the Church into the peace movement. However, they attempted to be as conciliatory as possible toward the regime. Declining participation in the 1949 Paris peace congress, the bishops declared that "[t]he Catholic Church's stand on the question of war and peace is so clear, that from the Hungarian Bench of Bishops' point of view any special statement would be superfluous."[98] In the aftermath of the March 1950 Stockholm peace meeting they reaffirmed their wish for peace, their condemnation of atomic weapons, and their desire for Hungary to stay out of any war. But they also resolutely forbade priests and members of the religious orders from participation in the movement.[99]

The regime had, however, finally succeeded in opening a rift between the upper and lower clergy. Without the bishops' approval, approximately twenty-five priests took part in a June 1949 peace meeting in Budapest.[100] Though not a large proportion of the clergy, this represented a real inroad and an opportunity to bypass and isolate the Episcopate. A big breakthrough came in connection with the March 1950 peace conference in Stockholm. It is not known how many priests attended this conference, but in the spirit of bringing the masses into peace work the participants drafted a petition condemning and banning atomic weapons. Known as the Stockholm Peace Appeal, the petition was to be signed by "all people of good will."[101] The Hungarian regime responded to this call zealously and by mid-1950 claimed to have obtained several million signatures and formed over 24,000 "peace defense committees."[102] Though this number is surely an exaggeration, there was a genuine effort to collect signatures and, by claiming such mass support, the regime could further isolate the bishops, who had forbidden priests and members of religious orders from signing the peace appeal.

According to József Révai, Minister of Culture, priests signed the peace appeal "in the hundreds."[103] There exists no independent confirmation of this number, and no evidence indicating the extent of intimidation used

[98] *Új Ember* April 17, 1949. Cited in Pál (1995: 9).
[99] Ibid.: 10–11. See also Salacz (1988: 69–70).
[100] Orbán (1996: 152) and Pál (1995: 10). The two authors differ on the exact number of participants. Orbán reports twenty-five, "from different Churches," while Pál lists twenty-three. Even if all twenty-five were Catholic, this represents a very small proportion of the clergy.
[101] Cited in Wittner (1993: 183).
[102] Sources differ on the exact number, but there were no fewer than 6.9 million signatures claimed, roughly the entire adult population of Hungary, and 24,583 peace defense committees. See Orbán (1996: 153) and Pál (1995: 11).
[103] Cited in Gergely (1985: 88). See also Orbán (1962: 208).

to obtain the signatures. However, the local peace committees charged with obtaining signatures sought out Church personnel and the priests who signed garnered publicity.[104] Clerical participation in the peace appeal proved to be a propaganda coup for the Party, which had intended to use the peace priest movement both to create internal divisions within the Church and to mobilize social strata, such as peasants and women, who tended to be religious and were the most likely to be under the influence of "clerical reaction."[105] Highlighting divisions between the upper and lower clergy, the Party claimed that within the Church those forces favoring cooperation with the regime were gaining ground against "anti-peace clerical reaction."[106] The bishops were also made to appear as enemies of the people. In the words of Révai, "[t]he Bench of Bishops has turned against the peace wish of millions of Hungarian working people, turned against the Hungarian People's Republic's peace policy, and excluded itself from the large and unified community of Hungarian workers struggling for peace."[107]

The Priests for Peace movement was officially founded on August 1, 1950, when approximately 300 priests, monks, religious instructors, and others came together for an inaugural meeting in Budapest. Nearly 100 of the participants were from Budapest, and the Bishoprics of Esztergom and Eger were also well represented. One hundred and seven were priests and assistant priests, some of whom were Protestant and Greek Catholic. The middle stratum of the Church was not well represented and included only one prelate, an episcopal notary, and two theology teachers. There were seventy members of religious orders.[108]

Based on the number and distribution of participants across regions and rank, the first meeting cannot be considered an unqualified success. Although 300 is a greater number than had previously taken part, a total of 7,500 had been invited, yielding a participation rate of only 4 percent.[109] Compared to the total number of priests and other clerics, the proportion is smaller still: only 2 percent.[110] Several reasons account for the low turnout, but one stands out: the bishops threatened to excommunicate priests who

---

[104] Pál (1995: 11). The number of signatories is cited here as "a few hundred."
[105] The Party's intentions are clearly spelled out in a confidential order of June 14, 1950. See Gergely (1985: 91).
[106] Ibid.: 88–9.
[107] Cited in ibid.: 88.
[108] Pál (1995: 26) and Gergely (1985: 93).
[109] Orbán (1996: 182).
[110] Ibid.

wished to overturn the bishops' rightful authority or who participated in or supported movements organized by the Communist Party.[111] There is evidence that clerics from the provinces attributed their absence not to a fear of reprisal, which would have alienated them from the hierarchy, but to the "inaccessibility" of Budapest.[112] This would have been a convenient excuse for the many clerics who sided with the bishops and were determined to resist all unnecessary cooperation with the regime.

It is also not clear how many of those who did attend felt pressure to do so. For example, the relatively large number from the religious orders is understandable given the uncertainty surrounding the future of the orders. Throughout 1950, the regime had been expelling monks and nuns from the schools and other social institutions. Beginning in June 1950, there were mass arrests and internments – 2,800 people in all.[113] Even if the monks were not overtly pressured to attend, it is easy to see why they would seek a rapprochement between Church and State. The presence of so many clerics from Budapest might also be the consequence of pressure and intimidation. The Party was far more powerful in Budapest than in the outlying provinces, and a poor showing of the capital's clergymen would have signaled others that the Party would not or could not ensure a proper turnout.

The ultimate importance of the priest for peace movement lay not in the numbers present at the founding meeting, or even in the circumstances under which the meeting took place, but in the movement's goals and aspirations. The organizers of the August 1 meeting had hoped to use the forum to expedite an agreement between the Church and the State. But, their conception of coexistence with the regime was quite different from that of the bishops. Indeed, they sharply criticized the bishops' stance toward the regime. Richard Horváth, a monk and founder of the movement, accused the bishops of leading the Church into a "blind alley" through their "bias against progress" and "desire to return to the old system."[114] For the leaders of the movement the way forward for the Church was to accept the arrival of socialism and to seek a place within it. This did not mean repudiating Roman Catholicism. "We are Roman Catholics, and that we remain,"

[111] Gergely (1985: 92). The bishops made reference to the Holy See's 1949 prohibition against cooperation with communists.
[112] Orbán (1996: 183). The evidence on accessibility comes from conversations the author claims to have had, though he never specifies with whom he spoke.
[113] Havasy (1993: 76–8). It was these arrests that finally brought the Bench of Bishops back to the negotiations for a concordat with the State.
[114] Excerpted from comments made during the proceedings. See Pál (1995: 29).

insisted Horváth.[115] However, he carefully distinguished between the sacred authority and political activity of the Holy See. Peace priests would remain loyal Catholics, but only in the the moral and ethical realm: "In politics we see our situation the best, and we experience our fate the most directly."[116] That meant joining in the struggle for peace and socialism. The movement saw no necessary contradiction between this struggle and Catholicism. Peace and human dignity were justified on both Christian and Marxist grounds. In this way, peace priests could be both loyal Catholics *and* loyal citizens of Hungary, and be allowed to practice their calling "for reconstructing the country and building a lasting peace."[117] In effect, the peace priests adopted socialism as a Catholic goal.

This movement posed great risks for the Church. As "loyal Catholics" and, apparently, loyal socialists, peace priests could blur the distinction among the faithful between Catholicism and socialism and reduce the Church to being a conduit for propagating the socialist project among the masses. It would then lose all moral authority as a force opposing the injustices perpetrated by the regime. This indeed appears to have been the plan. In the villages the peace committees were charged with diverse tasks. Their educational function was to spread socialist thinking. Regarding international affairs, this meant educating the people about the dangers of Western imperialism and the concomitant need to strengthen the socialist camp. But, it also involved disseminating information about the Five-Year Plan, the nationalization of businesses, and eventually agricultural collectivization. The committees also promoted work and civil discipline.[118]

The Reformed Church and the Peace Movement. The Reformed Church's path toward support for the peace movement and socialism more generally was not easy, but ultimately proved far less harrowing than the Catholic route to accommodation with the regime. The key difference lay in the divergent attitudes of the Church hierarchies. The Catholic Bench of Bishops, ever mindful of the Holy See's antipathy to communism, resisted the peace movement as long as possible. In the end the Catholic peace priest movement was founded without the bishops' consent.

---

[115] Ibid.: 30.
[116] Ibid.
[117] Ibid.: 32. For details of the founding meeting's concluding resolution, see Pál (1995: 31–3) and Orbán (1996: 189–90).
[118] Orbán (1996: 155).

The Reformed Church also opposed many aspects of the socialist project in the early postwar period. As described previously, Bishop László Ravasz had been no friend of communism. However, by the time the peace movement was launched in 1948, Ravasz had stepped down as leader of the Reformed Church. His position was assumed by Bishop Albert Bereczky, who had been leading a movement within the Church that sought a radical break with the past and acceptance of the new social circumstances. His assumption of power in July 1948 meant that the peace movement and socialism more generally came to enjoy Reformed support at the highest levels.

The Church's position was elaborated in the context of a new theology that justified socialism. This theology began with the notion that God's judgment was visible in the loss of the war and the subsequent social changes endured by society. It recognized "in the dissolution of bourgeois society and the formation of socialism God's just judgement and renewed grace."[119] In effect, God was passing sentence on the Church's entanglement with the old bourgeois system, a system that had pulled the country into war and was responsible for the murder of millions. The advent of socialism was "the meting out of God's sentence" for the Church's past.[120]

Socialism was not viewed, however, merely as punishment for past sins. The "great transformation of the world" initiated since the end of the war was seen as providing "new and better chances for the Church."[121] As we saw, the Church enjoyed many privileges during the Horthy era: bishops became members of the Upper House of Parliament; the State collected overdue obligatory church taxes and subsidized Church schools and the salaries of pastors. But in exchange, the State demanded formal recognition of the political order and reserved the right to intervene in Church affairs.[122] The new theology criticized the previous political system for having "put in fetters and worn down" the Church's work.[123] The separation of Church and State, a key communist aim, was seen as liberating the Church to pursue its mission.

That mission involved not merely spreading the Gospel. In April 1948, shortly after the resignation of Church leader Bishop Ravasz, the Synodal Council met and adopted a resolution in which it was "fully prepared to undertake all services in the new Hungarian State and social order which

---

[119] Kádár (1950: 19), cited in Takacs (1960: 66).
[120] Kádár (1950: 34).
[121] Cited in Kádár (1950: 19).
[122] Gombos (1960: 29).
[123] Kádár (1950: 40).

it can accomplish in the name of Jesus Christ and by the strength of the Holy Spirit."[124] What were these services? The Church considered "the abrogation of the big estates, the allotment of land to the agrarian population, and the nationalization of big enterprises to be in harmony with the Holy Scriptures."[125] In fact, Bereczky approved of the entire socialist project. Speaking on behalf of the Church in 1952, he declared "with the decision of faith that the advance of revolutionary socialism manifests God's just, merciful, and continuous judgment."[126] The Church was not a passive bystander, but rather insisted on taking an active role in bringing socialism about: "Our failure to work for social justice and real peace would be disloyalty to Jesus," declared one Bishop at the June 1949 meeting of the Hungarian Peace Commission.[127]

The relationship between peace and social justice and the need to struggle for both was a recurring theme of the Church's new theology. At the June 1949 world peace conference in Paris, Bereczky declared: "[T]he church's peace service cannot be a passive pacifism or a lukewarm neutrality, but it must be a courageous fight against the causes of war. This struggle also involves the effort to eliminate the social causes of war, it is therefore a bold decision in favor of social justice."[128] In one stroke Bereczky distances the Church from Western (pacifist) peace movements, and reiterates the communist view of social injustice as the main cause of war. As in the case of the Catholic peace priests, the Church left little doubt where injustice lay. In a 1950 message to Protestants outside Hungary the Lutheran and Reformed Church leaderships begged their co-religionists "to realize that the new threat of war to the whole of mankind is not lurking from the side of Socialism, but on the contrary, from the oppressors of the colonial people."[129] The fight for peace came to be considered the *sine qua non* of the Reformed faith. According to Bishop János Péter, "he who today does not fight for peace is essentially and decisively lacking in his faith and obedience."[130]

---

[124] Cited in Kádár (1958: 118–19). See also Takacs (1960: 294).
[125] Kádár (1958: 119).
[126] Cited in Gombos (1960: 64).
[127] Cited in Kádár (1950: 59).
[128] Cited in ibid.: 52.
[129] *Református Egyház II*, November 15, 1950, 22, p. 8. Cited in Takacs (1960: 353).
[130] *Református Egyház II*, November 15, 1950, 22, p. 11. Cited in Takacs (1960: 356). For an overview of the theological changes in the Reformed Church as it entered socialism, see Victor (1950: 32–8) and Poór (1986: 57–61). For a much more detailed treatment from a socialist perspective, see Kónya (1988). Takacs (1960) provides the best critical evaluation of the early impact of communism on the Reformed Church.

The enthusiasm expressed by the Church hierarchy gratified the Party. Bishops Albert Bereczky and János Péter and pastor Sándor Fekete were awarded the "Peace Order of Merit of the Hungarian People's Democracy" in April 1951. In celebrations honoring the awardees, top Church offical Roland Kiss reiterated the Church's view of peace, socialism, and the Hungarian rulers:

> The world peace movement is the freedom fight of the people, who now came to self-awareness, against the imperialist tyranny, which through its permanent threat of war wants to keep hundreds of millions of working people in the slavery of capitalism. But in vain. This great meeting would be lacking and false if we would not point to the decisive historical fact that under the leadership of the great Stalin, the Soviet Union's sacrifice of blood redeemed the Hungarian people from centuries of oppression and brought the nation into the peace camp of the free nations as an equal.... This change of destiny for the better was made possible for the Hungarians through the heroic sacrifice and the wisdom ... of Mátyás Rákosi. We express our gratitude for lifting up the Hungarian people and for his wise leadership.... The Reformed people of Hungary will remain the immovable support of the cause of peace until the final victory.[131]

3.4.3 Agreements between Church and State

Prior to the 1940s the status of all religious denominations in Hungary had been regulated through laws rather than formal agreements between Church and State.[132] The communists, however, sought to ensure the cooperation of the Churches through binding agreements. These agreements would spell out the rights and obligations of both Church and State. For the Churches this meant recognizing the republic and the desirability of the socialist project above all. Securing the Churches' recognition and cooperation would be crucial for the Party's efforts at enlisting the believing masses in the construction of socialism. This would be true even if the Churches were coerced into the agreements because the Church hierarchies would

---

[131] *Református Egyház III*, April 15, 1951, No. 8, p. 7. Cited in Takacs (1960: 358–9).

[132] Gsovski (1973: 101). Thus, unlike Austria, Germany, Italy, Poland, or Spain, Hungary never concluded a concordat with the Holy See. In a religiously mixed society neither party was eager to revive the conflicts that had plagued the country during the *Kulturkampf* of the 1890s. Thus, neither the State nor the Church felt it would improve it position by concluding an agreement. See Csizmadia (1971: 18–21) and Laszlo (1973: 212–13). The Reformed Church and other Protestant denominations had enjoyed religious freedom since the early seventeenth century and were permitted to administer themselves. The Horthy regime exercised the *right of supreme inspection* [*ius supremae inspectionis*] of the Churches' statutes. See Csizmadia (1971: 58–60).

be required to discipline members of the lower clergy who violated the agreement or other laws. The hierarchies would face further sanction if they failed to implement their end of the bargain.

The Reformed Church Agreement. The Reformed Church concluded its agreement with the State in October 1948, nearly two years before the Catholic Church. As we saw in the previous section, with the departure of Bishop Ravasz, the biggest roadblock to a compromise between Church and State was removed. In late April 1948, only two days after Ravasz's resignation, the Synodal Council approved a resolution in which it outlined its views on Church-State relations. The resolution went a long way toward assuaging fears that the Reformed Church would follow the Catholic Church in resisting the nascent socialist order. The council expressed its readiness to enter into negotiations for a formal agreement and stated its expectations about what such an agreement would look like. It recognized the legality and legitimacy of the Republic, praised the government for its actions to ensure the equality of religions, and gave official approval to the nationalization of industry and agrarian reform. It also exhorted the faithful to work diligently, seek peace, and resist the lure of slogans that would make the Church an instrument of war. In return, the Church expressed the hope that it would continue to enjoy the right of self-government and that its educational, missionary, and charity activities would be safeguarded.[133]

The agreement signed in October 1948 broadly conformed to the Church's previous resolution except in the sphere of education. The most important obligations undertaken by the Church were to:

1. "Recognize the Government of the Republic";
2. "Pray for the head of State and the welfare and peace of the Hungarian people";
3. "Accept the nationalization of confessional schools and taking over of all personnel by the State schools."[134]

---

[133] Tobias (1956: 440–1). The full text of the resolution can be found in ibid.: 465–8. The communists welcomed the resolution, seeing in it a rejection of the "sterile and harmful spirit of collaboration with the reactionary Catholic groups" in favor of "wholesome and fruitful cooperation with democracy." See *Szabad Nép*, May 1, 1948. Cited in Takacs (1960: 294–5).

[134] Tobias (1956: 446).

In return the State:

1. "Accepted and agreed to further the free exercise of religion including services and Bible classes in church, public buildings, homes, schools, parish houses, missionary activities in religious journals and books, distribution of Bibles and literature, holding conferences and retreats, compulsory religious education in the schools, and charitable activities";
2. "Left six educational institutions under Church control";
3. "Acknowledged the right of the Church to give (compulsory) religious instruction in State schools";
4. "Guaranteed the support of the Church on a decreasing scale until 1968, at which time the Church was expected to be self-supporting."[135]

Although the communists were in firm control of the government by the time of this agreement, they had not yet established a dictatorship. The agreement reflects this transitional period. The government pledged not only to respect freedom of religion, but to further its exercise in a variety of public ways. Parliament had approved the nationalization of most confessional schools in June 1948, but had maintained compulsory religious instruction in State schools. The agreement required the Church to acknowledge the nationalization of schools, but at the same time guaranteed that the clergy would retain control over religious instruction. However, as the communists consolidated their power it became clear that the parts of the agreement concerning the rights of the Church would be ignored. By December 1948, local authorities were already putting up obstacles to the free exercise of religion by denying the use of public facilities and discouraging public religious activities.[136] As described shortly, with the proclamation of the People's Republic in August 1949, the government passed many other laws and decrees, such as the abolition of compulsory religious instruction, that neutralized or abrogated Church rights.

The Catholic Church Agreement. The agreement concluded between the government and the Catholic Bench of Bishops on August 30, 1950 reflected the ongoing Sovietization of the country. By the middle of 1950, Hungary was in the grip of Stalinism: multiparty democracy had been eliminated, a

---

[135] Ibid.: 446–7. The full text of the agreement may be found in ibid.: 468–71.
[136] Ibid.: 446.

personality cult had arisen around Party leader Mátyás Rákosi, and the State was energetically implementing plans for the creation of a socialist society. The immediate cause of the Catholic Bench of Bishop's request to begin negotiations was the government's sharpened offensive against the Church. In a June 1, 1950, resolution, the Party accused alleged "reactionary" forces within the Church of a multitude of sins: 1) serving as a fifth column for the imperialists in Hungary; 2) supporting the "kulaks" and remnants of the old ruling classes in a struggle against the socialist transformation of agriculture;[137] 3) persecuting priests who were sympathetic to the government; and 4) mobilizing the youth.[138] The resolution declared that the religious orders were "the most important mass agitation institutions of clerical reaction" and intimated that they should be liquidated.[139] At the same time, however, the resolution stated that it was incumbent on the Party, the working class, and all working people to "help and support those elements of the Church that are sincerely drawing closer to the People's Republic and are ready to work honorably with working people."[140] This was a reference to "democratic" priests who were sympathetic to the peace movement.[141]

The religious orders came under immediate attack. Between June 7 and 9 the government expelled without prior warning approximately 1,000 monks and nuns from their residences near the Yugoslav border and interned them elsewhere in the country. Their presence was deemed "a danger to public order and security."[142] Another wave of expulsions, of approximately 2,000 members of religious orders, took place in mid-June. A third was ordered for July 10 through 12.[143] In the end, roughly 3,000 of 11,000 members of religious orders in Hungary suffered deportation. They would be released only in September 1950, when all religious orders were dissolved by government decree.[144]

---

[137] The term *kulak* was invented by the Soviets to stigmatize richer, more industrious peasants, who were most likely to resist collectivization.
[138] Gergely (1985: 89).
[139] Cited in Salacz (1988: 65).
[140] Gergely (1985: 90).
[141] The Party's resolution on "the battle against clerical reaction" may be found in "A Központi Vezetőség határozata a klerikális elleni harcról." *Pártmunkás*, June 10, 1950, 5–10. English excerpts from a speech of Révai before the Central Committee, on which the resolution was largely based, may be found in Gsovski (1973: 141–3).
[142] Havasy (1990: 120). The order is reprinted in Galter (1957: 235).
[143] Galter (1957: 236).
[144] For details of the deportation, see ibid.: 234–6 and Gussoni and Brunello (1954: 192–4). The Bench of Bishops considered the religious orders to be an organic component of the

Fearing further deportations and the possibility of a Church schism in the guise of the priests for peace movement, the Bench of Bishops concluded an agreement that was quite unlike the agreements with the other denominations. The government promised "complete religious freedom" according to the constitution of the People's Republic and "freedom of activity" to the Church in the discharge of its duties, but neither religious freedom nor the duties of the Church were defined concretely, as they had been in the case of the Reformed Church. The State would be free to interpret these provisions as it saw fit. The State also agreed to return eight of the Church's schools and pledged to subsidize the Church for eighteen years, after which time it was expected to be self-sufficient. In return the Church promised to:

1. "Recognize and support the political order and Constitution of the Hungarian People's Republic."
2. "Proceed under ecclesiastical laws against Church personnel who act against the law of the Hungarian People's Republic or against the constructive work of its government."
3. "Condemn subversive activities directed against the political and social order of the Hungarian People's Republic."
4. "Not permit the religious feeling of Catholic believers to be misused for political purposes against the State."
5. "Call upon Catholic believers to assume their share of the work in fulfilling the Five-Year Plan."
6. "Call upon the clergy not to resist the formation of agricultural cooperatives."
7. "Support the movement for peace, approve the efforts of the Hungarian Government to protect peace, and condemn warmongering and use of atomic weapons."[145]

The Bench of Bishops had capitulated. The Church agreed not only to recognize and support the Hungarian People's Republic, but also to support the Soviet-sponsored peace movement. Passive approval was not permitted: the Church would have to actively condemn subversive activities against

Church without which "true religious freedom is incomprehensible," and after the second wave of deportations initiated negotiations with the government. See the letter from the bench to the Minister for Religion and Public Instruction dated June 20, 1950, reprinted in Gergely (1990: 23–4).

[145] All citations from the agreement are from the English text in Gsovski (1973: 139–41). For the full Hungarian text see Gergely (1990: 317–19).

the government, discipline its own personnel when they are in violation of the law, and prevent the lower clergy from mobilizing the faithful against the State. Nor could the Church remain neutral on the issue of socialism: the agreement required the Church to exhort the faithful to fulfill the Five-Year Plan and forbade it from resisting the formation of agricultural co-operatives. The bishops did not consider this agreement a formal *Concordat* because it was concluded without the approval of the Holy See. Indeed, the Vatican refused to recognize the legality of the episcopal seal.[146] However, the government would proceed as if such a Concordat had been reached.[147]

3.4.4   State Office for Church Affairs

One of the most important institutions for asserting and maintaining control over the Churches was the establishment of the State Office for Church Affairs (*Állami Egyházügyi Hivatal*, hereafter ÁEH) in May 1951. Prior to this, religious affairs had been under the jurisdiction of the Ministry for Religion and Public Education. The ÁEH however, would enjoy much broader authority vis-à-vis the Churches. Its initial purpose was to "[settle] matters between the State and the religious denominations, especially for the purpose of carrying out the agreements and settlements concluded with the various religious denominations and of State support of religious denominations."[148] In practice, this meant broad authority over financial, administrative, and personnel matters within the Churches, and regulatory control over all matters relating to religious freedom, religious instruction, and the performance of religious ceremonies. The ÁEH was not simply an executor of government edicts. It also prepared and enforced

---

[146] Tobias (1956: 457).

[147] Hainbuch (1982: 39). That the bishops saw themselves compelled to come to agreement is clear from a draft pastoral letter in which they claimed to have considered discontinuing the negotiations and rejecting the proposed agreement in protest over the dissolution of the religious orders. The letter was changed at the request of religion and education minister Darvas, who did not think such language would contribute to the creation of an "atmosphere of peaceful coexistence between Church and state." The draft letter and response are reproduced in Gergely (1990: 319–24). Mindszenty considered it a humiliation that "priests were now forced to take a line directly contrary to their own inclinations.... They now had to ask citizens to collaborate with the atheists." Cited in Luxmoore and Babiuch (1999: 77).

[148] A translated version of the law establishing the ÁEH may be found in Gsovski (1973: 131). See also Galter (1957: 245–6, fn. 101).

statutes relating to the Churches and disbursed funds for religious instruction in the State schools and for maintenance of Church schools.[149] In the end, it also provided an extra layer of insurance against elements within the Churches who opposed the new relationship between Church and State. In October 1950, the Central Committee gave explicit expression to its suspicion regarding the Catholic Church in particular: "Many people regard the Agreement as merely an armistice making it possible for them to 'pull through the hard times.' We will keep that in mind and will be on the alert. We shall not allow the agreement to lull our vigilance and shall take care to prevent the reactionaries hiding behind the cloak of the Church from launching a fresh attack one day."[150]

Such broad powers over institutions as widespread and complex as the Churches could not be exercised without an extensive organization. The ÁEH was headquartered in Budapest and consisted of three departments: Church politics, personnel, and finance. Within the Church politics department there operated separate Catholic and Protestant groups. These groups were responsible for monitoring virtually all aspects of Church governance and operation, including encyclicals, benefices, the behavior of individual priests, and issues related to religious instruction. They also played a key role in training and supervising the ÁEH provincial bureaux, which operated in each of Hungary's nineteen provinces and Budapest. The personnel department handled all issues relating to the placement and transfer of individual priests and ministers and the collection of information on "oppositional" and other suspect Church personnel. These were important tasks because they would be used as tools to discipline uncooperative clergymen. The financial department dealt with matters concerning both the Church-State agreements and the operation of the ÁEH.[151]

The ÁEH's provincial organization operated as the "eyes and ears" of the State. There were deputies assigned to each Church diocese and the council of each county. Broadly speaking, these satellite offices, which worked very closely with the local councils, were responsible for supervising the activities of bishops, prelates, priests, and other clerical personnel. They ensured that Church personnel complied with the Church-State agreements and other edicts regulating Church activity. These deputies had the authority

---

[149] Decree No. 110 of 1951 lays out in detail the jurisdiction of the ÁEH. See Gsovski (1973: 132).

[150] Kádár (1958: 131–2).

[151] Szántó (1990: 18–20).

to directly engage with Church personnel on important matters and to discipline individuals who were not conforming to the law. In certain cases, such as the sudden death or illness of a priest, they could effect the transfer of a priest to a new location. In most instances, however, they were required to seek the central office's approval.[152] Even the smallest tasks were regulated. For example, ÁEH approval was required to have a parish seal made or changed, to print a parish bulletin or any pastoral letter, or to create and distribute devotional items.[153]

These provincial ÁEH offices played a crucial role in gathering and collating information from the towns and villages under their purview and transmitting this information to Budapest, where it could be analyzed in the context of similar reports from other provinces. To accomplish this surveillance, the ÁEH followed three strategies. First, in consultation with both local government and the Interior Ministry, it utilized "traditional" methods, such as wire tapping, intercepting mail, and videotaping. Second, it employed anonymous informants among Church personnel. According to one estimate, there were a total of 150 such informants spying on the Churches from within.[154] Finally, it employed cadres and other personnel loyal to the regime to oversee Church activities and report on what they observed. These individuals reported on registration for religious instruction, church attendance, festivals, such as Easter and Christmas, and other manifestations of church life.[155] Commissioners were placed in each bishop's office to ensure that the Church hierarchies were enforcing the Church-State agreements at the lower levels. As stated in the agreements, this meant that the Church had not just to refrain from actions directed against the State, but also to exhort the faithful to build socialism. The ÁEH made every attempt to fill Church positions with loyal personnel, in particular peace priests. This increased the chance that the Churches would be governed in ways preferred by the regime and also isolated more recalcitrant clergymen.[156] The struggle over what sort of priest would occupy which position in the Church hierarchies would be a continual point of conflict between Church and State throughout state-socialism.

[152] Ibid.: 17–18.
[153] András and Morel (1983a: 359).
[154] Szántó (1990: 23).
[155] According to one estimate, the number of these "observers" was at least as large as the number of anonymous informants employed by the Interior Ministry. See Szabó (2000: 81–2).
[156] Ibid.: 23.

3.5 Conclusion

This chapter has described the Churches' initial confrontation with the communist Party-State and, in particular, the rapid and dramatic diminution of Church influence between 1945 and the early 1950s. During this period, the State assumed responsibility for many of the services formerly provided by the Churches. The Party constructed an "apparatus of repression" to ensure that the Churches could be properly monitored and controlled and hoped to destroy the Churches from within by introducing a fifth column of "patriotic priests."

As we shall see, however, while the Churches may have entered state-socialism on the defensive, they were not completely defenseless. Chapters 4 and 5 retell from below the story of how the Churches exhibited surprising resilience in their battle for mass loyalties. Both Church and Party archival materials will reveal that although some clergymen cooperated with the regime, others resisted the many depredations of authoritarian rule, and in so doing preserved their local church communities.

4

The Battle for Souls, 1948–1956

4.1 Introduction

This chapter chronicles the opening skirmishes in the battle for mass loyalties between the Party and the Churches. During Hungary's Stalinist period the Party sought not merely to enforce outward compliance with the rules and rituals of communist life, but also to rid society of beliefs that contradicted the socialist values it hoped to instill. As we saw in Chapter 3, it went to great lengths to remove the Churches from the privileged position they had held in Hungarian society, and to fill their leadership positions with those sympathetic to socialism. Nonetheless, with churches in nearly every village to serve the faithful, the Churches remained the single largest impediment to the creation of a "new socialist man." For the Party to succeed they would have to be conquered from below as well as from above.

I devote a great deal of space, in this chapter and Chapter 5, to narrating the often ingenious ways in which the clergy attempted to foster church community. These clerical strategies can be read in two ways. First, in theoretical terms they represent efforts to manipulate how the population perceived the risks and rewards of public religious practice. As discussed in prior chapters, the clergy's goal was to maximize the reward and minimize the risk; the cadres attempted to minimize the reward and maximize the risk. Both the clergy and the cadres hoped that their respective actions would signal others as to the "correct" behavior. Second, in historical terms they reveal a neglected dimension of resistance to communist rule. As already noted, scholarly preoccupation with elite-level relations between Church and State has meant a neglect of the more quotidian clashes that allowed church community to survive. These stories also need to be told.

Section 4.2 surveys the Party's early view of its ideological tasks and how its idealized portrayal of the struggle against the Churches contrasted with the reality of the battle it would actually wage. Section 4.3 describes the Stalinist repression the Churches faced at the local level and clerical strategies of resistance. As we will see, even at the height of repression the Party's aims could be thwarted by recalcitrant priests or ill-informed local cadres. Section 4.4 depicts how some clergymen exploited the "thaw" following the death of Stalin to expand their mobilizational efforts on behalf of the church community and how the Party, in turn, employed new strategies to counter them. Section 4.5 addresses the 1956 uprising and what it showed about the Party's failure to effect real political change in society. Section 4.6 assesses the battle for souls by considering the strength of church community in different districts and villages. We will see that although the Party had made progress at weakening the church community, it could by no means declare victory.

4.2 Obstacles to Inculcating Socialism

Transforming the believing masses into loyal socialists would be, in the words of the Party, "terribly difficult, slow, requiring much time, patience, and effort."[1] In a speech at the founding of the Working Youth Association (*Dolgozó Ifjúság Szövetsége*, DISZ) Premier Rákosi outlined one of the central problems as being the continued existence of "habits and preconceptions" from the capitalist era. These included values such as attachment to property, selfishness, sloth, and working for yourself instead of your community. Quoting Stalin, Rákosi referred to such "bourgeois" values as "socialism's most dangerous enemy," and that "[i]n the era of proletarian dictatorship one of the Party's most essential tasks is the reeducation of the older generation and the education of the younger generation in the spirit of . . . socialism."[2]

Premier Rákosi singled out "clerical reaction" as a major hindrance to socialist development. Clerical reaction, as we saw in Chapter 3, had become the term of choice to refer to those elements within the Churches who were thought to oppose the socialist system. These forces were seen to be in opposition to the "democratic" or "progressive" movements within the Churches

---

[1] "Rákosi elvtárs beszéde a DISz alakuló kongresszusán," *Pártmunkás* vol. VI, no. 12, June 25, 1950, p. 3.
[2] Ibid.

that were ready to help build peace and socialism. "Democratic" clergymen were to be supported and encouraged, whereas "reactionary" ones were to be isolated and punished.[3] Rákosi identified the Catholic Church for its alleged oppositional activities (the speech was given before the agreement with the State), but acknowledged "reactionary" elements within the Protestant (and other) Churches. The Party attributed most of the problems that had been encountered in its attempt to implement socialism at the local level to clerical reaction. A June 1950 Party resolution accused such "reaction" of a multitude of "crimes," including (but not limited to): 1) being a fifth column for the imperialists; 2) disguising its political activities in religious garb; 3) undermining the working peoples' unity, discipline, and desire to work; 4) promoting the dropping out of worker and peasant students from school; 5) trying to arouse sympathy for the exploiting classes through its religious teachings; 6) organizing Church celebrations to interfere with work and school; 7) discrediting mass institutions, such as the Pioneers and the Youth Association, while infiltrating others, such as the parents council; 8) creating secret associations that turn people away from the socialist state under the guise of religion; 9) playing parents off against their children, and husband against wife; 10) propagandizing against voluntary religious instruction; and 11) intimidating and ridiculing children who did not attend religious instruction.[4]

Although this litany of accusations reads much like the inflated charges brought against the more prominent victims of show trials, beneath the hyperbole lay a grain of truth. As we saw in Chapter 3, the Party had made great strides in eliminating the Churches as competitors in the provision of education and services. Table 4.1 graphically illustrates the scale of the diminution of the Roman Catholic Church's institutional resources between 1945 and 1952. What remained of the Churches could not operate freely within society: the hierarchies were co-opted and all Church activities were subject to stringent regulation and supervision. Yet the Party's success in excising the Churches from their commanding role in society did not efface them as representatives of a non-Marxist view of history and human

---

[3] Terms such as democratic, progressive, and reactionary are in quotation marks to emphasize that these labels, part of the Stalinist vocabulary of the period, do not necessarily accurately describe the person to whom they refer. Hereafter I drop the quotation marks, it being understood that "democratic" priests were not necessarily procommunist, nor "reactionary" ones necessarily reactionary.

[4] "A Központi Vezetőség határozata a klerikális reakció elleni harcról," *Pártmunkás* vol. VI, no. 11, June 10, 1950, pp. 5–7.

4.2 Obstacles to Inculcating Socialism

Table 4.1 *Diminution of Catholic Institutional Presence.*

Institution	1945	1952
Asylums, homes	191	–
Elementary schools, 6 grades	1,216	–
General schools, 8 grades	1,669	–
Higher elementary schools	20	–
Gymnasiums (high schools)	49	8
Kindergarten teachers' schools	3	–
Professional high schools	22	–
Professional workers' schools	27	–
Nursing schools	1	–
Home economics schools	1	–
Commercial schools for girls	1	–
Apprentice schools	3	–
Commercial high schools	2	–
Divinity schools	1	–
Law schools	1	–
Teachers' colleges	4	–
Seminaries	22	6
Preparatory seminaries	8	–
Boarding schools	167	8
Monasteries (male)	187	6
Convents (female)	456	2
Hospitals	9	1
Association buildings	200	–
Printing companies	20	–
Newspapers and journal publishers	50	3

Source: András and Morel (1983a: 40–1) list similar numbers for 1965; Annabring (1953: 20); Gsovski (1973: 90–1).

development. Church buildings, often the largest and most ornate structures in the community, remained both as alternative spaces and powerful symbolic reminders of the influence the Churches once wielded. Moreover, Church sympathizers were still employed throughout the schools and local governments, and many in the lower ranks of the Party were still active participants in local church life. Their activities rarely, if ever, truly rose to the level of creating "secret associations," much less of being a fifth column for the imperialists. Yet the accusations do reflect the early obstacles the Party perceived in its attempts to disseminate socialist ideology.

The Party enunciated a rather subtle strategy for snuffing out the last remnant of clerical opposition. First, the resolution reinforced the distinction between democratic and reactionary Church elements: the former were to be supported, the latter isolated from the working masses, especially those who were believers. Reactionary religion teachers were not to be permitted to use religious instruction to turn the children against the socialist state. Educators and local Party organs were to cease any passivity in the battle against reaction. State administrative organs and democratic teachers would have to combat those educators who supported clerical reaction in the schools. Second, consistent with previous pronouncements and the constitution, the Party declared religious belief to be a private matter and thus not a justification for persecution. However, this did not apply to Party members, who were to act in the spirit of dialectical materialism. Party functionaries were to assist in the struggle against reaction through exemplary behavior. For example, they were not to remain neutral on the matter of whether their children were enrolled in religious instruction, and thus under the potential influence of "socialism's enemies." All Party members were to be informed that registering their children for religious instruction or attending church ceremonies unconsciously promoted clerical reaction, because such participation made it appear as if Party members were not committed communists, thus offering a tool with which reactionary clergy could encourage opposition to socialism.[5]

The reality of local conflict bore only faint resemblance to this idealized plan. There are three main reasons for this. First, Party practice proved less subtle than Party rhetoric. The Party's declared Church policy was cleverly crafted: the enemy was clerical reaction, not the Churches in general, or religious belief. Rhetorically, this position put the Party at odds only with "antidemocratic" forces within the Churches and permitted the faithful to join in the process of building socialism without feeling discriminated against. Thus the policy reflected a desire not to alienate potential allies among believers and the progressive clergy. However, despite its declared policy, in practice the Party vigorously sought to discourage religious practice, even that organized by the democratic clergy, and to "persuade" believers of the fallacy of religion. This might have led to great success in the struggle against the Churches, but these efforts were frustrated by often clumsy implementation. Thus, the second obstacle to victory against the Churches was the Party's reliance on often under-educated, ill-informed, and ill-prepared local cadres to wage the real battles. The dearth of qualified

---

[5] "A Központi Vezetőség határozata a klerikális reakció elleni harcról," *Pártmunkás* vol. VI, no. 11, June 10, 1950, p. 6.

socialist "foot soldiers" was of course not unique to Hungary. Peris (1998) notes how in the Soviet Union the Party had to go to great efforts to find and train enough cadres to propagate the regime's atheist message.[6] The third obstacle to victory over the Churches was the resilience of the lower clergy. Even ill-trained cadres might succeed in diminishing the Churches' influence where they faced no opposition. As this chapter documents, however, the clergy creatively used the maneuvering room available to it to frustrate these efforts whenever possible.

4.3 *Repression and Resistance, 1949–1953*

Even during the Stalinist period, the clergy seized upon the regime's own rules and policies to advance its interests. Chapter 3 described the lengths to which the Party went to ensure that the Churches' freedom of action was constrained by laws and regulations. We saw how the Party arrogated to itself the right to interpret these regulations, so that "freedom of religion," enshrined in the constitution and the agreements concluded between Church and State, did not prevent the regime from erecting numerous obstacles to the practice of that freedom. But the elasticity of the rules governing the Churches – the potential to reinterpret them for one's own benefit – worked both ways. The lower levels of the Party and the clergy often reinterpreted the rules in ways contrary to the Party elite's intentions.

The following example is illustrative of the tug-of-war between clergymen and cadres. In late 1949, a priest from Komárom county had intended to hold a three-day prayer meeting, consisting of sermons and other activities from church services. When the leader of the meeting showed up where the meeting was to be held, he was forbidden to enter. The police had canceled the event because the priest had never asked permission to hold such a session. Subsequently, the police commander ridiculed the priest and derided the religious beliefs of some of the faithful. The believers retorted that they were not ashamed of their religion and would always listen to the priest's "stupidities." The Bishop of Győr, to whom the clergyman complained, protested in a letter to the Interior Minister that the restriction represented a severe breaching of the legal guarantee of religious freedom and that the commander's behavior was contrary to the spirit of the constitution.[7]

---

[6] Peris (1998: 174–96).
[7] This is related in Bindes and Németh (1991: 143–4).

In this vignette we see many of the complexities and ambiguities that, multiplied countless times across villages and towns, would characterize the local Church-Party struggle. First, the local authorities felt constrained by the law. The meeting was not prevented for arbitrary reasons, but in reference to a law that purported to require advance permission for such an activity. Thus the regime could argue that the prohibition was legitimate. Second, the authorities reserved for themselves the right to determine the boundary between religious and political activity. Where this boundary lay was crucial because the constitution guaranteed freedom of religious practice, but did not permit such practice to be used for political purposes. We have no information on why the police chose to forbid this particular meeting. Perhaps they were unaware of the law. As we will see, misinterpretation and ignorance would be a hallmark of dealings with the authorities.

Third, neither the clergy nor the faithful quietly accepted their fate. The priest complained to his bishop, and the bishop attempted to use law to the Church's own advantage. Countering the authorities' claim, the bishop insisted that the purpose of the prayer meeting was religious, not political, and that the prohibition was a clear violation of the law. Moreover, he claimed, the officer's derisive remark about religion, while not contrary to law, was not in its spirit. It is not clear whether the bishop composed the letter in full knowledge that there was no "real" religious freedom or whether the bishop took the State naively at its word. Either way, the bishop was demanding that the State make good on its commitment to respect religious freedom. That commitment could not easily be openly disregarded, lest the Party lose legitimacy among the still largely religious peasantry and the naive lower levels of the government and Party. Even if the demand were to fail, then at least the Party-State's illegitimacy would be a little more visible. If the demand were to succeed, then the clergy would have one more opportunity to build community.[8]

Let us examine the two-way nature of regulations more closely. Consider the constitutional promise of "complete religious freedom" and "freedom of activity" for the Churches in the discharge of their duties. A highly confidential memo from the Party's propaganda department to each county

---

[8] This closely parallels the ways in which the Russian Orthodox Church harnessed the Soviet notion of "revolutionary legality" to circumvent Party dictates in the aftermath of the Russian Revolution. As Husband (2000: 145) notes, in their clash with the Bolsheviks, the clergy and the laity "cited law whenever possible in direct confrontations, and if unsuccessful at the local level they appealed to central authorities in the hope of having lower decisions overturned."

Party secretary, distributed less than one month after the conclusion of the agreement between the State and the Catholic Church, sheds light on the elasticity of these promises and their either naive or willful misinterpretation. The memo details several instances across the country in which lower-level Party members and others are interpreting the Church-State agreement in ways contrary to their intended spirit. For example, a Party leader from a heavy machinery factory in Borsod-Abaúj-Zemplén county declared at a meeting of educators that "we can happily report that the struggle against clerical reaction was now over." The Party secretary from a nearby village thought that his district Party committee could not possibly object if he were to attend church. In several other places around the country Party members and their wives once more began attending church. In some cases, the increase was substantial. In Szentpéterföld (Zala county), church attendance was reported to have doubled. Many others belatedly registered their children for religious instruction in the schools. At one meeting in Csongrád county people wondered why religious instruction was not once more made compulsory.[9]

The lower clergy and other Church personnel were no less immune from wishful thinking or apt to interpret the Church-State agreement in ways favorable to themselves. Peace priest leader Miklós Beresztóczy welcomed it, because it provided for punishment "not just for those who commit an offense against the Church, but for those who offend against the legal secular authority, whose constitution the bishops' agreement recognized."[10] This viewpoint is not that different from the Party's, which wanted the Church hierarchy to enforce the State's laws on the lower levels of the Church. Some priests took the agreement as a sign of the Church's acceptance of the regime and seized the opportunity to cooperate with the Party. A priest in Nadap (Zala county) used the pulpit to invite the peasants to join the local collective farm, so that the community could become socialist as soon as possible. Others joined the peace priest movement or protested against imperialists and atomic weapons.[11] The Catholic weekly *Új Ember* noted optimistically that on the basis of the agreement practicing Catholics would no longer be subject to "misunderstanding, suspicion, and discrimination" in the workplace or in life more generally.[12]

[9] Z5/1950.
[10] Cited in Salacz (1988: 95).
[11] Z5/1950.
[12] Ibid.

Many of the clergy, however, were not clear what was required of them as a consequence of the agreement and adopted a wait-and-see attitude, with the expectation that further instructions would be forthcoming. The bishops' pastoral letter explaining the agreement to the faithful was apologetic, and linked it directly with the bishops' efforts to relieve the situation of the religious orders, which were being persecuted. This provided fodder for priests who harbored little sympathy for the regime anyway. Some of these priests explicitly refused to participate on peace committees and openly denounced the agreement. One deacon from Tokaj (Borsod-Abaúj-Zemplén County) accused the bishops of being traitors and declared that he hoped the Holy Father did not sanction the agreement.[13]

The regime's distinction between democratic and reactionary priests provided both the Party and the clergy with opportunities to press their respective agendas. Recall that for the Party the declared enemy was clerical reaction, not the priesthood in general. However, the Party could arbitrarily label as reactionary virtually any activity that it did not like and was apt to see reaction lurking everywhere. According to a 1950 Interior Ministry report, the activities of religious groups had increased in the previous months, and "[t]he goal of these activities was to win the youth over to clerical reaction under the guise of religion."[14] The tendency to exaggerate the influence of reaction was not lost on the clergy, especially in the Reformed Church, which had made ardent attempts to accommodate the regime. In a speech before a clerical meeting in 1951, one pastor complained openly about the regime's usage of the fight against clerical reaction to prohibit any Church activity it deemed inappropriate: "[a]s I see it, they consider as clerical reaction any behavior that strengthens our Church life."[15] He expressed great regret that although the Reformed Church should be seen as capable of helping to achieve socialist goals, the Party did not wish to avail itself of the assistance. At a different meeting a pastor expressed similar concerns about the State Office for Church Affairs (ÁEH): "[the ÁEH] does everything in its power to cripple . . . religious life and education."[16] The pastor went on to recommend that the hierarchy be more careful in considering the regime's recommendations for further "building down" of the Church.

[13] Ibid.
[14] XIX-B-1-m Mo. 0069 of the Interior Ministry, cited in Orbán (1996: 221).
[15] Ref34/1951.
[16] Ref36/1951.

The clergy also harnessed the elasticity in the distinction between democratic and reactionary priests for its own advantage. In a number of provinces there were clergymen who, although of unknown political affiliation, declared themselves to be democratic, in the hope that parents would feel safe sending their children to them for religious instruction.[17] In response to a 1951 order requiring the Hajdúnánás (Hajdú-Bihar county) congregation to sell its copy machine, a Calvinist pastor appealed in a letter to the Interior Minister for an exception, citing the congregation's strong service in the struggle for peace. Not only had one of the congregation's pastors been an official delegate to the Budapest peace conference, the pastor argues, but the copy machine was used to promote progressive causes. As "proof" the pastor attached the Easter message sent to the congregants that outlined what was to be done in the struggle for peace.[18] Many priests who wrote letters to the ÁEH expressed the sentiment that they were "children of the people," language clearly meant to assuage official suspicion.[19]

The Party was acutely aware of the possibility that the clergy and other potential enemies might feign sympathy for the regime, and was by no means satisfied with vague, unsubstantiated declarations of loyalty. To gauge the opposition and probe for possible allies the authorities surveyed local activities. One 1950 report from Zala county detailed how the authorities in the county seat and elsewhere were going from apartment to apartment recording whether the occupants were Party members, whether they had a civil or religious marriage ceremony, whether they had enrolled their child for religious instruction, and to what confession they belonged. The author, the Party secretary, noted how dangerous this survey was for the clergy, because "[our] Party organizations are keeping a vigilant eye on their activities."[20]

The authorities also conducted regular visits with individual clergymen. These were designed both to communicate the regime's Church policies and to probe for possible opposition. The conversations covered topical issues. For example, in meetings conducted during 1951, the clergy were asked what they thought the purpose was of the newly created ÁEH, and how they felt about recent increases in their incomes, the fight for peace, and other timely political events. The clergy's responses were subsequently

[17] Z5/1950.
[18] Ref104/1951.
[19] Cited in Orbán (1996: 222).
[20] Zala Megyei Levéltár (1999: 142).

interpreted (more likely overinterpreted) for evidence either of sympathy, neutrality, or hostility to the regime.

Given the risk of retaliation, it would have been unusual if a clergyman had voiced open hostility. In fact, one might have expected attitudes to reflect those of the "peace priest" movement. However, the priests were aware that they would be held accountable for their statements, both by the Church and the Party, and thus remained largely evasive and noncommittal. For example, when asked about the ÁEH, one priest responded that he was not familiar with the order that created it, and thus had no opinion either way. He claimed to have no time to read the newspaper or follow domestic or foreign affairs, because he spent his days engaged in spiritual matters. When asked about the peace issue, he responded that both he and his fellow priests, as a matter of principle arising from their calling, believed in peace. This answer is, of course, not different from that of the Catholic hierarchy, which supported peace, but not the Soviet peace movement.[21] Another clergyman apparently was aware of the creation of the ÁEH, but portrayed it in purely technical terms, as a mechanism by which the State and the Churches could more efficiently communicate, to the benefit of both the Churches and the State. He too claimed to be removed from political events, adding that priests who politicize were not well liked anyway.[22] A third clergyman declined to opine on Church affairs, claiming that he was under the direction of the Catholic hierarchy and thus not free to express his personal opinion on such matters. This priest also employed Marxist discourse as a way of communicating sympathy for the regime, recommending the meetings with the local cadres as a way for the clergy to "better serve the affairs of the working people."[23]

The fact that the Reformed Church had been far more cooperative with the regime than the Roman Catholic Church did not spare it from undergoing the same comprehensive examination. The regime's thoroughness is illustrated in 1950 reports from Hajdú-Bihar county, where the population is predominantly Calvinist. These reports contain detailed assessments of each priest, pastor, preacher, religion instructor, and friar in the county. Among the items systematically reported were whether the person had traveled to the West, had been interned for any reason, and had, by May 1, signed the "peace appeal" (*békeív*), indicating support for the

[21] HB4/1951.
[22] Ibid.
[23] Ibid.

Soviet-sponsored peace movement. The latter datum was particularly important, because signing the peace appeal would be one of many litmus tests the regime would impose on democratic clergymen. The accounts often also included political assessments of the clergy's family members and speculation on their likely future stance vis-à-vis the regime.[24]

The Party also surveyed leading lay employees of the Churches. Data collected included the positions people held, their occupation, how much land they owned, and a characterization of their political views. One such report for the Reformed Church from the district of Biharnagybajom (Hajdú-Bihar county) revealed the work that lay ahead of the Party in infiltrating the lower levels of the Church. Of 146 people listed, only five were identified as Party members, and one as a candidate. A further five were listed as democratic without specifying a party affiliation. The majority of the people appeared as kulaks, right-wing, FKgP members, untrustworthy, or some other moniker indicating actual or potential hostility to the regime.[25]

It could be argued that the Party's preoccupation with clerical reaction predisposed the local cadres and other informants to blame the clergy for events over which they in actuality had little control. Clearly the upper echelons would be receptive to such accusations, given that it would have mirrored their own rhetoric. In doing so, the local Party organization might also have deflected criticism away from what may have been its own errors. Yet despite incentives to fault the clergy, in some cases they do not appear as the primary disruptive element. To see this, consider the problems the Party encountered in its efforts to establish "Houses of Culture" (*kulturotthonok*).

Houses of Culture were intended across Eastern Europe as an instrument in the socialist reeducation of the working peasantry, "an integral component of ideological work."[26] They were to become, according to the Hungarian Party, "in place of the pub and the church, the cultural and social center of the village."[27] The Party saw these Houses as a nerve center in efforts to spread the socialist message, part of an organizational network that included the schools and other cultural institutions.[28] Propaganda

---

[24] HB8/1950 and HB10/1950.

[25] HB1/1950. This document is missing some pages, and is therefore not exhaustive of all leading Church employees in the district. The list is organized by settlement. By examining differences across settlements in the text of the political characterizations, it is clear that each settlement was responsible for its own reporting.

[26] White (1990: 3).

[27] Z8/1951.

[28] Beke and Koncz (1985: 14–15).

activities to be conducted under the House of Culture aegis included training in the works of Lenin, Stalin, Rákosi, and other socialist leaders and intellectuals; lessons in the history of capitalist exploitation, working-class and colonial struggle, and the successes of the Soviet Union; and advice on proper economic, social, and political behavior under socialism.[29] The Houses were also to function as a forum in which other cultural and educational activities could take place under socialist supervision. The idea was to integrate them as much as possible with the everyday life of the community. They were used, for example, to popularize collective farming and disseminate information about industrial and agricultural methods. They hosted sports activities and housed natural science lectures, fine arts and performing groups, and reading circles.[30] In the course of 1950 alone, 645 such meeting places came into existence: 434 in villages, 192 in industrial plants, and 19 in cities.[31]

Given the importance the Party attached to these institutions, it would have been easy to attribute early difficulties in implementation to "clerical machinations." But apparently that was not where the problem lay. In a frank report detailing the steps to be taken to further develop the Houses of Culture network, the Party's agitation and propaganda department accused ill-informed lower-level Party members and other willfully disruptive local elements. Local Party organs apparently saw the Houses primarily as places of entertainment rather than as vehicles for serious political education. As a consequence, the Houses were not assigned political tasks and operated unsupervised.[32] Even when the Houses did operate as planned the results were not always what was expected. The cadres in charge of developing the Houses, for example, tended to be ill-trained in how to encourage participation. Thus the quality level of the events was often low, and only a small proportion of the community would get involved in the activities. At a conference of culture house directors in late 1953, a peasant is quoted as saying, "there's agitation indoors, there's agitation outdoors, but all we want to do is read."[33]

The Party also notes that oppositional elements within communities attempted to hinder the Houses' work, or at least influence their operation.

[29] Csende (1975: 142–3).
[30] Z6/1951 and Z8/1951.
[31] Z6/1951.
[32] Ibid.
[33] White (1990: 61).

126

It accuses "the enemy" of infiltrating the leadership boards of the Houses with "right-wing social democrats," "undesirable class elements," "choir-masters," cantors, and "former Horthy-era civil servants," under the pretext that they offered useful expertise.[34] Notably absent from this list is any mention of the clergy or clerical reaction, though the mention of cantors clearly indicates that the Churches were one possible source of opposition. The Party identifies taverns, not churches, as a main obstacle to developing the Houses in villages.[35]

No issue better illustrates the intricacies of local Church-State conflict than religious instruction in the schools. Chapter 3 described the bitter struggle waged after the war over the nationalization of confessional schools and the eventual introduction of voluntary religious instruction in the State schools. We saw how the regime attempted to limit the effectiveness of this instruction through a range of discriminatory decrees. However, the Party viewed religious instruction as far more than merely an annoyance to be legally regulated. It represented a direct challenge to the Party's monopolization of the schools. The schools were meant to serve a crucial role in ideological indoctrination. They would teach Marxism-Leninism, to be sure, but they would also imbue the youth with socialist patriotism and Party loyalty: "A central task of our schools, from the kindergartens to the universities, is to teach our young people... the significance, the leading role, the aims of our party... and... an open and partisan stand at the side of the people's democracies."[36] Achieving this would require a fundamental ideologization of the curriculum. József Révai, Minister of Education, put it best: "Naturally, there are no non-political subjects."[37] But religion could not easily be tailored to suit the political needs of the Party. Religious instruction constituted an important breach in the Party's ability to prevent the youth from hearing alternative views. The dangers the Party perceived in this breach are evident in a speech give by Révai before other Party members in mid-1950:

We must put up a firm and determined defense against the reactionary incitement going on during the lessons of religious instruction. The working parent who sends his child to religious instruction in schools entrusts his child's soul, in most cases, to the care of the people's foe, the agents of the imperialist warmongers. To send

[34] Z6/1951.
[35] Ibid.
[36] *Köznevelés*, 1949, cited in Juhasz (1952: 18).
[37] Cited in Magyar Dolgozók Pártja (1956: 94).

children to church or to religious education in schools given by reactionary priests means at the same time ... to take a stand against the People's Democracy.[38]

Enrollment in religious instruction was seen as a litmus test of loyalty to the regime. It is true that rhetorically this applied only to reactionary instructors, but as we have seen, the Party alone determined what counted as reactionary, and the boundary between that and democratic attitudes shifted as needed. In practice, the regime vigorously sought to diminish the proportion of children enrolled in religious instruction, in disregard of the loyalties of the instructor. For parents, requesting religious instruction was a great risk. To be seen as "against the People's Democracy" in mid-1950, during the Stalinist period, could mean incarceration or worse. It was during this period that hundreds of priests and members of religious orders were interned, thousands of peasants were convicted of "economic" crimes, and "class enemies" were being harassed.[39] High levels of enrollment were seen as Party failure and Church success. This was particularly true when Party members enrolled their children. For them, religion was not to be a private matter. According to Révai, "by going to church, by sending their children to religious instruction in schools, they [Party members] ... promote the efforts of the reactionary clergy."[40]

The Party erected obstacles to virtually all aspects of religious instruction. Beginning with the 1949–50 school year this instruction became voluntary. Registration was held at a special time, separate from general school registration, and required the written request of a child's parents. These conditions made such registration difficult and risky. The decree requiring parents to request the instruction was released on September 6, 1949, with the deadline for the request set for September 15. This gave the Churches little time to inform the laity of the changes, and parents little time to make the arrangements.[41] In the case of the railway training school in Debrecen (Hajdú-Bihar county), for example, there was no religious instruction that year, because the requests for enrollment did not arrive until after the fifteenth, and the school headmaster refused to grant an exception.[42] Many other parents almost certainly declined to register their children for fear of

[38] Cited in Gsovski (1973: 142).
[39] On the internal deportation of "class enemies," see the cases in Handler and Meschel (1997).
[40] Ibid.
[41] Gsovski (1973: 97).
[42] Ref92/1949.

being identified as an enemy of the regime. In Nagykaporna (Zala county) it was reported that during the 1951 registration period seven or eight parents appeared and wished to conduct the process orally. When the school headmaster requested a written declaration from them, they departed and went to their local priest, but never returned to register.[43]

The authorities went out of their way to make it as difficult and inconvenient as possible for parents. One 1953 complaint to the ÁEH from Győr-Moson-Sopron county accused the local authorities of neglecting to inform parents of the precise time in which registration was to take place (resulting in some people facing locked doors); of the need to bring the children with them to the registration; that those administering the registration would take a two- to three-hour lunch break (causing parents to miss work); that registration on the second day would last only until noon; that those children who failed another subject in school would not be permitted to enroll; that both parents' signatures were required for enrollment (forcing parents to identify themselves to the regime); and that those conducting the registration would spend ten to twenty minutes with each parent (resulting in long lines and more missed work). The authorities also attempted to discourage the industrial workers from exercising their rights and openly prevented orphaned and half-orphaned children from being registered.[44]

The regime employed numerous other "administrative measures" to discourage religious instruction. These included constraints on the time it could be offered (after all other classes finished), frequent changes in the schedule of instruction, withholding or delaying approval of instructors, assigning a room that was too small to hold the class, not providing study materials, and scheduling activities, such as movie showings, to conflict with the class.[45] The regime's power to deny permission to teach religion proved particularly powerful, because without an instructor there could be no instruction. For example, in cases where an instructor was unable to continue teaching (e.g., due to sickness), he or she could not be replaced without the authorities approving a replacement. That took time. Moreover, an instructor received approval to teach in a *particular* school. Special permission was required to move to a different school. Thus, when instructors stepped

[43] Z12/1952.
[44] Bindes and Németh (1991: 193–5). This is only one of many such complaints.
[45] Those responsible for organizing religious instruction in the Tiszántúli Reformed Church district sent detailed reports to the hierarchy complaining of these difficulties. See Ref92/1949, Ref96/1949, and Ref97/1950.

down it was not possible for a different instructor to immediately replace them, further delaying and disrupting the class.[46] In Győr-Sopron county during the 1950 school year there were many instances of religion teachers not getting the proper official certification and religious instruction, consequently, not taking place.[47]

The harassment extended to the classroom. A 1950 letter of complaint to a bishop from a Reformed teacher of religion in Dombrád (Hajdú-Bihar county) exemplifies the conditions under which instruction took place. Regulations stipulated that the religion teacher was permitted on school grounds only during the time that religious instruction was to take place. Throughout the school year, the school headmaster in Dombrád took this literally and demanded that the religion teacher wait outside the school building until the initial bell rang. The hope was that during inclement weather the teacher would cancel class, although he defied them and dutifully waited outside for the bell to ring. On several occasions, the school headmaster went up to the students as they were waiting for religion class and told them they should go home, because they did not have to go to that class. This led to some attrition. A couple of the other teachers did not permit the students to wait in the classroom for religious instruction and instead had them pack their things and wait outside. The religion teacher's complaints about this went unheeded. Sometimes the times of the different classes were changed at the last minute, in the hopes of reducing attendance even further. The school authorities also abused their oversight responsibilities. The rules required all courses to be overseen in equal measure. However, the religion teacher counted a total of eighty-six visits from the school headmaster or his deputy, far more than the other classes received. In many cases, these visits were intended to disrupt instruction by distracting the students from their lessons.[48] Despite all of these irritations, most of the students registered for religious instruction continued to attend class.[49]

---

[46] These and other complaints are relayed in Ref97/1950.

[47] Bindes and Németh (1991: 185–6).

[48] The problem of overzealous cadres was not limited to Hungary. Young (1997: 76–7) notes how in the aftermath of the communist revolution in Russia local communists responded with alacrity to the 1918 decree separating Church and State, suggesting that the motive behind abusive practices was pent up anger over the prior exclusion of nonreligious individuals from positions of influence within the village.

[49] Ref32/1950. The teacher wrote to the bishop in the hopes that the bishop would take the issue up with the county council.

Administrative harassment might have reduced enrollment and interfered with instruction, but it did nothing to decrease any underlying demands by parents to have their children receive religious training. The other
half of the battle against religious instruction consisted of efforts to win-
now down the "demand side" of religion. One important strategy in this was
propaganda aimed at discrediting the Churches as an alternative locus of
loyalty. The Party's use of the mass media, in particular newspapers, had begun in earnest in 1948 with open attacks against the Churches' intransigence
on the schools question, Church organizations, the Vatican, and especially
Cardinal Mindszenty. Later, the emphasis would broaden to the struggle
against clerical reaction and accusations against leading Church figures and
organizations, particularly Catholic. We may never know whether these
attacks served more to demoralize or empower the faithful. The Party certainly hoped that by exposing the Churches' "wrongdoings" people would
turn away from them. At the same time, however, the Party wanted to increase its own acceptability to the believing population by highlighting the
spirit of cooperation between Church and State. Thus, beginning in 1949
there was also increasing emphasis on progressive currents in the Churches
that were willing to work with the Party, in particular the peace movement.[50]

A second strategy involved efforts to disabuse people of their religious
beliefs. To avoid unnecessarily alienating believers, the Party rarely engaged in the type of frontal assault on religion that it employed against
the Churches. Indeed, official Party rhetoric held that religious belief was
a personal matter (*magánügy*). However, this represented more a tactic
than a statement of principle. First, it did not apply to Party members.
The Party considered it an obligation to train cadres and other functionaries in the spirit of dialectical materialism. Party members were to
be made to understand that participation in church life was not a neutral
behavior, irrespective of whether the clergyman in question was democratic or not. Rather, communist membership in the church community
only served the interests of clerical reaction.[51] The Party promised to
"hold accountable" (*felelőségre vonni*) those functionaries who did not carry
out the Party's wishes.[52]

---

[50] These are summary conclusions of a content analysis of the leading Party daily, *Szabad Nép*.
See Morel (1968: 84–6).

[51] "A Központi Vezetőség határozata a klerikális elleni harcról." *Pártmunkás*, June 10, 1950,
p. 6.

[52] Habuda et al. (1998: 164).

Third, although the Party stated its reluctance to coerce ordinary believers into abandoning their beliefs, it made no pledge to cease attempting to spread socialist ideas. In this regard, Houses of Culture represented only one possible tool. Radio, television, libraries, Winter and night schools, lecture series, and special academies for workers and peasants would all be used to educate the masses in scientific materialism.[53] In the schools "the textbooks, lesson plan, and curriculum should radiate Marxist-Leninist ideology."[54] Though there would later be debates on the compatibility between Marxism and Christianity, in the early 1950s the Party felt that "piety is not compatible with the communists' scientific worldview."[55]

At the local level, the Party increased its propaganda efforts against religious instruction in the period immediately preceding registration. A June 1952 resolution illustrates the gravity with which the Party viewed this task.[56] It ordered that the local press report the machinations of clerical reaction and any untoward activities relating to religious instruction.[57] It charged local Party committees with seeing to it that "educators, good activists from the teachers' union, and the most confident members of the parents' association ... decrease the numbers of registrants by as much as possible" by speaking to pious parents beforehand.[58] During the 1952 registration period in Zala county the teachers apparently visited each such set of parents, with special emphasis on those who worked in factories and on State and collective farms.[59]

The upper clergy, having been purged of any oppositional elements, joined the Party in urging the faithful to participate in the building of socialism. The Catholic bishops issued a series of pastoral letters supporting peace loans, prodding people to complete their agricultural tasks, and encouraging the development of collective farms. These were typically phrased not as secular advice for good citizens, but as part of Christian duty. Such phrasing greatly benefited the Party, because the truly pious would take their work even more seriously. Thus, for example, the June 4, 1953 letter urged

[53] "A MDP Politikai Bizottságának határozata az agitációs munkáról," *Pártépítés* vol. 6, no. 22, November 25, 1950, pp. 3–4.
[54] "A Magyar Dolgozók Pártja Központi Vezetőségének határozata a vallás- és közoktatásügyi minisztérium munkájával kapcsolatos kérdésekről," *Pártmunkás* vol. 6, no. 8, April 25, 1950, p. 5.
[55] Habuda et al. (1998: 164).
[56] Ibid.: 164–6.
[57] Ibid.: 165.
[58] Ibid.: 164.
[59] Z12/1952.

the peasants to work hard, even if it they were not private farmers: "After finishing the harvest it is just as important to gather and thresh the grain. He who finishes this work in time, and cleans his threshing floor and collects his wheat, is acting according to God's will.... It is God's will that the harvest provide as much bread as possible, not just to those who work the land, but to those in the factories, enterprises, and offices who are working for everyone's benefit."[60] The bishops also disciplined reactionary priests. In Hajdú-Bihar county, for example, five such priests were dismissed from duty in the period leading up to mid-1953. To further encourage cooperative democratic views, the Episcopate also assigned progressive priests to the more desirable parishes. Less docile clergymen were transferred to poor or rural areas.[61]

The Reformed hierarchy, as we saw in Chapter 3, also came to support socialism, and sought to rally the faithful behind the regime's programs. Church leader Bishop Albert Bereczky exuded praise for Rákosi in the following encomium on the occasion of his sixtieth birthday in early 1952:

Since the liberation we have learned and are continuously learning a new lesson taught to us primarily by his life, teaching and example.... We are increasingly aware of the great gift which was and is given to us by his wisdom, humaneness and knowledge. [He is] the great statesman whose wise and strong hand leads the life of our country.[62]

In a series of pastoral letters from 1952 and 1953, Church leaders expounded on a range of subjects, including the need to collect donations to aid victims of the Korean war,[63] gratitude that Hungary was free from oppression and servitude,[64] the importance of participation in the conservation of paper,[65] the need to maintain good relations with the local authorities,[66] and the obligation to work hard.[67] As in the Catholic letters, these points were justified in theological terms: "Careful, devoted, adequate, and timely completion of work is ... a command obligated by God's word...."[68]

---

[60] See Izsák (1985: 423–66), and p. 460 for the quotation.
[61] HB11/1953.
[62] Bereczky (1953: 297–8). Cited in Rácsok (2000: 15).
[63] Ref115/1952.
[64] Ref116/1952.
[65] Ref123/1953.
[66] Ref124/1953.
[67] Ref117/1952.
[68] Ibid.

The lower clergy was caught between a repressive Party and co-opted Episcopates that could offer little support in rallying the faithful to assert its claims. Religious instruction registration for the 1952–3 school year was particularly difficult, because the Party had just resolved to redouble its efforts to discourage religious instruction. In Zala county, for example, the registration period is reported to have been "mostly orderly, without the smallest problem."[69] The clergy was not completely passive, however. In some villages the priest announced details of the registration in church, or used bible study hours to reassure wavering individuals. In Pacsa (Zala county), it was noted that a flier announcing the registration had been hung on the church door, which the authorities promptly had removed. In other places, priests or other church members made visits to family homes or accompanied parents the entire way to the school on registration day.[70]

Some clergymen sought remedies to ameliorate the difficulties initiating and conducting religious instruction. Many who had their permission to conduct instruction suspended wrote to their bishops in hopes of either having the permission reinstated or finding replacement teachers.[71] In one village the Party had succeeded in preventing most of the desiring parents from registering their children, and the school administration was adamant that only those children officially registered could attend the class. The aggrieved parents complained to their priest, who subsequently asked the bishop to intercede so that those children who had been prevented from registering could also attend. Ultimately there was a supplementary registration, in which an additional fifty-three students were put on the rolls.[72] This is evidence that when the rights of the Church were unambiguously violated, the bishops were willing and ready to act.

More enterprising priests, realizing that the Party had determined to obstruct religious instruction in the schools, sought intensified contact with the students outside of school. They utilized all legal means, including catechism and preparation for first communion and confirmation. Enrollment levels for the 1952–3 school year in Hajdú-Bihar county testify to the importance of these rights of passage as an alternative or supplement to religious instruction in the schools. In Görbeháza, for example, not one of the 342 eligible students was enrolled in religious instruction, but fifty took

---

[69] Z12/1952.
[70] Z12/1952 and Sz63/1952.
[71] See, for example, Bindes and Németh (1991: 186–9).
[72] Ibid.: 190–1.

134

part in the preparation for First Communion. In Hajdúnánás, slightly more students took part in preparation for confirmation than attended religious instruction. These important rights of passage served not only to increase contact between the Church and the students, but also fostered a deeper relationship between the priest and the parents. As if to counteract the potential effects of the bishops' progovernment encyclicals, some priests refused to read them in church, feigned a coughing spasm while reading, or merely distributed typed versions.[73]

4.4 Exploiting Room to Maneuver, 1953–1956

Deteriorating economic conditions and Stalin's death in March 1953 set the stage for liberalization in Hungary. At Moscow's urging, the Party initiated the "New Course" in June 1953, with a resolution listing errors the Party had made in its efforts to implement socialism.[74] The resolution was wide-ranging, attributing the dramatically declining living standards to the Party's excessive emphasis on heavy industry, overly rapid industrialization and socialization of agriculture, too much military spending, and expansion of the State apparatus.[75] The ruling clique led by Rákosi was criticized for not recognizing "the proliferating breaches of the law, the incorrect, inimical conduct of the police and state-security organizations towards the workers, the activity of the councils, often bad, illegal, and unjust to the people, the high number of sentences by the courts, and so on."[76] Although the resolution did not focus on the Churches directly, the new prime minister, Imre Nagy, addressed them in a July 4 speech to the parliament (also publicized):

We have to show more tolerance in the field of religion. We can not allow the use of administrative measures which have been occurring in this field. In this matter the government maintains a tolerant attitude employing persuasion and enlightenment. The government disapproves of the use of administrative or other force.[77]

---

[73] See HB11/1953 for a catalog of various clerical activities.

[74] Habuda et al. (1998: 188–206). The Party leadership issued the resolution with reluctance. Although details would not be made public for decades, it nonetheless signaled a diminution in the influence of Rákosi and his allies. For details, see Rainer (2002), especially pp. 23–30.

[75] Habuda et al. (1998: 191).

[76] Quoted from Rainer (2002: 29). The resolution states that between 1951 and May 1953 the police, acting as a court, charged 850,000 people with petty offenses. This is nearly one in ten people.

[77] Juhász (1965: 156–63). For the original Hungarian, see Nagy (1954: 366–7).

The Churches took advantage of the "thaw" represented by Nagy's assumption of power. The Catholic Bench of Bishops initiated more general discussions with the government, leading to an informal agreement in late 1953. The most important provisions included an increase in the availability of Catholic publications and religion textbooks; the opening of homes for sick or elderly priests; permission to minister to hospital patients who request it; the cessation of the requirement that believers register by name for baptisms, first communion, confirmation, and weddings; and a pledge to work toward eliminating all irregularities in the registration and conduct of religious instruction.[78]

The Reformed Church reacted more timidly. The leadership's immediate response was to moderate its vigorous propagandizing on behalf of the peace movement and collectivization.[79] But there were no real efforts to increase the Church's autonomy or freedom of action. It was not until mid-1956 that the hierarchy felt pressure to change, and even then the demands concerned Church governance, not politics. A memorandum signed by 160 pastors, issued not long before the outbreak of revolution, expressed concern about the "[a]ccusations and counter-accusations, reports and denunciations" that were "poisoning the already difficult atmosphere of our church."[80] They called for a free discussion "without any fear of retaliation" and "within the framework of the Scriptures and our confession on the one hand and State and Church Agreement of October 7, 1948, on the other."[81] Although the memorandum did not challenge the terms of Church-State coexistence, it did seek democratization within the Church. The same tack was taken by a group of students and assistant ministers at the Reformed Theological Academy in Budapest. Their declaration, "The Confessing Church in Hungary," deplored "every counterrevolutionary attempt to bring back the past,"[82] yet considered "as fraudulent all despotic clique rule within the Church."[83] In greater detail than the aforementioned

[78] Gergely (1985: 139) and Izsák (1985: 461–2). Nagy had already pledged to remove obstacles regarding religious practice in the announcement of the government's program, so not all parts of the agreement represented genuine concessions.
[79] Takacs (1960: 397–8) and Kónya (1988: 193). Of course, forced collectivization fell out of favor in the New Course, so in any case there would have been less need to propagandize on its behalf.
[80] Cited in Takacs (1960: 405).
[81] Cited in ibid.
[82] Cited in Gombos (1960: 96).
[83] Gombos (1960: 97).

memorandum, this confession detailed the antidemocratic activities of the Church administration.[84] No substantive change in the Church administration would occur, however, until the outbreak of revolution.

The "thaw" was more than just rhetorical at the local level. The Party's 1955 and 1956 instructions to those overseeing religious instruction in the schools, for example, were distinctly civil in tone. The dates and times of registration were to be announced in advance and only one parent was required to be present, with or without the registrant. Although both parents' signatures were still required, in cases where one was a soldier, sick, or working a distance away this requirement could be relaxed. In cases where a child was missing one or both parents, a guardian could authorize the enrollment. Even children under State care could in principle be registered, provided a competent State representative was there to authorize it. Late registrations were also permitted, if the parents could show cause.[85] A 1956 report from Zala county on the situation of atheistic propaganda notes the general dearth of efforts to spread the materialist worldview since the beginning of the New Course. Not only were there few lectures detailing the counterrevolutionary role played by clerical reaction, the report stated, but almost no presentations on Hungarian humanism, the Enlightenment, or the Reformation's anticlerical literature. There were similarly few anticlerical plays.[86]

For all the improvement, however, the New Course did not ultimately represent a genuine shift in attitude toward the Churches or religion. First, the new policy did not prevent lower-level functionaries from using their discretion to impede Church activity. In the late summer of 1953, for example, Archbishop Gyula Czapik requested that the ordinaries under his direct authority in Győr-Moson-Sopron county report the illegalities surrounding the most recent registration for religious instruction, apparently in the hope that if he forwarded these to the ÁEH, they could be addressed. The ordinaries complied with his wish, but the ÁEH never followed up on the many problems reported.[87]

Second, and more importantly, once the initial confusion over the policy had died down, the regime became just as committed as ever to the battle

---

[84] For the full text of the declaration, see Takacs (1960: 409–13).

[85] Z17/1955 and Z21/1956.

[86] Z19/1956.

[87] For Czapik's letter and a summary of the reported illegalities, see Bindes and Németh (1991: 202–4). Salacz (1988: 123) notes how the ÁEH refused to act in the spirit of the New Course.

against the Churches. Between the announcement of the New Course and the outbreak of revolution in 1956 it continued to mobilize against religious instruction in the schools, harass perceived "reactionary" elements, and propagandize in favor of socialism and against religion.[88] As before the New Course, for example, the Party's Agitation and Propaganda department prepared detailed action plans to convince people not to register their children for religious instruction. County, district, and municipal Party committees were to commence "individual propaganda," employing only "ideologically solid" functionaries and Party members who possessed the requisite experience and preparation. Their energies were to be concentrated on "important industrial and agricultural centers, collectives, State farms... and those areas where clerical influence is stronger than average."[89] Reactionary clergymen who employed "spiritual terror" (*lelkiterror*) against the parents to get them to register were to be held responsible for their actions, and all Church officials were to be cordoned off from the registration, lest they exert influence at the last moment.[90] In 1955, one Lutheran pastor regretted that the State still required written permission to enroll. "If an oral application had been sufficient, then registration rates would be 98%, but many were frightened by the paper."[91]

Special efforts were devoted to individuals who by virtue of their positions could influence the behavior of the majority by their actions. These included State functionaries, Party members, and "local notables" – those who were held in high esteem by a given community. As noted in Chapter 1, such personnel had an extraordinary signaling effect that reduced the perceived risk of participation. Lower-level Party members and State functionaries proved particularly troubling because many of them continued to enroll their children in religious instruction or participated in other activities, such as Easter and Christmas processions. Whatever patience the Party was showing toward ordinary citizens, it certainly did not tolerate religious practice among its own allies. The Party kept detailed records

---

[88] These activities continued with seeming independence of the ebb and flow of power during this period between Prime Minister Nagy, who represented the New Course, and Party leader Rákosi, who advocated a more orthodox line. Even with the resurgence of Rákosi in early 1955, however, the level of repression of society would never again reach what it had been before the New Course. For details on the struggle between Rákosi and Nagy, see Kovrig (1979: 257–84) and Ignotus (1972: 220–35).

[89] Z21/1956.

[90] Z17/1955.

[91] Szépfalusi (1984: 127).

on those who participated, noting particularly when a person was a Party leader, or held a job from which he or she would be able to exert influence, such as teacher, tavern-keeper, worker on a collective or State farm, or member of the local council.[92] In part, this behavior was surely due to uncertainty about what the Party actually stood for. As late as 1955 there were calls in Hajdú-Bihar county for the Party's Agitprop department to keep cadres updated on Church politics through organized discussions.[93] During the 1956–7 registration period in Szentkozmadomb (Zala county), a communist declared that the local teacher did not dare speak against religious instruction because every Party person had told him that he could enroll his child, and that even in the high school the communists were enrolling their children.[94] The influence of religion on some teachers was worrisome enough that the Ministry of Education had to request that these teachers not mobilize against materialist education and in favor of religious instruction.[95] The Party conducted more targeted political education for its own lower-level functionaries.[96]

The Party continued to pursue a dual strategy, repressing reactionary Church elements, but encouraging progressive ones to support socialism. We saw previously how even before the New Course both the Catholic and Reformed upper clergy, pursuant to the agreements between Church and State, had issued pastoral letters urging the laity to fulfill its socialist obligations. The authorities assiduously monitored the lower clergy to determine which priests were properly exhorting the faithful and which were not. To ensure that the priests were behaving properly, the local functionaries and cadres would pay regular visits, updating them on the latest political, economic, and social developments that should be incorporated into sermons. Surveillance was meticulously planned. During the February 1 to April 30, 1955 period in Hajdú-Bihar county, for example, local cadres were to report every two weeks on the activities of the priests in their jurisdictions who had been elected to local offices. The head of the county council pledged to speak with at least one such priest once a week, in the hopes of getting him to spread the socialist message without also strengthening religious life.

[92] See, for example, Sz37/1955, Sz38/1956, Sz39/1956, and Sz67/1954.
[93] HB16/1955.
[94] Z20/1956.
[95] Z17/1955.
[96] Sz69/1955, which describes how before the 1955/56 period of religious instruction registration Party members went out to "educate" other members who had enrolled their children in the previous year.

Fearing that the clergy would not reveal its true intentions when surrounded by Party and government representatives, the council leader also planned to use religious individuals, who might have more privileged access, as informants. Other meetings were held with members of the local Catholic peace committee and respected priests, so that the records of the twice-yearly meetings of all the clergy in a bishopric (*koronagyűlés*) could include references to the development of socialist agriculture, the struggle for peace, and other elements of the Party's program. Those clergymen perceived as working against the spirit of the Church-State agreements would also be visited. Where that proved ineffectual, the council head would recommend punishment, such as withholding the priest's supplemental income.[97]

The New Course emboldened the lower clergy. As we have seen, local functionaries and cadres were often ignorant of what the New Course meant in concrete terms for church life. The masses were even more in the dark. This provided the clergy an opening, because it could employ its own interpretation to deepen religious life. Some priests may also have acted out of ignorance of what the New Course actually represented. Probably more knew that the Party's aims remained the same and used it as a pretext. In either case, the clergy were able to exploit popular uncertainty by pushing the envelope of what the Party would tolerate.

As in the aftermath of the Church-State agreements, for example, the priests acted as if the new policy were more radical than it actually was. Just before the supplemental religious instruction period in 1953, priests in the Zalaegerszeg district (Zala county) went from house to house telling everyone that there was an agreement with the school headmaster and that the headmaster would gladly receive them at registration.[98] The priests became quite adept at spreading false ideas. In some communities they claimed that the political situation had entirely changed, and that the government would now not try to intrude into people's religious feelings, even into the beliefs of communists.[99] The priest in Csesztreg (Zala county) let the parents know that at Christmas time it was possible to go to confession every day, and that they should see to it that their children attend.[100] In several other villages

[97] HB16/1955. The workplan goes on to describe measures to be taken to combat clerical reaction, which is taken to mean not only priests perceived as hostile to the regime, but also the local activities of the remnants of the religious orders and devotional associations.
[98] Z13/1953.
[99] Z16/1954.
[100] Z15/1953.

the clergy claimed that registration for religious instruction was compulsory.[101] In Rédics (Zala county) the priest claimed in one sermon that, "it is the obligation of every Hungarian citizen to practice his religion and take part in Sunday services."[102]

A second clerical strategy was to develop friendly relations with the local authorities. Priests' participation in the peace movement and in organs of local government afforded contact with influential cadres and functionaries, and some used these connections to gain a free hand in conducting religious affairs. In several areas in Zala county, for example, they used official connections to convince peasant members that they should support reinstituting mass in those schools where it did not usually take place.[103] In other cases, the clergy exploited friendly relations with the school headmaster to request that religious instruction be held in the middle of the school day and to conduct religious instruction in church rather than in the school.[104]

While some courted the local authorities, others attempted to isolate them within the community. The teachers, especially if they were Party members, were a favorite target. During the 1953 supplementary religious instruction registration period in Zala county, for example, the priests attempted to rally the parents against the teachers in the period just before registration. In Dióskál, the priest convinced the parents to demand that he be allowed to register the children for religious instruction rather than the headmaster, because the latter was a communist.[105] One parent, enraged that a teacher would not register his child, called the teacher a "filthy communist," and threatened to throw him out of the school.[106] Sensing the vulnerabilities of the local functionaries, other priests told parents that any trouble they had with teachers should be reported, so that the teacher could be "dealt with." This was possible, according to the clergy, because the government was now giving "every advantage."[107]

The clergy's main effort was directed toward encouraging the faithful to participate in church life. Having just experienced Stalinist excesses, the masses were not keen on antagonizing the authorities. Although the New Course brought a widespread sense of relief, there were still few guideposts

---

[101] Z13/1953.
[102] Z15/1953.
[103] Z16/1954.
[104] Ibid.
[105] Z13/1953.
[106] Z20/1956.
[107] Z15/1953.

on which activities were permitted and which were not. Aware that the masses might be reticent about asserting their rights, the clergy resorted to a variety of quotidian tactics. In Szabolcs-Szatmár-Bereg county, for example, some priests traveled on motorcycles to outlying farms to encourage increased registration for religious instruction. They relied on their own powers of persuasion, but also enlisted the assistance of local peasants to go door to door and organize bible readings.[108] Similar phenomena were observed in Zala county, where some priests enlisted the help of old women from the "rose garland" society.[109]

The youth were of particular concern. As with the teachers, the clergy used a combination of carrots and sticks to keep them in the church community. During the 1956 Easter season in Eszteregnye (Zala county), for example, the priest attempted to gather the young people together two or three times a week to teach them the Passion Play.[110] In Pakod (Zala county) the priest gave a prayerbook and picture of a saint to the children, so that they could more easily pray.[111] In Páka (Zala county) the priest tried to entice the students by playing card games with them.[112] When the youth were uncooperative the clergy sometimes took them to task. In Eszteregnye, for example, the priest used the pulpit to chastise the young people who preferred cultural events to church attendance.[113]

The clergy was not beyond resorting to more intimidating methods. In Zala county priests or their assistants sometimes informed parents that whoever did not enroll a child in religious instruction would not receive the Holy Sacraments and that the child would be denied the right to undergo confirmation or participate in Holy Communion.[114] In the Zalaszentgrót district, leaflets were discovered in 1953 that vilified the regime and the educators who supported it.[115] In Fityeház the priest prepared several women to contact parents in preparation for the 1956–7 religious instruction registration.

[108] Sz66/1954.

[109] Z15/1953.

[110] Z18/1956.

[111] Z13/1953.

[112] Z18/1956. As we will see, this strategy of gathering people together for nonreligious purposes, such as work, game playing, or outdoor activities, became more widespread in the years after 1956.

[113] Z18/1956. The Party, of course, purposefully scheduled such events opposite church activities. This prompted one priest to request that the Young Pioneer events be rescheduled so as not to conflict with Sunday Mass. See Z15/1953.

[114] Z20/1956.

[115] Z13/1953.

When these women encountered resistance from individuals who did not wish to enroll their children, harsh words were exchanged.[116] With the clergy's encouragement, in many places a large number of mothers with their children appeared well before 8:00 A.M. on registration day, demanding that the registration begin. When the teachers tried to reason with them, the women became unruly. In Gelse, the priest had apparently whipped up such a frenzy that several parents entered the school and demanded that the registration continue even during lunchtime.[117] Even Party members were insistent. According to one, "every Party member told me that I could register my child . . . only religion can nurture." After registering her child she asked others to keep an eye on the teacher, and if he raised any difficulties or failed to register a child, she would find another Party member and together they would see to it that he was disciplined.[118]

4.5   1956

The revolutionary uprising of October–November 1956 holds a drama all its own. Yet rather than recount this heroic and ultimately futile effort to escape Soviet domination, I use the events to illustrate the fragility of the political changes that had occurred since 1948.[119] At the elite level, efforts to restore the immediate postwar democracy commenced even as the dictatorship was melting away. A week into the revolution the reformist government led by Imre Nagy announced the abolition of the one-party system and a desire to reconstitute the government based on multiparty elections. Upon the request of the Council of Ministers, the Independent Smallholders Party (FKgP), Social Democratic Party (SZDP), and National Peasant Party (NPP) quickly reorganized. The FKgP, victor in the 1945 parliamentary elections, was the first to reemerge. Béla Kovács, former Secretary-General of the FKgP and victim of several years in Soviet captivity, was reelected to his old position. Communist collaborators, such as former Prime Minister Lajos Dinnyés and others, were refused readmission to the party. Shortly thereafter the SZDP was reestablished, led by former party leaders who had all spent time in prison. Fellow travelers of the Communists were excluded from the party. The Catholic-oriented

[116] Z20/1956.
[117] Z13/1953.
[118] Z20/1956.
[119] The revolution has spawned a large literature. For a recent overview, see Romsics (1999: 301–11).

Democratic People's Party reemerged, as did the NPP, renamed the Petőfi Party.[120]

The Catholic Church also sought to reverse the changes it had been forced to undergo. Cardinal Mindszenty remained Archbishop of Esztergom even as he languished in prison and unquestionably remained the preeminent symbol of resistance to communism. Released from house arrest, one of his first acts was to restore the Church's ability to govern itself by cleansing the Church of collaborators. After conferring with Archbishop Grősz and others, he moved to liquidate "the coercion and deception of the toppled regime" within the Church, the peace priest movement.[121] In a radio address shortly thereafter, he declared that Catholics expected "the immediate granting of freedom of Christian religious instruction and the restoration of the institutions and societies of the Catholic Church – among other things, her press."[122] He also called for free elections and for the restoration of private property, "justly limited by social interests."[123]

The Reformed Church's attitude was informed by the hope of coexistence with the State guided by the principle of a "free Church in a free State," in keeping with Calvinist tradition. In his radio address of November 1, 1956, Bishop László Ravasz, newly reinstituted temporary leader of the Church, enunciated this impulse to the Hungarian people. He scolded the former Church elite who "yielded even more than was necessary to the violence and machinations of a political power which is a mortal foe of the Church."[124] Ravasz, unlike Mindszenty, did not call for a return to bourgeois democracy, but he did praise the revolution for upholding the national honor.[125]

The revolution was not confined to the elite. As Lomax (1976: 115) notes, it was a "spontaneous revolutionary mass movement in which the

---

[120] This is taken from Váli (1961: 293, 296–8). See also Szántó (1992: 84–6).

[121] Mindszenty (1974: 211) and Orbán (1996: 322–3).

[122] See "Mindszenty's Radio Address, November 3, 1956," reprinted in Mindszenty (1974: 331–3). There is disagreement about the degree of restoration Cardinal Mindszenty desired. Gergely (1985: 152–3) argues, for example, that although Mindszenty did not explicitly call for the return of Church estates, this was implied because there would be no other way of generating the funds for operating the vast network of Catholic institutions. Others (e.g., Hutten [1967: 192]) emphasize Mindszenty's declaration that the Church did not oppose the historical progress that had been made.

[123] Mindszenty (1974: 333).

[124] Cited in Kádár (1958: 156).

[125] Gombos (1960: 103).

people threw themselves at the symbols of the old regime."[126] Party influence and government control melted away from provincial towns and rural areas within days after the outbreak of the revolt. The initial transition was seldom violent, as local functionaries, having heard of the revolutionary demonstrations, usually handed over power without resistance. The regime could not even count on its own local officials to fight. Some people took the opportunity to efface the recent past. Soviet war memorials were often dismantled and in the more devout areas crosses and crucifixes returned to school classrooms. In retaliation for the years of harassment, the latter task was often assigned to the local Party secretary. Roughly 40 percent of the cooperatives disbanded and 50 percent of the remaining membership left.[127] Sixty-three percent of the land cultivated by the cooperatives was returned to its original owners.[128] A better picture of what partisan preferences looked like after eight years of dictatorship would have emerged from the promised free elections, but the revolution was crushed only days after it began.

4.6 Assessing the Battle for Souls

The rapid dissolution of the Communist Party, abandonment of collective farms, resurrection of precommunist parties, and mass involvement in the aborted revolution all point to Party failure at making much headway in spreading sympathy for socialism between 1948 and 1956. However, this does not imply that there was no progress in weakening mass ties to the Churches. Recall from the introductory chapter that there is a difference between the erosion of old commitments and the formation of new ones. The collapse of the Party during the 1956 revolution is a poignant illustration that even most Party members had not yet internalized socialist loyalties. The question, however, still remains: How successfully had the Party chipped away at the church community by 1956?

Table 4.2 displays the percentage of children enrolled in religious instruction in the schools for the entire country and the major administrative divisions of Zala county for the period leading up to 1956.[129] Nearly

---

[126] Cited in Ekiert (1996: 49).

[127] Rona-Tás (1997: 61).

[128] Váli (1961: 293).

[129] Primary sources materials differ slightly on the exact levels of enrollment. Where possible I have recomputed the percentages from raw enrollment numbers reported. Where these were unavailable I rely on the reported percentages.

Table 4.2 *Religious Instruction Enrollment, 1952–1956.*

Region	1949	1952	1953	1954	1955	1956
Lent d.	–	2.6	6.6	–	36.0	48.4
Letenye d.	–	1.8	11.7	–	16.0	22.0
Nagykanizsa d.	–	10.9	41.9	–	17.0	27.0
Zalaegerszeg d.	–	8.5	42.3	–	38.0	48.5
Zalaszentgrót d.	–	6.2	27.1	–	23.9	32.3
Nagykanizsa town	–	6.4	24.8	–	13.0	15.0
Zalaegerszeg town	–	0.1	3.5	–	0.6	1.0
Zala county	–	6.4	28.0	38.8	23.4	30.2
Hungary (elementary)	86	–	27.2	35.5	29.4	30.2
Hungary (middle)	80	–	0.7	1.9	0.8	0.5

Note: The dash indicates the data are unavailable. In cases where the percentages are incorrectly reported in the original source I have recalculated them from the raw numbers also given. The "d." is an abbreviation for *district* (*járás*).
Source: Bangó (1970: 149), Bango (1978: 67), Zala Megyei Levéltár (1999: 414), and Z12/1952, Z13/1953, Z20/1956.

90 percent of the children were enrolled in 1949, the year voluntary religious instruction was introduced, in both elementary and middle schools. This illustrates the baseline level of religious commitment against which the Party had to struggle. The drop in registration resulting from the introduction of State repression is most evident in comparing 1949 and 1953: from 86 percent to roughly 27 percent in elementary schools. The more precipitous drop in middle school enrollment is due to the fact that in many of those schools even voluntary instruction was discontinued. The 0.7 percent for the country as a whole in 1953 may thus represent a higher enrollment level in the minority of schools where instruction was still offered.[130]

The increase and decrease within geographic units between 1952 and 1956 reflect the ebb and flow of State repression. The upturn from 1952 to 1953 coincides with the introduction of the "New Course." The drop again in 1955 (especially visible between 1954 and 1955 for Zala county as a whole) and subsequent rise in 1956 coincides with the temporary "refreezing" associated with Imre Nagy's ouster in early 1955 and his reemergence

[130] Bangó (1970: 149). He notes that teacher training, industrial, agricultural, and economic trade schools were mostly likely to lack religious instruction. The drop would appear even more striking if compared with data from 1952, at the height of the repression.

once again in 1956.[131] The generally lower levels of enrollment in towns are evidence of differential treatment by the Party. First, as the more desirable places to live, the towns attracted the higher-ranking Party members, who would have received more favorable housing than others. This alone would depress registration, because such people would have been drawn disproportionately from those who were not regular churchgoers. Second, the Party attempted to secure the more comfortable urban parishes for the most cooperative priests. So urban parishioners would less likely experience the sorts of clerical mobilizing activities that were occurring in more rural areas.[132] There is also some evidence that the clergy, aware of the difficulties of evangelizing in the larger towns, chose to focus their activities on the smaller communities.[133]

To what extent can the battles between the local clergy and cadres account for the variance in enrollment levels? The uniformly low levels in the 1952 column show that when sufficiently determined, the regime could suppress enrollment, regardless of local conditions. Beyond this general observation, however, the district-level data are too highly aggregated to be very informative. To investigate the effects of Church and Party activity it is necessary to have enrollment information from geographic units that coincide with the activity areas of the local clergy and cadres. Districts and towns are too large to isolate the effects of an individual priest and any opposition he may have encountered. Settlement-level registration data illustrate the importance of moving to the lower level of aggregation. Zala county's Nagykanizsa district alone contained fifty-eight settlements, whose 1953 enrollment levels ranged from 3 percent to 92 percent.[134] In Letenye district (Zala county), the range across thirty-two communities was 4 percent to 83 percent, averaging 41 percent.[135] The same year communities in the Berettyóújfalu district (Hajdú-Bihar county) ranged from

---

[131] Bangó (1970: 149) and Ignotus (1972: 226–8). This table contradicts Gergely (1985: 144), who argues that plans to reinvigorate the fight against the clergy in 1955 were never really implemented.

[132] HB11/1953 notes that five of the most reactionary Catholic priests were discharged, while a friendly priest was placed in the Hajdú-Bihar county seat, Debrecen.

[133] Z29/1962.

[134] Z125/1953. I do not consider communities with zero enrollment, because this was likely due to an outright cancellation of religious instruction. Such irregularities occurred even during the "New Course." See, for example, Sz.P.L. Acta Cancellariae 1049/1953.

[135] Z130/1951.

30 percent to 77 percent, averaging 53 percent.[136] The district level data are clearly aggregating quite disparate outcomes.

At the village level, there are multiple streams of evidence that clerical activities boosted enrollment. Consider Gelse (Zala county, Nagykanizsa district) between 1952 and 1953. For 1952 in this district the villages of Alsórajk, Felsőrajk, Kilimán, and Murakeresztúr are listed as having higher enrollments, with the highest being 14 percent.[137] Because Gelse is also in this district and was not mentioned in the list, it can be presumed to have a 1952 enrollment of less than 14 percent. We know that during the 1953 registration period, the priest in Gelse mobilized the parents, who ultimately succeeded in getting the local teacher to continue registering the children even beyond official registration hours. Between 1952 and 1953 religious instruction shot up from 14 percent to 71 percent, well above the district average of 42 percent.[138] Another example is Orosztony (Zala county). Here the school headmaster was religious and regularly went to church, and the priest used his influence to gain a free hand in religious instruction. Registration for religious instruction in Orosztony jumped from 3 percent in 1953 to 50 percent in 1954.[139] This village is illustrative of the dilemmas the authorities faced in permitting friendly priests to continue their activities while encumbering reactionary ones. The regime's own informant admitted that the priest in Orosztony had qualified as a democratic, yet he nonetheless seized available opportunities to deepen religious life.[140]

Ethnographic studies of individual villages support the theoretical claim, advanced in Chapter 1, that decisions to engage in public religiosity, which can result in such jumps in enrollment, are premised on how others in the community are acting or are expected to act. In order words, outcomes reflect a tipping dynamic. For example, in 1959 the Head of the ÁEH in Hajdú-Bihar county noted that in villages where a majority of children are enrolled the parent thinks "most people are registering their children, so there can't be a problem if I register mine. Indeed, it might even be disadvantageous."[141] Community expectation was strong enough even to

[136] HB6/1952.
[137] Z12/1952.
[138] Z125/1953.
[139] Z16/1954 and Z125/1953.
[140] Z16/1954.
[141] HB43/1959.

sweep up those who would not normally go to church. To be a "proper peasant" in Átány (Heves county) meant "living according to the rules of the Reformed Church."[142] According to one villager in Lapos (Heves county), who claimed not to be a believer, it was traditional to participate in rites, such as baptism, confirmation, and church weddings and funerals. He had his daughter confirmed because doing otherwise risked community ostracism.[143] This was true even for Party members. In Lapos, for example, a new Party member was asked not to register his daughter for First Communion. He ultimately had it done in another town to preserve his anonymity with his local Party elite.[144] Thus, even those who violated Church norms recognized the hold they exerted.[145] Bolstering this community expectation was one of the clergy's most valuable tools in the struggle to preserve church community. Of course, such expectation could work to depress as well as elevate enrollment: The aforementioned report on Hajdú-Bihar villages noted that where a minority of children were registered, the parental feeling was that "few parents are registering their children, and no harm is coming to them . . . why should I enroll mine?"[146]

Elevated enrollment levels during parts of the early 1950s are indirect evidence of clerical involvement. The level in a given settlement depends on both the underlying demand for religious instruction and the distribution of risk thresholds within the community, neither of which we have much direct evidence for during this period. However, during the early years of state-socialism, when Stalinism was in its heyday, but only a few years into the battle against religion and the Churches, we should expect a high demand for instruction, but also high-risk thresholds. Prudence would have demanded, during the Stalinist period, that believing parents not be seen to defy the regime. Yet on average we do not observe particularly low enrollments. For Letenye district (Zala county) in 1951 the average across villages was 41 percent, with a maximum of 83 percent; for Berettyóújfalu (Hajdú-Bihar county) during the same period the average was 53 percent with a high of 90 percent. The clergy seems likely to have played a role in this stubborn refusal to be cowed by the authorities.

---

[142] Fél and Hofer (1969: 305).
[143] Bell (1984: 152). See also Vasary (1987: 236) and Z18/1956.
[144] Bell (1984: 152–3).
[145] Jávor (1983: 285).
[146] HB43/1959.

If we think of registration levels as a consequence of a cascade of enrollment, then it is necessary to address the question of why the cascade ends before engulfing the entire settlement. Why do some villages have high, others middling, and still others low enrollment levels? One factor may be the presence of determined local cadres. Active priests might have attempted to mobilize the faithful, but been frustrated by the communists. The uncertain outcomes of localities with determined cadres and active priests are evident during 1953 in Zala county's Lent and Nagykanizsa districts. Here seven communities are listed as having influential reactionary clergymen: Murakeresztúr, Galambok, Magyarszerdahely, Zalaszentbalázs, Hahót, Pórszombat, and Csesztreg. Given the relatively liberated atmosphere of the New Course we might expect high levels of enrollment in these places. Of the five for which we have data, three are over 50 percent, but two are under 20 percent. In Zalaszentbalázs only 3 percent of students were enrolled. We lack detailed knowledge of what happened in these communities, but a reasonable conclusion would be that the Party countered these priests with its best cadres, as it so often declared its willingness to do, with varying success.[147] In other cases, the Party managed to stamp instruction out entirely. For example, in Bakonycsernye (Veszprém county) nearly every student was enrolled in religious instruction in 1951, but none enrolled in 1952, because neither the pastor nor assistant pastor were given permission to conduct instruction.[148]

Another factor lay in confessional differences between the Roman Catholic and Calvinist Churches. Recall from Chapter 1 that Catholic priests enjoyed more authority than Calvinist pastors over their respective flocks, and thus greater ability to foster church community. We will see much more evidence of the greater resilience of Catholic community in the next chapter, when we consider more systematically rates of religious instruction in Zala and Hajdú-Bihar counties, but one account of the situation in Tázlár (Bács-Kiskun county) epitomizes the differing role of the clergy in the two Churches:

The total percentage of [Catholic] children attending was 76 percent in 1957, but has since fallen to under 50 percent. The priest, of course, rails against this system, which allows him to enter the school, but then to reach only a declining percentage of the pupils, and to find that even these may be reluctant listeners, as the instruction

---

[147] See Z125/1953 for the data and Z14/1953 for the Party's characterization of these villages.
[148] Kardos (1969: 90). For this reason, I exclude from the analysis years where enrollment levels were actually zero.

falls outside normal lesson time. In contrast the [Protestant] pastor has adopted a low profile and throws the decision wholly onto families by making attendance voluntary outside school hours. He attracts an even smaller percentage of the Protestant pupils.[149]

4.7 Conclusion

This chapter has described the opening salvos in the battle for souls waged between the Churches and the Party. The Churches, once proud institutions, suffered greatly throughout the first half of the 1950s: leading clerics had been tainted with collaboration, a peace priest movement had been introduced to spread socialism through the churches, and religious practice met with persistent harassment. Yet although the Church leaderships were largely co-opted, at the local level the clergy and the communists often engaged in tumultuous struggles to undermine each other's influence. Far from being the powerless victim of oppression, the priesthood exhibited remarkable resilience and ingenuity in countering the Party's attempts to erode the church community. The Party-State, belying its all-powerful image, often suffered tactical defeat at the hands of determined clergymen. The residue of these clashes can be seen in registration levels for religious instruction in the schools, which serve as a marker for the strength of church community across settlements. Although the Party had made inroads, the Churches had survived Stalinism.

Ironically, however, Stalinism was not the greatest threat to the Churches' influence. As we will see in Chapter 5, the socialist reorganization of agriculture, reintroduced not long after the failed revolution, would pose far greater risks to church life than had the repression of the early 1950s. Countering these and other new perils after 1956 would prove to be one of the clergy's greatest challenges. Chapter 5 recounts the Party's reinvigorated efforts to corrode church community and the clerical efforts to circumvent them.

[149] Hann (1980: 115).

5

The Battle for Souls after 1956

5.1 Introduction

János Kádár arrived in Budapest with the Soviets on November 7, 1956. Though nominally head of a "new Hungarian revolutionary worker-peasant government," he initially enjoyed little real authority. The army had sided with the revolution, requiring the establishment of a "Hungarian revolutionary home guard militia" composed of loyal communists. The Hungarian Workers Party (MDP) had dissolved, reemerging as the Hungarian Socialist Workers Party (MSZMP). The new party declared its adherence to the same principles as its predecessor, but explicitly distanced itself from both the "left-wing" errors of the Rákosi era and the "right-wing" deviation represented by Imre Nagy. However, in December 1956 the newly christened party could boast only 37,000 members, as against several hundred thousand before the revolution.[1]

Although formal armed resistance to the Soviet army had ended by the second week of November, it cannot be said that resistance per se ceased, or that victory could be declared. Cardinal Mindszenty took refuge in the U.S. embassy; Imre Nagy escaped to the Yugoslav. In late November, some intellectuals and students demanded a Soviet withdrawal, the return of Nagy, and the establishment of representative democratic socialism. A general strike was called and a women's demonstration organized for early December. Later that month, the State Office for Church Affairs (ÁEH) was abolished and its functions subsumed under the Ministry of Education.

Yet the Party moved quickly to assert its authority. It disbanded revolutionary groups, suspended the operation of tainted organizations, such as

[1] Romsics (1999: 311 and 315–23).

152

the Writers' Association and the Journalists' Club, and arrested those suspected of participating in the revolution or organizing resistance. Once it was clear which way the wind was blowing Party ranks swelled, with membership increasing to 125,000 by early 1957 and to 400,000 by the end of 1957. Retribution proceeded apace. By the end of 1959, around 35,000 people had been rounded up, with most receiving prison terms, and approximately 350 executed.[2] Among those murdered was Imre Nagy, who was lured out of the Yugoslav embassy on the promise that he would be spared. Cardinal Mindszenty, as we will see, remained a thorn in Hungarian-U.S. relations. He would remain in the U.S. embassy until finally permitted to leave the country in 1971.

This chapter describes the battle for souls between the Churches and the Party-State in the years after the aborted 1956 revolution. Although the Party would never return to the brutal tactics employed during the Stalinist heyday, we will see that it continued its struggle against both any sign of independence or autonomy within the Churches and the religious worldview within the population. The success with which the Party was able to induce the upper clergy and a portion of the lower clergy into passive acquiescence if not active cooperation with the regime has been well documented.[3] Although we will summarize the actions of both the Party and the cooperating clergy, the purpose of this chapter is to highlight the ways in which some clergy not only resisted the regime's many efforts at co-optation, but also actively sought to preserve church community. Section 5.2 describes the contours of Church-State relations in the years immediately after 1956. Section 5.3 moves to the local level, charting the Party's renewed offensive against the Churches through the mid-1960s. Section 5.4 chronicles the variegated strategies the clergy employed to combat the Party's depredations. In Section 5.5 we examine the recollectivization of agriculture, the most important single event in the life of post-1956 rural Hungary. By the end of agricultural reorganization the patterns of interaction between parish priests and local cadres had been set. Section 5.6 describes the resulting *modus vivendi* between Church and State. Section 5.7 reassesses the successes and failures in the battle for souls by examining the evolution of religiosity in Hajdú-Bihar and Zala counties. We then review more general trends in religiosity and religious belief in section 5.8.

---

[2] Ibid.: 320 and 323.

[3] For the Reformed Church the most comprehensive is Tibori (1996, 1998, and 2000). For the Catholic Church, see Mészáros (1994 and 1995).

5.2 Normalization

Reformist elements within the Roman Catholic and Reformed Church leaderships attempted to capitalize as best they could on the Party's temporary weakness in the immediate aftermath of the Soviet invasion. For example, in a November 13 encyclical letter to all congregations, Reformed Bishop László Ravasz concisely expressed both the wrongs perpetrated against the Church and his dissatisfaction with the Church's leaders:

This system took deep root in the life of the Hungarian Reformed Church and inhibited its holy service. It mingled preaching with political propaganda, narrowed the Church's life, and progressively seized from the Church's spirit, history, and constitution every basic freedom that had guaranteed its democratic character through the centuries, installing in its place a tyranny. In vain were there complaints, outcries, warnings. In vain appeared striking signs that the Hungarian people were turning away from the Church's leadership. In all of Hungary in our Church alone did things remain unchanged.[4]

Ravasz was careful, however, to couch demands for reform within parameters acceptable to the Kádár regime. The encyclical went on to demand the excision of antidemocratic elements from the organization and administration of the Church, and a return to traditional modes of Church governance, albeit within the framework of the 1948 agreement with the State. He emphasized that the Church rejected all attempts at restoring the bourgeois order, and indeed approved and would promote the country's socialist transformation. In essence, Ravasz was calling on the Party to respect in spirit as well as letter the separation of Church and State.[5]

The Catholic Bench of Bishops also attempted to recover some of its previous influence and autonomy. In a letter to his ordinaries written just after hearing of the impeding disappearance of the ÁEH (into the Education Ministry), Archbishop József Grősz expressed what he thought ought to be negotiated in any new agreement with the regime. Some of these, such as the cessation of government interference in Church governance, complete freedom in the appointment of Church personnel, and a halt to the politicization of sermons, echoed the requests of the Reformed leadership.[6]

---

[4] Barcza (1999: 186).
[5] Ibid.: 187. Ravasz was not alone in seeking these changes. There was a flurry of activity in November and December 1956, when it appeared as if the Party, chastened by the MDP's dramatic collapse and eager to demobilize society, might show more willingness to compromise. For details, see Barcza (1994: 90–103).
[6] This letter is reprinted in Salacz (1988: 148–9).

154

But he also hoped to secure the free operation of Catholic associations and religious orders, even if not in the numbers that had existed before communism. In February 1957, the Bench of Bishops submitted these and other perceived violations of the Hungarian constitution's guarantee of religious freedom to the government.[7]

One victim of the 1956 revolution was the peace priest movement. Although institutions such as the National Peace Council were never officially abolished, in practical terms the movement had collapsed, its members having been ejected from influential Church positions. In the hopes of preventing its reorganization, in May 1957 the Bench of Bishops, in consultation with the National Peace Council, formed a new peace organization, *Opus Pacis*. Headed by Archbishop József Grősz, it included prominent peace priests as members. Like the former peace priest organization, it was designed to "serve the cause of universal peace."[8] But it was overseen by the Church hierarchy and had more limited membership. According to Mindszenty (1974: 222–4), the bishops hoped that if *Opus Pacis* could monitor the lower clergy, there would be no need for the government to reorganize the peace priests, or to insist that such priests receive favorable placements within the Church administration.[9]

Ultimately the Churches' hopes would go unfulfilled, as the Party had every intention of continuing its struggle against the Churches and the religious worldview. In early January, the Party enunciated its principles of Church-State relations. It stated its readiness to ensure the continuation of voluntary religious instruction in the schools and of the Churches' independence, but within the framework of prior agreements, which it considered still valid. In exchange it expected that in the interests of a return to normalcy and the lessening of tension, Church leaders and members would obey the law. The Churches were also expected not to permit their institutions to be used by "political reaction," and not to punish those Church members who exhibited progressive (i.e., procommunist) views.[10] By February, the government had rejected Grősz's proposal and suggested that unless peace priests were reinstated into leading positions, ministerial commissioners would be installed to oversee the bishops. When the bench

---

[7] Ibid.: 151–2.
[8] Hutten (1967: 196).
[9] For details of the fate of the priest movement in the months after the revolution, see Gergely (1985: 158–61) and Pál (1995: 123–34).
[10] Gergely (1985: 156).

demurred, noting that only the Vatican had that authority, overseers were promptly placed in all bishoprics.[11]

In March 1957 the government reinstated two of the more divisive features of pre-1956 Church-State relations: the regulation of voluntary religious instruction in the schools and the right of the government to intervene in the filling of clerical positions.[12] The old, restrictive rules concerning religious instruction had been in force right up until the outbreak of revolution, but were relaxed in the revolution's aftermath. For a brief period it was possible to attend religious instruction without having registered in advance, with the instruction held during normal school hours rather than outside them. The changed atmosphere, in combination with a desire to show opposition to the new Soviet-imposed regime, had raised attendance for religious instruction to 80–90 percent.[13] The March regulations put an end to this brief liberalized atmosphere, but in the hope of mollifying believers, were notably more liberal than the pre-1956 rules. First, they threatened legal action against those who employed "force, threat, or misinformation" not just against those who desired religious instruction, but against those who attempted to *hinder* it. Formally at least, then, religious instruction was to be genuinely voluntary. Second, in instances where there was no room at school available for religious instruction, it became possible to use Church property. Third, when it caused no disruption to the curriculum, it was possible to hold both hours of weekly religious instruction one after the other rather than on separate days. Fourth, the Churches were given greater voice in the nomination and appointment of religion instructors. These instructors, who before 1956 would have been automatically excluded if they were deemed to have oppositional views, would face such exclusion only if they demonstrated oppositional behavior. Finally, the Churches were given a greater role vis-à-vis educators in the supervision of the instruction.[14]

The regulation regarding appointment to Church positions gave the State even greater authority over Church personnel than it had previously enjoyed. Prior approval of the Presidential Council of the People's Republic

---

[11] Mészáros (2001: 14–15).

[12] See Government Regulation 21/1957 (March 4), Implementary Provision 39/1957, and Legal Regulation 22/1957. English translations of these may be found in András and Morel (1983b: 159–66, 175–7).

[13] Nagy Péter (2000a: 121).

[14] See Nagy Péter (2000a) for a subtle analysis of the liberalizing aspects of the 1957 re-regulation of religious instruction.

became required for any appointment or other issue that would normally fall within the purview of the Holy See, or for appointments to top positions in other Churches. The Ministry of Education's permission became compulsory for virtually all appointments (or changes in appointments) normally under the jurisdiction of Church officials, including jobs at theological academies, leading positions at confessional secondary schools, and, most significantly, local pastors and parish priests. The order was made retroactive to October 1, 1956, which means that all the personnel changes in the Churches that had been effected in the course of the revolution became vulnerable to reversal. With this regulation the regime gained unprecedented authority over the Churches, which were open to even stricter control than before 1956.[15]

Despite asserting its right of approval for all Church positions, the regime did not immediately demand prominent places for progressive clergymen. This was less of an issue with respect to the Reformed Church because Vatican approval for such positions was not required, and the return of the pliant pre-1956 leadership, while by no means without problems, was proceeding apace.[16] However, the Catholic Bench of Bishops, fearful of the return of the peace priests, kept close watch on the clergymen, lest they give the Party a reason to intervene. They were careful not to appoint anyone to a vacant post without the proper approval. On April 10, 1958 they declared their support for "the government's legal efforts on behalf of the Hungarian people's welfare" and condemned "every effort directed against the State and social order of the Hungarian People's Republic."[17] In return, the Party had been allowing the bishops to accede to Vatican demands that no peace priests be given prominent positions. But the situation changed later in 1958. Speaking on behalf of the government, Premier Gyula Kállai declared:

We support the *Opus Pacis* movement initiated by the Bishops. We believe, however, that *Opus Pacis* can be a strong and successful peace movement if it is not limited to the narrow circle of the higher clergy. It must be founded on the broadest possible mass base of the democratically minded clergy. *Opus Pacis* cannot be set in opposition to the mass movement of the democratic priests, which is rooted in the life of the Hungarian people. If the Bishops sincerely desire cooperation with

---

[15] For a summary from a Catholic perspective of the political discussions surrounding this regulation, see Salacz (1988: 156–63).

[16] Barcza (1994: 98–103).

[17] Cited in Gergely (1985: 158–9).

the state they must base their activities upon those friends who through the years have demonstrated by their work that they are fighting alongside the masses of the people for peace and the building of socialism. ... The relationship between Church and state must be placed upon the firm ground of principles, so that it does not become a mere matter of peaceful but passive coexistence. Rather, it must be an active, positive collaboration aiming solely and firmly at the building of socialism.[18]

As in the earlier agreements between the Churches and the State, the regime demanded not just the absence of opposition, not just passive support, but active cooperation between Church and State in the building of socialism. This would be accomplished through the work of those "fighting alongside the masses of the people" – the peace priests. The Church hierarchies would be responsible for policing their own ranks, to ensure that individuals favorable to the regime were not excluded from positions of authority. That same year the Reformed Church became a "founding member" of a "Christian Peace Conference" (*Keresztyén Békeconferencia*).[19]

The principles that would guide the Party's attitude toward the Churches for the next three decades were laid out in two resolutions of mid-1958, one addressing clerical reaction, the other the struggle against the religious worldview.[20] Taken together, these resolutions represent more a codification of pre-existing experience and practice than a new strategy. Three separate issues, each requiring different action, were identified: clerical reaction, the Churches as such, and the religious worldview. Against clerical reaction, understood as any clerical effort to achieve temporal (secular) power, the Party would use political methods, as it would against any other political reaction. Such methods included, according to Kádár, everything "from propaganda to bombs," because "clerical rule has no business in a proletarian dictatorship."[21]

The Party's attitude regarding the Churches was more muddled. The Party recognized that the Churches as such were its principal competitor for mass influence, and not just "extreme" elements within the Churches. In 1958, Kádár noted with delightful understatement that "we communists don't like it if the Church is socially influential, and the Church doesn't like

---

[18] Cited in Mindszenty (1974: 224).
[19] Ladányi (1999: 138).
[20] The resolution on clerical reaction of June 10, 1958 may be found in Urbán (1991: 53–8). The July 22, 1958 resolution on the religious worldview is reprinted in Vass (1979: 268–76).
[21] Kádár's remarks are taken from the minutes of a July 25, 1958 meeting of the Central Committee. See Soós (1997: 424).

it if the communists are influential."[22] Such attitudes are the reason that the battle against clerical reaction had, as we saw in the last chapter, so often spilled over into attacks on progressive clergymen and the believing masses. However, the Party also explicitly recognized the necessity of supporting and working with the Churches, at least for some period of time, to further the country's socialist development. The Party hoped that by fostering democratic clerical elements it could benefit from the Churches' assistance without also encouraging them as alternative sources of loyalty.[23]

The Party considered the religious worldview to be inherently reactionary, "in implacable opposition to marxism-leninism."[24] Yet it acknowledged that frontal attacks, of the sort applied to clerical reaction, tended to create messianism and martyrdom, which increased rather than decreased religious belief. It would be necessary to proceed with patience, and to avoid offending believers' religious sensibilities or limiting their freedom of religious practice.[25] After all, even believers could help build socialism. Religion was seen as having two, interrelated roots: ignorance and the continuing existence of "backward" peasant and petit-bourgeois social strata. For the Party, the main question, at least formally, was not who was religious and who was atheist, but a person's class origins and political attitudes and behavior. The class roots of religion would, in the Party's view, disappear when the working class, the peasants, and intellectuals together succeeded in building socialism.[26] In the meantime, however, ignorance would be addressed through materialist education, "scientific explanatory work" (*tudományos felvilágosító munka*). As before 1956, such education was to be all-encompassing, occurring not just in the schools and other formally educational fora, but also through exhibits, radio, television, and similar means. To achieve this it was necessary to restrict the Churches' regular contact with the youth to religious instruction and preparation for First Communion and Confirmation. The clergy was to be forbidden from

---

[22] See the minutes of a July 25, 1958 meeting of the Central Committee. Reprinted in Soós (1997: 424–5).

[23] Ibid.: 424–5.

[24] Vass (1979: 269).

[25] This recognition follows on both the Hungarian experience prior to 1956 and the Soviet experience before that. Indeed, during the Soviet Communist Party's Eighth Party Congress in 1919, it was recognized as necessary "to avoid offending the religious sensibilities of believers which leads only to the strengthening of religious fanaticism." Quoted in Tobias (1956: 16).

[26] Vass (1979: 269–70).

engaging the youth through sport, film, singing groups, and other nonreligious activities. This applied in particular to the Catholic Church, which was seen as a center of opposition.[27]

The Party reiterated its view that for Party members religion was not to be a private matter, as it was for other believers.[28] Religious belief was portrayed as fundamentally alien to Marxism and thus upsetting to the unity of the Party, which by extension endangered working class power. The Party forbade its members from participating in religious processions, festivals, and other practices, but differentiated between "active" and "passive" participation. No one who of her own accord enrolled her child for religious instruction, arranged for a religious wedding or funeral, or otherwise initiated religious activities was permitted to fulfill a Party function. However, it was recognized that Party members would be invited or otherwise would feel pressure to attend christenings, church weddings, and other such affairs. In such cases participation was acceptable. As we will see, it was not uncommon for Party members to attribute their attendance at religious festivities to the need to keep the peace with their wives or their mothers. Personnel who were not in the Party but occupied important positions, such as teachers and State employees, were permitted to participate in church life, but were to be taught Marxism-Leninism, so that they too might abandon their religious views.[29]

By the end of 1959, relations at the elite level between the Churches and the State had, by all appearances, become "normalized." According to the original agreements between the Churches and the State, State subsidies to the Churches were supposed to have been cut by 25 percent in 1958. In the hope of further securing the Church elites' cooperation these cuts were postponed. In April 1959 the government approved the implementation rules for its 1957 regulation on the filling of Church positions. No appointments could be made without government approval. For the filling of important posts the Churches had ninety days to make arrangements. After that time the government would make its own appointment. This prevented the Churches from indefinitely dragging out decisions in critical cases. All appointees had sixty days in which to sign another loyalty oath to the State.

---

[27] Mészáros (1991: 95–6).

[28] Again, this policy goes back at least to Lenin, who asserted that "we demand that religion be regarded as a private matter as far as the State is concerned, but under no circumstances can we regard it as a private matter in our party." Quoted in Goeckel (1990: 26, fn. 31).

[29] Vass (1979: 272–4).

160

In June, the ÁEH was resurrected as an independent entity. According to László (1990: 161) the only difference between the "new" and the "old" ÁEH was that the "mustached bishops" – the civilian administrators of the dioceses – were never permanently reinstated.[30]

5.3 The Party Offensive at the Local Level

The prospects for maintaining the Churches as an alternative locus of loyalty must have appeared bleak in the years following the aborted uprising. It is true that registration for religious instruction in the schools skyrocketed across the board between 1956 and 1957. Registration rose from 2 percent to 32 percent in the city of Miskolc, from 7 percent to 26 percent in Budapest, from 33 percent to 51 percent in Zala county, from 22 percent to 36 percent in Hajdú-Bihar county, and from 30 percent to 47 percent nationally.[31] This increase included the children of local Party leaders, teachers, and others occupying important State positions, although the bulk of the attendees were of peasant origin.[32] As gratifying as this surge in religious practice must have been for the Churches, it represented more a statement of opposition to the new, Soviet-imposed regime than a mass rediscovery of church life per se. Consolidating such elevated levels of attachment to the Churches would require a great deal of ingenuity, because the Soviet occupation extinguished any hope that the regime would disappear any time soon. The believing masses would have to resign themselves to the reality of socialism, both inside and outside the churches.

The Party was prepared to take its battle against clerical influence and the religious worldview directly to the people. The foot soldiers in this battle were to be ordinary Party members, who had to be educated in the contradictions between religion and communism. The Party elite recognized the tendency to think of the struggle against religion as a task for ideologues and teachers, and took pains to ensure that ordinary Party members understood what was required of them. One memo from Zala county reminded Party members that a good communist could not be religious or attend religious events, and that they had to be good examples for the workers, who were vulnerable to clerical manipulation. Against the then prevalent view that

---

[30] The decrees on the ÁEH and Church positions may be found in András and Morel (1983b: 171–3 and 177–9), respectively. For a brief discussion, see Gergely (1985: 166–8).

[31] M40/1958. These levels refer to grade school [*általános iskola*] only.

[32] M39/1958.

lack of religious education created misbehaved, disrespectful children, the Party averred that the situation was worse before communism, when the clergy threatened children with hell and damnation, and society was built on ignorance and fear. Party members were warned not just to avoid rearing their own children in a religious way, but to "evangelize" other Party members and State functionaries against such action.[33]

Organizing atheist propaganda went beyond instilling revolutionary fervor in the local cadres. To counter the contact between Church and society associated with religious festivals and traditions, in 1959 the Party introduced a set of civil ceremonies for family events. Christenings, for example, were to be replaced with name-giving ceremonies and funerals with farewells, each of which would have a set of rituals associated with them. The idea was to imbue each citizen with the feeling that "from the cradle to the grave his path in life is being attentively followed and sincerely participated in by society, that he is being supported by the comradeship of his fellow workers. He should become used to the idea that our fate is not decided by supernatural powers, but rather by us, through human society, and through the laws of life itself."[34] These ceremonies gained legal status in 1962 and by 1970 there existed a network of offices to promote civil celebrations.[35] We will have occasion later in the chapter to examine the evolution of participation in these practices. It is worth noting here, however, that the data, which are available only at the regional and national levels, provide contradictory evidence on the strength of church community. Thus, whereas by 1984 only around 55 percent of Roman Catholics were having church weddings, 71 percent were still christening their children, and 91 percent were demanding Catholic burials.[36]

Those who observed up close the struggle between the Party and the Churches knew that clerical influence stemmed from more than merely popular religious belief. A 1959 report from the Hajdú-Bihar ÁEH representative outlined a set of recommendations to advance the Party's goals. The report surmised that the presence of priests and pastors in local councils, the Patriotic Peoples' Front, agricultural collectives, peace committees, sporting clubs, culture houses, and other organizations served to broaden the Churches' influence. Wherever possible the clergy were to

[33] Z23/1958. Similar views are expressed by the ÁEH in Hajdú-Bihar. See HB46/1959.
[34] András and Morel (1983b: 97).
[35] Ibid.: 97–8. See also András and Morel (1969: 93–5; 131–2).
[36] Tomka (1988b: 510–77).

162

be excluded from these organizations. Tensions within the Churches between reactionary and progressive clergymen were to be fostered to divert the Churches' energies away from their missions. Party-approved sporting events, hiking outings, and similar social activities were to be organized for the youth. The Womens' Council (*Nőtanács*) was to be enlisted to gain the support of women, who were the most religious group. As before 1956, all cultural and educational venues, such as the theater, exhibitions, and libraries, were to be used to further the atheist message.[37]

The Party continued to discourage, impede, and disrupt religious instruction in the schools, belying its stated promise that the decision to participate or not would remain free of coercion.[38] Before the registration period teachers made home visits and chaired meetings to convince parents not to enroll their children. Special attention was devoted to wavering local cadres and factory workers. To the extent such discussions were aimed at ensuring that parents understood the difference between a "materialist" and "idealist" education, such visits could be excused. However, the Party did not limit itself to that. According to one priest, in mid-1958 a rumor was circulating in his parish that upperclassmen who attend religious instruction would not be permitted to continue their education. In other cases, the authorities intimated that a parent could lose his or her job. This practice was particularly pronounced when the parents were educated, and could thus set a bad example for others.[39]

Where such mobilization did not work, "administrative measures" could still be employed. Denying a religion instructor permission to teach remained a potent weapon. In Marcaltő (Veszprém county), the priest complained to his bishop that such problems had resulted in three consecutive years without regular religious instruction.[40] In one instance, the head of the local council and the school headmaster requested that the priest not use the pulpit to inform the parishioners when the registration was to take place, suggesting that it was enough simply to hang printed instructions from the church door. Sowing confusion over when registration was

---

[37] HB46/1959 and HB49/1959. These represent only a sample of a very detailed set of recommendations.

[38] For a recent overview of Catholic education in the post-1956 period, see Mészáros (1994: 216–46).

[39] Such events occurred in numerous places and times, and can be found in both Party and Church sources. See, for example, M46/1958, M47/1958, Bindes and Németh (1991: 217–18), Ve13/1959, and HB44/1959.

[40] Ve4/1957.

actually supposed to happen was a favorite ploy. Party members were explicitly instructed not to volunteer such information[41] and many parents simply did not know when the appropriate time was. One religion instructor complained that the authorities intervened even if he asked one of his students to tell her classmates when the registration was to take place.[42] Yet there were other obstacles even for parents that managed to figure that out. In another case, a parish priest was forbidden from teaching religion because on the day of registration a number of parents entered the rectory, which the government interpreted as illegal clerical interference. Local Party leaders, teachers, and other functionaries supervised the registration process, and there were many reports of parental signatures requesting instruction not being accepted.[43]

The continuing difficulties the Churches faced with respect to religious instruction may be better appreciated by considering what happened in 1959 in the village of Pacsa (Veszprém county), where in a letter to Church authorities the local priest relates how during the registration period the authorities went far beyond their customary antireligious propaganda, employing "the crudest forms of intimidation." Apparently, the head of the Executive Committee of the local council and his secretary stood at the school gate as parents were entering to enroll their children and harangued them for endangering their children's future and depriving them of any hope for success. The teachers continued the intimidation during the registration process. Parents who nonetheless insisted on going through with it were further threatened with the loss of their livelihoods. Some parents, fearing they would no longer be able to support themselves, withdrew their registration. Others pointed out that the constitution and the agreements between Church and State guaranteed their right to religious instruction. The functionaries responded that such toleration was merely propaganda aimed at the international community and had little real meaning. The priest went on to express his profound disappointment that government regulations were being enforced against the Church, but not against the State, and that this was causing much fear and suffering among his parishioners.[44]

---

[41] Z23/1958.

[42] M48/1959.

[43] HB45/1959 and Bindes and Németh (1991: 218–20).

[44] Ve25/1959. A brief note from the bishop's office sent two weeks later indicated that the complaint had been forwarded to the appropriate authorities.

Clerical response to this new harassment ranged from acceptance of the new regime (the peace priests) to passive neutrality and active opposition. The return of the Party after the aborted 1956 uprising removed a glimmer of hope, kept alive since 1948, that somehow the regime could not last, that it would be consumed by its own excesses. Whereas before 1956 the Churches could hope to outlast the regime, after the failed revolution there was little reason to believe that socialism would end any time soon. Reaction to the renewed offensive against the Churches reflected a sense of both resignation at the seeming inevitability of diminishing Church influence and determination to make the best of a bad situation. Such perseverance is illustrated in descriptions of efforts to preserve the Szentimreváros (Budapest) Catholic youth movement. The leaders of the movement knew that their organizational activities were considered illegal and that the Party would interpret them as reactionary. Movement leaders simply wanted to impart to their members the religious mentality that they had grown up with and had become increasingly difficult to obtain in religious classes where the Party oversaw the content. There was little question of expanding the movement, as that carried great risk. The leadership had more modest aims, which were simply to preserve what was already there.[45]

5.4 Clerical Resistance

In hopes of combatting the depredations of the Party-State, the clergy employed and built upon many of the same strategies that had been developed between 1948 and 1956. It is convenient to divide the post-1956 period into two phases. The first extends from the failed revolution to roughly the mid-1960s. Hungarian rural life underwent a dramatic transformation during this period, with the re-collectivization of agriculture. As we will see, the imposition of socialist agriculture provided the clergy with unprecedented opportunities to reconnect with the faithful, but also dealt a severe blow to its efforts to preserve church community. The second phase, beginning in the mid-1960s, represented for both the Roman Catholic and Reformed Churches a recognition of their statuses as "Churches within socialism." In 1964, the Vatican and the Hungarian State signed a "partial agreement," the first between the Vatican and any communist State, marking a definitive normalization in relations. For the Reformed Church the "Theology of Service" developed during this period likewise constituted another attempt

---

[45] Kamarás (1992: 80–1).

to reconcile the Church with the reality of socialist society. Clerical resistance would continue after the mid-1960s, but with diminished scope. By the 1970s the most important location for religious instruction had shifted from the schools to churches. The slide into insignificance of the last "outpost" of the Churches within the school system represented a victory for the Party, which had long sought to confine clerical influence to the inside of the church building. Yet, for the transmission of partisan attachments it was enough for the Churches to have survived through the early 1970s. As will be illustrated in the next chapter, areas where church community declined only in the 1970s better preserved their preferences for the Right than areas where the Church eroded in the 1960s or earlier.

As before 1956, religious instruction in the schools remained a site of continued tumultuous conflict between the parish clergy and local cadres. The Party acknowledged that clerical efforts to counter the Party's offensive remained largely within the law,[46] but noted with regret that the clergy was taking advantage of every available opportunity to ensure the success of the instruction. Before the registration period, for example, the Church hierarchies were careful to send out encyclical letters informing the local clergy of their responsibility to announce the timing and rules for registration at all religious services, bible studies, and other gatherings.[47] In the period leading up to the 1962 registration period, the priest in Páka (Zala county) used the pulpit no fewer than twelve times to remind parishioners of their responsibility to show up at the appointed time.[48] In other instances letters were sent to individual families.[49]

For many clergymen, however, these strategies were too passive. A common tactic remained exaggerating the degree of cooperation between Church and State as a way of reassuring wavering parishioners or intimidating ill-informed local cadres. In Zala county in 1958, for example, numerous priests exploited the putatively "normal" Church-State relationship. They pointed to Archbishop Grősz's recent receipt of an award from the government as evidence that the Party was now respecting religious freedom, and that it was safe to fulfill all commitments to the Church.[50] In Hajdú-Bihar county in 1959 a Reformed clergyman pointed out that his congregation

[46] M39/1958 and M45/1958.
[47] Ref138/1957 is an example of such a letter, sent from the Reformed Universal Convent to every church. It details both clerical duties and the Church's rights under the law.
[48] Z80/1962.
[49] M45/1958 and M47/1958.
[50] Z22/1958.

had just received 20,000 forint to repair the church, and that with such State support there could be no problem with religious instruction.[51] The Catholic clergy would make similar exhortations after the signing of the partial agreement between the Hungarian State and the Vatican in 1964.[52] An assistant priest in Murakeresztúr (Zala county) took this strategy one step further, noting that "the laws of our People's Republic ensure religious instruction, and whoever mobilizes against that instruction also mobilizes against those laws."[53] In yet another twist, the priest in Lent (Zala county) accused the local officials of not upholding the constitution, suggesting that it was they, and not he, that would be held to account.[54] Many clergymen argued that the only difference between religious teachings and communist teachings was that the former wanted to achieve common goals with God, the latter without God.[55]

The laity resorted to similar subterfuge. In 1958, the Party noted that mothers and grandmothers often registered the children for religious instruction without the father's knowledge or against his will. Normally this would prevent the child from being enrolled, but the women insisted to the local authorities that they would work out the details with the father and that registration should go ahead anyway.[56] Many of these fathers, having learned of what happened, returned to the school to have the child removed from the religious instruction rolls. This was particularly prevalent among Party members, who had no desire to be seen as setting a bad example for the rest of the community.[57]

A widespread practice was visits to the faithful. Many priests went from house to house, urging parents to enroll their children.[58] One clergyman rode a motorcycle through several villages, telling people that only religious instruction could ensure that children become ethical adults. Others enlisted the help of parishioners to call on those who might not wish to risk registration. This could, of course, dramatically increase the Church's

---

[51] HB43/1959. See also HB44/1959, where a Catholic priest encouraged parishioners to take advantage of their rights as guaranteed under the constitution.

[52] Z38/1965.

[53] Z30/1962.

[54] Z80/1962.

[55] Sz7/1964.

[56] M45/1958.

[57] HB39/1960. One cadre, however, declared that he would rather leave the Party than raise his child without religion.

[58] See, for example, Z80/1962.

outreach, particularly among those who might not attend church regularly. Women were often tapped for this task. Sometimes these would be former nuns or the wives of Protestant pastors. Other times they were simply devoted believers who wanted to perform good works.[59] As before 1956, there were numerous accusations that priests also employed "terror tactics" to pump up registration. Typically these involved threats to withhold certain services that only the Church provided, such as confession, confirmation, and Holy Communion. Sometimes the clergy would encourage the more devout to pester those parents who did not enroll their children the previous year.[60]

The clergy also sought to enhance the students' experience during the instruction. As noted in Chapter 4, the conditions the regime imposed on these classes – held after school hours, without grades, and with the instructor barred from disciplining students – virtually ensured unruly, ill-attended sessions. Indeed, one 1958 report from the Ministry of Education noted that in many places 50 to 60 percent of the enrolled children did not regularly attend class, and that this percentage depended in part on the character of and methods employed by the teacher.[61] Aware of the difficulties of holding the students' attention, the clergy sought to liven up the lessons. Some distributed pictures of saints as a reward for answering questions correctly. Others would begin to narrate an interesting story, leaving the most exciting parts for the following meeting. Still others would show films in class.[62]

The youth remained an important clerical focus even beyond religious instruction. In regard to spiritual education, for example, the clergy continued to devise numerous means of contact outside officially sanctioned channels.[63] One was the holding of church services designed especially for children, where there would be singing, worship, and the learning of aphorisms to hold the children's interest. Another was the holding of "childrens hours" where the group would be involved in fun activities, such as story telling and learning poetry. A third involved bible reading, especially for young people who may already have left school and were preparing for marriage. A fourth focused on preparing children for confirmation, which

---

[59] M45/1958 and HB44/1959.
[60] See, for example, HB43/1959, HB45/1959, Z75/1962, and M43/1958.
[61] M40/1958.
[62] M39/1958.
[63] HB21/1962.

lasted many months and involved not just the children, but also their parents. The celebration brought together the entire church community. A fifth was the staging of church celebrations and "religious evenings" for adults and children alike, complete with joyful song and refreshments. This was in addition to the regularly scheduled feasts and other events held throughout the year. A sixth brought the clergy into the homes of the faithful. Many priests and pastors made it a point to visit the homes of those just baptized, preparing for confirmation, getting married, or anyone else requiring spiritual assistance. One pastor summed up the purpose of these visits as "anchoring to the Church the children through their parents and the parents through their children."[64]

Clerical involvement with younger parishioners was not limited to activities directly related to religious life. To maintain influence priests employed tactics that, in the Party's view at least, were "more flexible and variegated" than before.[65] For example, the clergy, traditionally a privileged class and socially distant from ordinary believers, threw itself into everyday community affairs. In many settlements, priests organized and participated in sporting events. They arranged group TV watching, and helped form photography clubs, do-it-yourself repair groups, and hikes and outings. They distributed stamps, pictures, postcards, and sugar to the smaller children. Nothing was demanded in return for these gifts. Rather they were used to forge relationships that might result in greater participation in church life. In Galambok (Zala county), for example, the priest made wooden letters and gave a letter to a child each time he or she would attend church. If a child could collect enough letters to spell the name of a saint, then he or she would be rewarded with a snack or being able to watch TV. In Zalaszentgrót (Zala county) the priest constructed an automatic piggy bank in the church building that draws a picture of a church. If money was deposited, an angel appeared. If more money was deposited, a bell rang.[66] In Csömő and Hencida (Hajdú-Bihar county) singing groups were organized.[67]

The rest of the community was fair game, too. In one village, the priest regularly went to the movies and afterward would lead the viewers in discussing the film. In other places the priest helped workers get placed in

---

[64] HB21/1962. These strategies are taken from a report compiled by the ÁEH representative in Hajdú-Bihar county. Similar strategies are also listed in HB19/1959.
[65] Z36/1964.
[66] Z36/1964 and Z22/1958.
[67] HB21/1962.

factories and arranged students' school enrollments. When the time of social activities coincided with mass, many clergymen tried to reschedule the service rather than mobilize against attending the event, as they might have done previously. It became more common for the clergy to join in very simple work to gain respect. In Gellénháza, (Zala county), for example, the priest was seen dressing in "shabby clothes, rubber boots, and a worn out hat." He regularly performed manual labor, rode a motorcycle, and went hunting with other members of the community. He even visited the workers in the fields and drank wine and talked with them. According to one observer, the peasants thus became proud of "their" priest, a priest of the simple people.[68] The clergy's ability to branch out in this way was predicated in part on popular expectations of what a priest ought to be doing. In one survey, a majority of respondents thought that one of the priest's main jobs was to tend to the community of religious people. By contrast, only 17 percent felt that maintaining friendly relations with the local authorities should be a main task.[69]

Rather than attempt to subvert local social institutions, as was common before 1956, the clergy increasingly tried to cooperate with them. Some priests offered, for example, to hold combined name-giving and baptism ceremonies. Others visited the houses of culture or the Communist Youth Alliance (KISZ) club. Younger clergymen sometimes strove to maintain friendly contacts with local Party cadres and State functionaries by joining them in various recreational activities.[70] Many held positions in Patriotic People's Front organizations, peace committees, or served on local or provincial counsels. In Hajdú-Bihar in 1959 no fewer than 85 out of 513 clergymen and other Church employees were serving in some official capacity or another. Although many of these were local positions, some were countywide: four in the Patriotic People's Front, five on the Peace Committee, and an additional five people holding influential positions in Debrecen, the provincial capital.[71]

For the Party, clerical participation in secular State institutions was a mixed blessing. On the positive side, the greater the clerical participation in the machinery of government, the greater popular legitimacy the regime could be presumed to enjoy. In the years immediately following the 1956

[68] Z36/1964.
[69] Tomka (1991b: 40).
[70] Z36/1964.
[71] HB19/1959.

revolution the government could use all the help it could get, as it had to fight the popular conception that it was merely a Soviet puppet. The sight of clergymen working side by side with Party members and other functionaries sent the right signal to those who might doubt the wisdom of joining the project to build socialism. Indeed, this is why the Party exerted a great deal of effort to reinvigorate the peace priest movement. The hope was, as it had been before 1956, that these patriotic priests would use their moral authority to proselytize for the regime.

However, similar advantages could also accrue to the Churches. First, the same activities that signaled acceptance of the regime by the Churches *also* signaled acceptance of the Churches by the regime. As noted previously, the clergy often pointed to the agreements between the Churches and the State as evidence of the State's acceptance of a legitimate social role for the Churches. The presence of Church functionaries in governing positions provided even more fodder for those clergymen who sought to pursue their pastoral activities without harassment. Second, there was no guarantee that the clergymen filling these official positions were in fact genuinely democratic in outlook. The Party's original distinction between democratic and reactionary priests proved far too inelastic to capture the grey area between full collaboration with the regime and open opposition to it. We saw in Chapter 4 how some clergymen exploited the regime's favoritism toward progressive priests by feigning democratic attitudes. The Party's continuing fear that the government would be infiltrated by clerical reaction led it to expend much energy observing the priesthood, even the putatively democratic portion of it, for any signs of disloyalty. Of particular concern were the "passive" priests. They were numerous, but did not consistently exhibit behavior that would have permitted the Party to classify them as either progressive or reactionary. Their inscrutability aroused the authorities' suspicion, as it was often unclear whether or not such neutrality was serving as a cloak for oppositional activity. Nonetheless, such priests often succeeded in gaining places on local and regional governing committees. The Party usually labeled them "careful" or "passive" to express this uncertainty, or "forthcoming" (*közeledő*) if it thought a priest was basically sympathetic to socialism.[72]

---

[72] See HB19/1959 and Z26/1960, both detailed reports on the situation of Church politics in Hajdú-Bihar and Zala counties, respectively. The Hajdú-Bihar report contains tables identifying and politically evaluating the clerical personnel then in government.

Where a clergyman proved particularly effective or popular, or demonstrated reactionary tendencies, the government had numerous levers of influence. First, it could withhold privileges. The Head of the ÁEH in Hajdú-Bihar county noted in 1959 that overzealous pastors would be denied the extra money due them for teaching the religion class.[73] Similarly, the ÁEH conducted numerous visits with priests it deemed reactionary, in the hope of gauging the extent of their opposition and perhaps even persuading them to change their ways. Where such persuasion did not work, the authorities might withdraw their right to teach religion class, reduce their pensions, or withdraw their subventions altogether.[74]

Second, the government could request that the Church assign a priest to a new post or settlement. For example, remarking on the events surrounding the 1958–9 registration period for religious instruction in the schools in Zala county, the ÁEH representative noted the vigor with which the clergy was mobilizing the population for registration, to a degree not witnessed since 1948. As a penalty for the perceived abuse of the Church-State agreement, it was recommended that several of the most successful parish priests be relocated to new areas.[75] The Churches, eager to preserve what few resources they could, typically assented to these transfers. For example, in the Tiszántúl Reformed Diocese, which spans a portion of eastern Hungary, no fewer than eighty-five transfers were effected between March 27 and May 9, 1958 alone. Of course, not every transfer involved a priest or was a consequence of Party pressure. Pastors, priests, and other Church employees often had personal reasons for wanting to relocate and the Churches sometimes succeeded in placing the most effective clergymen where they were most needed. Indeed, in a report detailing the Church political situation in Hajdú-Bihar in 1959, the county ÁEH representative, cognizant of this administrative tool, recommended that Church transfers be limited only to those that benefited the government's Church policy.[76] Some transfers

---

[73] HB44/1959.

[74] See, for example, the reports of conversations with five reactionary priests, in HB26/1962. It is worth noting that of these five, three were Greek Catholic and two were Roman Catholic. According to HB19/1959, in Hajdú-Bihar county there were ninety Reformed pastors, twenty-seven Roman Catholic priests, and only thirteen Greek Catholic priests. These data are evidence that reactionary tendencies were much less prominent in the Reformed than in the other two denominations.

[75] M43/1958.

[76] HB19/1959.

went against the wishes of the congregation. One anguished letter from a Reformed believer to the bishop of the Tiszántúl diocese wondered why a popular pastor was being transferred without the congregation's permission and why there was no democracy within the Church.[77] In the Catholic diocese of Veszprém there were 138 transfers in 1957, at least 139 in 1958, and 130 in 1959.[78]

Third, there was always the option of arrest. Although the Kádár regime never resorted to the mass deportations characteristic of the pre-1956 period, it was nonetheless prepared to incarcerate those it deemed in violation of Church-State agreements. For example, in the "Black Raven" affair of 1961, eighty-one Church functionaries were convicted of illegally organizing against the People's Republic, for attempting to create an "underground Church," and seeking to establish a "Christian Republic." Of these, twenty two were priests.[79]

5.5 *Collectivization*

The single most important transformation rural Hungary underwent in the years after 1956 was the re-collectivization of agriculture. Recall from Chapter 4 that nearly two-thirds of the land that had been previously collectivized reverted to its original owners during the 1956 revolution. As a consequence, Hungary's socialist agricultural sector had become the smallest in Eastern Europe after Poland's.[80] In December 1958, the Party published its plans for a new drive toward collectivization, to be completed by April 1961. Although the Party renounced the coercive methods that had been employed during the previous wave of collectivization in the early 1950s, it also recognized that the peasants were unlikely to voluntarily give up their lands. "The peasant," according to Party Secretary Kádár, "had struggled all his life to get a hold of at least a small piece of land. Everything he had ever seen and experienced told him that land was the only security, that land was life. Is it surprising that he clung to it?"[81]

The Party opted instead to apply a combination of economic incentives and "persuasion" through an intensive propaganda campaign. Both

---

[77] Tibori (1996: 61–70).
[78] Veszprém Érseki Levéltár Egyházmegyei Iktató 1957, 1958, and 1959.
[79] Kiszely (2001: 101–2). Havasy (1990: 183) reports as seventy the number of priests brought before the court.
[80] Kovrig (1979: 341).
[81] Quoted in Kádár (1985: 115).

"carrots" and "sticks" were used on the economic front. To make private farming less economically attractive, the regime raised prices on industrial goods and lowered prices on agricultural produce. The hope was that farmers would then join out of economic necessity. At the same time the regime offered pensions, health insurance, and retirement benefits to cooperative members and agreed to pay rent to those who surrendered their land. It was hoped that social insurance would reassure older peasants that they would not be endangering their livelihoods by forfeiting their only source of income. The rent payments were to be compensation for the wealthier peasants.[82] A more relaxed policy toward private household plots, which under Rákosi had been viewed as a threat to socialism, further decreased the risk of joining.[83] As a final inducement, subsidies were offered to the cooperatives for the purchase of livestock, buildings, and machinery.[84]

In many ways, the propaganda campaign in favor of collectivization resembled the Party's mobilization efforts during the religious instruction registration period. In villages targeted for collectivization, committees composed of local cadres, State functionaries, and sympathetic workers were enlisted to go from house to house evangelizing for the collective movement. In hopes of winning the peasants over, collectives were portrayed in idealistic terms: as an extended family; as offering a lighter workload; and as a vehicle for achieving the emancipation of women, who would participate equally as producers alongside men.[85] These village visits could last for days or weeks in areas with reluctant peasants. Bell (1984: 132–3) notes that in Kislapos (Heves county) initial efforts proved fruitless: "The peasants ... were very skeptical of the claims and conditions made by people far less familiar with agriculture than they. Many household heads hid or left home for days to avoid the constant pressure of argument and persuasion." As in the case of religious instruction, there were reports of psychological and physical abuse where persuasion did not work. As Bell (ibid.) says, even when the men succeeded in avoiding the problem, "wives often caved in under the stress and joined in their stead." Likewise, Hann (1980: 40) reports that some peasants "claimed to have been threatened with firearms." Of course, the anger could run both ways. In Zala county in 1959 there were

---

[82] Donáth (1980: 287) and Lampland (1995: 176–7).
[83] Goven (1993: 124).
[84] Donáth (1980: 288).
[85] Lampland (1995: 176–84).

reports of peasants threatening to beat the newly arrived organizers. In one case the organizers fled the village, with peasants shouting that "there will still be a peasant revolution!"[86]

Special efforts were focused on local elites, especially the middle and wealthier peasants, who had the most to lose from any redistribution of land. When such elites joined the cooperative it sent two kinds of signals. First, to the extent participation appeared voluntary, it could convince wavering peasants that it might actually be in their interest to join. Second, where participation was coerced, or at least perceived to be coerced, the peasants would likely view as futile their own prospects for resistance. Thus, much like the demonstration effect of "converting" a Party member in the case of registration for religious instruction, the surrender of a peasant elite to the cooperative was often sufficient to induce those still remaining outside to give up.[87]

The Party would have preferred to implement the collectivization without any input from the Churches. As summarized in 1962 by the president of the Hajdú-Bihar county council's Executive Committee, "the main task was to use them [the Churches] where necessary, to keep them at a distance where possible," and to remember that "the main goal was to prevent them from preventing the reorganization."[88] At a time when the Party was still striving to increase its membership in the wake of the aborted 1956 uprising, however, it recognized that the clergy could play a key role in its propaganda campaign. After 1956, the Reformed Church press began filling up with articles praising the moral superiority of collectives as a "communal, unselfish" way of life, and urging "true" Christians to join them.[89] The Catholic peace priest movement expressed similar views: "Communal life is more Christian than individual life...therefore the collective movement is not un-Christian."[90] Unconditional support was given: "Our oath to the State and the Church-State agreement demands that we support the collective movement...we should emphasize our collective task from the pulpit and the confessional, in both private and public discussions."[91] In meetings of both Reformed and Catholic clergymen fulsome praise could be heard for the idea of

---

[86] Z29.5/1959.
[87] Bell (1984: 132–8), Donáth (1980: 285–6), and Lampland (1995: 179–92).
[88] HB23/1962.
[89] Takacs (1960: 436) and Kónya (1988: 234).
[90] *Katolikus Szó*, September 18, 1960, quoted in Pál (1995: 158).
[91] *Katolikus Szó*, April 2, 1961, quoted in Pál (1995: 159).

joining the peasantry in its journey toward the socialist transformation of agriculture.[92]

The Party hoped to limit clerical involvement to the propaganda sphere, to prevent priests from infiltrating the collectives in the same way they had managed to secure positions in various governing bodies. It even went so far as to advise individual priests to avoid joining the face-to-face mobilizational efforts conducted under Party aegis.[93] Yet it was difficult to prevent such "spillover," especially among the peace priests, some of whom may truly have believed in the righteousness of the collective movement. In Kehida (Zala county), for example, many of the peasants were initially unwilling to join, despite great efforts by the local organizers. Only after the priest spoke individually with leading members of the congregation was the majority of the village willing to participate. Likewise, in Kiskanizsa (Zala county) the local priest went from house to house, urging individuals to sign the declaration of participation. The Evangelical priest in Liszó (Zala county) was singled out for his progressiveness. He entered the cooperative and became a brigade leader.[94] Similar overzealous clergymen were observed in Hajdú-Bihar county.[95] Significantly, the clergy appeared to be most effective when they linked the merits of agricultural organization to the successful performance of the Church's mission rather than to appeals to patriotism or socialism. Indeed, many of those elected to leading positions in the collectives were openly religious.[96] The Party thus feared that the socialist character of the collectives could be undermined.

Few priests openly opposed collectivization, but many refused to adopt a position either for or against. In part this reticence was an attempt to steer a course between the Party and episcopates that in some cases were less than enthusiastic about the reorganization. Observers noted, for example, that the Reformed Church leadership did far more to encourage collectivization than the Catholic hierarchy. Whereas Reformed pastors were urged to join the collectives and work alongside their congregants in building socialism, Catholic priests were merely cautioned to not express opposition to them. As one pro-reorganization Catholic clergyman put it, "the

[92] For Catholics, see Ve27/1959, Ve28/1959, and Ve29/1959; for the Reformed, more general comments in support of socialism may be found in Ref140/1958.

[93] See the comments made in October 1959 by a series of Catholic priests in a meeting where the Church's attitude toward collectivization was being discussed, in Ve28/1959.

[94] Z29/1962.

[95] HB23/1962.

[96] Z29/1962 and HB23/1962.

Bench of Bishops asks the priesthood not to oppose the collective movement. But this is too little! With prudence and understanding we need to advise our farming believers that collectives are the only possible way."[97] By not taking sides, a priest could hope to avoid alienating both the Party and his clerical superiors. The more recalcitrant of these passive priests might evince opposition by refusing to accommodate to the new work rhythms of the collectives. In parts of Zala county, for example, some discouraged the peasants from working on Church holidays, and declined to reschedule Mass, thus preventing a full day's work.[98]

Sometimes there were open confrontations between the priests and the local authorities. These are exemplified by the experience of the Greek Catholic priest János Kisfalusi. He notes in his memoirs how in 1959 the ÁEH secretary in Borsod county, who bragged about his fourth-grade education, but who in fact "was stupid and only had a big mouth," called him to a meeting to discuss his poor relations with the president of the collective in the village of Rakaca, one István Görcsös. As Kisfalusi further recounts it:

> István Görcsös, whom they could not place elsewhere, was handed to the inhabitants of Rakaca. Every week he sent a report that he was unable to be effective because I was preventing it. I clarified: Görcsös does more damage to himself with his boorishness than 100 priests could do. If he would speak nicely with the people of Rakaca things would go much better, but because he is stupid and rude he will never succeed anywhere.
>
> Görcsös once asked me to preach in church that everyone should join the collective, that they should not steal. At the time I was still inept, and I promised nothing. But I should have dealt with it by promising everything and doing nothing, since that's what everyone did. That's when it was reported that I had accused the president of the collective of stealing. (Which would have been true, because he stole everything for himself, the stone, the lime, the wood, everything possible.)[99]

In the end, collectivization was rapid and intense and transformed the face of Hungarian villages. Between 1958 and 1961 the number of private farms larger than half a hectare decreased from over 1,300,000 to just over 150,000. The percentage of arable land farmed by cooperatives increased from around 11 percent to roughly 75 percent. The number of cooperative members skyrocketed from 140,000 to 1,115,000.[100] By the end of

---

[97] Ve28/1959.
[98] Z29/1962.
[99] Kisfalusi (1992: 101–3).
[100] Donáth (1980: 290).

1961 only 6 percent of Hungary's peasants were still engaged in private farming as their primary occupation. The feeling of loss, combined with the increasing mechanization of agriculture, accelerated a flight from the land that was already being encouraged by the regime's industrialization policies. Between 1959 and 1963 the percentage of wage earners deriving their living from agriculture declined from 41 to 30.[101]

5.6 Elite Conciliation, Local Conflict

Elite-level relations between the Churches and the State would ultimately prove more conciliatory than the daily battles taking place from below. What Ignotus (1972: 260–1) terms the "uneasy friendship" that emerged beginning in the early 1960s between the regime and the Catholic Church resulted in the so-called partial agreement concluded between Hungary and the Vatican in 1964. For Monsignor Casaroli, who represented the Vatican in the negotiations, the document represented neither a "modus vivendi" nor an "accord," but an agreement that addressed the pressing issue of Church administration in Hungary.[102] The terms of the agreement were indeed modest. Each side agreed to certain Episcopal appointments. The oath of allegiance to the Hungarian People's Republic that was required for certain Church officeholders was to remain binding on the Church, but only to the extent that laws did not violate Christian principles. Finally, each Hungarian diocese would be allowed to send one priest to the Hungarian Papal Institute in Rome for training. The administrator of that institute, however, would have to be acceptable to the Hungarian government. The significance of the agreement lay in its symbolism: the Holy See had explicitly recognized the authority of a state-socialist government regarding Church affairs. The Vatican had previously excommunicated all communists, and all previous agreements between the Church and the communist States had been concluded without its approval. The partial agreement thus represented an enormous leap toward a normalization of Church-State relations.

The 1971 departure of Cardinal Mindszenty from the U.S. embassy – where he had been granted asylum in the aftermath of the failed 1956

---

[101] Romsics (1999: 331). It should be noted that this discussion has glossed over the fact that there were several different kinds of collectives, each with different rules of ownership and membership, and that the recollectivization process took place in discrete waves. For details, see Varga (2001).

[102] András and Morel (1983a: 38–9) and Polgar (1984: 19–21).

revolution – marked a further step forward in the normalization of relations between the Catholic Church and the Hungarian State. Soon thereafter the Holy See reversed its prior ex-communication of the peace priests.[103] Within a few years, the regime and Vatican had agreed on a series of Episcopal appointments. In the interests of the Church the pope relieved Mindszenty of his post as Archbishop of Esztergom, primate of Hungary. For the first time in decades there was a resident bishop in each of Hungary's dioceses. In 1977 János Kádár was received by the pope in a private audience.[104] The following year Kádár pronounced as "settled" the relationship between the State and the Catholic Church.[105]

The Church hierarchy underscored this peaceful relationship in its public statements. Bishop József Cserháti (1980) noted that at the time of the 1950 Church-State agreement the "social aims...of the practitioners of the people's power...were identical in ethical content to men of the Gospel being called to the fraternal brotherhood."[106] Though it was contrary to canon law, in 1985 three Catholic priests were elected to the Hungarian parliament, with the approval of Archbishop of Esztergom Lékai.[107] Lékai declined a seat in parliament only after the intercession of Pope John Paul II.[108] Cardinal Lékai did accept the Order of the Banner of Rubies of the Hungarian People's Republic in recognition of his "exceptional efforts to promote good relations between the Hungarian State and the Catholic Church."[109] A total of thirty-one Catholic Church personnel were elected to parliament and national council offices in 1985.[110] The Church had, at last, made peace with the regime, but apparently on the regime's terms. So concerned was the Hungarian hierarchy to maintain its "modus vivendi" with the State that Pope John Paul II at least twice requested that the bishops more vigorously defend the Church's rights, singling out the right to conduct religious instruction.[111]

In the years after 1956 the Reformed Church leadership continued its effort to develop a theology that would justify the Church's support for

---

[103] Mindszenty (1974: 238).
[104] These events are briefly discussed in László (1990: 161–2).
[105] Kádár (1985: 429).
[106] Cited in Wildmann (1986: 165).
[107] Ramet (1987: 71).
[108] Michel (1991: 26).
[109] Ramet (1987: 71).
[110] ÁEH (1987: 98–9).
[111] Ramet (1987: 146).

socialism. By the latter part of the 1960s this culminated in what has been termed the "Theology of Service." The basic idea was similar to the doctrine put forth by Bishop Bereczky and other members of the leadership in the late 1940s: the Church had sinned in previous historical periods and "in the new period of humankind binds itself, in a free and contributive association, to the progressive trends of true humanity and shares in the building of socialism." Following Christ's example, then, the duty of the Church was to serve humanity and to reject any form of political power.[112] One Church leader, on the twentieth anniversary of the country's liberation in 1945, declared gratefulness to God for granting the Church new possibilities to serve in the new system, which was much more humane than the old, and ensured the Church's freedom.[113] In one observer's by no means unique opinion, the Reformed leadership had "made the church the collaborator with an atheist secular authority."[114]

The State authorities were apparently pleased. In 1972, Bishop Tibor Bartha, President of the General Synod of the Reformed Church, was awarded the First Class of the Banner Order of the Hungarian People's Republic "in recognition of his services in working for the good relations developed between the Hungarian State and the Reformed Church as well as his efficient activity in the international peace movement."[115] In 1980, Bishop Bartha spoke glowingly of the Church-State relationship: "the Churches – including Calvinist believers – with pleasure shoulder the burden of and take part in the realization of our society's humanitarian and patriotic goals."[116] Later he claimed that the socialist program "suits the requirements of love of humanity, love of country, and esteem for life."[117]

Notwithstanding the cordial relationship between the State and the Church leaderships, and even recognition by the authorities that the Churches were not just tolerated, but needed to ensure the maintenance of moral values,[118] the battle to limit contact between the clergy and society

---

[112] Szabó (1989: 198).

[113] This is a paraphrase of a statement before a Church, not a Party, audience. See Tibori (1998: 29).

[114] Pungur (1992: 134). Similar views are held by Majsai (1991) and Pásztor (1995).

[115] Beeson (1982: 279).

[116] Cited in Tibori (2000: 100).

[117] Cited in Ref186/1982.

[118] See, for example, the remarkable 1977 statement by the Chairman of the ÁEH, in which he acknowledges the positive role the Churches can play "in spreading ideas of humanism, of love for the people, [and] in the fight against crime. . . . " Quoted in László (1990: 163).

proceeded in broad outline much as it had before. A 1976 report from Zala county on religious instruction in the schools and another on reducing the influence of clerical reaction do reflect the evolution of the Church-State relationship, but also make clear that the Churches remain a foe to be defeated rather than a partner to work with. The report on religious instruction dutifully notes that the local Party organizations, village councils, and educators were "generally prepared well" for the registration, and lists the communities where registration levels remain unusually high. It records the number of Party and council members who enrolled their children and which priests were thought to be in violation of Church-State agreements.[119] The clergy's tactics remained as they had been: some threatened to withhold Communion to those children who do not attend class; another complained that one of the teachers had convinced a parent to have his child unenrolled.

The report on clerical reaction does note that the majority of "the Churches, Church personnel, and religious people stand on the side of the socialist system." However, it also assures that the local Party and State organs are prepared to further reduce the Churches' influence.[120] Indeed, other parts read as if they could have been written in the 1950s rather than the 1970s. Clerical reaction is accused of hindering the Party's resocialization efforts, discrediting the peace priests by referring to them as traitors and diminishing the population's trust in socialism. These accusations are not rantings against an imaginary class enemy, but made, as in previous years, in the context of concrete observations about specific clerical activities. Numerous clergymen, for example, are accused of traveling over the border to Yugoslavia to strengthen their ties with the West and thus "infecting" home areas with new ideas. More illuminating are the accusations that the clergy, rather than engage in open confrontation, instead prefers to cloak its opposition in terms of the legalities of the constitution and other agreements that the State had entered into. These are precisely the strategies, of course, that permitted so many priests to avoid serious punishment. The communities in which reactionary clergymen worked are identified (at least 19 out of some 200 settlements). In most cases, the Party intended to effect a solution by meeting with each priest, in the hopes of dissuading them from their activities. In the more serious

---

[119] Z72/1976.
[120] Z72.5/1976.

instances (three in all), the Party intended to have the priests transferred elsewhere.[121]

Elements of the lower clergy rebelled against not just the Party, but also their own Church leaderships. For example, in the late 1970s a Renewal Movement within the Reformed Church was secretly formed among ministers who were not collaborating with the authorities. In 1978, the movement published a memorandum criticizing the State for "forcing ministers to preach political sermons; for turning church leaders into state officials; [and] for the comedy of church election practices."[122] The ministers accused the Church leadership of working against the true interests of the Church, and thus assisting in the gradual liquidation of the Church. The movement clandestinely organized resistance to collaboration between the leadership and the regime, and in the summer of 1989 openly called for reform.[123]

Within the lower Catholic clergy perhaps the best-known example of dissent is that of Father György Bulányi, a nonconforming charismatic priest who rejected the Church's subservience to the authorities and founded a community of Catholic believers who refused military service and sought to live the simpler spiritual lives of the early Christians, outside of the institutional Catholic Church. Numbering perhaps in the thousands, these "base communities" began to spring up in the 1970s (and not just in Hungary) and were considered a threat by both the State *and* the Church. The bishops considered Bulányi and the priests who followed him a danger to the unity of the Church and the stability of their relations with the authorities. Bulányi "spoke truth to power," complaining that "the concessions made by the state are mere formalities that did not make any substantial change in the situation of the Church."[124] On a visit to Rome, the bishops submitted a formal complaint against Bulányi to the pope, who decided against Bulányi and ordered him and his followers to submit to the Hungarian Church hierarchy. In June 1982, the Bench of Bishops formally relieved Bulányi of his duties.[125]

Pressure on the church community would continue into the 1980s. Tomka (1991a) relates how during this period young churchgoers were

[121] Z72.5/1976.
[122] As formulated by Pungur (1992: 150).
[123] Ibid.: 150–1.
[124] Cited in Ramet (1987: 145).
[125] András and Morel (1983a: 264–79), László (1990: 168–72), Michel (1991: 118–22), and Ramet (1987: 145-6).

refused admittance to summer camps and denied access to higher education, and how religious educators still faced obstacles to promotion. He notes instances of the regime using selective incentives to encourage people to discontinue religious practice. Employers, for example, would still provide financial subsidies for socialist name-giving, wedding, and funeral ceremonies if a church ceremony were foregone. The Churches had neither the human nor the financial resources to reconnect to those who had already been lost, but pastoral efforts might still succeed with those who showed a modicum of belief. This sentiment was expressed by Father Tibor Hegedűs of the village of Sümegcsehi in an interview I conducted in 1996. A priest since 1959, he elegantly summed up his role: "My predecessors created the religiosity; I only tried to preserve what was already there. Anything more was not possible."[126]

5.7 Reassessing the Battle for Souls

This chapter has documented the continuing struggle between the Party and the Churches for mass allegiance in the years after 1956. We have seen that although the Party abandoned the Stalinist methods of the early 1950s, it still devoted a great deal of effort to whittling away at Church influence. Agricultural collectivization represented an additional weapon in the Party's arsenal, even if it was rarely portrayed in those terms. As we saw, the reorganization of agriculture meant the introduction of socialism into even the smallest rural outposts, and the disruption of what were often tightly knit communities. The Churches themselves were split between those who professed fealty to the new system and the need for full cooperation with it and those who, either overtly or more subtly, sought to preserve the Churches as an independent object of identification. We have seen how many of the lower clergy devised ever more-clever strategies for skirting the many obstacles the Party placed between them and the faithful.

Table 5.1 illustrates the evolution of registration for religious instruction in the schools and the progress of collectivization (on the right side of the table) across the rural districts and towns of Hajdú-Bihar and Zala counties between 1958 and 1970. The data stop in 1970 for two reasons. First, there is monotonic decline after 1970. By 1975, for example, registration rates in Zala county are only 7.3 percent, and in Hajdú-Bihar county

---

[126] Interview conducted by the author in the parish church, Sümegcsehi, August 8, 1996.

Table 5.1 *Religious Instruction Enrollment and Collectivization, Hajdú–Bihar and Zala Counties, 1958–1970.*

Region	District	Percentage Enrolled in Religious Instruction								Percentage Collectivized	
		1958	1959	1960	1961	1962	1963	1965	1970	1959	1962
Zala county	Lent d.	61.0	48.1	38.3	32.4	29.5	25.2	20.5	12.0	14	63
	Letenye d.	–	–	–	17.0	12.0	13.2	11.2	1.7	18	59
	Nagykanizsa d.	67.0	47.0	35.4	30.2	27.6	25.3	26.1	17.9	38	71
	Zalaegerszeg d.	–	46.1	39.5	29.1	25.7	26.6	18.3	18.0	40	61
	Zalaszentgrót d.	59.0	38.2	–	20.6	18.0	17.1	16.9	6.9	42	67
	Nagykanizsa t.	–	–	–	3.3	2.1	2.1	1.2	0.04	–	–
	Zalaegerszeg t.	–	–	–	0.6	0.4	0.9	0.5	0.8	–	–
	TOTAL	50.6	35.6	28.2	21.3	18.3	17.4	13.8	8.2	–	–
Hajdú-Bihar county	Berettyóújfalu d.	46.1	41.4	29.4	20.4	16.8	13.8	11.8	4.1	59	75
	Biharkeresztes d.	26.8	21.5	17.2	10.6	7.1	5.4	1.6	0.1	53	74
	Debrecen d.	35.1	33.5	32.3	21.7	19.5	14.6	11.7	6.6	9	53
	Derecske d.	33.6	31.0	24.6	18.8	17.4	14.6	7.8	0.5	16	81
	Polgár d.	25.0	16.9	10.9	6.3	4.0	4.2	3.0	0.2	35	61
	Püspökladányi d.	30.1	20.8	11.8	5.7	2.8	1.5	0.6	–	47	66
	Debrecen t.	–	3.0	1.0	0.4	0.04	0.06	–	–	–	–
	Hajdúböszörmény t.	21.5	13.6	7.1	2.2	1.6	2.3	0.5	0.1	11	63
	Hajdúnánás t.	16.4	14.4	6.2	2.3	2.1	0.8	0.4	0.1	13	68
	Hajdúszoboszló t.	21.6	11.1	3.8	2.3	0.6	0.1	–	–	12	41
	TOTAL	31.2	26.1	19.6	13.0	10.8	8.9	6.1	2.5	–	–

Note: The – indicates the data are unavailable. In cases where the percentages are incorrectly reported in the original source I have recalculated them from the raw numbers also given. Sources for collectivization: computed from data in KSH (1959a, 1959b, 1960a, 1960b, 1962a, 1962b). The "d." is an abbreviation for *district (járás)*; the "t." for town.

Source: Sources for enrollment in Hajdú-Bihar are: HB28/1962, M63/1964; HB89/1965, HB116/1970; in Zala: M43/1958, M50/1962, Z35/1964, Z36/1964, Z38/1965, Z90/1960, Z137/1960, Z74/1959, Z136/1959, Z139/1963, Z80/1962, Z81/1964, Z138.5/1962, Z73/1964, and Z8/1962.

184

they are a mere 1.2 percent.[127] They decline even further in the ensuing years, and including these data only clutter an already large table. For Hungary as a whole registration rates are a mere 3.2 percent by 1987.[128] Second, and more importantly, the State introduced church religious instruction beginning in 1975. This instruction was subject to many of the same rules as its counterpart in the schools. For example, the instructors were not to question the children and could not employ visual aids. Moreover, limitations on the maximum number of children that could attend per parish meant that fewer than half of all age-eligible Catholic children could actually attend. Nonetheless, the churches represented a venue that might prove less troublesome than the schools.[129] By 1976, in Zala county church instruction had put a considerable dent into the number of students attending school religious instruction. The priests were seen to be focusing more on the church version and attendance seemed to be climbing in rough proportion to the decline of school instruction. In the village of Belezna, for example, not a single student attended religion class at school, but over 90 percent did so at church.[130] By the 1984–5 school year, as many as ten times as many Catholic students in some Church bishoprics had their religious instruction in the churches as in the schools. The church was a more popular venue for this instruction across all eleven bishoprics.[131] Clearly, then, after the mid-1970s school instruction data do not reflect the true state of the church community.

Perhaps the most striking feature of Table 5.1 is the dramatic drop in registration levels and concomitant rise in collectivization in the years after 1958, across all districts. One measure of the decline is the percentage of the 1958 level remaining by 1963 (obtained by dividing the 1963 level by the 1958 level). Thus, for example, in Zalaszentgrót district (Zala county) the level of registration in 1963 is only 28 percent of its 1958 level. In Püspökladányi (Hajdú-Bihar county) the 1963 level is only 5 percent of the 1958 level. The towns (with a "t.") fell even faster than the rural districts,

[127] Z70/1975 and HB134/1975.
[128] Tomka (1991b: 33).
[129] András and Morel (1983a: 285–6) note that since 1950 there had already been limited church instruction for children preparing for First Communion and Confirmation, and that some instructors had expanded its scope with the tacit approval of the local authorities. Thus, what finally happened in the 1970s was in part a codification of preexisting informal practice. For a discussion of the evolution of this instruction, see ibid.: 285–90.
[130] Z150/1976.
[131] Tomka (1988b: 555–9), especially Table 30.

accelerating a trend that, as we saw in Chapter 4, had already begun before 1956.[132] The two columns on the far right of the table represent the percentage of families that were members of collective farms in 1959, at the beginning of the recollectivization drive, and 1962, when it was nearing its end.[133] In both counties the rapid introduction of collectivization is illustrated in the substantial jump in the proportion of families participating between 1959 and 1962.

There is no denying that the sharp decline in religious instruction represented a blow to the Churches and a failure, in the aggregate, for the clergy. In some ways these trends validate Marxian views of the relationship between production relations and adherence to religion. The decline between 1958 and 1963 was too rapid to be attributable solely to the Party's energetic if often clumsy indoctrination efforts or other slow-moving processes of secularization. Rather, it appears to be directly related to the success with which the Party had managed to restructure the way in which agricultural workers relate to each other and to their land. Empirical studies in the Soviet Union show that membership in collectives (and other official institutions) work against loyalty to the Church in two ways. First, they are thought to have served as vehicles through which to disseminate socialist ideology to rural folk who may not otherwise have had much contact with it. Much as children get exposed to socialism in schools, so too are their parents, on an almost daily basis, in the collectives. Second, they are said to have offered an alternative source of recreation or companionship. Those engaged in private farming have, in this

[132] Note, however, that these data comprise the sum of the registration levels for the lower grades [alsótagozat] and the upper grades [felsőtagozat]. The principal difference between the two is that the former was necessary in preparation for Confirmation and First Communion, whereas the latter was optional from that perspective. This is important because over time attendance in the upper-division classes fell more steeply than in the lower-division classes. The decline evident in the table would thus have appeared much less drastic had data only for the lower grades been used. For example, in the Zalaegerszeg district of Zala county in 1965, 18% of all students were enrolled in religious instruction. This figure represents an average of 28% of the lower division and only 10% of the upper division. See Z141/1965. Moreover, in some cases registration levels for the lower division actually rose over time, bucking the almost universal downward trend. In the Zalaegerszeg district, for example, lower-division registration grew from 28% to 32% between 1965 and 1969. See Z141/1965 and Z142/1969. Despite the evident advantages of employing this measure, I prefer to use the combined figures because they are a worse-case scenario for my argument on the resilience of church community.

[133] Figures represent the situation as of December 31 of each year and have been rounded off to the nearest percent.

argument, a far greater need for the community provided by their fellow believers.[134]

Ethnographic accounts of religiosity suggest that collectivization contributed to a decline in religiosity by eroding the prevailing community expectation that had nurtured it. In Pécsely (Veszprém county), for example, villagers "unanimously mark 1960 as the turning point in religious practice and relationship to the Church, both for Protestants and Catholics...."[135] This date coincided with collectivization. Some villagers argued that the need to work household plots on Sundays precluded them from regularly attending church. Others claimed they were too old, ill, or tired, and that in any case the church seemed to fill up only on religious holidays and for funerals.[136] These sentiments, which acknowledge no expectation to engage in religious practice, stand in contrast to those expressed before 1956 (see Chapter 4). In Bakonycsernye (Veszprém county) villagers offered a similar litany: "the mines and the collectives divert people from church" and "people are interested in money, not religion."[137] For Kislapos (Heves county), Bell (1984: 150–4) relates a similar story. Although church attendance remained relatively high among the elderly in the aftermath of collectivization, those of working age explained their absence by citing the need to work on Sunday or the importance of family time in cases where family members commuted to work or school. In Kislapos, the collective became the forum where the entire community came together, obviating the need for church. This stands in sharp contrast to Vársány (Nógrád county), a village where far fewer people were employed in collectives. There the church reigned supreme in community life. For those villagers, "religion unites the community" and "a person has to belong somewhere."[138]

The nexus between collectivization and the decline of religiosity should not be overstated. If the connection were really that direct, then we would expect to see religiosity fall in rough proportion with rises in collective participation rates. The empirical patterns, however, are more subtle. First, contrary to expectation, the correlation between 1962 participation rates and 1963 religious instruction rates (see Table 5.1) is positive (0.20), not

[134] Powell (1975: 140–1).
[135] Vasary (1987: 236).
[136] Ibid.: 237.
[137] Kardos (1969: 99).
[138] Jávor (1978: 336).

negative.[139] In this admittedly small sample, higher rates of collectivization in 1962 are weakly associated with higher rates of religiosity in 1963.
This is probably a chance event (statistically speaking), but it does illustrate that one cannot take as given the necessarily disruptive nature of
collectivization. Second, within districts the pace of collectivization can be
far more pronounced than the collapse of religiosity. Thus, for example,
in Debrecen district participation in collectivization roughly sextupled between 1959 and 1962 (9 percent to 53 percent), while between 1960 and
1963 religiosity declined by only just over a half (from 32.3 percent to
14.6 percent). Similarly, in Derecske district during the same periods, collectivization quintupled (from 16 percent to 81 percent), while religiosity
declined by only 41 percent (from 24.6 percent to 14.6 percent). Finally,
moving from the district to the village level, it becomes clear that there were
many cases in which religiosity was maintained even with collectivization.
In Hajdú-Bihar county in 1961, for example, 93 percent of the families in
Bihartorda had joined collectives and 45 percent of children were registered for religious instruction. Excepting the extremely unlikely possibility
that the 7 percent of families who were not in collectives were having
45 percent of the children, it is clear that many of those in collectives must
have been registering their children for religious instruction. Similar arguments can be made for the villages of Csökmő, Körösszakál, Nagykereki,
Váncsod, and many others.[140] Survey research in other parts of Hungary
from the early 1970s further backs up the claim: 30 percent of collective
members in Somogy county and 27.3 percent in Heves county attended
church weekly. In three strongly Catholic communities in Heves county
44 percent attended church *daily*.[141]

To what extent can trends in religious practice be attributed to clerical
mobilization (or the lack thereof)? Isolating any one factor is difficult. First,
it bears repeating that district- and town-level data are too highly aggregated
to shed much light on the tactics of individual clergymen, their adversaries
among the cadres, or other settlement-level activities. The continuing

[139] The dates used for the two factors are different because of differences in the time of year
when each piece of data is collected. The collectivization data are as of December 31 of
the relevant year, while religious instruction registration occurs midyear. To evaluate the
effect of collectivization on religiosity, it is thus necessary to use collectivization data from
the previous year.
[140] Sources for collectivization are the same as for Table 5.1. Religious instruction data for
1961 are taken from HB37/1961.
[141] Tomka (1979b: 65).

188

wide range of enrollment levels lurking beneath the district-level averages can be illustrated using 1958 data from Nagykanizsa district. As shown in Table 5.1, the overall level was 67 percent. The range of enrollment across this district's fifty-eight villages, however, ranged from 0 percent to 92 percent. In 19 percent of these villages fewer than 50 percent of children were enrolled, and in 26 percent of the villages greater than 80 percent were. The level reported in the table is thus an average of quite disparate quantities.[142]

Second, as in the pre-1956 period limitations in the source material complicate efforts to assemble the requisite contextual information for enough settlements to disentangle clerical from other factors. That is, there are data on the activities of the clergy and the cadres for far fewer settlements than for which we know the level of religious instruction and other demographic characteristics. As we have seen, the Party was assiduous in monitoring local religious life. However, it tended to focus its reporting activities on the most oppositional elements within the clergy and on the most zealous or blundering local officials. Only in exceptional cases do the data correspond for any one settlement in a way that can illuminate religiosity as a joint result of both active priests and weak cadres. Consequently, while we can employ a "large-N" analysis to identify a number of correlates of elevated religious enrollment, the influence of the local clergy cannot be established in a similar fashion.

Nonetheless, there is substantial evidence of clerical success. It is most easily seen in instances where enrollment levels jumped significantly from one year to the next. For example, Zoltán Lőrincz, a young Roman Catholic priest in Kismarja (Hajdú-Bihar county), was known to have reactionary views. He openly complained of the harassment the Party dealt to the faithful and attempted to reach out to young people beyond church services. His efforts succeeded: the number of Roman Catholic children registered for religious instruction doubled between 1958 and 1959.[143] Another

---

[142] See Z126/1958 for the data. Even village-level data may not be disaggregated enough. Confessionally mixed villages, like the larger towns, had more than one priest. Because religious instruction in the schools was not generally divided by confession, the level of enrollment in such a village would have reflected the possibly disparate enrollment rates across each confession.

[143] HB44/1959. Lőrincz's experience also illustrates the dangers of appearing to be too reactionary. In an interrogation by the ÁEH in 1962, he was unapologetic about his actions, which he insisted were necessary in the service of the Church. The ÁEH ultimately recommended that his supplemental income be revoked. See HB26/1962.

creative priest sought to bypass the obstacles put forth by the local cadres by announcing that the church would serve as an alternative site for registration. This resulted in a jump in registration from 48 percent to 72 percent.[144] A similar incident occurred in Zalaszabár (Zala county) the same year.[145]

It is not necessary, however, to focus merely on cases of unusual fluctuation. Striking evidence of clerical efficacy is also visible in differing rates of enrollment between settlements where local cadres enroll their children and those where they do not. Recall that in the battle over registration for religious instruction local communists and State functionaries were pivotal actors. For the Party they were to be the front line in efforts to frustrate the clergy and dissuade parents from enrolling their children. For the Churches the local representatives of the regime were special targets of evangelization: if they could be convinced to register their children, it would send an unmistakable signal to others that there need be no fear in them also doing so. As one Party member summed it up, "it causes unbelievable damage in the countryside when communist parents create a precedent with their enrolled children."[146] In short, settlements might tip toward high enrollment levels.

The Churches' expectations and the Party's fears were well-founded. The Party oversaw the collection across settlements not only of the number of children enrolled in religious instruction, but often the number of Party members and State functionaries. By comparing the rates of enrollment of settlements where no Party cadres or functionaries enrolled their children with settlements where at least one such pivotal person did, we can evaluate the advantage accruing to the Churches of "turning" a Party cadre or functionary. In Nagykanizsa district (Zala county) in 1958, there were thirteen settlements where neither Party members nor council members enrolled their children, and the average rate of registration was 50 percent. Among the remaining forty-five settlements it was 70 percent, a twenty percentage point difference.[147] In Baktalóránthaza district

---

[144] M47/1958.
[145] M43/1958.
[146] M39/1958.
[147] See Z126/1958 for the data. A two-sample *t*-test confirms that this difference is too large to have occurred by random chance (at a 0.05 confidence level). The relationship also holds, albeit less strongly, when the analysis is run separately for Party members and council members. Interestingly, the average rate of registration is 63% for settlements where no Party members' children were enrolled, but only 50% where no council members' children were enrolled. One might have thought Party members, for whom religion was

(Szabolcs-Szatmár-Bereg county) we can see more clearly the comparative advantage for the Churches of focusing on Party members. In 1964, across twelve settlements without Party enrollment, registration levels averaged 16 percent, versus 36 percent for the remaining seven settlements. In 1966, the corresponding levels were 18 percent and 30 percent respectively.[148] When State employees registered their children, by contrast, there was a lesser boost in registration, 2 percentage points in 1964 and 6 in 1966.[149] This may reflect the fact that many State functionaries were not Party members, which would render their behavior less effective as a signal of potential Party acquiescence.

Less dramatic outcomes can also furnish evidence. One of the key assumptions of the pre-1956 discussion was that the underlying demand for customary public religious observance remained relatively high, even if State repression prevented people from actually participating. It was this demand that fueled the tipping process in favor of religious instruction once the clergy had provided the spark. What limited registration levels in the early 1950s for most people was a combination of red tape, harassment, and the fear of persecution or discrimination in education and employment. By the 1960s, however, the presumption of high latent demand for religious practice was becoming less tenable because the Party's battle against religious belief was making inroads, particularly among young people. One survey of high school students in 1966-7 found that 57.5 percent declared themselves atheists, 20 percent were uncertain, and only 20.2 percent considered themselves religious.[150] That roughly half of the respondents admitted atheism is dramatic evidence of the Party's progress. In a different

---

not a personal matter, would have provided better signals than council members. This result may be an artifact of the data: some settlements may be so religious, or so small, that there were no Party members at all. In Lenti district in 1958, for example, the average rate for settlements with no Party children enrolled was 69%, versus only 59% where there were such children. See Z129/1958.

[148] In both cases two-sample *t*-tests are significant at the 0.05 level. Note that these jumps do not represent the direct effect of adding the children of Party members. In most cases, only one or two cadres per settlement enrolled their children, far less than would be mathematically necessary to effect such substantial jumps in rates.

[149] In neither case are these differences statistically significant.

[150] The survey is discussed in Medyesy (1980: 128). Two issues should be noted regarding the use of communist-era survey data. First, samples may not have been randomly chosen, so the results may not reflect the beliefs of the country's students as a whole. Second, on an issue as sensitive to the Party as adherence to the materialist worldview, some respondents may be reticent about revealing their true beliefs. Thus, the results for a given sample may underestimate the number of believers.

survey, of high school students just in major cities, 45.5 percent declared themselves "definitely atheist," while only 8.7 percent admitted being a believer.[151] In a 1965 survey of rural eighth graders in one village, 45 percent gave a scientific explanation for the origin of the universe, but 53 percent gave a religious explanation.[152] As in all surveys, the numbers can be sensitive to question wording. Thus, while 87 percent of collective members in Somogy county "believed in God," only 45 percent believed in an afterlife.[153]

There is a twofold significance to the increase in the number of declared nonbelievers. First, in theoretical terms, these nonreligious individuals, presumably outside local church institutions, would have been particularly vulnerable to Party blandishments. Leaving the Churches did not automatically imply the acceptance of socialist views: as noted in the introductory chapter, there is a difference between dropping your old loyalties and adopting new ones. But it did render them susceptible to pressures in that direction. Second, from an empirical perspective, the more religious belief erodes, the greater the clerical effort required to achieve a given level of mobilization, and the less likely we will see macrolevel evidence of tipping in favor of more religious instruction. Whereas in the early years of the regime the principal obstacle to increasing religiosity was facing down overeager local cadres and assuaging popular fears of retribution, by the 1960s the clergy began to face the problem of persuading people that religious practice was worthwhile at all. This would require far more evangelization and organizational effort. To the extent the pool of people who might be members of the church community shrunk, so too would the prospect of observing the effects of tipping, even at the village level. To see this, consider a settlement consisting only of "atheists" and "believers." The larger the pool of atheists relative to believers, the more difficult it will be to gauge changes in religiosity among believers, which is observed at the settlement level. Put another way, if the population of a hypothetical settlement were only 10 percent believers, then even if religiosity jumped from 0 percent to 100 percent of believers, the observed level for the settlement would rise by only 10 percentage points.[154]

[151] Ibid.: 131.
[152] Ibid.: 130.
[153] Tomka (1979b: 64).
[154] This assumes that there is no simultaneous change in the fraction of "atheists" engaged in religious practice.

192

5.7 Reassessing the Battle for Souls

Under these circumstances clerical success should also be measured one person at a time. In Fülöp (Hajdú-Bihar county) in 1964, for example, the Catholic priest induced local council members to enroll their children by threatening to deny Communion to those children who did not attend religion class.[155] Sometimes success meant preventing a decrease in religiosity rather than facilitating an increase. Because of the local priest, in Sárhida (Zala county) religious instruction remained at 28 percent rather than declining from 1961 to 1962. Apparently, past experience had led some parents to fear that enrolled children would have a more difficult time getting into high school. In 1962, however, it became known that the high school admitted three students who had been attending religious instruction continuously for eight years. The priest exploited this fact to reassure wary parents that their children would face no discrimination for having been enrolled.[156]

Even decreases in religiosity from year to year can, in principle, be consistent with clerical mobilization. Consider a hypothetical village in which 100 percent of the children are enrolled in religious instruction in a given year and the Party decides to focus resources on reducing this number. Suppose the following year the Party succeeds in ensuring that only 50 percent of the children are signed up. Suppose further that the decrease was a result not of red tape or intimidation, but of a concerted effort at educating parents in the principles of materialism and the peccadillos of the Churches. In one sense such a dramatic decline represents a great victory for the Party: if the goal is 0 percent religiosity, then then half the battle is won. However the nature of the victory – and of the clerical failure – depends in part on the scale of the effort the Party devoted to the task. Given enough resources strategically deployed the Party would be able to steamroll all but the most devout of parents. The parish clergy was no match for the local cadres when the latter were determined enough. In such circumstances, a 50 percent enrollment level could be interpreted as a triumph for the clergy, because in the absence of any countervailing factors the level might have been reduced much further.[157]

---

[155] HB64/1964.

[156] Z138.5/1962. It is worth noting that other members of the local church establishment often engaged in mobilizational activities. In one village in Hajdú-Bihar county, for example, the high level of religious instruction in 1959 is attributed not to the priest, but to the efforts of the religion instructor. See HB45/1959.

[157] There is ample evidence that the Party targeted religious villages for extra attention. However, we cannot know, in cases of decline, what the level would have been had the clergyman in a particular settlement not been present.

Of course, not all clerical activities were necessarily successful. In several communities in Hajdú-Bihar county, for example, the number of young people preparing to take First Communion dropped steadily between 1958 and 1961, despite energetic organizational efforts by the priests.[158] One Reformed minister noted the difficulties in finding lay church leaders: "to the extent that members of the congregation focus their energies on communal work, they evince less interest toward religious life, the Church, and their local church."[159] Inactive or unpopular priests could do damage. The clergy in several Zala county villages in 1960 did not concern themselves with deepening religious life and were sometimes observed to engage in drunkenness and other objectionable behavior. Consequently, they lost the respect of their parishioners, who kept their distance from the church.[160] These observations are consistent with Hann's observation that "a great deal depends on the character of the ministers."[161] In Tázlár during the 1960s, the ministers maintained neutrality with regard to affairs of State, using the pulpit for occasional diatribes on declining moral standards, but otherwise not engaging with the secular world of the village. Hann notes that "the quietest stance of the Church is rendering it increasingly isolated in the new community and at the same time preventing it from expressing the conservative opinions of the old."[162] The Churches apparently ceded the capital Budapest to the Party. A report from 1964 relates how the clergy was not seen to expend a great deal of effort evangelizing, an observation all too clear from the registration data for the 1964–5 school year: on average only 0.98 percent of students were enrolled in religious instruction.[163]

It is difficult to pin down accurate figures on what proportion of all clergymen engaged in mobilizational activities. The Party, as we have seen, tended to view the clergy in terms of its perceived loyalty to socialism: reactionary priests were thought to oppose socialism; progressive (peace) priests were seen to support it; and neutral or passive priests were viewed as vacillators. This classification suited the Party's need to gauge its progress in "converting" the priesthood to socialism. As of 1960 in Zala county, for example, the Party classified as peace priests 22 percent of 158 clergymen.[164]

---

[158] HB31/1961.
[159] Cited in HB22/1962.
[160] Z26/1960.
[161] Hann (1980: 120).
[162] Ibid.: 121.
[163] M61/1964.
[164] Z26/1960.

By 1959, an estimated 30 percent of the Catholic priests in Hajdú-Bihar county were similarly classified.[165] These numbers are important insofar as they roughly indicate the proportion of clergy who continued to resist the various rewards available to the progressive priests.[166] In terms of local church life, however, the most important distinction was between active and inactive priests, which cut across the Party's politically inspired categories. As one observer noted, both reactionary and progressive priests attempted to deepen religious life; they differed only in the methods employed.[167]

Some evidence of the breath of mobilization emerges from Zala county. Recall that in the aftermath of the 1956 revolution the regime passed a law asserting its right to approve of all Episcopal and clerical appointments, including those that were made by the Churches during the revolutionary period. The Party kept a particularly watchful eye on the latter and compiled reports on these priests. One such report from 1967 details, for each of seventeen clergymen, whether the priest's behavior was positive, neutral, or negative vis-à-vis the regime; his political activities, if any; and how active or inactive he was in fostering religious life.[168] The assignations appear to be based entirely on the impressions of an ÁEH functionary, but they do provide a glimpse, however small, into the state of the priesthood as of the mid-1960s. Of the seventeen clergymen, eleven were peace priests and four were reactionaries. Only two of the seventeen were considered inactive, nine were fairly active, and six were active. Thus 35 percent of the priests were considered active in deepening religious life and fully 88 percent were either active or fairly active. There is no way to know what activities the priests engaged in to earned these monikers, or whether they were active enough to have effected changes in religiosity. But it does illustrate a lingering resilience against a determined foe.

Who were these recalcitrant clergymen? Catholic priests were noticeably more resistant than Reformed pastors, a finding consistent with

---

[165] HB19/1959.

[166] The actual proportion of reactionary priests is almost certainly higher than the numbers indicate because some clergymen were undoubtedly feigning progressiveness to benefit from the Party's largess. The Party continued to expend resources trying to ferret out suspected closet reactionaries, but the process was by no means a witch hunt. A 1962 report notes that several clergymen that had previously been classified as either neutral or reactionary were, upon further investigation, actually more progressive than had been believed. See HB22/1962.

[167] HB22/1962.

[168] Z48/1967.

the differences between the two Churches identified in Chapter 1. The Reformed Church's more sympathetic stance toward socialism led to greater clerical participation in government. For example, disproportionately more Reformed pastors occupied seats on the countywide Patriotic Peoples Front committees.[169] This is not in itself evidence of resistance, as some of these priests may well have assumed these positions to obstruct rather than facilitate government policy. However, for Hajdú-Bihar we also know that only two out of eighteen (11 percent) of Reformed pastors in key positions were considered reactionary, versus four out of nine (44 percent) Roman Catholics and one out of four (25 percent) Greek Catholics.[170] Even outside of government the Catholic priesthood was more oppositional: as of the late 1950s in Hajdú-Bihar roughly 10 to 12 percent of the Reformed pastors were considered reactionary, versus 15 to 18 percent of the Roman Catholic priests, and 20 to 22 percent of the Greek Catholic priests.[171]

The Calvinist clergy also appeared to devote less energy to preserving church life. One Party informant in Hajdú-Bihar noted that "the Greek Catholic and Roman Catholic priests and parents engage in more activity during the year than the Reformed."[172] Another remarked how the Catholic episcopate dealt with the collectivization issue with notably less vigor than the Calvinist leadership.[173] This pattern of relative inactivity existed nationally: according to one report, the counties with the lowest levels of religious instruction were predominantly Protestant, and that one reason was that "in comparison with the [Roman] Catholic Church, the Protestant Churches in general did not perform adequate preparatory work."[174] The Catholic Church continued to perform better than the Reformed Church even as it lost proportionally more priests. Between 1960 and 1967 the number of active Catholic priests and preachers declined from 4,400 to 3,733, a 15 percent drop. The Reformed decrease was only 9 percent, from 1,610 to 1,460.[175]

---

[169] M05/1959.

[170] HB19/1959.

[171] HB19/1959. Greek Catholics (Uniates) comprised approximately 8% of the population in Hajdú-Bihar. Though this confession has not figured prominently in the discussion thus far, local observers considered these priests to be the most reactionary of all. For comparison's sake I include information on this confession here even though I do not focus on the resistance activities of Greek Catholic priests.

[172] HB39/1960.

[173] HB23/1962.

[174] M45/1958.

[175] Tibori (1998: 133).

The preponderance of Roman (and Greek) Catholics among students registered for religious instruction can be unambiguously demonstrated for Hajdú-Bihar. As of the early 1960s, the Hajdú-Bihar population was comprised of approximately 68 percent Reformed, 15 percent Roman Catholic, and 8 percent Greek Catholic.[176] Yet in 1960, the Reformed constituted only 55% of the children enrolled in religious instruction, Greek Catholics made up 24 percent, and Roman Catholics an additional 20 percent. Thus Roman and Greek Catholics were overrepresented among the religion students and the Reformed were underrepresented.[177] In terms of raw numbers all three confessions had many fewer religion students in 1964, after collectivization, than in 1960. Greek Catholic enrollment dropped from 2,810 to 1,970; Roman Catholic fell from 2,346 to 1,032. But the drop was catastrophic for the Reformed: 6,323 to 1,625. The Reformed comprised only 35 percent of the religion students, the Roman Catholics 22 percent, and the Greek Catholics 42 percent. Thus, not only was the Reformed Church less well represented before socialist agriculture transformed the village, it also proved less able to combat collectivization's pressures on the church community.[178] The absolute decline for all Churches and the disproportionate Reformed deterioration continued throughout the 1960s. Between 1965 and 1970 the number of Reformed students in religion class dropped from 1,216 to 222, or roughly 82 percentage points. Roman Catholics sunk from 1,001 to 345, or 66 percentage points. Greek Catholics remained the most resilient, decreasing by "only" 57 percentage points, from 1,780 to 773.[179]

Hajdú-Bihar county was not unique, though the scale of decline differed in other places. In the Baktalórántháza district of Szabolcs-Szatmár-Bereg county, for example, the absolute number of students enrolled in religious

---

[176] M63/1964. This estimate is only slightly different from the distribution obtained in the 1949 census: 70% Reformed, 18% Roman Catholic, and 8% Greek Catholic. See KSH (1996: 11).

[177] See HB39/1960 for the data. In principle, this effect could be due to differential birthrates across confessions. If Catholics have more children than the Reformed, then the confessional distribution of children in school will not reflect the distribution in the population. However, according to Kamarás (1995: 121) the relative proportion of the different denominations remained relatively stable during the communist period.

[178] Compare the numbers in HB39/1960 and M63/1964. Also, we see again that the losses were much greater for upper-division religious instruction. The absolute number of lower-division students dropped by "only" 50%, whereas for the upper-division it was 62%.

[179] Compare the numbers in HB89/1965 and HB116/1970.

instruction dropped from 1816 in 1964 to 898 in 1969, but the decline hit each confession more evenly than in Hajdú-Bihar: the Reformed component of the totals dropped from 46 percent to only 44 percent.[180] Religious belief (as opposed to practice) was also decaying more rapidly among Calvinists. One national survey from the first half of the 1970s found that 49 percent of Catholics but only 41 percent of Calvinists declared themselves to be religious. Catholics were substantially more pious than Calvinists across all education groups, major occupational groups, and age groups except the over-sixty crowd.[181] These confessional patterns of belief and religiosity are wholly consistent with the findings in Table 5.1, which show lower religiosity in predominantly Calvinist Hajdú-Bihar. One cannot help but marvel at how well these findings reflect doctrinal differences between the Roman Catholic Church, which puts such emphasis on ritual, and the Calvinist Church, whose operating principle is *sola fide* (faith alone).[182]

5.8 Beyond Religious Instruction

It would have been far beyond the scope of this book to have given a full accounting of the Churches' experience under state-socialism, yet it should be acknowledged that religious instruction is only one of many possible indicators of religiosity, and an imperfect indicator of underlying religious beliefs. In this section, I briefly summarize trends in other indices of church life, focusing in particular on the Catholic Church. Most reflect the downward pattern of the religious instruction data, lending extra confidence that these data portray the actual level of church community with fair accuracy. Church attendance, for example, remained at roughly 80 percent until 1951 (aggregating all confessions), and then began a dramatic decline, to approximately 20 percent, by the beginning of the 1980s. The percentage of people who never attended church grew in the same period to over 30.[183]

---

[180] Computed from data in Sz6/1964, Sz9/1966, and Sz10/1969.

[181] For example, among those in their 20s, 30% of Catholics were religious versus only 18% of Calvinists. Among university graduates the proportions were 25% and 16%; among intellectuals 19% and 9%. See Tomka (1979a: 123–4).

[182] This curt formulation comes from Molnár and Tomka (1989: 214).

[183] Froese (2001: 254). Note that these are retrospective data, constructed by asking participants in one 1991 survey to recall their childhood experiences in church. As such, they are likely to suffer from recall bias and ought to be seen only as approximate indicators of the true underlying religiosity.

Rites of passage remained one of the Catholic Church's most cherished means of maintaining contact with the laity. Christenings, weddings, and funerals presented opportunities to reinforce the faith of those who might have wandered from the Church, and to maintain the connection between religiosity and the everyday life of parishioners. As discussed previously, the State initiated substitute civil ceremonies in the late 1950s. We lack systematic longitudinal data on the popularity of civil ceremonies, but we can chart the evolution of adherence to the Catholic rites. Between 1951 and 1984, the percentage of Catholic newborns that were christened declined from 100 to 71, or roughly 29 percentage points. The percentage of Catholic couples undergoing church weddings declined by 33 percentage points during the same period, from 74 to 41 percent.[184]

If christenings and church weddings were losing their allure, the same cannot be said for religious burials: they declined by only 9 percentage points. Thus, while christenings declined by a third, and weddings by nearly a half, Catholic funerals remained nearly as popular in 1984 as they had been in 1951.[185] This confirms the remark of one villager in Kislapos (Heves county) that "[e]ven the greatest Communist when he dies, or before death, calls for the priest to give last rites."[186] For most communists and their sympathizers, then, it was better to be safe than sorry. More significantly, the percentage of all Hungarians who self-declare as religious, which reached a low point of 44.3 percent in 1977, rose to 58.1 percent by 1988, and nearly 71 percent by 1993.[187] This new spirituality manifested itself in the Catholic base communities and evangelical Protestant groups. These "parallel Churches" lacked the established Churches' resources, but also their onus of collaboration. They strove "for the totality of Christian life and witness."[188]

---

[184] Tomka (1988b: 533–5).

[185] Tomka (ibid.: 539). Csanád (1976) compares religiosity in 1932 and 1971 using a composite index involving christenings, weddings, and funerals, and finds that religiosity had declined by only 16 percentage points. Interestingly, he also finds that Catholic religiosity is significantly higher in Zala county than it is in Hajdú-Bihar county. This suggests that the roots of religiosity lay not just in features of the confession, but in "contextual" features of where the churches are located.

[186] Cited in Bell (1984: 152).

[187] Froese (2001: 259).

[188] Tomka (1988a: 175–6).

5.9 Conclusion

This chapter has recounted the battle from below between the Churches and the Party for mass allegiance, documenting the many twists and turns in efforts by each side to undermine the influence of the other. Using registration rates for religious instruction in the schools as an empirical marker, it chronicled the evolution of church community through repression, materialist education, and economic transformation. Parish priests and local cadres played starring roles in this drama as the "shock troops" for their respective institutions. We discovered that as socialism wore on, and society became more secular, the clergy was compelled to devise ever-more creative methods to prevent the decline of the church community. Catholic priests proved far more adept at maintaining church institutions than Calvinist pastors, who labored under a leadership far more sympathetic to socialism.

We have not yet, however, illustrated any of the macropolitical consequences of these clerical activities. How is the maintenance of local church institutions related to the transmission of rightist partisan attachments between pre- and post-communism? How strong did church community have to be for transmission to take place? Did confessional differences during state-socialism carry over into the postcommunist period? It is to these questions that we now turn.

6

Church Community and Rightist Persistence

STATISTICAL EVIDENCE

6.1 Introduction

Chapter 2 illustrated extraordinary electoral continuities and discontinuities between pre- and postcommunism. Chapters 3 through 5 retold the Churches' battle against the Party's efforts to remake partisan attachments in society, documenting the often brave struggle of the local clergy and the laity to preserve church community through decades of repression and informal incentives to abandon the Churches. We saw that Roman Catholic priests tended to more actively mobilize their parishioners against the communists than Calvinist pastors, and that church community tended to be higher among Catholics than among Calvinists. This chapter brings together the quantitative findings of Chapter 2 with the historical arguments of Chapters 3 through 5. It demonstrates through a series of statistical analyses that church community transmitted precommunist rightist attachments into postcommunist politics.

There are numerous pitfalls on the path toward generating statistical estimates of the effect of church community, each of which must be recognized and, if possible, addressed. First, as in prior chapters, I employ the fraction of children registered for religious instruction in the schools as a proxy for church community in each settlement. Although these data are the richest available that can also be matched with pre- and postcommunist electoral outcomes, it bears repeating that they are an imperfect measure and almost certainly underestimate the actual level of church community. For example, the elderly are ignored entirely. They are more likely to attend church, but have no children to boost religious instruction. In a village with only elderly people, "church community" would be zero, but actual church community would be quite high. Moreover, as documented in Chapter 5, religious instruction in the schools was in decline by the 1970s as more and more people took advantage of church instruction. That development, and an apparent jump in Hungarians' religiosity between 1978 and 1990, is not reflected at all in the school data.[1] Fortunately, the bias is systematic in one direction. If we assume that the magnitude of the deviation is uniform across settlements, then the statistical results would be identical to those using actual church community data.

Second, theory provides little guidance on how church community should be specified in a statistical model. We know that higher levels of church community during communism ought to be associated with greater persistence in rightist attachments, but not how best to characterize the religious trajectories of settlements. To ensure the robustness of the results, I thus employ multiple indicators, including the average level of church community over time within settlements, the actual level of church community in select years, and indicator variables describing different possible trajectories for church community through time. I describe each of these more fully later in the chapter.

Third, the settlement is not the ideal level of analysis to reveal the effects of church community if these effects do exist. If church community is associated with rightist persistence, it is because individual church affiliates prefer rightist parties. Recall from previous chapters, however, that such individuals are not directly "visible" with settlement-level data, because most settlements are composed of both church affiliates and those not affiliated. To estimate the individual-level relationship between church affiliation and support for rightist parties from aggregate data I perform cross-level inferences using the $\mathfrak{E}I$ model described in King (1997). This will yield the estimated fraction of church affiliates that support rightist, leftist, and liberal parties. As explained shortly, the use of ecological inference in this case involves some heroic assumptions. To ensure that the results are not simply an artifact of these assumptions or the estimation method, I estimate similar outcomes with individual-level data from International Social Survey Program surveys from 1991 and 1998.

---

[1] The proportion of people declaring "I am religious" rose from 44% in 1978 to 66% by June 1990. See Froese (2001). Of course, we don't know what proportion of this increase reflects an increase in loyalty to the established Churches as opposed to a more general increase in spirituality. In either case, it represents a dramatic reversal of prior trends in secularization.

Fourth, it is necessary to account for competing explanations of rightist persistence. We identified one such possibility, underlying social and economic stasis, in the instrumental approaches discussion from Chapter 1. Postcommunist survey data reveal other correlates of rightist voting. To truly isolate the impact of church community it is necessary to embed it in a multivariate model. This can pose certain problems for analyses based on aggregate data, because some factors that are known to be correlated with rightist voting at the individual level may vary too little across geographic units for their effects to appear in an aggregate analysis. For example, surveys tell us that the rightist bloc is disproportionately composed of the elderly, but this effect might not appear in aggregate data because age may not vary much across settlements. Employing the aforementioned survey data I show that church community retains its explanatory importance even after controlling for the effects of age and other factors.

This chapter proceeds first by describing the sample of settlements on which the analysis is based. Section 6.3 replicates for the sample a portion of the analysis in Chapter 2. That is, it estimates the overall influence of the distant (precommunist) electoral past on postcommunist electoral outcomes, omitting all nonelectoral variables. Section 6.4 offers graphical evidence for the importance of church community in minimizing the differences between pre- and postcommunist rightist support. Sections 6.5 and 6.6 introduce and discuss multivariate statistical models of the postcommunist rightist vote. They show that church community accounts for rightist persistence even when controlling for other possible correlates of the rightist vote. Section 6.7 demonstrates that Catholic areas have stronger church community than Calvinist areas and that there exists confessional variation in party choice. Section 6.8 verifies through ecological inference and survey research that the aggregate relationships also hold at the individual level.

6.2 Sample Characteristics

Although the Party assiduously documented many skirmishes between clergymen and cadres, the registration numbers did not survive for each settlement in each year. However, the data for a couple hundred settlements spanning Veszprém and Zala counties in western Hungary, gleaned from the same archival materials that were used to document Church-Party struggles, happen to be particularly rich. In some cases the data go back to the early 1950s, but for more than 200 settlements it is possible to reconstruct the trajectory of the church community from the early 1960s through the early 1970s. For a smaller portion of the sample the series can be extended to 1979.

Reflecting national trends, the proportion of students enrolled in religious instruction in the schools declined in the sample throughout the 1960s. Whereas on average 61 percent of students were enrolled in 1961, in 1966 only 45 percent were enrolled, and by 1970 only 36 percent were enrolled.[2] But there were dramatic variations across settlements. Roughly one-quarter of all settlements in 1970 had enrollment levels greater than 55 percent. Five percent of them had levels above 75 percent, and another 5 percent had no enrollment at all. Even in 1979, when the average enrollment level had fallen to only 13 percent, nine settlements had levels over 50 percent. The overall decline in religious instruction was not exhibited by every settlement. In only 129 out of 220 places was there a monotonic decline between 1961 and 1970. In other cases there were increases or a fluctuation. The existence of longitudinal cross-sectional registration data renders this sample far more useful for statistical analysis than the larger number of settlements for which there exist scattered data for different years. In all cases, the data represent registration in both elementary and high schools.

It should be noted that this sample is not statistically representative of the universe of Hungarian settlements. Although these Western localities display wide variation both in their support for the Right and across a battery of demographic variables, they are nonetheless more rightist, more Catholic, and less Calvinist than the average. These differences between the sample and the universe of settlements are illustrated in Table 6.1. Note that this table shows averages across settlements (in percent), not the overall proportion of Catholics and Calvinists or the percentage support for the rightist bloc in the population.[3]

The nonrepresentativeness of the sample poses a problem only under two conditions, neither of which holds in the present case. The first would be if the only goal were to make inferences about all Hungarian settlements. Although it would have been preferable to be able to make such inferences,

[2] Where the 1966 data are missing, 1965 data are used instead.
[3] As in Chapter 2, I analyze only the vote for regional party lists. The major postcommunist rightist parties through 1998 include the Alliance of Young Democrats (Fidesz), the Hungarian Democratic Forum (MDF), the Christian Democratic People's, Party (KDNP), the Independent Smallholders Party (FKgP), the Hungarian Democratic People's Party (MDNP), and the Hungarian Justice and Life Party (MIÉP).

6.2 Sample Characteristics

Table 6.1 *Sample Demographic and Political Characteristics.*

	Sample	Hungary
Right Vote 1945	77%	68%
Right Vote 1990	55	49
Right Vote 1994	44	37
Right Vote 1998	67	59
% Catholic	79	63
% Calvinist	12	27

Note: The number of observations used to compute these quantities may vary. For Hungary $N = 2,800$ for the vote and $N = 928$ for the religious data. For the sample $N = 220$. These quantities represent averages across settlements.

the sample still yields valuable information on the church community's role in transmitting rightist attachments. The second condition would be if the sample were chosen in a way that was intended to maximize the church community's effect. Fortunately, that is not the case. There is no reason to believe that the vagaries of data collection and archiving that allowed such rich data to survive in these regions are or could be in any way related to electoral outcomes that none of the principals involved could even know about.

One advantage of settlements from the Catholic heartland in the West rather than the Protestant areas of the East is a much denser settlement structure. Veszprém and Zala counties each consist of more than 200 municipalities, and the average 1990 population across settlements is less than 2,000. The eastern county of Hajdú-Bihar, by contrast, consists of roughly eighty settlements, with an average population of more than 7,000. The median Hajdú-Bihar settlement has more than 2,000 inhabitants, while in Veszprém and Zala the number is under 600. All other things being equal, smaller settlements provide more information, because the population of interest is broken up into smaller units. Ultimately this increases variation across settlements while decreasing variation within settlements, resulting in better inferences all around.[4]

---

[4] At one time, all of Hungary had the dense structure of "microcommunities" visible in the North and West. The emergence of two different settlement structures can be traced back to the Turkish occupation of the sixteenth and seventeenth centuries. Turkish influence was greatest in South-East Hungary, where new administrative divisions with much larger settlements were introduced. The predominance of Protestantism was also preserved in Turkish-controlled areas. Well to the West of the Danube, by contrast, Hapsburg power

6.3 The Influence of the Past

I begin the analysis by revisiting for the sample the preliminary statistical analysis in Chapter 2, where the magnitude of electoral persistence was quantified by regressing the postcommunist vote on the precommunist vote. Our first task is to estimate the relative importance of distant and recent partisan patterns on contemporary electoral patterns. As in Chapter 2, I define the rightist vote margin as the difference between the rightist and leftist vote proportions in each settlement in each election year. Thus, as before, for 1998, $R98 = Right\ Vote\ 1998 - Left\ Vote\ 1998$, where $R98$ represents the rightist victory margin, with analogous transformations for 1990 and 1994. To gain a rough estimate of the influence of the electoral past I employ an Ordinary Least Squares (OLS) regression for each postcommunist election, as expressed in the following three equations, where i indexes over settlements:

$$R98_i = \beta_{08} + \beta_{18}R94_i + \beta_{28}R90_i + \beta_{38}R45_i + \epsilon_{i8} \qquad (6.1)$$
$$R94_i = \beta_{04} \qquad\qquad + \beta_{14}R90_i + \beta_{24}R45_i + \epsilon_{i4} \qquad (6.2)$$
$$R90_i = \beta_{00} \qquad\qquad\qquad\qquad + \beta_{10}R45_i + \epsilon_{i0} \qquad (6.3)$$

In this model, $R98$, $R94$, $R90$, and $R45$ represent the rightist vote margin. The β coefficients associated with these vote margins can be interpreted as the influence of a prior electoral outcome on the electoral outcome listed on the left-hand side. (The β_0 coefficients represent the general partisan swing because they are constant over settlements in any given election.) The error terms ϵ_i capture the idiosyncratic factors at work in each election and settlement.

The statistical results, with robust standard errors, are displayed in Table 6.2.[5] Each column of Table 6.2 represents a different postcommunist election, and each row represents the influence of past electoral outcomes. All results are statistically significant at the 0.05 level except those in italics. There are four noteworthy features of this table. First, the legacy of the

remained strong enough to preserve the original structure and ensure the success of the Counter-Reformation.

[5] Robust standard errors are computed because the wide range in sizes of settlements (ranging from less than 100 to more than 60,000) produces significant heteroscedasticity, with the smaller settlements exhibiting significantly higher vote variance than the larger settlements. Weighted least squares is not employed because it is theorized that traditions are locally transmitted, regardless of settlement size. Consequently, each settlement ought to be given equal weight in the estimation.

6.3 The Influence of the Past

Table 6.2   *OLS Regression: The Influence of the Past.*

Explanatory Variable	Election Year		
	1990	1994	1998
R94	–	–	0.55(0.07)
R90	–	0.61(0.06)	*0.02(0.06)*
R45	0.26(0.04)	0.17(0.03)	0.09(0.03)
Constant	0.30(0.02)	−0.18(0.03)	0.19(0.02)
R^2	0.16	0.55	0.53
N	295	295	274

Note: The table lists OLS regression coefficients and corresponding robust standard errors (in parentheses) for each explanatory variable and the constant term. All coefficients except the influence of $R90$ on $R98$ (listed in italics in the table) are significant at $p < 0.05$.

1945 outcome continues to persist through the 1998 election, even controlling for earlier postcommunist outcomes. That is, whatever partisan traditions are being created after 1990, they are not subsuming preexisting local political traditions. Second, the 1990 result does not influence the 1998 result once the 1994 result is controlled for (the 0.02 in the third column of results is statistically insignificant). That is, within the postcommunist regime it is necessary only to know the most-recent electoral outcome because it subsumes the previous outcomes within the same political regime. Thus, within postcommunism electoral loyalties are "updated" from the previous election. Third, these coefficients illustrate the significant electoral volatility within the postcommunist era. A coefficient of 1 represents a situation in which an outcome replicates an earlier outcome. Neither the 1994 influence on 1998 (0.55) nor the 1990 influence on 1994 (0.61) comes close to such replication. Finally, the difference in R^2 between the 1990 result and the other two outcomes is a result of the inclusion of the previous electoral outcome as a regressor in the 1994 and 1998 equations. These estimates, in particular the continued salience of the 1945 result, provide a baseline amount of persistence that needs to be explained.[6]

---

[6] For reference all three regressions were also run using the raw vote fractions for the Right. Given the different scale of these variables, the estimated magnitudes of the resulting coefficients are different, but their signs and statistical significance are similar.

6.4 *The Importance of Church Community:* Prima Facie *Evidence*

This section offers preliminary *prima facie* graphical evidence that church community transmitted precommunist rightist electoral traditions. Consider Figure 6.1, which displays scatterplots of the pre- and postcommunist rightist vote margins for settlements with "high" and "low" levels of church community. "High" and "low" are defined with respect to the average level across all settlements in the three snapshot years of 1961, 1966, and 1970. These specific dates are not in themselves of any special importance, but they do represent cut points between the 1945 and the postcommunist elections. I computed the average levels of church community in each year. Then I determined, for each settlement in each year, whether it fell above or below this average. A settlement with high community is defined as one whose level remained at least one-half of a standard deviation above the sample average in all three years. Similarly, settlements with low community fell at least one-half of a standard deviation below the sample average. This definition excludes a proportion of the sample from the graph – only 67 settlements fall into either the high or low category – but it permits a graphic illustration of the working hypothesis in more clear-cut cases. We will see shortly that these results hold even when this restriction is relaxed.

Each settlement in Figure 6.1 is represented by either an "X", if it had high church community, or an "O", if it had low church community. The diagonal lines in each panel represent the situation in which the pre- and postcommunist support for the Right exactly coincides. Similarly to the graphs in Chapter 2, if a settlement appears below the diagonal line, then its support for the Right has fallen relative to 1945. If a settlement is above the diagonal, then the Right has gained since 1945. The greater support for the Right in areas with high church community is visible in the general pattern of Xs being above Os in all three panels. That is, conditional on a given level of precommunist rightist vote margin, settlements with high church community during communism give more support to the postcommunist Right than settlements with low church community during communism. Because the Xs are closer to the diagonal – on average – than the Os, these settlements can be said to have better preserved the level of support they gave before the communists came to power. Difference of means tests for postcommunist rightist vote margin in high and low church community localities for all three elections support this

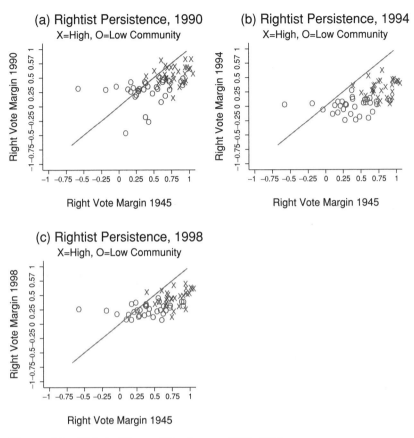

Figure 6.1 Rightist Electoral Persistence, 1945–1998.

conclusion: the differences visible in the graphs are not the result of random chance.[7]

There are two other important characteristics of this figure. First, the strength of church community and a settlement's precommunist support for the Right are not independent of one another. The Xs, or high community localities, tend to occur in the more conservative settlements, which cluster toward the upper right-hand portion of each panel. The Os, by contrast, are

---

[7] For each election, the average postcommunist vote margin for high localities was compared with that of low localities, to see if they were statistically different. In all three cases the margin for high settlements was higher than that for low settlements.

more numerous in settlements that before communism were more evenly divided between Left and Right. These are visible for all three panels on the horizontal axis where the rightist vote margin was less than or equal to 0.25. This pattern of Xs and Os is graphical evidence of the need for an interaction term in a statistical specification: church community matters more the more rightist a settlement is. The Os are especially prominent among those few places where the Left obtained a majority of the vote in 1945. Interestingly, the Right gained ground in these settlements. There are too few of these to make reliable generalizations, but it does serve as a reminder that there is a trajectory, largely unexamined in this book, leading from precommunist leftist support to postcommunist rightist support. Second, the national swing between the Left and the Right between 1994 and 1998 is visible in panels (b) and (c) in the number of settlements that move from having a negative rightist vote margin (meaning the Left received a plurality) to a positive rightist vote margin. This phenomenon is particularly visible among settlements with low church community, as evidenced by the upward movement of many Os between panels (b) and (c). This is evidence that the shift to the Right in 1998 was a feature of settlements where partisanship was not "anchored" in the legacy of local church institutions.

6.5 Multivariate Evidence

Figure 6.1 provides preliminary evidence that settlements with high church community better preserved their preferences for rightist parties than settlements with low church community. However, it is possible to do much better than draw inferences from a graph. First, as previously mentioned, I threw away a lot of potentially useful information to generate the high and low categorizations. Registration for religious instruction is a fraction that can range from 0 to 1, permitting a much more nuanced estimation than that achievable with dichotomous data. Second, the graph does not provide for any statistical controls. To discern the genuine effect of church community it is necessary to specify a multivariate model.

Instrumental approaches to voting behavior rely in some form on underlying social or economic stagnation to explain electoral persistence. Where there is little economic or social development, the argument runs, there is not likely to be dramatic change in electoral preferences. Cursory comparison of 1949 and 1990 census data in Chapter 1 showed that this scenario was unlikely to hold generally: the aggregate change wrought under state-socialism was simply too great. However, the argument might be valid for more peripheral settlements. Although no area of the country lay untouched by the communist experience, not all areas experienced the same degree of economic and social transformation. Consider relative levels of industrialization in 1949 and 1990, as indicated by census data on the number of industrial wage earners per settlement. For Hungary as a whole, the average settlement saw an increase in industrialization of roughly 30 percentage points, but 5 percent of settlements had increases of less than 10 percentage points. A similar result is obtained for the sample.[8] It is possible that those settlements experiencing the least change also retained more of their precommunist electoral preferences. To put it another way, greater change in the level of industrialization between 1949 and 1990 might be associated with greater losses for the Right.

As an initial test of this hypothesis I correlated the change in support for the Right between 1945 and each of the first three postcommunist elections with the change in the level of industrialization. Given the rapid economic restructuring since 1990, the 1990 census data on industrial workers are, at best, a crude indicator of the actual level of industrialization in 1994 and 1998. But they nonetheless provide a clue to the magnitude of economic transformation. Moreover, even though the proportion of industrial workers declined under the post-1989 reforms, unless these workers returned to the kinds of occupations held by their forebears in the 1940s, the economic structure of the settlement would still have changed dramatically. For the country as a whole, the correlation between change in levels of industrialization and support for the Right in 1990 is 0.09 and drops for subsequent elections. In seven out of nineteen provinces (Veszprém among them) the correlation is negative, indicating that greater changes in level of industrialization are associated with *greater* levels of rightist persistence. For our settlement sample, the correlation never rises above 0.09 for any election. Thus, whatever is accounting for rightist persistence and volatility, it is not the magnitude of industrial change in the settlements.

I now introduce a series of multivariate models. The outcomes to be explained are, as before, the rightist margins in 1990, 1994, and 1998. The key explanatory variables are the rightist vote margin in 1945, a measure

---

[8] The data I employ for 1949 comprise the fraction of wage earners in industry and mining, whereas the 1990 comprise only industry, so the actual growth in industrialization is somewhat larger than reported here.

of church community for each settlement, and an interaction between the 1945 rightist vote margin and church community. There are few theoretical priors to guide the choice of indicators of church community. As noted in the preceding text, the dichotomous classification into high and low settlements sacrifices too much information given that the raw data consist of numerical measures for each settlement at different points in time during the communist period. Moreover, it could be that church community effectively transmitted rightist attachments not just where it remained high throughout the period, but where it remained high long enough such that the resulting networks were maintained until communism ended. To capture these possibilities and to ensure that the results are not sensitive to any particular specification, I estimated separate models on the full sample using church community from 1961, 1966, 1970, and the average of these three values. An interaction is included because the expectation is that church community enhances the transmission of *rightist* attachments, not leftist or other attachments.

I include the fraction of the population older than sixty years of age, the fraction of the population completing the eighth grade, and the fraction of dwellings built in a settlement before 1945 as control variables. The first two are included even though survey data offer conflicting evidence on their correlation with rightist voting. Older cohorts preferred both the Smallholders (FKgP) and the Hungarian Democratic Forum (MDF) in the 1990 and 1994 elections. But the Young Democrats (Fidesz - MPP) drew disproportionate support among younger voters in 1998. Education is even more problematic: FKgP and Christian Democratic (KDNP) voters tended to be less educated, but MDF and Fidesz voters more educated.[9] The fraction of pre-1945 dwellings is used as a proxy for the level of development (or rather underdevelopment) of a settlement. The age of the housing stock in 1990 should be directly related to the amount of investment a settlement received during the communist period. A settlement with an older housing stock indicates a dearth of capital and a stagnant or declining local economy. This provides another way of evaluating instrumental explanations, which predict a positive relationship between economic stagnation and rightist persistence.[10] The equations to be estimated with OLS are

---

[9] Enyedi (2000), Tóka (1995a), Tóka (1999), and Tóka and Enyedi (1999).

[10] See Angelusz and Tardos (1999a) for a slightly different measure of wealth in a model of voter turnout across localities. The 1990 census data are available in machine-readable form from the Hungarian Central Statistical Office.

listed as follows, where the i subscript indexes over settlements:[11]

$$R98_i = \beta_{08} + \beta_{18}R45_i + \beta_{28}Church_i + \beta_{38}R45*Church_i +$$
$$\beta_{48}Underdeveloped_i + \beta_{58}Over60_i + \beta_{68}Educ_i + \epsilon_{i8} \qquad (6.4)$$
$$R94_i = \beta_{04} + \beta_{14}R45_i + \beta_{24}Church_i + \beta_{34}R45*Church_i +$$
$$\beta_{44}Underdeveloped_i + \beta_{54}Over60_i + \beta_{64}Educ_i + \epsilon_{i4} \qquad (6.5)$$
$$R90_i = \beta_{00} + \beta_{10}R45_i + \beta_{20}Church_i + \beta_{30}R45*Church_i +$$
$$\beta_{40}Underdeveloped_i + \beta_{50}Over60_i + \beta_{60}Educ_i + \epsilon_{i0} \qquad (6.6)$$

The statistical results, with robust standard errors, are displayed in Table 6.3.[12] For each election four specifications are displayed, each with a different measure of church community: levels from 1961, 1966, 1970, and the average between 1961 and 1970. The key variables are the first three listed in each model: $R45$, *church community*, and their interaction, $R45*church$. Because there is so much going on in this table, it is easiest to interpret it in stages. First, all effects of the key variables are either zero (in the conventional statistical meaning) or in the predicted direction, positive. On the whole, the more conservative a locality before communism, or the higher the level of church community during communism, the greater the postcommunist rightist vote margin. This finding, which is in accord with expectation, is fairly robust across all specifications and postcommunist elections.

Second, however, there is significant collinearity among the three key variables. This could have been predicted based on Figure 6.1, which showed that church community was strongest in areas of precommunist

[11] OLS regression with vote fraction as the dependent variable is technically inappropriate for the multiparty electoral data under analysis here. First, it assumes that the vote for a party is theoretically unbounded and could fall anywhere on the real number line, whereas in reality its fraction of the overall vote must lie between 0 and 1. Second, it estimates a rightist party's vote independently, whereas in actuality it is not completely independent: the sum of the proportions for all parties in any given election must sum to one. Although convenient methods exist to account for these special features of multiparty data (Tomz, Tucker, and Wittenberg [2002]; Jackson [2002]), in the present case there is little need for such statistical razzle-dazzle. My research indicates that this more sophisticated approach yields virtually identical results to OLS for the data under analysis here. In such a case OLS is preferable because it is more familiar and generates intermediate results that are easy and intuitive to interpret.

[12] Education proved to be insignificant across a range of different specifications, so it was dropped from the analysis. This does not imply that education levels had no influence on the vote. As noted previously, significant differential effects across individual parties might have washed out in aggregating up from parties to blocs. Also, education might vary too little across settlements for its effects to appear at the aggregate level.

Table 6.3 *OLS Regression: Did Church Community Matter for Persistence?*

Explanatory Variable	Postcommunist Election											
	1990				1994				1998			
	(61)	(66)	(70)	(AVG)	(61)	(66)	(70)	(AVG)	(61)	(66)	(70)	(AVG)
R45	0.01	0.05	0.23**	0.07	0.01	0.14**	0.22**	0.10	0.05	0.20**	0.20**	0.15*
	(0.11)	(0.09)	(0.08)	(0.10)	(0.08)	(0.07)	(0.06)	(0.08)	(0.08)	(0.07)	(0.05)	(0.08)
Church community	0.01	−0.03	0.29**	0.15	0.05	0.11	0.11	0.13	0.13	0.17	0.18*	0.23**
	(0.12)	(0.14)	(0.11)	(0.15)	(0.08)	(0.10)	(0.09)	(0.11)	(0.08)	(0.11)	(0.09)	(0.11)
R45*church	0.37**	0.42**	−0.05	0.31	0.38**	0.21	0.10	0.28*	0.19	−0.03	−0.05	0.03
	(0.18)	(0.21)	(0.17)	(0.21)	(0.14)	(0.14)	(0.13)	(0.16)	(0.14)	(0.16)	(0.14)	(0.17)
Underdeveloped	0.14*	0.15*	0.11	0.11	0.16**	0.17**	0.14**	0.14**	0.12*	0.13**	0.09	0.09
	(0.08)	(0.08)	(0.08)	(0.08)	(0.07)	(0.07)	(0.07)	(0.07)	(0.06)	(0.06)	(0.06)	(0.06)
Over60	0.16	0.06	−0.09	−0.02	0.74**	0.62**	0.55**	0.54**	0.28	0.21	0.15	0.14
	(0.23)	(0.23)	(0.22)	(0.23)	(0.23)	(0.24)	(0.25)	(0.25)	(0.18)	(0.18)	(0.18)	(0.18)
Constant	0.16**	0.21**	0.17**	0.17**	−0.25**	−0.23**	−0.21**	−0.22**	0.06	0.08	0.11**	0.09*
	(0.07)	(0.06)	(0.05)	(0.06)	(0.05)	(0.05)	(0.05)	(0.05)	(0.05)	(0.05)	(0.04)	(0.05)
R^2	0.26	0.28	0.30	0.29	0.44	0.44	0.41	0.44	0.30	0.28	0.27	0.29
N	229	227	220	218	229	227	220	218	227	225	218	216

Note: The table lists OLS regression coefficients and corresponding robust standard errors (beneath in parentheses) for each explanatory variable and the constant term. Note that for each election four specifications are displayed, each differing in the specification of church community. Coefficients with two asterisks are significant at $p < 0.05$; coefficients with one asterisk are significant at $p < 0.10$.

rightist strength. Further evidence emerges if we examine the coefficients in the *AVG* model of the 1990 election (the fourth column of data), which at first glance seems the least supportive of my argument. Although none of the effects individually are different from zero, their joint effect is positive and highly significant, a textbook example of collinearity.[13] This problem almost certainly accounts for the shift of statistical significance between the interaction term and the main effects across specifications and elections. Thus, in four models the interaction term is significant and the main effects not significant, whereas in three models the reverse is true.

Collinearity renders the interpretation of individual coefficients more difficult, but does not affect estimates of their joint importance. This is crucial because in almost all of the models the joint effect of *church community* and *R45 * church* is, as we expect, positive: church community is most effective in localities that were most rightist before communism. From the perspective of my argument, however, the ideal situation is where the interaction term is significant and the main effects are zero, as occurs twice in both 1990 and 1994. The disappearance of the main effects illustrates that what matters most for the preservation of precommunist rightist attachments is not church community or precommunist conservatism alone, but *both together*. The 1994 results are particularly amazing. More than 40 percent of the variance (as indicated by R^2) can be explained knowing only the rightist vote margin in 1945, the level of religiosity in the 1960s, the fraction of apartments built before 1945, and the fraction of the population older than the age of sixty.

Third, the positive effect of *Underdeveloped* across the majority of models shows that instrumental theories of persistence cannot be entirely ruled out. The less "modern" a settlement, at least in terms of the prevailing housing stock, the greater the congruence between pre- and postcommunist support for the Right. This "backwardness" factor operates in addition to church community. The existence of still other unexplored transmission mechanisms can be inferred from the coefficient on *R45*. As an explanatory factor, *R45* is unlike the others in that there is no causal mechanism directly linking it to the postcommunist vote. Precommunist vote does not "cause" postcommunist vote in the same way as church affiliation or even age can. If all mechanisms linking pre- and postcommunist support for the Right were included in these models, then we would expect the

[13] Greene (2000: 256). I computed the joint significance of the three key coefficients using Stata's test command.

coefficient on $R45$ to be zero, because true explanatory factors ought to absorb any residual correlation between the pre- and postcommunist outcomes. Collinearity between $R45$ and *church community* prevents a definitive conclusion about the independent effect of $R45$, but it is probably safe to say that neither underdevelopment nor church community collectively exhaust the theoretical links between pre- and postcommunist rightist attachments.

Equations 6.4 through 6.6 represent the total influence of precommunist rightist partisan patterns on postcommunist rightist loyalties. However, it is possible to divide the influence of the distance past into two distinct components. The first is indirect, through its effect on the first postcommunist outcome in 1990. In this component, the distant past's effect on subsequent postcommunist outcomes in 1994 and 1998 is felt through the partisan pattern established in 1990 (note in Table 6.2 that the 1990 outcome is a powerful predictor of the 1994 outcome). The second path is direct. Here church community and precommunist rightist attachments may influence the 1994 and 1998 outcomes even after controlling for the 1990 result. As we saw in Chapter 2, there have been elements of instability and stability across Hungary's first three postcommunist elections. Some of the effects of the more distant past may well not have become visible until after the 1990 election.

Ideally, these effects would be modeled by inserting $R90$ into equations 6.4 through 6.6 as control variables and reestimating the system. $R90$, modeled again as in equation 6.6, would then be treated as endogenous. In this way, we could simultaneously estimate both the influences of the recent and distant past on the 1994 and 1998 outcomes and the separate influence of the distant past on the 1990 outcome. However, the introduction of a lagged dependent variable ($R90$) as an explanatory factor adds a number of methodological complications that could render the resulting estimates highly speculative.[14] Instead, I alleviate the problem by modeling the *change* in vote margin between 1990 and 1994 and between 1990 and 1998 rather than the vote margin *level* in 1994 and 1998. This involves absorbing the endogenous variable $R90$, which would be an

[14] Achen (2000) provides a clear and concise explanation of the pitfalls of including lagged dependent variables as regressors. OLS estimation in this case gives biased results. The appropriate technique is instrumental variable estimation, which in the present case requires finding a variable that is correlated with $R90$, but not correlated with $R94$ and $R98$. However, employing a bad instrument may be just as misleading as OLS. For a nonmathematical introduction to instrumental variables, see Kennedy (1985: 115–16).

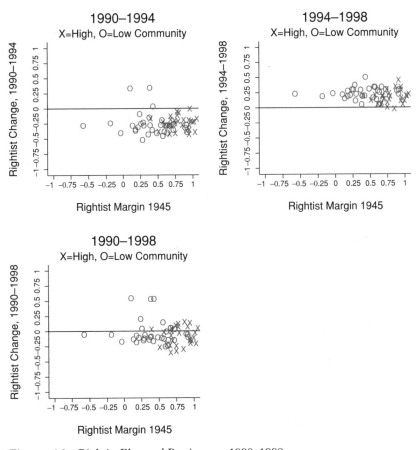

Figure 6.2 Rightist Electoral Persistence, 1990–1998.

explanatory variable, into the dependent variable. Thus, the outcomes to be explained become $R98 - R90$ and $R94 - R90$, or postcommunist rightist persistence.

There is no need to actually estimate these models, because it is easy to see graphically that once the 1990 outcome is assumed as a baseline, partisan movement *within* the postcommunist period is only slightly related to the precommunist partisan pattern or the level of church community. Figure 6.2 plots the change in rightist margin between 1990 and 1994, 1990 and 1998, and 1994 and 1998 as a function of the rightist margin in 1945 for localities with high and low church community (defined as for Table 6.2 and Figure 6.1). Thus, as before, each settlement is represented by either an X, if it had high church community, or an O, if it had low church community. The horizontal line at the zero point in each panel indicates exact persistence between elections. The weak relationship between rightist, church-oriented settlements and postcommunist rightist persistence can be seen in all three panels by observing where the Xs and Os tend to cluster with respect to the vertical axis. If the distant partisan past mattered for rightist persistence between 1990 and 1998, then settlements with high church community (Xs) ought to be less volatile than settlements with low church community (Os). In other words, the Xs ought to be clustered closer to the horizontal zero line than the Os. Difference in means tests confirm that only in the 1994–8 panel is the average value of rightist change for the Xs (0.15) significantly lower ($p < 0.001$) than for the Os (0.24). The distant past mattered, but principally in fostering initial postcommunist partisan conditions.

Raw statistical results are informative, but it still remains to determine the magnitude of the effect of church community on the postcommunist rightist vote margin. We would like to know how big a "boost" in postcommunist rightist vote margin is expected for different hypothetical values of key explanatory variables. Using the model in equations 6.4 through 6.6, and the AVG indicator of church community, I thus computed the change in the expected value of the postcommunist rightist margin in 1990, 1994, and 1998 given a wide array of hypothetical changes in 1945 rightist vote margin and church community, holding other variables at their means.[15] More specifically, I varied the change in both the 1945 rightist vote margin and church community from 0 (meaning no change) to 100 percent, in gradations of 25. One hundred percent represents a substantial change. In the case of the vote, it is equivalent to a move from a 50-50 percent Left-Right split to a total rightist victory before communism. For church community the shift represents a move from the lowest to the highest possible level. These extreme hypotheticals fall somewhat outside the actual values in the sample (particularly for the 1945 rightist margin), but they will serve to identify the limits of the model's predictive ability. Such an analysis permits us to answer counterfactuals about what would have happened to postcommunist rightist support if the 1945 rightist vote margin

---

[15] I use the average value of church community between 1961 and 1970 not because it performed best according to Table 6.3 (the 1961 value arguably performed better), but because as an average it presumably contains fewer idiosyncratic factors than a measurement from a given year.

6.5 Multivariate Evidence

Table 6.4 *How Much Did the Distant Past and Church Community Matter?*

	Change in Church Community (% points)					
	0	25	50	75	100	
	0	*3*	*7*	*10*	*13*	1990
0	0	*3*	*7*	*10*	*13*	1994
	0	*5*	*11*	*16*	*21*	1998
	2	7	12	18	23	
25	*3*	8	13	18	23	
	4	9	15	20	26	
Change in	*3*	*10*	18	25	33	
Right Margin 50	*5*	12	**19**	26	33	
1945	7	13	19	25	31	
(% points)	*5*	14	24	33	43	
75	*8*	16	25	34	42	
	11	17	23	29	36	
	6	18	29	41	52	
100	*10*	21	31	42	52	
	14	21	27	34	40	

Note: Hypothetical boost in postcommunist vote for the Right (in percentage points) for different combinations of changes in 1945 rightist margin and church community (also in percentage points), with other variables held at their means. The three numbers arrayed columnarly represent the expected boost for 1990 (top), 1994 (middle), and 1998 (bottom). For clarity I do not report standard errors, but italicize those values whose 95 percent confidence intervals include zero.

and church community had been different from their actual values in the data.[16]

Table 6.4 displays these expected boosts in postcommunist rightist electoral margins and provides more striking evidence of the importance of church community in transmitting precommunist rightist attachments. Hypothetical boosts in 1945 rightist electoral margin are arrayed to the left of the cells of the table and identical boosts for church community run across the top. These values are in percentage points. Thus, for example, a change of 50 percentage points for the 1945 rightist margin in an evenly divided locality implies a shift from a 50-50 percent vote split to 75-25 percent in favor of the Right. A similar change in church community implies a boost

[16] All expected values are computed using Clarify. For details see King, Tomz, and Wittenberg (2000) and Tomz, Wittenberg, and King (2003). Unless otherwise specified, all such marginal effects are computed with Clarify.

Church Community and Rightist Persistence

of 50 percentage points, from, say, 25 percent to 75 percent. For each value of change in rightist margin and church community, three expected boosts in the rightist margin are listed: 1990 (top), 1994 (middle), and 1998 (bottom). Thus, for example, the expected boost in the 1994 rightist electoral margin, given a 50 percentage point boost in both the 1945 rightist margin and church community would be 19 percentage points (the bolded number in the center of the table). Italicized values have associated confidence intervals that include zero.

The advantage of this table is that it permits an assessment of both the individual effects of precommunist attachments and church community separately, as well as their interaction. I will refer to "cells" in the table by their row and column indices. Thus, the (0,0) cell refers to the column of three zeroes at the top left. The weakness of either factor independently may be seen by examining the first row (change in rightist margin equals zero) and column (change in church community equals zero) of cells. The first row of cells represents the independent impact of church community because the impact of precommunist attachments is set to zero. Likewise, the first column of cells represents the independent impact of precommunist rightist support. All estimates are statistically zero in both the first row and column of cells. In other words, absent precommunist rightist attachments, church community is irrelevant for postcommunist rightist attachments. Absent church community, it is irrelevant how strong rightist attachments were before communism.

The *joint* importance of church community and precommunist attachments can be seen by scanning the table from the top left (near 0,0) toward the bottom right (near 100,100). In the purely hypothetical case of a complete shift to the right and maximum levels of religiosity (i.e., 100,100), the boost in postcommunist right support would be a whopping 52 percentage points in 1990 and 1994. But such a dramatic counterfactual is beyond the bounds of the values in the sample. Within the sample the average precommunist rightist margin equaled 51 percent, with a standard deviation of 30. The average level of church community was 47 percent, with a standard deviation of 20. A more realistic counterfactual would be to vary both factors by two standard deviations, from one below the mean to one above. In each case that represents an increase of approximately 50 percentage points, or a shift from a leftist community with low religiosity to a rightist community with high religiosity. As seen in the middle cell (50,50) of Table 6.4, the expected boost in such a case is at least 18 percentage points, regardless of which postcommunist election is considered.

220

The magnitude of this boost may perhaps best be appreciated by considering how much of a difference it would have made in the actual postcommunist electoral outcomes. For each settlement in Hungary I determined which electoral bloc won the plurality of the vote for each postcommunist election. Where either the liberal or leftist bloc came out on top, I computed the difference in vote between the winning bloc and the rightist bloc. Out of a total of 766 localities in which the rightist bloc lost the popular vote in 1990, the difference between its outcome and the victorious bloc's outcome was less than 18 percentage points in 557 (73 percent) of the cases. In other words, if the Right in these 557 localities had benefitted from an 18 percentage point boost in support, it would have emerged victorious. In 1994, the boost would have changed the result in 65 percent of the 1,639 places the Right lost; in 1998, the Right would have won every single locality. Thus, precommunist partisan patterns and church community really did matter for postcommunist rightist support.

6.6 Unpacking "Church Community": Religious Trajectories under Communism

The measures of church community used thus far have served as a convenient summary, but they abstract away from the dynamic evolution of religiosity during communism. The fate of church community can be broken up into three general trajectories, depending on how it evolved between 1961 and 1979. As previously noted, there was a general decline in church community during this period, from 61 percent in 1961 to 36 percent in 1970. By 1979 that had fallen to 16 percent.[17] To construct trajectories, I rely on these yearly cross-sectional averages and how the level of church community within each settlement compares to the average level for a given year. One trajectory is where a locality's church community remained low – below the yearly average – throughout the 1961–79 period. This occurred in 61 out of 221 places, including most of the larger settlements – Ajka, Balatonfüred, Pápa, Sümeg, Tapolca, and Veszprém (the county seat). In Sümeg, for example, church community was never above 16 percent in this period and was 0 percent by 1979. In Balatonfüred, the level was already 40 percent by 1961 (21 percentage points below the average) and only 6 percent by 1979.

---

[17] In cases where the 1979 data are missing, 1977 data are used instead. This occurred for 40 out of 163 settlements for which 1979 or 1977 data are available.

A second trajectory is where it remained high (above average) in 1961, but then became low (below average) some time before 1979. This occurred in forty localities. Twenty had declined by 1966, eleven more by 1970, and a further nine by 1979. Settlements in this group tend to be mid-sized and to have undergone middling levels of population change under communism. The largest locality is Csabrendek, with just under 3,000 people in 1990. The median change in population between 1949 and 1990 is a loss of 318 people. This is in contrast to a median loss of 237 for all localities (in the sample) and a loss of only 168 for areas where church community fell early on. A third trajectory is where high levels of church community were preserved throughout the 1961–79 period, which happened in fifty-five localities.[18] Settlements following this trajectory tend to be smaller, with a median 1990 population of 425, versus 958 for places where church community had declined by 1961. But they do not feature the greatest absolute demographic change, suffering a median loss of 208 people between 1949 and 1990, a smaller loss than for settlements where church community declined between 1966 and 1979. The average level of church community in 1979 in this trajectory was 43 percent, versus only 3 percent for settlements where it became low by 1970 or 1979.

A total of sixty-five localities do not fit any of the preceding trajectories. For example, in a few places church community monotonically increased between 1961 and 1970, bucking the general downward trend. In many cases, localities missed qualifying for one of the trajectories because of fluctuating levels. Thus, some localities had low levels in 1961 and high levels in 1966 or 1970, only to fall again by 1979. Others had high levels in 1961 and 1979, but low levels in between. These are interesting patterns and may reflect the vagaries of local church institutions in particular places. Chapters 4 and 5 illustrated how priests and pastors were often shuffled from one area to another. Disparate patterns of church community could reflect the distribution across settlements of active and inactive priests. This is as true for our three trajectories as it is of those paths that are more mixed. But there are too few with any one pattern to include them in the analysis.

The degree to which these different trajectories can account for rightist persistence may be explored in much the same way as in previous sections.

---

[18] Due to the large numbers of missing data for 1979, a locality is also counted as having high levels of church community between 1961 and 1979 if it had high levels through 1970 and its data are missing for 1979. Twenty-one of these fifty-five localities had missing data for 1979.

6.6 Unpacking "Church Community"

The expectation is that the longer church community remained high in a given settlement, the greater the electoral "boost" in that settlement for the postcommunist Right. To explore this possibility I created a series of indicator variables, identifying each of the three trajectories for 1961–79: where church community was low (below average) for the entire period; where it was high in 1961, but became low sometime thereafter; and where it remained high throughout the period. By definition, a settlement cannot experience more than one of these trajectories, though some fall into the "mixed" category. To estimate the effects I employ a modified version of equations 6.4 through 6.6, where $Church_i$ is replaced by indicator variables identifying trajectories and the interaction term is dropped altogether.[19]

The results of this analysis appear in Table 6.5. *LowAll* refers to the trajectory where church community is low throughout the 1961–79 period. *GoLow* indicates the trajectory where church community was still high in 1961, but became low some time thereafter. *HighAll* refers to the trajectory in which church community remained high through the period. The other variables are as in the earlier analysis and the "mixed" trajectory is excluded. The importance of church community for the preservation of rightist preferences may be seen in the coefficients on the trajectory variables: *LowAll*, *GoLow*, and *HighAll*. As expected, there is a positive boost in rightist vote in settlements where it remained high (*HighAll*). Where it began high, but subsequently became low (*GoLow*) there is a slightly positive boost, at least in 1994. It is likely that this weak effect is a consequence of aggregating places where church community dropped soon after 1961, where we would not expect any boost, with areas that declined only in the late 1970s, and where it is likely there would be a boost. Settlements where church community remained low (*LowAll*) experienced a loss in rightist support. The continuing significance of the precommunist rightist vote (*R45*) is more evidence that while church community is important, it does not constitute the only means by which rightist attachments were transmitted through the communist period.

How big is the rightist boost associated with each trajectory? To generate these values I computed the expected change in rightist vote for a hypothetical shift from the *LowAll* trajectory to the *HighAll* trajectory, holding

---

[19] The interaction term is dropped to increase the efficiency of estimation. The inclusion of 1979 data results in a significant drop in the number of observations, which exacerbates preexisting problems of collinearity.

Table 6.5 *OLS Regression: Church Community Trajectories and Persistence.*

Explanatory Variable	Postcommunist Election		
	1990	1994	1998
R45	0.20**	0.24**	0.19**
	(0.05)	(0.04)	(0.04)
Underdeveloped	0.22**	0.25**	0.11
	(0.10)	(0.08)	(0.07)
Over60	−0.38	0.22	0.12
	(0.33)	(0.27)	(0.25)
LowAll	−0.10**	−0.06*	−0.07**
	(0.04)	(0.03)	(0.03)
GoLow	0.04	0.06*	0.03
	(0.04)	(0.03)	(0.03)
HighAll	0.10**	0.08**	0.08**
	(0.05)	(0.04)	(0.03)
Constant	0.28**	−0.14**	0.17**
	(0.08)	(0.06)	(0.06)
R^2	0.27	0.42	0.35
N	146	146	145

Note: The table lists OLS regression coefficients and corresponding robust standard errors (beneath in parentheses) for each explanatory variable and the constant term. Coefficients with two asterisks are significant at $p < 0.05$ and coefficients with one asterisk are significant at $p < 0.10$.

other factors constant at their average values. In other words, all other things being equal, how much of a difference did having consistently high church community make versus always having low church community? In 1990, the net boost was 19 percentage points for the Right. In 1994 and 1998, the boost was 14 and 15 percentage points, respectively.[20] Thus, church community trajectories mattered a great deal for rightist attachments.

6.7 Confessional Differences

Thus far I have not considered the impact of religious confession. One lesson of Chapters 4 and 5 is that the level of religiosity within a locality depends a great deal on whether that locality is predominantly Roman

[20] The standard error is 5 points in 1990, and 4 points in both 1994 and 1998.

Catholic or primarily Calvinist. Ample archival evidence showed that, on average, Catholic priests were more likely than Calvinist pastors to mobilize their parishioners to confront the Communist Party and, ultimately, more successful in preserving church community. To see the extent to which religiosity was higher in Catholic localities, I divided the sample into two parts according to whether Roman Catholicism or Calvinism was the predominant religion. Predominance is defined as greater than 50 percent of the population belonging to a confession, as recorded in the 1949 census. This yielded sixteen Calvinist localities and 171 Catholic localities. I then compared the average values of church community in each of the subsamples. Catholic settlements had higher religiosity (49 percent) than Calvinist ones (39 percent). A difference of means test confirms that this result is unlikely to have occurred by chance.[21]

Confessional differences also appear to be significant in support for individual parties within the rightist bloc. Recall from Chapter 2 that immediate postwar political conditions meant that the only rightist party permitted to run in the 1945 national parliamentary election was FKgP. Consequently, it attracted all the votes of those opposed to the leftist parties, Protestant and Catholic, rural and urban. Its "catchall" status, however, does not mean that under circumstances of greater electoral choice it would have been equally acceptable to these disparate constituencies. Gati (1986: 70–1) notes, for example, that the 1945 FKgP represented significant "bourgeois-democratic" and "populist-agrarian" interests. Confession mattered too. This became apparent by 1947, by which time, as we saw in Chapter 2, the Communist Party had succeeded in employing "salami tactics" to weaken the bourgeois opposition. By the 1947 national parliamentary elections the rightist bloc was represented by a host of different parties, including a smaller FKgP and also the Democratic People's Party (DNP). These parties had distinct confessional profiles, with the FKgP assuming a Protestant (largely Calvinist) profile and the DNP attracting an inordinate share of the Catholic vote.

---

[21] A linear regression of church community on the proportions of the population that are Calvinist and Catholic yields a similar conclusion: Catholicism is significantly and positively related to church community, while Calvinism exhibits no relationship at all. As noted earlier in this chapter, however, the subset of settlements for which we have systematic data on church community is considerably less Calvinist than the full Hungarian sample. The limited variation in the distribution of Calvinists across these localities means that a linear regression of church community on the proportion of the population that is Calvinist risks yielding insignificant results even if in reality there were a significant relationship.

The postcommunist FKgP and KDNP have portrayed themselves as the revived successors to the precommunist FKgP and DNP, respectively. The legitimacy with which these parties can claim to have assumed the mantle of these older parties was addressed in Chapter 1. What is germane here is that despite a leveling of differences between Catholics and Calvinists as a consequence of communist repression, and a society far more secular than it had been in the 1940s, the vote for these "successor" parties divides along similar confessional lines. To illustrate this I estimated a model only slightly different from the ones already estimated for the rightist bloc as a whole. First, the dependent variables are support for KDNP, FKgP, and MDF in 1990, 1994, and 1998. Second, all variables involving vote margins are replaced with vote fractions.[22] Third, church community is measured using the average between 1961 and 1970. Finally, 1949 census data on the fraction of Catholics and Calvinists across settlements are added as explanatory variables. The results appear in Table 6.6.

Table 6.6 illustrates that communism did not succeed in eradicating the interrelationship between confession and electoral attachments. This can be seen by examining the coefficients on *Catholic49* and *Calvinist49*, which have been put in boldface in the table. The strongest relationship is that between Catholicism and KDNP, which remained even in 1998, by which time KDNP had virtually collapsed, receiving only a few percent of the vote. This relationship stands in stark contrast with the lack of correlation between Catholicism and FKgP. The opposite story, albeit more weakly, holds for Calvinism: correlation with FKgP support, but a general lack of relationship with KDNP. This mimics the precommunist partisan pattern. The link between Catholicism and KDNP is stronger than that between Calvinism and FKgP in part because KDNP was founded as a Catholic "subcultural" party.[23] FKgP, by contrast, appealed rhetorically to Christian values, as had its precommunist predecessor, but not to Calvinism per se. By 1998, it had become a party of the "losers" of the postcommunist transition.

Note that the 1945 rightist vote (*RVote45*), *church community*, and their interaction are significant for KDNP and insignificant for FKgP in all elections. This is evidence that in the present heavily Catholic sample KDNP "stood for" precommunist rightist traditions to a greater extent than FKgP and that church community mattered more for Catholics than it did for

---

[22] I abandon electoral margins because there were six parliamentary parties in 1990 and 1994, and it is not clear how to compute a meaningful margin in this case.
[23] Enyedi (1996).

Table 6.6 *OLS Regression: Persistence in Catholic and Calvinist Areas.*

Explanatory Variable	Postcommunist Election								
	1990			1994			1998		
	FKgP	KDNP	MDF	FKgP	KDNP	MDF	FKgP	KDNP	MDF
RVote45	0.19	−0.14**	−0.08	0.05	−0.19**	0.17**	−0.09	−0.05**	0.01
	(0.10)	(0.06)	(0.10)	(0.07)	(0.04)	(0.06)	(0.06)	(0.02)	(0.02)
Church community	0.04	−0.08	−0.23	0.02	−0.32**	0.13	−0.10	−0.10**	0.002
	(0.16)	(0.14)	(0.17)	(0.13)	(0.08)	(0.12)	(0.12)	(0.04)	(0.03)
RVote45*Church	−0.08	0.41**	0.23	0.03	0.58**	−0.22	0.24	0.18**	0.02
	(0.21)	(0.17)	(0.22)	(0.15)	(0.11)	(0.15)	(0.15)	(0.05)	(0.04)
Underdeveloped	0.13**	−0.05	0.06	0.06**	−0.03	0.07**	0.11**	−0.01	0.04**
	(0.05)	(0.04)	(0.05)	(0.04)	(0.02)	(0.04)	(0.04)	(0.01)	(0.01)
Over60	0.38**	−0.09	−0.25	0.03	0.14**	0.30*	0.06	0.02	−0.03
	(0.15)	(0.12)	(0.18)	(0.08)	(0.07)	(0.18)	(0.10)	(0.05)	(0.03)
Catholic49	**−0.02**	**0.17**	**0.13**	**0.04**	**0.12**	**0.03**	**0.03**	**0.03**	**0.008**
	(0.05)	(0.03)	(0.05)	(0.03)	(0.02)	(0.04)	(0.03)	(0.01)	(0.005)
Calvinist49	**0.12***	**0.04***	**0.12**	**0.08**	**0.01**	**0.03**	**0.02**	**0.004**	**0.02***
	(0.07)	(0.03)	(0.05)	(0.04)	(0.02)	(0.04)	(0.04)	(0.01)	(0.01)
Constant	−0.08	−0.001	0.24*	0.02	0.07**	−0.08	0.14**	0.03	−0.005
	(0.09)	(0.06)	(0.09)	(0.05)	(0.04)	(0.07)	(0.06)	(0.02)	(0.02)
R^2	0.19	0.43	0.06	0.10	0.57	0.15	0.17	0.28	.13
N	202	202	202	202	202	202	201	201	201

Note: Calvinist areas prefer FKgP, Catholic ones prefer KDNP. The table lists OLS regression coefficients and corresponding robust standard errors (beneath in parentheses) for each explanatory variable and the constant term. Coefficients with two asterisks are significant at $p < 0.05$; coefficients with one asterisk are significant at $p < 0.10$. Confessional factors are in boldface.

Calvinists. Just how much religious factors mattered may be seen in the fit (R^2) of the KDNP models, which rises to nearly 60 percent for the 1994 KDNP vote. For all the changes wrought under communism, over half the 1994 vote can be explained knowing only the popularity of the right in 1945, the fraction of Catholics in 1949, and religiosity in the 1960s. This finding is consistent with survey research, which shows that among rightist parties KDNP had the most religious constituency, with 56 percent of its voters in 1994 attending church at least once a week.[24]

6.8 Who Supported the Right? Ecological Inferences and Survey Results

The foregoing analyses show that the stronger church community was in a settlement, the more likely that settlement retained its precommunist preferences for rightist parties. The historical arguments in Chapters 4 and 5 clearly indicate that the source of this rightist support ought to be members of the church community. But it would be committing an "ecological fallacy" to infer this directly from the regression results. What are required are cross-level inferences, from the locality level to individuals within localities.[25] As detailed in this section, performing ecological inferences with the church community data involves strong empirical assumptions that cannot be verified. Thus, to ensure that the results are not an artifact of either the data or the estimation method, I also estimate the electoral preferences of the church community through surveys. The survey outcomes, which are based on national random samples, will not match the ecological estimates derived from the settlement sample, but they should be in broad qualitative agreement.

6.8.1 Ecological Inferences

The goal of ecological inference in the present case is to estimate, for each settlement, the proportion (or percentage) of church affiliates (and nonaffiliates) that support a given political bloc. The data to be used are the number of church affiliates (i.e., the strength of church community) and the number of votes a bloc obtains in each settlement. The quantities that we

---

[24] Stumpf (1994) and Tóka (1994).

[25] Three lucid, recent treatments of ecological inference are Achen and Shively (1995), King (1997), and King, Rosen, and Tanner (2004).

6.8 Who Supported the Right?

Table 6.7 *Ecological Inference for the Three-Bloc System, 1990–1994.*

	Vote for Blocs				
	Left	Liberal	Right		
Non-Church	β_i^{nLe}	β_i^{nLi}	β_i^{nR}	$1 - C_i$
Church	β_i^{cLe}	β_i^{cLi}	β_i^{cR}	C_i
	V_i^{Le}	V_i^{Li}	V_i^{R}	

Table 6.8 *Ecological Inference for the Two-Bloc System, 1998 and After.*

	Vote for Blocs			
	Left	Right		
Non-Church	β_i^{nLe}	β_i^{nR}	$1 - C_i$
Church	β_i^{cLe}	β_i^{cR}	C_i
	V_i^{Le}	V_i^{R}	

know and the unknowns to be estimated may be conveniently displayed as in Tables 6.7 and 6.8. There are two tables because the number of quantities to be estimated decreases as we move from the three-bloc party system of 1990–4 to the two-bloc system in 1998 and thereafter. In these tables the V_i^{Le}, V_i^{Li}, and V_i^{R} represent the fraction of the vote obtained by the leftist, liberal, and rightist blocs, respectively. C_i represents the proportion of the community that is church affiliated. Each quantity is subscripted with i to indicate that the table represents a single locality. The Vs and C are known. The βs are to be estimated and represent the fraction of church affiliates and nonaffiliates who support a given bloc. For example, in Table 6.7, β_i^{cR} (in the lower right-hand corner) represents the estimated fraction of church affiliates who support the Right; β_i^{nLe} represents the fraction of non-affiliates who support the Left. As I include in the analysis only voters who choose one of the blocs, the fractions across each of the rows of this table must sum to one.[26] Thus, in Table 6.7, $\beta_i^{cLe} + \beta_i^{cLi} + \beta_i^{cR} = 1$; in Table 6.8, $\beta_i^{cLe} + \beta_i^{cR} = 1$. The constraint on the βs means that within

---

[26] I exclude nonvoters from the present model. These could be included by adding another column to the table, in effect creating a fourth "bloc." However, doing so does not change the qualitative results and adds unnecessary complications to the estimation process. The entire analysis is performed using only votes cast for the three blocs.

each row in each table, only $k - 1$ unknowns are estimated, where k is the number of blocs appearing in the table.

One of the assumptions of ecological inference is that the population from which the row variable is taken be the same as that of the column variable. In the present case, this means that the population for which we have church affiliation information should be the same as the population going out to vote during the postcommunist period. This permits us to make conclusions of the form, "the fraction of church affiliates who voted for the Right is 0.65." Tables 6.7 and 6.8 clearly violate this assumption: church community relies on data from the 1960s and 1970s, while voting data are from the 1990s. In performing these ecological inferences, then, there is an implicit assumption that the strength of church community remained constant between the 1970s and the 1990s.[27]

I employ King's (1997) $\mathfrak{E}I$ method to generate estimates of church affiliates' and nonaffiliates' electoral preferences in 1990, 1994, and 1998. The results, stated in percentages, appear in Table 6.9. The bottom row of numbers represent the estimated percentage of church affiliates supporting leftist, liberal, or rightist parties across three postcommunist elections. For reference, support for rightist parties is in bold. Thus, for example, 57 percent of church affiliates are estimated to have voted for the Right in 1994. The top row reports analogous estimates for nonaffiliates. Note that for each election, each row of estimates adds up to 100 percent, because I exclude nonvoters and votes for parties that fall outside the three blocs. For clarity standard errors are not reported.[28]

Table 6.9 strongly supports the hypothesis that church affiliates preferred rightist parties. Their support for the Right never falls below 50 percent,

---

[27] How the resultant ecological inferences are thereby biased depends on the nature of the bias in church community. If the overcounted or undercounted church affiliates are as likely to vote for rightist, leftist, or liberal parties as those that are counted, then no systematic bias should occur.

[28] Although $\mathfrak{E}I$ generates estimates for each locality, I report only the population-weighted average over the whole sample of localities. These estimates thus represent our best guess of regionwide electoral preferences. The 2×3 tables in 1990 and 1994 were estimated using the $\mathfrak{E}I2$ routine. Ferree (2004) reports inconsistencies in $\mathfrak{E}I2$, with estimates varying depending on the order in which the column variables are entered into the analysis. To double check my results I reran the analysis varying the order in which the blocs get entered. The differences among the results are not substantial (differing by approximately 7 percentage points). The outcomes reported here represent the worst-case scenario for my argument. That is, I report the results where church affiliate support for the Right is estimated to be the lowest.

6.8 Who Supported the Right?

Table 6.9 *Ecological Regression: Bloc Preferences of Church Affiliates.*

| | Postcommunist Election | | | | | | | |
| | 1990 | | | 1994 | | | 1998 | |
	Left	Liberal	Right	Left	Liberal	Right	Left	Right
Non-Church	24	36	41	39	35	26	44	56
Church	5	26	**69**	17	26	**57**	25	**75**

Note: The table lists population-weighted estimates of the overall percentage (in the settlement sample) of church affiliates and non-affiliates voting for leftist, liberal, and rightist parties. For clarity I do not display standard errors.

even in the three-bloc party system of 1990–4. There is over twice as much support for the Right as for the liberals and at least three times the level of support for the Left. The unpopularity of the Left among church affiliates is not surprising given their experience during the socialist period. This confirms that whatever the success of the former communist parties at repackaging themselves as moderate social democrats, the "regime divide" continues to separate church affiliates from those with sympathies for the old ruling party.

Equally striking are the differences in electoral preferences between church affiliates and nonaffiliates. Nonaffiliates comprise a decisive majority of the population, so their preferences may be taken as a baseline with which to interpret affiliates' preferences. In all three elections church affiliates preferred the Right to a far greater extent than the rest of the population. Even in 1990, when the Right sailed to victory, the difference was 28 percentage points (69–41 percent). Church affiliate preferences for the Right are matched by a distaste for the Left. Even in 1994, the year the Socialists triumphantly returned to power, the Left succeeded in obtaining only 17 percent of the church vote, versus 39 percent of the rest of the population's. (The Socialists obtained approximately 33 percent of the nationwide popular vote on regional lists in the first round.)

6.8.2 *Survey Results*

Survey research adds an extra layer of confidence that church affiliates' preference for the Right is not epiphenomenal of other social and economic factors, and also compensates for the fact that the settlement sample underrepresented Calvinists and probably overrepresented smaller villages.

231

I analyze two surveys conducted under the auspices of the International Social Survey Program (ISSP), one in 1991 and the other in 1998, each of which is based on national random sampling and had religion as a motivating theme.[29]

In addition to a battery of demographic and religion questions, respondents were asked which party they intended to vote for "if there [were] a general election next Sunday." From this question I constructed dependent variables (one for each survey, according to the memberships in Appendix 3) to indicate which bloc was favored. For 1991, the categories were Left, Liberal, and Right; for 1998, they were simply Left and Right. The explanatory variables common to both models are church attendance (religiosity), religious confession (Roman Catholic or Calvinist), size of settlement respondent dwells in (rurality), education, income, and age. For 1991, I also ran analyses with religious belief explanatory factors, such as whether religious leaders should influence people's vote choice, whether it would be better to have believers in office, and whether religious leaders should influence government decisions. Though some of these factors turned out to predict rightist support, none washed out the effects of religiosity. Rightist support is thus not merely about religious belief. I do not present results from these more expanded models.[30] OLS regression is no longer appropriate because the outcomes are discrete choices. Instead, I use limited dependent variable models: multinomial logit for 1991 and logit for 1998.[31]

[29] Each consisted of personal interviews of 1,000 respondents. Both datasets with complete documentation are available from the Interuniversity Consortium for Political and Social Research (ICPSR) under study 6234 for 1991 and 3065 for 1998.

[30] With a few exceptions the variables from the surveys were used without recoding. For 1991, the unchanged variables include religiosity (V65), size of settlement (V122), education (V99), income (V118), and age (V78). For 1998, this pertains to size of settlement (V254), education (V205), and age (V201). Confession (V106 in 1991 and V217 in 1998) was recoded to include only Roman Catholics (coded as "1") and Calvinists (coded as "2"). In 1991, *confession* refers to the religion in which the respondent was baptized or registered; in 1998 it refers to the religion the respondent "now feels he belongs to." In the 1998 model, religiosity was recoded so that lower values reflect less frequent attendance, and higher values more frequent, in keeping with the 1991 coding. Income (V216 in 1998) was recoded into three categories so that the effect coefficient, which (inversely) reflected the scale of the income variable, would be more easily presentable in the table. I have found in my analyses that the statistical significance of these factors is robust to such coding changes. Religious belief variables include V26–V29.

[31] Both models can be used to estimate the probabilities of supporting one bloc over another. The multinomial logit reduces to the logit when there are only two outcomes. See Long (1997) for a clear explanation of how these models work.

6.8 Who Supported the Right?

The results appear in Table 6.10, with the 1991 multinomial logit results as the first column of numbers and the 1998 logit results as the second column. Although the two models are displayed side by side, the magnitudes of the coefficients are not directly comparable, because the number of possible outcomes differs across the two models. Note that in multinomial logit separate effects are listed for both the Right and the Liberal blocs, which reflect the differing odds of an individual supporting the Right or the Liberal blocs given the other factors in the model. The logit has only one set of effects, representing the odds of supporting the Right, because there are only two outcomes.

Although the magnitudes of the effect coefficients are not directly interpretable in either model, three important conclusions can still be drawn from this table. First, religiosity, understood now as church attendance, is a robust predictor of rightist support, even after controlling for a bevy of alternative possibilities. Indeed, the relationship held even as the composition of the rightist bloc changed dramatically between 1991 and 1998 with the decline of MDF and KDNP and the rise of Fidesz. Although we have not yet computed the magnitude of the effect, we can nonetheless safely conclude that settlements with strong church community retained their preference for the Right because church affiliates voted for the Right. Second, support for the Right cannot be interpreted merely as a reaction to antipathy for the Left. In 1991 church affiliates could have supported liberal parties but they did not: religiosity had no effect either way. This is all the more remarkable because by 1991 people may have already begun to feel the bite of economic and social reforms, and might have been expected to punish the ruling rightist coalition. Third, even controlling for religiosity, Calvinists (coded on *Confession* with a higher number than Catholics) may have been less likely to support the Right in the early 1990s. This is tantalizing evidence that the sympathy for the socialist regime evinced by the Reformed Church leadership and concomitant doctrinal changes may have rendered churchgoing Calvinists more vulnerable to socialist influence than their Catholic counterparts.[32]

To estimate just how big the effects of religiosity and confession are, I computed the predicted probabilities that both Catholics and Calvinists

---

[32] The coding for *Settlementsize* increases in value for smaller places. Thus, rural folk have a higher estimated probability of supporting the Right in 1991 than city dwellers. Similarly, older people are estimated to have a lower probability of voting liberal in 1991 than younger people.

Table 6.10 *Multinomial Regression: Church Affiliate Support for the Right, 1991 and 1998.*

		Vote Intention	
	Explanatory Variable	Multinomal Logit 1991	Logit 1998
Right	Religiosity	0.32**	0.25**
		(0.10)	(0.07)
	Confession	−0.90*	−0.29
		(0.48)	(0.26)
	Settlement size	0.59**	−0.07
		(0.29)	(0.14)
	Education	0.005	0.11
		(0.15)	(0.11)
	Income	0.06	0.10
		(0.06)	(0.16)
	Age	−0.0003	0.0004
		(0.01)	(0.008)
	Constant	−0.20	−0.55
		(1.37)	(0.92)
Liberal	Religiosity	0.08	
		(0.10)	
	Confession	−0.28	
		(0.46)	
	Settlement size	0.007	
		(0.30)	
	Education	0.20	
		(0.15)	
	Income	0.05	
		(0.06)	
	Age	−0.05**	
		(0.01)	
	Constant	2.95*	
		(1.39)	
	$Pseudo - R^2$	0.19	0.04
	N	396	373

Note: The dependent variables here are preference for the Left, Liberals, or the Right in 1991, and the Left or the Right in 1998. Each of these was constructed based on respondents' party preferences, and reflects only those who intended to vote. In the multinomial analysis the Left is the base category. In the logit analysis the Right is coded as "1" and the Left "0". The table lists coefficients and corresponding robust standard errors underneath in parentheses. Coefficients with two asterisks are significant at $p < 0.05$; Coefficients with one asterisk are significant at $p < 0.10$.

6.8 Who Supported the Right?

Table 6.11 *Catholic and Calvinist Rightist Support, 1991 and 1998.*

| Church Attendance | Probability of Rightist Support | | | |
| | 1991 | | 1998 | |
	Catholics	Calvinists	Catholics	Calvinists
Never	0.31	0.19	0.45	0.38
	(0.04)	(0.05)	(0.05)	(0.06)
Occasionally	0.43	0.28	0.52	0.45
	(0.03)	(0.06)	(0.04)	(0.06)
Often	0.72	0.57	0.74	0.68
	(0.05)	(0.09)	(0.04)	(0.06)

Note: The table lists predicted probabilities and associated standard errors. All values are statistically different from zero.

support the Right at certain levels of church attendance, holding all other factors constant at their average values. These results appear in Table 6.11. Here "Occasionally" means at most a few times a year and "Often" means weekly or more. Several features of this table buttress the arguments I have made throughout this chapter. First, for both elections and within each confession, the greater the religiosity, the greater the predicted probability of supporting the Right. For Catholics in 1991, a hypothetical shift on religiosity from never attending church to attending weekly boosted the probability a whopping 41 percentage points (from 0.31 to 0.72). The difference was also large, if less dramatic, for the Calvinists. Second, within each category of church attendance and for each election, the Catholics support the Right in greater proportion than the Calvinists. Thus, for example, the probability of voting Right among those who occasionally attended church in 1991 was 0.43 for Catholics and only 0.28 for Calvinists, a difference of 0.15 points. Indeed, in 1998 Catholics who never attended church were just as likely to support the Right as Calvinists who occasionally did.

The nexus between religiosity and rightist preferences is remarkably robust. Analysis of both the September 1992 and April 1994 waves of the Central European University electoral study (see CEU [1994]) shows that support for the Right increases with frequency of church attendance even after controlling for a variety of issue positions, including views on the economic situation, abortion, and whether atheists are fit for public office. Religiosity predicts respondents' self-placement on a Left-Right scale as well as their preference for rightist over leftist parties. Taken together with similar findings from the ISSP data, this shows that church adherents' party

235

preferences are rooted not just in an alignment of policy interests (e.g., restricting abortion rights or keeping atheists out of office), but also in more diffuse partisan loyalties to the Right. Local church institutions matter even independently of religious beliefs that the most faithful churchgoers are most likely to hold.

6.9 Conclusion

This chapter has shown, through a variety of graphical and statistical methods across multiple data sets, that church community preserved attachments to parties of the Right between pre- and postcommunism. Although all Churches suffered during the communist period, the Roman Catholic Church proved far more resilient than the Reformed Church. Even for equal levels of religiosity, Catholics retained their conservative loyalties to a greater extent than Calvinists. These robust statistical results complement the empirical links between pre- and postcommunism established in Chapters 4 and 5. We now know both how local church institutions transmitted rightist attachments and the magnitude of these effects in the postcommunist period.

Local priests and pastors could not foresee the end of communism, and could no more anticipate the consequences of their actions than the Communist Party could the effects of its own efforts at liberalization. What is clear is that rightist electoral persistence is, in part, the unintended consequence of clerical actions during the communist period. In battling local cadres for mass allegiance and thereby galvanizing church institutions, the clergy unwittingly fostered a constituency that would provide a rich source of rightist votes once the communist regime fell. I now turn to the question of what this study can tell us about politics beyond Hungary.

7

Conclusion

7.1 Introduction

Why do mass political loyalties persist even amid prolonged social upheaval, disruptive economic development, and demographic transformation? The paradox of political persistence has bedeviled researchers ever since Siegfried (1913) first identified it. After nearly a century of research there remains little consensus even on how to identify continuity, much less what might account for it. This book has tackled these problems by zeroing in on countries emerging from communism. If there were ever cases in which mass political attitudes should have been transformed, it would have been during state-socialism, when Communist Party dictatorships strove so vigorously to create loyal socialist citizens. Drawing on extensive archival research and an original database of election results, this study has documented and explained the remarkable persistence of rightist partisan attachments during Hungary's journey from multiparty politics to communism and back to multiparty politics in the twentieth century. This chapter first summarizes the book's main findings, and then elaborates on their broader implications.

The microfoundations of rightist persistence are rooted in the power of local institutions, even those under extreme duress, to act as focal points for mutual interaction. Once the Communist Party assumed power, the Churches became the last refuge for those with right-wing loyalties and battled the Party for mass influence for the remainder of the communist period. This epic struggle pitted parish priests and pastors, who encouraged robust religious practice, against Party activists, who sought to restrict church life. Hemmed in and harassed by Party cadres, clergymen employed a variety of ingenious tactics to maintain adherence to church rites and rituals. The outcomes of these struggles were not easy to predict: crafty priests might outfox Party cadres, or themselves be outmaneuvered. The successful clergyman engaged in enough mass mobilization to keep the church alive, but not so much as to incur Party wrath. The resulting social interaction created a community of practice that girded individuals against pressures to adopt the dominant political values. By the end of communism this community, having resisted political assimilation into the socialist milieu, provided a natural constituency for emerging parties of the Right. This occurred even in areas that underwent extensive economic and social change and despite virtually complete discontinuity in political party organizations between pre- and postcommunism. In the end, rightist continuity resulted from the outcomes of localized conflicts, not merely a serendipitous cluster of social and economic conditions.

7.2 Implications

7.2.1 Hungary

The reappearance of older partisan configurations after so many tumultuous decades overturns two shibboleths about Hungary. The first, widespread in both popular and scholarly circles, is that the victory of the former communists in the 1994 national parliamentary elections represented a break with the country's much-ballyhooed conservative political culture. This view is superficially correct, but untrue at a deeper level. The Socialist victory did represent the first time in Hungarian history that the Left had been freely voted into power. However, this was as much a reflection of the peculiarities of the electoral system as of mass sentiments. The statistical analysis in Chapter 2 compares pre- and postcommunist election results across virtually all towns and villages. It shows that the 1994 outcome is far more congruent with the precommunist past than the 1990 rightist victory, hailed by so many as a "return to tradition."

The second shibboleth is that the Churches, their resistance broken during the 1950s, no longer effectively opposed communist encroachment. Although this might be true for much of the Church leaderships, there remained significant pockets of opposition within the clergy, particularly among Roman Catholics. As Chapters 4 and 5 illustrate, Catholic priests proved far more effective than Calvinist pastors in countering the depredations of communist rule. Contrary to conventional wisdom, this outcome is less a consequence of greater Calvinist sympathy for the communist project than of advantages accruing to the Catholic Church under conditions of oppression. Whereas for Catholics there is no salvation outside the Church, for Calvinists heaven may be reached through faith alone. Calvinists thus enjoyed far more autonomy than Catholics in determining the compatibility between their faith and communism. In a political context where the Party aggressively sought to discourage religious affiliation, and where co-eval loyalties to both Church and Party proved difficult to sustain, it thus proved far easier for Calvinists to abandon their Church.

7.2.2 State-Socialism

The manner in which rightist attachments reemerged after communism also challenges two cherished notions about state-socialism. One concerns the nature of popular opposition to dictatorship. There has always been a pronounced tendency to view "irrepressible" mass democratic values as having limited the ability of the communist parties to fulfill their most transformative goals. The Party might beat the nation down and hold it captive, but it could not, in this view, extinguish the equity and equality that "resonate in the human spirit."[1] As Paul (1979) notes, such enduring values testify to the "cultural limits of revolutionary politics." This study suggests a markedly different conclusion. The roots of Hungarian continuity lay ultimately in institutions rather than ideas, in structure rather than culture. Rightist loyalties survived not because they were too deeply rooted, but because the Party failed to destroy the institutional context that reproduced them over time. Where local church institutions withered, so too did rightist attachments. Indeed, my findings hearken back to modernization theory. That approach's teleology of social development may have been misguided, but I validate one of its principal tenets: removed from their web of social affiliations, people become far more amenable to political resocialization.[2]

The other myth is the "freezing hypothesis" for postcommunist politics. As argued in Chapter 1, the notion of state-socialism as a "deep freeze" was very much in vogue in the early years of the transition, when many elites were attempting to revive long moribund political traditions and tap into what they perceived as long-suppressed, authentic identities. The emergence of revived precommunist parties, lively discussions of long-taboo

---

[1] Almond (1983: 138).
[2] See Deutsch (1961) and Kornhauser (1959) for classic statements of the modernization thesis.

historical subjects, and reinvigorated bickering between Serbs and Croats, Czechs and Slovaks, and Hungarians and Romanians certainly presented the illusion of a "revival of the past." There were even a few groups that, like Rumplestiltskin, seemed out of place in a world that had passed them by. Gordon (2002: 86), for example, describes a group of Catholic nuns in postcommunist Romania who, having survived an exceptionally brutal communist dictatorship, emerged as if "coming out of a time warp," with "no experience of a Church touched by Vatican II." Yet these are exceptional cases, more representative of journalistic fascination with European variants of the "noble savage" than of the true state of affairs. Those embedded within local church institutions did not emerge from communism as throwbacks to a bygone political era, having, on the whole, favored moderate rightist parties over those elements making antediluvian political appeals. The moral of the story is that continuity is not tantamount to fixedness. It should be viewed as a consequence not of the recrudescence of precommunist political cleavages, which in any case were largely irrelevant for the problems Eastern Europe faced in the 1990s, but of the reinterpretation of already-existing attachments in light of ever-changing realities. This interpretive process is no different than what has happened in places such as the U.S. South, where there has been no inconsistency between being a lifelong Democrat and having views on issues, such as race, that evolved dramatically over the decades.

7.2.3   Path Dependence

Hungarian political continuity is "path dependent," but in a different way from current conceptions. As summarized by Pierson (2004), the predominant image of path dependence is that of a branching process from some common initial starting point. Once a particular historical trajectory is followed, it is increasingly costly to reverse course and embark on a different trajectory. Consequently, political outcomes are often determined by decisions made at choice-points much earlier in time. A textbook example comes from Moore (1966), who explains how countries end up as either dictatorships or democracies depending on the particular historical trajectory they follow. Consider an abbreviated form of the argument for England and Germany. Although both endured royal absolutism in the premodern period, England eventually developed a middle-class stratum that allowed for the development of democracy, whereas in Germany middle-class weakness in comparison with the landed aristocracy ultimately led to the emergence of fascism.

Moore describes many causal links that led to democracy in England and fascism in Germany. The key feature of his argument from my perspective is that to account for regime outcomes it is necessary to know only the next to last links in the causal chains. Thus, once England came to have a strong middle class and Germany a weak one, there is sufficient information about each country to predict their respective regime outcomes. In Moore's now famous formulation: no bourgeois, no democracy. However, *how* England came to have a strong middle class and Germany a weak one is, while historically interesting, logically irrelevant to his conclusions. Put differently, history matters, but only insofar as it takes us further and further back in the causal chain for each country.

Hungarian political continuities point to a very different situation, in which it is *more* important to know events further back in the causal chain than those closer to the outcome of interest. Table 6.5 in Chapter 6 shows that the nature of the trajectory of church community in a municipality during communism mattered for postcommunist rightist loyalties. As expected, settlements where church community was low the whole time had lower support for the Right than those where the church had once been strong. What was not discussed, however, is that by late in the communist period the average level of church community for each trajectory was virtually the same. This means that what mattered for postcommunist outcomes in these cases was not the *level* of church community at a particular point in time but the *path* settlements took to arrive at that level. To make the analogy with Moore's argument, it is as if what mattered most for a fascist outcome was not the weakness of the middle class, but the historical process by which the middle class became weak. We have a situation in which the path mattered more than the endpoint of the path. In this sense, local church institutions in Hungary "remembered" their own pasts, and Hungarian rightist loyalties are truly path dependent.

This conclusion implies an indispensable role for large-N analysis in path dependence arguments. It is unfortunate that the detailed knowledge of individual cases deployed in typical applications has precluded such analysis.[3]

---

[3] See, for example, Mahoney and Rueschemeyer (2003b) and Pierson (2004). Mahoney and Rueschemeyer (2003a: 13) claim that having a small number of cases is an indispensable feature of comparative historical analysis. Yet the trade-off between extensive knowledge of a few cases and superficial knowledge of many cases is more a practical than a theoretical

Most of the outcomes of interest to political scientists have multiple potential causes, and only through consideration of many observations, each of which has varying values on potential alternative explanatory factors, is it possible to isolate the path dependence of a particular outcome from other possible causes. Large-N analysis ought to be not only a desirable feature of historical approaches, but a necessary component of them.

7.3 Toward a General Theory of Persistence

How "portable" is the argument? As explained in the introductory chapter, the paradox of political persistence has occurred not just in former communist countries, but in many redemocratizing authoritarian regimes and stable democracies. However, the argument I have offered does not lend itself to immediate application either to other types of partisan persistence or to rightist persistence in other countries. Parish priests in Hungary may have successfully fostered local church institutions, and those institutions may have preserved loyalties to parties of the Right. But there is no guarantee that in other countries priests performed a similar function, that churches were the relevant institutions, or that rightist loyalties were transmitted. The vocabulary of "rightist" and "leftist" might even need to be changed in some other political contexts. In short, to borrow the language of Przeworski and Teune (1970: 24), my argument remains more "historically based" than "abstractly formulated." The task, then, is to begin thinking about how to formulate a theory that will be valid for other political systems, and for other partisan attachments.

The best place to begin is "close to home" – with other redemocratizing former communist regimes. As postcommunist countries the former Czechoslovakia and Poland share many of the same background conditions that made political persistence so paradoxical in Hungary: decades of Party rule, forced industrialization, and socialist reeducation. Both countries have had political palettes in which parties that could be labeled as leftist and rightist competed for popular support. Thus, the basic paradox of persistence as formulated for Hungary – the transmission of rightist partisan loyalties against the concerted efforts of an authoritarian leftist regime – remains the same. However, it is not clear whether such

---

limitation. Given sufficient time and resources, there is no obstacle in large-N research to the sort of detail found in small-N studies. Tarrow (2004) has a nice discussion of how qualitative and quantitative methods can and should coexist within the same research program.

persistence is rooted in the Churches, though in both instances there is good reason to think so.

The Polish case is perhaps the easiest to make because the Catholic Church there was the strongest Church in the bloc and actually *gained* organizational strength during the communist period.[4] Unlike in Hungary, most Poles retained loyalties to the Church through the 1960s and beyond.[5] However, it would still be necessary to show empirically that variations in the strength of church community – however that might be measured in the Polish context – corresponded with varying congruence between pre- and postcommunist rightist parties. In the former Czechoslovakia the Churches were severely repressed during state-socialism, and seemed to enjoy little mass loyalty.[6] However, Buerkle (2003) shows that continuities in support for "populist" parties – the precommunist Slovak Peoples Party and Meciar's postcommunist Movement for a Democratic Slovakia – are correlated with the presence of Catholic institutions and associations. She does not explore the links between the pre- and postcommunist periods, but does provide strong *prima facie* evidence for a Church connection.

As we move from former state-socialist countries to other redemocratizing authoritarian countries, the character of the paradox begins to change. First, under an authoritarianism of the Right, it is leftist political elites that are arrested, killed, or forced into exile. Leftist trade unions and other organizations are broken up or infiltrated. Thus, it is leftist and not rightist continuity that becomes puzzling, and the argument must be extended to include both kinds of loyalties. Second, continuity becomes less paradoxical, for although leftists may be persecuted, on the whole rightist authoritarian regimes have been less intrusive into society than their leftist counterparts. With the exception of Nazi Germany, no rightist authoritarian regime implemented programs to create a "New Man," and preauthoritarian institutions of civil society survived to a greater degree. There are thus more potential avenues whereby partisan attachments could be transmitted, and the menu of institutional candidates has to be correspondingly extended beyond the Churches.

Spain provides a wonderful example of the way in which a different set of institutions, nurtured by different entrepreneurial elites, could transmit an alternative partisan attachment. The Franco regime lasted roughly four

---

[4] Osa (1989: 275) refers to Polish "exceptionalism" in this regard.
[5] Diskin (2001: 132).
[6] Michel (1991).

decades, a similar duration to state-socialism in Eastern Europe, and left-ist leaders and institutions endured a long period of repression and exile. Nonetheless, Maravall (1982: 175) reports a high ecological correlation between the 1936 and 1977 votes for the Spanish Socialist Party (PSOE). He notes the importance of intergenerational partisan continuity, and adds that it "was much stronger... in those enclaves where the PSOE and the UGT [General Union of Workers] survived under the dictatorship – the protective communities of Asturian miners and of steel and metal workers from Vizcaya."[7] This argument, too, is "historically based," and the exact mechanism of this protection remains unclear. Yet, in so many ways it is the mirror image of my own. In both Hungary and Spain semiautonomous local institutions survived as foci of loyalty, facilitating the transmission of partisan attachments that were in opposition to the dominant set of values.

If we consider stable democracies, the character of the paradox evolves even further. The affinity between religiosity and rightist partisan attach-ments in Hungary might appear unremarkable to many who study Western European politics, where regular churchgoers have evinced far greater sup-port for conservative and Christian democratic parties than their less fervid fellow citizens.[8] Seen from Western Europe, then, the Hungarian finding appears less than puzzling. However, this study has done more than merely document an association. It explains *why* there should be a high correlation. In retelling the story of clerical resistance to communist rule, in specifying the mechanism of partisan reproduction over time, it has transformed the empirical relationship between religiosity and rightist attachments from the realm of association into that of causation.[9] Indeed, my argument might explain the Western European correlation, and with little modifi-cation could account for the less visible, but equally interesting, minority of the religious that has opted for leftist and other parties.[10]

---

[7] Maravall (1982: 176).

[8] The literature is voluminous. Striking evidence for this in postwar Germany may be found in Schmitt (1989). See also Lipset (1960).

[9] See Laitin (1995) on the importance of having a "story" linking independent and dependent variables.

[10] Kalyvas (1996: 168–9) describes the influence of liberal Catholics in nineteenth century Belgium. Berenson (1984: 128) documents how the "democ-socs" in mid-nineteenth-century France sought to promulgate their vision of socialist democracy and "unorthodox religiosity." As Harris (1999: 141) notes, in the United States before the Second World War, churches sometimes acted to draw African-Americans into *communist* organizations. More recently, liberation theology in Latin America illustrates that at least some in the Catholic Church were willing to ally with the Left in defense of the downtrodden. Tarrow

What can Hungary really tell us about the roots of political continuity in stable democracies? The reason former communist regimes are such interesting cases is that the peculiarly intrusive nature of state-socialism renders them "causally sparse" – the theories developed to explain continuity in Western Europe and North America are excluded *a priori*. Local church institutions transmitted rightist attachments without repeated election campaigns and political participation to "bind in" electoral loyalties, without parties and their satellite organizations to "encapsulate" voters, and in the midst of much economic and social turbulence. In a world of multiple causation there is no reason why this new explanation must necessarily apply to other parts of the world. Economic stability and political encapsulation might very well account for many pockets of persistence in stable democracies. Yet, this book points to a further wrinkle because the theory it propounds relies on few of the accoutrements of democratic politics that limit other theories' domains of applicability. It just might be the case that hidden underneath the mechanisms adduced to explain continuity in Western Europe and North America there operates a simpler logic, one that requires virtually no democratic politics, but wherein individuals embedded in particular institutional contexts are able to reproduce core attachments that orient them within an ever-evolving political firmament. If this is true then we will have discovered the core of the paradox of political persistence.

(1988) documents the existence of leftist Catholic "base communities" in Italy. For other contemporary examples, see the contributions in Broughton and ten Napel (2000).

Appendices

Appendix 1. Deviation between the Database Results and the Official Results

Party	Regional List 1998 Used Here		Regional List 1998 Official	
	Vote	(%)	Vote	(%)
MSZP	1,423,765	32.24	1,497,231	32.92
SZDSZ	348,109	7.88	344,352	7.57
MDF	137,365	3.11	127,118	2.80
FKgP	607,491	13.76	597,820	13.15
KDNP	114,208	2.59	104,892	2.31
FIDESZ-MPP	1,244,539	28.19	1,340,826	29.48

Party	Regional List 1994 Used Here		Regional List 1994 Official	
	Vote	(%)	Vote	(%)
MSZP	1,759,828	32.98	1,781,504	32.99
SZDSZ	1,054,436	19.16	1,065,889	19.74
MDF	626,629	11.74	633,770	11.74
FKgP	469,492	8.80	476,272	8.82
KDNP	374,623	7.02	379,523	7.03
FIDESZ	374,872	7.02	379,344	7.02

.

.

.

.

.

.

.

.

.

.

.

.

.

.

.

.

.

.

.

.

.

.

.

Party	Regional List 1990 Used Here Vote	(%)	Regional List 1990 Official Vote	(%)
MSZP	531,237	10.90	535,064	10.89
SZDSZ	1,042,997	21.39	1,050,799	21.39
MDF	1,205,570	24.73	1,214,359	24.73
FKgP	573,110	11.75	576,315	11.73
KDNP	313,097	6.42	317,278	6.46
FIDESZ	436,436	8.95	439,649	8.95

Party	Regional List 1947 Used Here Vote	(%)	Regional List 1947 Official Vote	(%)
MKP	1,078,714	23.12	1,112,990	22.3
SZDP	701,146	15.06	744,671	14.9
FKGP	748,989	16.08	769,580	15.4
DNP	768,623	16.50	820,453	16.4
KNT	63,677	1.37	69,586	1.4
PDP	48,386	1.04	50,374	1.0
NPP	409,116	8.78	415,465	8.3
FMDP	208,502	4.48	260,411	5.2
MFP	664,798	14.27	670,547	13.4
MRP	83,711	1.80	89,179	1.7

Party	Regional List 1945 Used Here Vote	(%)	Regional List 1945 Official Vote	(%)
FKGP	2,686,450	57.37	2,697,503	57.30
SZDP	820,446	17.52	823,314	17.41
MKP	799,165	17.06	802,122	16.95
NPP	322,987	6.90	325,284	6.87
PDP	76,219	1.63	76,424	1.62
MRP	5,757	0.12	5,762	0.12

Sources: 1998 Published: Körösényi (1999: 121); 1994 Published: Luca et al. (1994: 574); 1990 Published: Szoboszlai (1990: 596–7); 1947 Published: Izsák (1983: 200–1); 1945 Published: Vida (1986: 142–3).

Appendix 2. Guide to Party Abbreviations

1990–1994–1998

MSZP: Hungarian Socialist Party
SZDSZ: Alliance of Free Democrats
MDF: Hungarian Democratic Forum
FKgP: Independent Smallholders Party
KDNP: Christian Democratic People's Party
FIDESZ: Alliance of Young Democrats
MDNP: Hungarian Democratic People's Party
MIÉP: Hungarian Justice and Life Party

1945–1947

FKgP: Independent Smallholders Party
MKP: Hungarian Communist Party
DNP: Democratic People's Party
SZDP: Social-Democratic Party
MFP: Hungarian Independence Party
NPP: National Peasant Party
FMDP: Independent Hungarian Democratic Party
MRP: Hungarian Radical Party
KNT: Christian Women's Camp
PDP: Civic Democratic Party

Appendix 3. Members of the Leftist, Liberal, and Rightist Blocs

Leftist 1990: Hungarian Socialist Party (MSZP), Hungarian Socialist Worker's Party (MSZMP), Worker's Party (Munkáspárt), Hungarian Social-Democratic Party (MSZDP).
Leftist 1994: Hungarian Socialist Party, Worker's Party, Hungarian Social-Democratic Party.
Leftist 1998: Hungarian Socialist Party, Worker's Party, Hungarian Social-Democratic Party, Alliance of Free Democrats (SZDSZ).
Liberal 1990: Alliance of Free Democrats, Alliance of Young Democrats (Fidesz), Entrepreneur's Party (VP).
Liberal 1994: Alliance of Free Democrats, Alliance of Young Democrats, Entrepreneur's Party, Republic Party (KP).

Rightist 1990: Hungarian Democratic Forum (MDF), Independent Smallholders Party (FKgP), Christian Democratic People's Party (KDNP), National Smallholders Party (NKgP), Independent Hungarian Democratic Party (FMDP), Somogy Christian Coalition, Freedom Party, Hungarian Independence Party (MFP).
Rightist 1994: Hungarian Democratic Forum, Independent Smallholders Party, Christian Democratic People's Party, Compromise Smallholders Party, United Smallholders Party (EKgP), Hungarian Justice and Life Party, Conservative Party.
Rightist 1998: Alliance of Young Democrats–Hungarian Civic Party (Fidesz-MPP), Hungarian Democratic Forum, Independent Smallholders Party, Christian Democratic People's Party, Hungarian Justice and Life Party, Hungarian Democratic People's Party.
Leftist 1945: Hungarian Communist Party (MKP), Social-Democratic Party (SZDP), National Peasant Party (NPP).
Leftist 1947: Hungarian Communist Party, Social-Democratic Party, National Peasant Party.
Rightist 1945: Independent Smallholders Party.
Rightist 1947: Independent Smallholders Party, Democratic People's Party (DNP), Hungarian Independence Party, Independent Hungarian Democratic Party, Christian Women's Camp (KNT).

Appendix 4

Results of bivariate regressions of 1998, 1994, and 1990 rightist vote margins on 1945 rightist vote margins, by county. Blocs and election years are listed across the page, and counties are listed down the page. The results are presented in columns of three numbers for each election and county. The top number in the column is the estimated bivariate regression coefficient. The second number in the column is the estimated constant. The third number in the column is the estimated R^2. (In some cases I also list the number of observations.) Thus, for example, the regression coefficient after regressing the Right bloc margin in 1998 on that in 1945 for the settlements within Baranya county is 0.10. Likewise, the constant from the regression is 0.04, and the R^2 is 0.02. (See the top left column of three numbers.) To reduce clutter, values marked with an asterisk are *not* significant at $p < 0.10$. Values of less than 0.001 are reported as 0.

Appendix 4

County	Right Bloc Regression of 1998 on 1945	Right Bloc Regression of 1994 on 1945	Right Bloc Regression of 1990 on 1945
Baranya	0.10	0.07*	0.08*
	0.04*	−0.39	0.28
	0.02	0.01	0.03
	(N = 240)	(N = 238)	(N = 240)
Bács	0.22	0.26	0.10
	0.07	−0.12	0.21
	0.15	0.21	0.04
	(N = 275)	(N = 274)	(N = 275)
Békés	0.13	0.13*	0.08*
	0.12	−0.07	0.27
(N = 53)	0.08	0.07	0.03
Borsod	0.34	0.26	0.25
	0.16	0.02*	0.29
(N = 83)	0.24	0.22	0.23
Csongrád	0.10	0.04*	0.07
	0.19	0.02*	0.41
(N = 37)	0.12	0.02	0.05
Fejér	0.19	0.21	0.20
	0.07	−0.09	0.17
	0.09	0.12	0.11
	(N = 91)	(N = 91)	(N = 90)
Győr	0.14	0.16	0.11
(N = 141)	0.22	0.07	0.32
	0.07	0.12	0.06
Hajdú	0.10	0.20	0.17*
	0.09	−0.10	0.19
	0.04	0.18	0.13
	(N = 68)	(N = 67)	(N = 68)
Heves	0.06*	0.13	0.13
(N = 102)	0.01*	−0.11	0.23
	0.02	0.07	0.05
Jász-Nagykun-Szolnok	0.09*	0.15	0.12
	0.03	−0.12	0.20
	0.04	0.13	0.07
	(N = 57)	(N = 57)	(N = 56)
Komárom	0.29	0.24	0.20
	0.05	−0.09	0.34
	0.34	0.32	0.37
	(N = 61)	(N = 60)	(N = 61)

County	Right Bloc Regression of 1998 on 1945	Right Bloc Regression of 1994 on 1945	Right Bloc Regression of 1990 on 1945
Nógrád	0.27	0.27	0.30
(N = 105)	0.07	−0.06	0.23
	0.26	0.28	0.35
Pest	0.13	0.23	0.18
(N = 151)	0.19	−0.001*	0.35
	0.08	0.25	0.19
Somogy	0.27	0.26	0.25
(N = 211)	0.01*	−0.20	0.08
	0.13	0.10	0.11
Szabolcs	0.13	0.19	0.10
	0.13	−0.05	0.31
	0.04	0.10	0.03
	(N = 179)	(N = 178)	(N = 179)
Tolna	−0.04*	−0.11	−0.01*
(N = 99)	0.17	0.06	0.38
	0.01	0.05	0.001
Vas	0.27	0.29	0.13
	0.15	0.001*	0.35
	0.12	0.14	0.06
	(N = 187)	(N = 185)	(N = 186)
Veszprém	0.27	0.34	0.32
(N = 192)	0.21	−0.02*	0.23
	0.20	0.25	0.20
Zala	0.21	0.17	0.06*
	0.22	0.11	0.43
	0.11	0.07	0.01
	(N = 211)	(N = 210)	(N = 211)
TOTAL	0.21	0.22	0.15
	0.11	−0.05	0.28
	0.14	0.16	0.09
	(N = 2,547)	(N = 2,541)	(N = 2,550)

Appendix 5. A Note on Data Sources

This study is heavily data-reliant. I have attempted to specify both the patterns of Hungarian electoral continuity and discontinuity and the role of local church institutions during communism in transmitting rightist partisan attachments. I describe the electoral patterns by integrating freshly collected municipality-level data from the 1945 national parliamentary elections for virtually all of Hungary's towns and villages with preexisting postcommunist datasets. To reconstruct the struggle between priests and local communists for mass loyalties, I rely on a broad range of archival materials. Because these documentary sources were created in a period and under a regime in which falsification frequently occurred, I want to address their origin and how I used them.

The November 1945 national parliamentary elections were not free, but are considered by scholars to be fair. Thus, although the Allied Control Council prohibited "fascist" parties from competition, there were few reports of intimidation or chicanery during the election. Because I measure partisan attachments at the level of blocs rather than individual parties, the exclusion of the most right-wing parties does not bias my analysis. As noted, the Smallholders (FKgP) absorbed these rightist votes. Survey data from the period are also broadly consistent with the election outcomes. The Hungarian News Agency's Public Opinion Research Institute polled 6,000 people in October 1945 on their opinions concerning the elections upcoming in November. While the results do not exactly mirror the electoral outcome, they are close enough to lend extra confidence that the results actually reflect underlying preferences. For example, 48 percent of respondents said they would support the rightist FKgP, which ultimately won 57 percent of the vote. Twenty-five percent said they would vote for the Social Democrats, which ultimately garnered 17 percent. The prediction for the Communists was 18 percent, only 1.1 percent higher than their actual result of 16.9 percent.[1]

I tell the struggle from below between the Churches and the Party largely through archival materials. The question is, how accurate are these portrayals? How well do they reflect what really happened on the ground? It is well documented that the regime manufactured evidence when no real evidence could be found to incriminate someone it deemed undesirable. Cardinal Mindszenty was condemned using such "evidence," as were countless lesser-known victims. It is also true that documents could be deliberately falsified if by not doing so the party responsible for the "bad news" would incur sanction from the authorities. This may be particularly prevalent in organizations such as the State Office for Church Affairs (ÁEH), which was responsible not just for documenting church activities, but also for implementing government edicts aimed at reducing clerical influence.

---

[1] Magyar Távirati Iroda (1945: 17).

If the ÁEH inflated reports on the progress against the Churches it stood to gain standing with Party elites, but in the longer term risked losing relevance. (An ÁEH would not be necessary in a society in which the Churches had withered [or were reported to have withered] away.) If it understated its progress, on the other hand, then it might succeed in staking a greater claim on resources, but it also might result in the replacement of key figures in the organization. There was also the ever-present risk that the falsification would be discovered and punished.

Falsification certainly occurred, but not every report was falsified, and we are not without tools for evaluating the validity of particular claims. First, the greater number of independent documents about a certain fact or event, the greater confidence we have in the validity of that fact or event. Although the Party was the ultimate authority and data gathering on the Church was centralized in the ÁEH, there were sometimes different accounts of the same events. For example, both the Party and the Churches kept records on the pastoral activities of the lower clergy. The Churches kept their own archives and although these, as everything else, were supervised by the ÁEH, there is little evidence that these reports were written by the same individual whose reports appeared in the Party archives. Second, the greater the detail on a particular item, the more confidence we may have in it. For example, are there merely vague references to clerical "terror tactics," or is there also mention of specific people and acts? A detailed document does not preclude the possibility that a truly enterprising cadre would deliberately invent details to appear trustworthy, but in the aggregate it seems unlikely that many of them would go to such trouble.

How can we know that a document, as a whole, plausibly reflects events on the ground and not merely reproduces the Party preference for progress against the Churches? First, the narrower the circle of people with access to the document and its contents, the more confident we can be in it. It is one thing to fill popular newspapers and periodicals with glowing reports of the progress toward socialism, but why print lies when only the top officials are granted access? Many of the sources used here were marked "top secret" or "strictly confidential."[2] Second, reports that contain mixed messages are, typically, more reliable than those that are more homogeneous. Real life under state-socialism was never as unremittingly uniform as much of the early literature made it out to be. Reliable reports will reflect this plurality

---

[2] In Hungarian, *szigorúan titkos* and *szigorúan bizalmas*, respectively.

of belief and action, documenting both good and bad news. For example, a document that differentiates between progressive and reactionary priests, as most under consideration here did, is far more reliable than one accusing every clergyman of being reactionary. Third, in cases where a report is released a certain number of times per year, such as the "monthly bulletin" (*"havi jelentés"*) describing the general political atmosphere in particular localities, successive reports were compared with one another for evidence that they were more than mere formalities. For example, do the details of particular activities remain the same from month to month? If the number of church attendees is given in one month, does exactly the same number appear the next month? This reduces the reliability of a document. Finally, the same kind of reports from different provinces were compared for similarities and differences. One would expect some parallels given that the ÁEH gave common instructions to all provincial offices. For example, all monthly bulletins were required to mention any oppositional activity on the part of the clergy. Moreover, the language in which the bulletins were written would have reflected the common idiom in use at the time. In the 1950s this meant frequent references to "clerical reaction" (*klerikális reákció*), "imperialists" (*imperialisták*), "Church machinations" (*egyházi aknamunka*), and other such phrases. But behind the rhetoric, the declared magnitude and details of clerical and other activity usually differed across provinces. Zala county documents paint a different picture of Church-Party struggle from those in Hajdú-Bihar.[3] On balance, then, we can have confidence in the archival materials this study employs.

[3] For a subtle discussion of the sociology of such reports from the field, see Szabó (2000: 70–83).

Bibliography

Secondary Sources

Abramson, Paul R. 1992. "Of Time and Partisan Instability in Britain." *British Journal of Political Science* 22:3, 381–5.

Achen, Christopher H. 2000. "Why Lagged Dependent Variables Can Suppress the Explanatory Power of Other Independent Variables." Paper prepared for the Annual Meeting of the Political Methodology Section of the American Political Science Association, UCLA, July 20–2, 2000.

Achen, Christopher H. and W. Phillips Shively. 1995. *Cross-Level Inference*. Chicago and London: The University of Chicago Press.

Adriányi, Gabriel. 1974. *Fünfzig Jahre Ungarisher Kirchengeschichte, 1895–1945*. Mainz: Hase & Koehler Verlag.

ÁEH [Állami Egyházügyi Hivatal]. 1987. *Tájékoztató a Magyarországon Működő Egyházakról és Felekezetekről*. Budapest: ÁEH.

Allardt, Erik and Stein Rokkan, eds. 1970. *Mass Politics: Studies in Political Sociology*. New York: The Free Press.

Almond, Gabriel A. 1983. "Communism and Political Culture Theory." *Comparative Politics* 15:2, 127–38.

Andorka, Rudolf, Tamás Kolosi, and György Vukovich, eds. 1994. *Társadalmi riport 1994*. Budapest: Tárki.

András, A. Gergely. 1996. "Máig tartó hagyományok." *Magyar Nemzet*. March 25, 1996, 8.

András, Emmerich and Julius Morel. 1969. *Bilanz des Ungarischen Katholizismus*. München: Heimatwerk Verlag.

András, Emeric and Julius Morel. 1983a. *Church in Transition: Hungary's Catholic Church from 1945 to 1982*. Vienna: Hungarian Institute for Sociology of Religion.

András, Emeric and Julius Morel. 1983b. *Hungarian Catholicism: A Handbook*. Vienna: Hungarian Institute for Sociology of Religion. Toronto: St. Elizabeth of Hungary Parish.

Angelusz, Róbert and Róbert Tardos. 1999a. "Electoral Participation in Hungary, 1990–1994." In Tóka and Enyedi, *Elections to the Hungarian National Assembly 1994: Analyses, Documents and Data*. Berlin: Sigma, 168–97.

257

Angelusz, Róbert and Róbert Tardos. 1999b. "A választói erőtér blokkosodása, 1994–98." In Kurtán et al., *Magyarország politikai évkönyve 1998–ról.* Budapest: Demokrácia Kutatások Magyar Központja Alapítvány, 619–36.

Annabring, Matthias. 1953. "Die katholische Kirche im kommunistischen Ungarn." *Südost-Stimmen,* 3:8, December, 1–32.

Balogh, István, ed. 1994. *Törésvonalak és értékválasztások.* Budapest: MTA Politikai Tudományok Intézete.

Balogh, István. 1999. "Szabad és demokratikus választás–1945." In Földes and Hubai, *Parlamenti választások 1920–1998.* Budapest: Politikatörténeti Alapítvány, 208–34.

Balogh, Sándor, István Birta, Lajos Izsák, Sándor Jakab, Mihály Korom, and Péter Simon, eds. 1978. *A magyar népi demokrácia története 1944–1962.* Budapest: Kossuth Könyvkiadó.

Bangha, Béla, ed. 1931–3. *Katolikus Lexikon.* Four Volumes. Budapest: A Magyar Kultúra kiadása.

Bangó, Jenő. 1970. "Vallásszociológia Magyarországon." *Katolikus Szemle* XXII:2, 143–55.

Bangó, J. 1978. "L'influence des facteurs politiques et socio-culturels sur la religiosite de la jeunesse hongroise." *Revue des Pays de L'est* 1: 63–83.

Barany, Zoltán. 1990. "First Session of New Parliament." *RFE/RL Research Report,* May 25.

Barcza, József. 1994. "Az 1956-os forradalom megtorlása a magyarországi református egyházban." *Confessio* 18:1, 90–103.

Barcza, József. 1999. "Egyházunk az 1956. forradalom idején és Ravasz László jelentősége." In Barcza and Dienes, *A magyarországi református egyház története 1918–1990.* Sárospatak: A Sárospataki Református Kollégium Teológiai Akadémiája, 173–90.

Barcza, József and Dénes Dienes, eds. 1999. *A magyarországi református egyház története 1918–1990.* Sárospatak: A Sárospataki Református Kollégium Teológiai Akademiája.

Barron, J. B. and H. M. Waddams. 1950. *Communism and the Churches: A Documentation.* New York: Morehouse-Gorham Company.

Bartels, Larry M. 1998. "Electoral Continuity and Change, 1868–1996." *Electoral Studies* 17:3, 301–26.

Bartolini, Stefano and Peter Mair. 1990. *Identity, competition, and electoral availability: The stabilisation of European electorates 1885–1985.* London: Cambridge University Press.

Bartosek, Karel. 1993. "A történelem visszatérése–cseh módra." *Világosság* XXXIV: 1 (January), 10–15.

Beal, John P., James A. Coriden, and Thomas J. Green. 2000. *New Commentary on the Code of Canon Law.* New York: Paulist Press.

Beeson, Trevor. 1982. *Discretion and Valour: Religious Conditions in Russia and Eastern Europe.* rev. ed. Philadelphia: Fortress Press.

Beke, Pál and Gábor Koncz. 1985. "Művelődési otthonok: gondok, lehetőségek." *Magyar Építőművészet* 4, 14–15.

Bibliography

Bell, Peter D. 1984. *Peasants in Socialist Transition: Life in a Collectivized Hungarian Village*. Berkeley: University of California Press.

Bennett, Anne. 1998. "Party System Change in Redemocratizing Countries." In Pennings and Lane, *Comparing Party System Change*. London and New York: Routledge, 185–201.

Benoit, Kenneth. 1999. "Votes and Seats: The Hungarian Electoral Law and the 1994 National Parliamentary Election." In Tóka and Enyedi, *Elections to the Hungarian National Assembly 1994: Analyses, Documents and Data*. Berlin: Sigma, 108–38.

Bereczky, Albert. 1953. *A keskeny út*. Budapest: Református Egyetemes Konvent.

Berelson, Bernard R., Paul F. Lazarsfeld, and William N. McPhee. 1954. *Voting: A Study of Opinion Formation in a Presidential Campaign*. Chicago: University of Chicago Press.

Berend, Ivan. T. 1996. *Central and Eastern Europe, 1944–1993: Detour from the Periphery to the Periphery*. New York: Cambridge University Press.

Berend, Ivan T. and György Ránki. 1974. *Economic Development in East-Central Europe in the Nineteenth and Twentieth Centuries*. New York: Columbia University Press.

Berenson, Edward. 1984. *Populist Religion and Left-Wing Politics in France, 1830–1852*. Princeton: Princeton University Press.

Bergquist, William and Berne Weiss. 1994. *Freedom! Narratives of Change in Hungary and Estonia*. San Francisco: Jossey-Bass.

Bindes, Ferenc and László Németh. 1991. *Ha engem üldöztek . . . Válogatott dokumentumok a győri egyházmegye életéből 1945–1966*. Budapest: Mécs László Lap-és Könyvkiadó.

Blalock, H. M. 1964. *Causal Inferences in Nonexperimental Research*. Chapel Hill: University of North Carolina Press.

Blumstock, Robert. 1977. "Public Opinion in Hungary." In Connor and Gitelman, *Public Opinion in European Socialist Systems*. New York: Praeger, 132–66.

Blumstock, Robert. 1981. "Hungary." In Welsh, *Survey Research and Public Attitudes in Eastern Europe and the Soviet Union*. New York: Pergamon Press, 319–88.

Bociurkiw, Bohdan R. and John W. Strong, eds. 1975. *Religion and Atheism in the U.S.S.R. and Eastern Europe*. London: Macmillan.

Bodrogi, Tibor, ed. 1978. *Vársány: Tanulmányok egy észak-magyarországi falu társadalomnéprajzához*. Budapest: Akadémiai Kiadó.

Bőhm, Antal, Ferenc Gazsó, István Stumpf, and György Szoboszlai, eds. 2000. *Parlamenti választások 1998: Politikai szociológiai körkép*. Budapest: Századvég Kiadó, MTA Politikai Tudományok Intézete.

Bolyki, János and Sándor Ladányi. 1987. "A református egyház." In Lendvai, *A magyar protestantizmus 1918–1948: Tanulmányok*. Budapest: Kossuth Könyvkiadó, 25–127.

Books, John W. and Charles L. Prysby. 1991. *Political Behavior and the Local Context*. New York: Praeger.

Box-Steffensmeier, Janet M. and Renée Smith. 1996. "The Dynamics of Aggregate Partisanship." *American Political Science Review* 90:3, 567–80.

Bibliography

Brady, Henry E. and David Collier, eds. 2004. *Rethinking Social Inquiry: Diverse Tools, Shared Standards*. Oxford: Roman & Littlefield.

Broughton, David and Hans-Martien ten Napel, eds. 2000. *Religion and Mass Electoral Behaviour in Europe*. London and New York: Routledge.

Brown, Archie, ed. 1985. *Political Culture and Communist Studies*. Armonk, NY: M. E. Sharpe.

Brown, Archie and Jack Gray, eds. 1979. *Political Culture and Political Change in Communist States*. 2nd ed. London: MacMillan.

Brown, Archie and Gordon Wightman. 1979. "Czechoslovakia: Revival and Retreat." In Brown and Gray, *Political Culture and Political Change in Communist States*. 2nd ed. London: MacMillan, 159–96.

Brustein, William. 1988. *The Social Origins of Political Regionalism: France, 1849–1981*. Berkeley: University of California Press.

Bruszt, László and János Simon. 1991. "A 'választások éve' a közvélemény-kutatások tükrében." In Kurtán et al., *Magyarország politikai évkönyve*. Budapest: Demokrácia Kutatások Magyar Központja Alapítvány, 607–46.

Bruszt, László and János Simon. 1994. "Az Antall-korszak után, a választások előtt." In Kurtán et al., *Magyarország politikai évkönyve*. Budapest: Demokrácia Kutatások Magyar Központja Alapítvány, 774–802.

Buerkle, Karen. 2003. *Democracy before Civil Society: Associations and Vote for National Populism in Slovakia and the Czech Lands 1918–1938; 1994–2002*. Ph.D. diss., University of California, San Diego.

Burdick, Eugene and Arthur J. Broadbeck, eds. 1959. *American Voting Behavior*. Westport, CT: Greenwood Press.

Burnham, Walter Dean. 1968. "American Voting Behavior in the 1964 Election." *Midwest Journal of Political Science* XII:1, February, 1–40.

Butler, David and Donald Stokes. 1969. *Political Change in Britain: Forces Shaping Electoral Choice*. New York: St. Martin's Press.

Campbell, Angus et al., eds. 1966. *Elections and the Political Order*. New York: John Wiley and Sons.

Campbell, Ted A. 1996. *Christian Confessions: A Historical Introduction*. Louisville, KY: Westminster John Knox Press.

Carey, George. 1985. *A Tale of Two Churches: Can Protestants & Catholics Get Together?* Downers Grove, IL: InterVarsity Press.

Carey, John M. and Matthew Soberg Shugart. 1995. "Incentives to Cultivate a Personal Vote: A Rank Ordering of Electoral Formulas." *Electoral Studies* 14:4, 417–39.

CEU [Central European University, Budapest]. 1994. "The Development of Party Systems and Electoral Alignments in East Central Europe: Hungarian panel study, Fall 1992-Spring 1994." SPSS data files from the September 1992, December 1993, April 1994, and May 1994 general population surveys in Hungary. Budapest: Department of Political Science, Central European University. Distributors: Tárki data archive, Budapest; Zentralarchiv, Cologne.

Chambers, William Nisbet and Walter Dean Burnham, eds. 1967. *The American Party Systems: Stages of Political Development*. New York: Oxford University Press.

Bibliography

Colburn, Forrest D., ed. 1989. *Everyday Forms of Peasant Resistance*. Armonk, NY: M. E. Sharpe.

Connor, Walter. D. and Gitelman, Zvi. Y., eds. 1977. *Public Opinion in European Socialist Systems*. New York: Praeger.

Converse, Philip E. 1966. "The Concept of a Normal Vote." In Campbell et al., *Elections and the Political Order*. New York: John Wiley and Sons, 9–39.

Converse, Philip E. 1969. "Of Time and Partisan Stability." *Comparative Political Studies* 2:2, July, 139–71.

Converse, Philip E. and Roy Pierce. 1986. *Political Representation in France*. Cambridge, MA: Belknap Press.

Cotta, Mauricio. 1996. "Building Party Systems after the Dictatorship: The East European Cases in a Comparative Perspective." In Pridham and Vanhanen, *Democratization in Eastern Europe: Domestic and International Perspectives*. London and New York: Routledge, 99–127.

Csanád, Béla. 1976. "A katolikus vallásosság mérése hazánkban." *Vigilia* XLI évf. 5. szám, 294–303.

Csende, Béla. 1975. *A művelődési otthonok negyedszázada Békés megyében 1949–1974*. Békéscsaba: A Békés Megyei Tanács V.B. Művelődésügyi Osztálya.

Cserháti, József. 1980. "Tovább a nyitott utakon." *Vigilia* XLV évf. 10. szám. October, 651–9.

Csizmadia, Andor. 1966. *A magyar állam és az egyházak jogi kapcsolatainak kialakulása és gyakorlata a Horthy-korszakban*. Budapest: Akadémiai Kiadó.

Csizmadia, Andor. 1971. *Rechtliche Beziehungen von Staat und Kirche in Ungarn vor 1944*. Budapest: Akadémiai Kiadó.

Daalder, Hans and Peter Mair, eds. 1983. *Western European Party Systems: Continuity and Change*. Beverly Hills: Sage.

Dalton, Russell J., Scott C. Flanagan, and Paul Allen Beck, eds. 1984. *Electoral Change in Advanced Industrial Democracies: Realignment or Dealignment?* Princeton: Princeton University Press.

DeBoef, Suzanna. 2000. "Persistence and Aggregations of Survey Data over Time: From Microfoundations to Macropersistence." *Electoral Studies* 19:1, March, 9–29.

de Certeau, Michel. 1984. *The Practice of Everyday Life*. Berkeley: University of California Press.

Desan, Suzanne. 1990. *Reclaiming the Sacred: Lay Religion and Popular Politics in Revolutionary France*. Ithaca and London: Cornell University Press.

Deutsch, Karl. 1961. "Social Mobilization and Political Development." *American Political Science Review* 55:3, September, 493–514.

Diskin, Hannah. 2001. *The Seeds of Triumph: Church and State in Gomułka's Poland*. Budapest and New York: Central European University Press.

Dogan, Mattei. 1967. "Political Cleavage and Social Stratification in France and Italy." In Lipset and Rokkan, *Party Systems and Voter Alignments: Cross-National Perspectives*. New York: The Free Press, 129–95.

Dogan, Mattei and Stein Rokkan, eds. 1969. *Quantitative Ecological Analysis in the Social Sciences*. Cambridge, MA: MIT Press.

Donáth, Ferenc. 1980. *Reform and Revolution: Transformation of Hungary's Agriculture 1945–1970*. Budapest: Corvina Kiadó.

Downs, Anthony. 1957. *An Economic Theory of Democracy*. New York: Harper & Row.

Drake, Paul and Ivan Jaksic, eds. 1999. *El modelo chileno: democracia y desarrollo en los Noventa*. Santiago: LOM ediciones.

Dunn, Dennis. 1977. *The Catholic Church and the Soviet Government, 1939–1949*. Boulder, CO: East European Quarterly.

Ekiert, Grzegorz. 1996. *The State Against Society: Political Crises and Their Aftermath in East Central Europe*. Princeton: Princeton University Press.

Ekiert, Grzegorz and Stephen Hanson, eds. 2003. *Capitalism and Democracy in Central and Eastern Europe*. New York: Cambridge University Press.

Enyedi, Zsolt. 1996. "Organizing a Subcultural Party in Eastern Europe: The Case of the Hungarian Christian Democrats." *Party Politics* 2:3, 377–96.

Enyedi, Zsolt. 2000. "Religious and Clerical Polarisation in Hungary." In Broughton and ten Napel, *Religion and Mass Electoral Behaviour in Europe*. London and New York: Routledge, 157–75.

Erdő, Péter, ed. 2001. *A magyar katolikus egyház 1945-től 1965-ig*. Budapest: Márton Áron Kiadó.

Farkas, György. 1988. "Katolikus Agrárifjúsági Legényegyletek Országos Testülete." In Turányi, *Magyar katolikus almanach II*. Budapest: Stent István Társulat, 292–312.

Fél, Edit and Tamás Hofer. 1969. *Proper Peasants: Traditional Life in a Hungarian Village*. Chicago: Aldine Publishing Company.

Felak, James. 2000. "Relations between the Communist and Social Democratic Parties in Hungary in 1945." *East European Quarterly* XXXIV:1, March, 95–130.

Ferree, Karen E. 2004. "Iterative Approaches to RxC Ecological Inference Problems: Where They Can Go Wrong and One Quick Fix." *Political Analysis* 12:2, Spring, 143–59.

Fiorina, Morris P. 1976. "The Voting Decision: Instrumental and Expressive Aspects." *Journal of Politics* 38, 390–415.

Földes, György and László Hubai, eds. 1999. *Parlamenti választások 1920–1998*. Budapest: Politkatörténeti Alapítvány.

Froese, Paul. 2001. "Hungary for Religion: A Supply-Side Interpretation of the Hungarian Religious Revival." *Journal for the Scientific Study of Religion* 40:2, 251–68.

Furtak, Robert K., ed. 1990. *Elections in Socialist States*. New York: Harvester Wheatsheaf.

Gabriel, Oscar W. and Klaus G. Troitzsch. 1993. *Wahlen in Zeiten des Umbruchs*. Frankfurt: Peter Lang.

Galter, Albert. 1957. *The Red Book of the Persecuted Church*. Dublin: M. H. Gill and Son Ltd.

Gannon, Thomas M., ed. 1988. *World Catholicism in Transition*. New York: MacMillan.

Gati, Charles. 1986. *Hungary and the Soviet Bloc*. Durham: Duke University Press.

Bibliography

Gazsó, Ferenc and Tibor Gazsó. 1994. "Választói magatartás és pártpreferenciák Magyarországon." In Balogh, *Töresvonalak és értékválasztások*. Budapest: MTA Politikai Tudományok Intézete, 109–46.

Geddes, Barbara. 1995. "A Comparative Perspective on the Leninist Legacy in Eastern Europe." *Comparative Political Studies* 28:2 July, 239–74.

Gergely, Jenő. 1977. *A politikai katolicizmus Magyarországon (1890–1950)*. Budapest: Kossuth Könyvkiadó.

Gergely, Jenő. 1985. *A katolikus egyház Magyarországon 1944–1971*. Budapest: Kossuth Könyvkiadó.

Gergely, Jenő. 1990. *Az 1950-es egyezmény és a szerzetesrendek felszámolása Magyarországon*. Budapest: Vigilia Kiadó.

Gergely, Jenő. 1997. *A katolikus egyház története Magyarországon 1919–1945*. Budapest: ELTE-Újkori Magyar Történeti Tanszék.

Gitelman, Zvi Y. 1977. "Public Opinion in Czechoslovakia." In Connor and Gitelman, *Public Opinion in European Socialist Systems*. New York: Praeger, 83–103.

Goeckel, Robert F. 1990. *The Lutheran Church and the East German State: Political Conflict and Change under Ulbricht and Honecker*. Ithaca and London: Cornell University Press.

Golden, Miriam. 1988. "Historical Memory and Ideological Orientations in the Italian Workers' Movement." *Politics & Society* 16:1, March, 1–34.

Gombos, Gyula. 1960. *The Lean Years: A Study of Hungarian Calvinism in Crisis*. New York: The Kossuth Foundation.

Gordon, Mary. 2002. "Women of God." *The Atlantic Monthly*, 289, January, 57–91.

Goven, Joanna. 1993. "The Gendered Foundations of Hungarian Socialism: State, Society, and the Anti-Politics of Anti-Feminism, 1948–1990." Ph.D. Diss., University of California, Berkeley.

Greene, William H. 2000. *Econometric Analysis*. 4th ed. Upper Saddle River, NJ: Prentice Hall.

Gsovski, Vladimir. 1973. *Church and State behind the Iron Curtain*. 2nd ed. Westport, CT: Greenwood Press.

Gussoni, Lino and Aristede Brunello. 1954. *The Silent Church*. New York: Veritas Publishers.

Gyáni, Gábor. 1993. "Political Uses of Tradition in Postcommunist East Central Europe." *Social Research* 60:4, Winter, 893–913.

Habermas, Jürgen. 1990. *Die Moderne–ein unvollendetes Projekt: Philosophisch-politische Aufsätze 1977–1990*. Leipzig: Reclam-Verlag.

Habuda, Miklós, Sándor Rákosi, Gábor Székely, and György T. Varga. 1998. *A Magyar Dolgozók Pártja határozatai 1948–1956*. Budapest: Napvilág Kiadó.

Hainbuch, Friedrich. 1982. *Kirche und Staat in Ungarn nach dem Zweiten Weltkrieg*. München: Dr. Dr. Rudolf Trofenik.

Handler, Andrew and Susan V. Meschel, eds. 1997. *Red Star, Blue Star: The Lives and Times of Jewish Students in Communist Hungary (1948–1956)*. Boulder, CO: East European Monographs.

Hann, C. M. 1980. *Tázlár: A Village in Hungary*. Cambridge: Cambridge University Press.

Harris, Frederick. 1999. *Something Within: Religion in African American Political Activism*. Oxford: Oxford University Press.

Hart, Henry O. 1983. "The Tables Turned: If East Europeans Could Vote." *Public Opinion* 6, October/November, 53–7.

Havasy, Gyula. 1990. *A magyar katolikusok szenvedései 1944–1989*. Budapest: self-published at INFO Kft.

Havasy, Gyula. 1993. *Martyrs of the Catholics in Hungary*. Budapest: Gyula Havasy.

Hays, Samuel P. 1967. "Political Parties in the Community-Society Continuum." In Chambers and Burnham, *The American Party Systems: Stages of Political Development*. New York: Oxford University Press, 152–81.

Heclo, Hugh and Henrik Madsen. 1987. *Policy and Politics in Sweden: Principled Pragmatism*. Philadelphia: Temple University Press.

Henn, Matt. 1998. "Opinion Polling in Central and Eastern Europe under Communism." *Journal of Contemporary History* 33:2, 229–40.

Herf, Jeffrey. 1993. "Multiple Restorations: German Political Traditions and the Interpretation of Nazism, 1945–1946." *Central European History* 26:1, 21–55.

Hervay, Ferenc. 1988. "Szerzetesrendek." In Turányi, *Magyar Katolikus almanach II*. Budapest: Szent István Társulat, 157–321.

Hoensch, Jörg K. 1996. *A History of Modern Hungary 1867–1994*. London and New York: Longman.

Hollos, Marida and Bela C. Maday, eds. 1983. *New Hungarian Peasants: An East Central European Experience with Collectivization*. New York: Social Science Monographs – Brooklyn College Press.

Hoschka, Peter and Hermann Schunk. 1978. "Regional Stability of Voting Behavior in Federal Elections: A Longitudinal Aggregate Data Analysis." In Kaase and von Beyme, *Elections and Parties*. London and Beverly Hills: Sage, 31–52.

Houska, Joseph J. 1985. *Influencing Mass Political Behavior: Elites and Subcultures in the Netherlands and Austria*. Berkeley, CA: Institute of International Studies.

Hubai, László. 2001. *Magyarország XX. századi választási atlasza 1920–2000*. 3 vols. Budapest: Napvilág Kiadó.

Hubai, László. 2002. "A választói magatartás kontinuitása 1990-2002." *Politikatudományi Szemle* 11:1–2, 93–119.

Huckfeldt, Robert and John Sprague. 1995. *Citizens, Politics, and Social Communication: Information and Influence in an Election Campaign*. Cambridge: Cambridge University Press.

Huckfeldt, Robert, Eric Plutzer, and John Sprague. 1993. "Alternative Contexts of Political Behavior: Churches, Neighborhoods, and Individuals." *Journal of Politics* 55:2, 365–81.

Hunt, Lynn. 1984. *Politics, Culture, and Class in the French Revolution*. Berkeley: University of California Press.

Husband, William B. 2000. *"Godless Communists": Atheism and Society in Soviet Russia 1917–1932*. DeKalb: Northern Illinois University Press.

Hutten, Kurt. 1967. *Iron Curtain Christians: The Church in Communist Countries Today*. Minneapolis: Augsburg Publishing House.

Ignotus, Paul. 1972. *Hungary*. London: Ernest Benn Limited.

Bibliography

Izsák, Lajos. 1983. *Polgári ellenzéki pártok Magyarországon 1944–1949*. Budapest: Kossuth Könyvkiadó.

Izsák, Lajos. 1985. "A katolikus egyház társadalompolitikai tevékenysége Magyarországon (1945–1956)." *Századok* 119:2, 423–66.

Izsák, Lajos. 1999. "A parlamentarizmus vesztett csatája – 1947." In Földes and Hubai, *Parlamenti választások 1920–1998*. Budapest: Politikatörténeti Alapítvány, 235–58.

Jackson, John E. 2002. "A Seemingly Unrelated Regression Model for Analyzing Multiparty Elections." *Political Analysis* 10:1, 49–65.

Janos, Andrew C. 1982. *The Politics of Backwardness in Hungary: 1825–1945*. Princeton: Princeton University Press.

Janos, Andrew C. 2000. *East Central Europe in the Modern World: The Politics of the Borderlands from Pre- to Postcommunism*. Stanford, CA: Stanford University Press.

Jávor, Kata. 1978. "Kontinuitás és változás a társadalmi és tudati viszonyokban." In Bodrogi, *Vársány: Tanulmányok egy észak-magyarországi falu társadalomnéprajzához*. Budapest: Akadémiai Kiadó, 295–373.

Jávor, Kata. 1983. "Continuity and Change in the Social and Value Systems of a Northern Hungarian Village." In Hollos and Maday, *New Hungarian Peasants: An East Central European Experience with Collectivization*. New York: Social Science Monographs-Brooklyn College Press, 273–300.

Jehlička, Peter, Tomas Kostelecký, and Ludek Sykora. 1993. "Czechoslovak Parliamentary Elections 1990: Old patterns, New Trends and Lots of Surprises." In O'Loughlin and van der Wusten, *The New Political Geography of Eastern Europe*. London and New York: Belhaven Press, 235–54.

Jowitt, Kenneth. 1974. "An Organizational Approach to the Study of Political Culture in Marxist-Leninist Systems." *American Political Science Review* 68:3, September, 1171–91.

Juhasz, William. 1952. *Blueprint for a Red Generation: The Philosophy, Methods, and Practices of Communist Education as Imposed on Captive Hungary*. New York: Mid-European Studies Center of the National Committee for a Free Europe.

Juhász, William. 1965. *Hungarian Social Science Reader*. München: Heller and Molnar.

Kaase, Max and Klaus von Beyme, eds. 1978. *Elections and Parties*. London and Beverly Hills: Sage.

Kádár, Imre, ed. 1950. *Five Years of Hungarian Protestantism*. Budapest: Hungarian Church Press.

Kádár, Imre. 1958. *The Church in the Storm of Time*. Budapest: Bibliotheca.

Kádár, János. 1985. *Selected Speeches and Interviews*. Budapest: Akadémiai Kiadó.

Káldi, Georg. 1956. "Die Kirche in Ungarn." *Sociaal Kompas* 4:2, July/August, 37–67.

Kalyvas, Stathis N. 1996. *The Rise of Christian Democracy in Europe*. Ithaca, NY: Cornell University Press.

Kamarás, István. 1992. *Búvópatakok*. Budapest: Márton Áron Kiadó.

Kamarás, István. 1995. "Tendencies of Religious Changes in Modern Hungary." *Hungarian Studies* 10:1, 121–30.

Bibliography

Kardos, László. 1969. *Egyház és vallásos élet egy mai faluban (Bakonycsernye – 1965)*. Budapest: Kossuth Könyvkiadó.

Kende, Péter. 1992. "Vissza – de milyen hagyományhoz?" *Világosság* XXXIII, December, 881–7.

Kennedy, Peter. 1985. *A Guide to Econometrics*. 2nd ed. Cambridge: MIT Press.

Kertzer, David I. 1980. *Comrades and Christians: Religion and Political Struggle in Communist Italy*. Cambridge: Cambridge University Press.

Key, V. O., Jr. 1949. *Southern Politics in State and Nation*. New York: Vintage.

Key, V. O., Jr. and Frank Munger, 1959. "Social Determinism and Electoral Decision: the Case of Indiana." In Burdick and Broadbeck, *American Voting Behavior*. Westport, CT: Greenwood Press, 281–99.

Kharkordin, Oleg. 1998. "First Europe–Asia Lecture: Civil Society and Orthodox Christianity." *Europe–Asia Studies* 50:6, 949–68.

King, Gary. 1997. *A Solution to the Ecological Inference Problem: Reconstructing Individual Behavior from Aggregate Data*. Princeton: Princeton University Press.

King, Gary, Ori Rosen, and Martin A. Tanner. 2004. *Ecological Inference: New Methodological Strategies*. New York: Cambridge University Press.

King, Gary, Michael Tomz, and Jason Wittenberg. 2000. "Making the Most of Statistical Analyses: Improving Interpretation and Presentation." *American Journal of Political Science* 44:2, April, 347–61.

Kisfalusi, János. 1992. *Ne félj, veled vagyok!* Hungary: Rakaca.

Kiss, Csilla. 2003. "From Liberalism to Conservatism: The Federation of Young Democrats in Post-Communist Hungary." *East European Politics & Societies* 16:3, 739–63.

Kiszely, Gábor. 2001. *Állambiztonság (1956–1990)*. Budapest: Korona Kiadó.

Kitschelt, Herbert. 1992. "The Formation of Party Systems in East Central Europe." *Politics & Society* 20:1, 7–50.

Kitschelt, Herbert. 2003. "Accounting for Postcommunist Regime Diversity: What Counts as Good Cause?" In Ekiert and Hanson, *Capitalism and Democracy in Central and Eastern Europe*. New York: Cambridge University Press, 49–86.

Kitschelt, Herbert, Zdenka Mansfeldova, Radoslaw Markowski, and Gábor Tóka. 1999. *Post-communist Party Systems: Competition, Representation, and Interparty Cooperation*. New York: Cambridge University Press.

Klandermans, B., Hanspeter Kriesi, and Sidney Tarrow, eds. 1988. *From Structure to Action: Comparing Social Movements across Cultures*. International Social Movement Research Series, vol. 1. Greenwich, CT: JAI Press.

Kolosi, Tamás, Tóth István György, and György Vukovich, eds. 1999. *Social Report 1998*. Budapest: Tárki.

Kónya, István. 1988. *A "keskeny úton" a "szolgáló egyház" felé*. Budapest: Akadémiai Kiadó.

Kornhauser, William. 1959. *The Politics of Mass Society*. Glencoe, IL: Free Press.

Kornis, Julius. 1932. *Education in Hungary*. New York: Teachers College, Columbia University.

Körösényi, András. 1991. "Revival of the Past or New Beginning? The Nature of Post-Communist Politics." *The Political Quarterly* 62:1, January–March, 52–74.

Bibliography

Körösényi, András. 1999. *Government and Politics in Hungary.* Budapest and New York: Central European University Press.

Kostelecký, Tomáš. 1994. "Economic, Social and Historical Determinants of Voting Patterns in the 1990 and 1992 Parliamentary Elections in the Czech Republic." *Czech Sociological Review* 2:2, 209–28.

Kostelecký, Tomáš. 2002. *Political Parties after Communism: Developments in East-Central Europe.* Baltimore and London: Johns Hopkins University Press.

Kovács, András. 1996. "Did the Losers Really Win? An Analysis of Electoral Behavior in Hungary in 1994." *Social Research* 63:2, 511–30.

Kovács, Ernő. 1995. "Négy választás Magyarországon: Gondolatok az 1945 utáni demokratikus választásokról." *Acta Academiae Paedagogicae Agriensis Nova Series Tom* XXII, Eger, 97–111.

Kovrig, Bennett. 1979. *Communism in Hungary: From Kun to Kádár.* Stanford: Hoover Institution Press.

Kowalski, Mariusz and Przemysław Śleszyński. 2000. *Uwarunkowania Zachowań Wyborczych W Województwie Słupskim.* Dokumentacja Geograficzna nr 21. Warszawa: PAN IGiPZ.

Krivý, Vladimír. 1997. "49 Städte: Wandel und Kontinuität." in Mannová, *Bürgertum und bürgerliche Gesellschaft in der Slowakei 1900–1989.* Bratislava: AEP, 37–59.

Krivý, Vladimír. 2003a. "The HSL'S Heritage in Terms of Territorial Voting Patterns." Unpublished manuscript, Institute of Sociology, Slovak Academy of Sciences.

Krivý, Vladımir. 2003b. "Slovak Regions: Changes and Continuities in Voting Patterns." Paper prepared for the European Consortium for Political Research, Marburg, 2003.

KSH [Központi Statisztikai Hivatal]. 1959a. *Hajdú-Bihar megye fontosabb statisztikai adatai.* Budapest: KSH.

KSH [Központi Statisztikai Hivatal]. 1959b. *Zala megye fontosabb statisztikai adatai.* Budapest: KSH.

KSH [Központi Statisztikai Hivatal]. 1960a. *1960. évi népszámlálás 3. Hajdú-Bihar megye és Debrecen személyi és családi adatai.* Budapest: KSH.

KSH [Központi Statisztikai Hivatal]. 1960b. *1960. évi népszámlálás 3. Zala megye személyi és családi adatai.* Budapest: KSH.

KSH [Központi Statisztikai Hivatal]. 1962a. *Hajdú-Bihar megye fontosabb statisztikai adatai.* Budapest: KSH.

KSH [Központi Statisztikai Hivatal]. 1962b. *Zala megye fontosabb statisztikai adatai.* Budapest: KSH.

KSH [Központi Statisztikai Hivatal]. 1973. *A Magyar Népköztársaság helységnévtára 1973.* Budapest: Statisztikai Kiadó Vállalat.

KSH [Központi Statisztikai Hivatal]. 1985. *A Magyar Népköztársaság helységnévtára 1985.* Budapest: Statisztikai Kiadó Vállalat.

KSH [Központi Statisztikai Hivatal]. 1987. *Pótfüzet A Magyar Népköztársaság 1985. évi helységnévtárához 1987.* Budapest: Statisztikai Kiadó Vállalat.

KSH [Központi Statisztikai Hivatal]. 1990. *A Magyar Köztársaság államigazgatási helynévkönyve 1990. január 1.* Budapest: KSH.

KSH [Központi Statisztikai Hivatal]. 1993. *1990. évi népszámlálás: települési adatok és településhatáros térképek mágneslemezen.* Budapest: KSH.

KSH [Központi Statisztikai Hivatal]. 1996. *1949. évi népszámlálás: vallási adatok százalékos megoszlása településenként.* Budapest: KSH.

Kuran, Timur. 1995. *Private Truths, Public Lies: The Social Consequences of Preference Falsification.* Cambridge, MA and London: Harvard University Press.

Kuran, Timur and Cass R. Sunstein. 1999. "Availability Cascades and Risk Regulation." *Stanford Law Review* 51, April, 683–768.

Kurtán, Sándor, Péter Sándor, and László Vass, eds. 1991. *Magyarország politikai évkönyve.* Budapest: Demokrácia Kutatások Magyar Központja Alapítvány.

Kurtán, Sándor, Péter Sándor, and László Vass, eds. 1994. *Magyarország politikai évkönyve.* Budapest: Demokrácia Kutatások Magyar Központja Alapítvány.

Kurtán, Sándor, Péter Sándor, and László Vass, eds. 1999. *Magyarország politikai évkönyve 1998-ról.* Budapest: Demokrácia Kutatások Magyar Központja Alapítvány.

Ladányi, Sándor. 1999. "Vázlatos történelmi áttekintés a magyarországi református egyház közelebbi múltjának alakulásáról." In Barcza and Dienes, *A magyarországi református egyház története 1918–1919.* Sárospatak: A Sárospataki Református Kollégium Teológiai Akadémiája, 101–39.

Laitin, David. 1986. *Hegemony and Culture: Politics and Religious Change among the Yoruba.* Chicago and London: The University of Chicago Press.

Laitin, David. 1995. "National Revivals and Violence." *Archives européennes de sociologie* 36, 3–43.

Lampland, Martha. 1995. *The Object of Labor: Commodification in Socialist Hungary.* Chicago: University of Chicago Press.

Lányi, Gusztáv. 1993. "Föltámadás és/vagy restauráció?" *Magyar Tudomány* XXXVIII:2, February, 168–76.

László, Gábor Dobos. 1987. "Belmisszió és irányzatok a protestáns egyházakban és vallásos szervezetekben." In Lendvai, *A magyar protestantizmus 1918–1948: Tanulmányok.* Budapest: Kossuth Könyvkiadó, 263–313.

Laszlo, Leslie. 1973. "Church and State in Hungary, 1919–1945." Ph.D. Diss., Columbia University.

László, Leslie. 1990. "The Catholic Church in Hungary." In Ramet, *Catholicism and Politics in Communist Societies.* Durham and London: Duke University Press, 156–80.

Leith, John H., ed. 1963. *Creeds of the Churches: A Reader in Christian Doctrine from the Bible to the Present.* Garden City, NY: Anchor Books.

Leithner, Christian. 1997. "Of Time and Partisan Stability Revisited: Australia and New Zealand 1905–1990." *American Journal of Political Science* 41:4, 1104–27.

Lendvai, Ferenc, ed. 1987. *A magyar protestantizmus 1918–1948: Tanulmányok.* Budapest: Kossuth Könyvkiadó.

Lenin, Vladimir Ilyich. 1943. "Attitude of Worker's Party Toward Religion." *Selected Works.* vol. XI. New York: International Publishers.

Levine, Marc V. 1976. "Standing Political Decisions and Critical Realignment: The Pattern of Maryland Politics, 1872–1948." *Journal of Politics* 38:2, May, 292–325.

Bibliography

Levitsky, Steven. 2003. *Transforming Labor-Based Parties in Latin America: Argentine Peronism in Comparative Perspective.* New York: Cambridge University Press.

Lewis, Paul G. 2000. *Political Parties in Post-Communist Eastern Europe.* London and New York: Routledge.

Lewis-Beck, Michael S. 1984. "France: The Stalled Electorate." In Dalton et al., *Electoral Change in Advanced Industrial Democracies: Realignment or Dealignment?* Princeton: Princeton University Press, 425–48.

Linz, Juan J. 1980. "The New Spanish Party System." In Rose, *Electoral Participation: A Comparative Analysis.* Beverly Hills, CA: Sage, 101–89.

Linz, Juan J. 2000. *Totalitarian and Authoritarian Regimes.* Boulder, CO: Lynne Rienner.

Linz, Juan J. and Alfred Stepan. 1996. *Problems of Democratic Transition and Consolidation: Southern Europe, South America, and Post-Communist Europe.* Baltimore and London: The Johns Hopkins University Press.

Lipset, Seymour Martin. 1960. *Political Man: The Social Bases of Politics.* Garden City, NY: Anchor Books and Doubleday & Company.

Lipset, Seymour M. and Stein Rokkan. 1967. "Cleavage Structures, Party Systems, and Voter Alignments: An Introduction." in Lipset and Rokkan, *Party Systems and Voter Alignments: Cross-National Perspectives.* New York: The Free Press, 1–67.

Lipset, Seymour M. and Stein Rokkan, eds. 1967. *Party Systems and Voter Alignments: Cross-National Perspectives.* New York: The Free Press.

Loewenberg, Gerhard. 1968. "The Remaking of the German Party System: Political and Socio-economic Factors." *Polity* 1:1, Fall, 86–113.

Lohmann, Susanne. 1994. "The Dynamics of Informational Cascades: The Monday Demonstrations in Leipzig, East Germany, 1989–91." *World Politics* 47, October, 42–101.

Lomax, Bill. 1976. *Hungary, 1956.* New York: St. Martin's Press.

Long, J. Scott. 1997. *Regression Models for Categorical and Limited Dependent Variables.* Thousand Oaks, CA: Sage Publications.

Luca, Gábor, Ádám Levendel, and István Stumpf, eds. 1994. *Parlamenti választások 1994.* Budapest: Osiris-Századvég.

Luther, Kurt Richard and Kris Deschouwer, eds. 1999. *Party Elites in Divided Societies: Political Parties in Consociational Democracy.* London and New York: Routledge.

Luukkanen, Arto. 1994. *The Party of Unbelief: The Religious Policy of the Bolshevik Party, 1917–1929.* Helsinki: SHS.

Luxmoore, Jonathan and Jolanta Babiuch. 1999. *The Vatican and the Red Flag: The Struggle for the Soul of Eastern Europe.* London and New York: Geoffrey Chapman.

MacEoin, Gary. 1951. *The Communist War on Religion.* New York: Devin-Adair.

Magyar Dolgozók Pártja. 1956. *A szocializmus építésének útján: A Magyar Dolgozók Pártja II. kongresszusának anyagából.* 2nd ed. Budapest: Szikra.

Magyarországi Református Egyház. 1967. *A Magyarországi Református Egyház Törvénykönyve.* Budapest: Egyetemi Nyomda.

Magyar Távirati Iroda. 1945. "Jelentés az 1945 októberi országos közvéleménykutatás eredményéről." Budapest: Magyar Közvéleménykutató Szolgálat.

Mahoney, James and Dietrich Rueschemeyer. 2003a. "Comparative Historical Analysis: Achievements and Agendas." In Mahoney and Rueschemeyer (2003b), *Comparative Historical Analysis in the Social Sciences*. New York: Cambridge University Press, 3–38.

Mahoney, James and Dietrich Rueschemeyer, eds. 2003b. *Comparative Historical Analysis in the Social Sciences*. New York: Cambridge University Press.

Mair, Peter. 1997. *Party System Change: Approaches and Interpretations*. Oxford: Clarendon.

Mair, Peter. 1990. "Continuity, Change, and the Vulnerability of Party." In Mair and Smith, *Understanding Party System Change in Western Europe*. London: Frank Cass, 169–87.

Mair, Peter and Cas Mudde. 1998. "The Party Family and Its Study." *Annual Review of Political Science* 1, 211–29.

Mair, Peter and Gordon Smith, eds. 1990. *Understanding Party System Change in Western Europe*. London: Frank Cass.

Majsai, Tamás. 1991. "Protestants under Communism." *The New Hungarian Quarterly* 32:123, 58–67.

Mannová, Elena, ed. 1997. *Bürgertum und bürgerliche Gesellschaft in der Slowakei 1900–1989*. Bratislava: AEP.

Maravall, José. 1982. *The Transition to Democracy in Spain*. London & Canberra: Croom Helm.

McAuley, Mary. 1985. "Political Culture and Communist Politics: One Step Forward, Two Steps Back." In Brown, *Political Culture and Communist Studies*. Armonk, NY: ME Sharpe, 13–39.

Medyesy, Laslo. M. 1975. "Evolution of the Socialist 'New Man' in Hungary: A Study of Political Socialization of the Post-1956 Generation." Ph.D. diss., Indiana University.

Medyesy, Laslo. 1980. "Evolution of the Socialist 'New Man' in Hungary: A Study of Political Socialization (1956–1975)." Vienna: UKI Reports.

Mészáros, István. 1991. "Vallásos nevelés, állami iskolák, 1949–1990." *Magyar Egyháztörténeti Vázlatok* 3:3, 89–106.

Mészáros, István. 1994. *Kimaradt tananyag: A diktatúra és az egyház 1957–1975 II*. Budapest: Márton Áron Kiadó.

Mészáros, István. 1995a. *Kimaradt tananyag: A diktatúra és az egyház 1957–1975 III.A*. Budapest: Márton Áron Kiadó.

Mészáros, István. 1995b. *Kimaradt tananyag: A diktatúra és az egyház 1957–1975 III.B*. Budapest: Márton Áron Kiadó.

Mészáros, István. 1995c. *Kimaradt tananyag: A diktatúra és az egyház 1957-1975 III.C*. Budapest: Márton Áron Kiadó.

Mészáros, István. 2001. "A 'megegyezések' kora (1950, 1957, 1964). Adalékok e megegyezések természetéhez." In Erdő, *A magyar katolikus egyház 1945-től 1955-ig*. Budapest: Márton Áron Kiadó, 7–30.

Michel, Patrick. 1991. *Politics and Religion in Eastern Europe*. Cambridge: Polity Press.

Bibliography

Miller, William L. 1977. *Electoral Dynamics in Britain since 1918*. London: Mac-Millan.

Mindszenty, József. 1949a. *Four Years Struggle of the Church in Hungary*. London: Longmans, Green and Co.

Mindszenty, József. 1949b. *Cardinal Mindszenty Speaks: Authorized White Book*. London: Longmans, Green and Co.

Mindszenty, József. 1974. *Memoirs*. New York: MacMillan.

Molnár, A. and M. Tomka. 1989. "Youth and Religion in Hungary." *Religion in Communist Lands* 17:3, 209–29.

Moore, Barrington, Jr. 1966. *Social Origins of Dictatorship and Democracy*. Boston: Beacon Press.

Morel, Julius. 1968. *Religion in der kommunistischen Presse: Eine Inhaltsanalyse*. Innsbruck, Austria: Im Kommissionsverlag Österreichischen Kommissions-buchhandlung.

Morin, Edgar. 1970. *The Red and the White: Report from a French Village*. New York: Random House.

Nagy, Imre. 1954. *Egy évtized: Válogatott beszédek és írások (1948–1954)*. Budapest: Szikra.

Nagy Péter, Tibor. 2000a. "Hittanoktatás és világnézeti nevelés 1956. után." *Iskolakultúra* 6–7, 121–9.

Nagy Péter, Tibor. 2000b. *Járszalag és aréna*. Budapest: Új Mandátum Könykiadó.

Nardulli, Peter F. 1994. "A Normal Vote Approach to Electoral Change: Presidential Elections, 1828–1984." *Political Behavior* 16:4, 467–503.

Niesel, Wilhelm. 1962. *The Gospel and the Churches: A Comparison of Catholicism, Orthodoxy, and Protestantism*. Philadelphia: The Westminster Press.

Offe, Claus. 2004. "Capitalism by Democratic Design? Democratic Theory Facing the Triple Transition in East Central Europe." *Social Research* 71:3, 501–28.

O'Loughlin, John and Herman van der Wusten, ed. 1993. *The New Political Geography of Eastern Europe*. London and New York: Belhaven Press.

Orbán, József Gyula. 1996. *Friedensbewegung katholischer Priester in Ungarn, 1950–1956*. Budapest: METEM.

Orbán, Sándor. 1962. *Egyház és állam: A katolikus egyház és az állam viszonyának rendezése 1945–1950*. Budapest: Kossuth Könyvkiadó.

Osa, Maryjane. 1989. "Resistance, Persistence, and Change: The Transformation of the Catholic Church in Poland." *East European Politics & Societies* 3:2, Spring, 268–99.

Pál, József. 1995. *Békepapok: Katolikus békepapok Magyarországon (1950–1989)*. Budapest: Egyházfórum.

Panebianco, Angelo. 1988. *Political Parties: Organization and Power*. New York: Cambridge University Press.

Pásztor, János. 1995. "The Theology of the Serving Church and the Theology of Diaconia in the Protestant Churches and Their Consequences in Hungary during the Time of Socialism." *Religion in Eastern Europe* 5:6, December, 22–36.

Paul, David W. 1979. *The Cultural Limits of Revolutionary Politics: Change and Continuity in Socialist Czechoslovakia*. Boulder, CO: East European Quarterly. Distributed by Columbia University Press.

271

Paul, David. W. 1985. "Czechoslovakia's Political Culture Reconsidered." In Brown, *Political Culture and Communist Studies*. Armonk, NY: ME Sharpe, 134–48.

Pennings, Paul and Jan-Erik Lane, eds. 1998. *Comparing Party System Change*. London and New York: Routledge.

Peris, Daniel. 1998. *Storming the Heavens: The Soviet League of the Militant Godless*. Ithaca and London: Cornell University Press.

Péter, László. 1995. "Church-State Relations and Civil Society in Hungary: A Historic Perspective." *Hungarian Studies* 10:1, 3–33.

Petersen, Roger D. 2001. *Resistance and Rebellion: Lessons from Eastern Europe*. New York: Cambridge University Press.

Pierce, Roy. 1992. "Toward the Formation of a Partisan Alignment in France." *Political Behavior* 14:4, December, 443–69.

Pierson, Paul. 2004. *Politics in Time: History, Institutions, and Social Analysis*. Princeton and Oxford: Princeton University Press.

Póka, György. 1988. "Az egyházközségek és egyesületek." In Turányi, *Magyar Katolikus almanach II*. Budapest: Szent István Társulat, 275–91.

Polgar, Steven. 1984. "A Summary of the Situation of the Hungarian Catholic Church." *Religion in Communist Lands* 12:1, 11–41.

Poór, József. 1986. *A protestáns teológia Magyarországon, 1945–1985*. Budapest: Kossuth Könyvkiadó.

Powell, David E. 1975. *Antireligious Propaganda in the Soviet Union: A Study of Mass Persuasion*. Cambridge, MA: MIT Press.

Pridham, Geoffrey and Paul G. Lewis, eds. 1996. *Stabilising Fragile Democracies: Comparing New Party Systems in Southern and Eastern Europe*. London and New York: Routledge.

Pridham, Geoffrey and Tatu Vanhanen, eds. 1996. *Democratization in Eastern Europe: Domestic and International Perspectives*. London and New York: Routledge.

Przeworski, Adam and Henry Teune. 1982 [1970]. *The Logic of Comparative Social Inquiry*. Malabar, Florida: Krieger Publishing.

Pungur, Joseph. 1992. "Protestantism in Hungary." In Ramet, *Protestantism and Politics in Eastern Europe and Russia: The Communist and Postcommunist Eras*. Durham and London: Duke University Press, 107–56.

Putnam, Robert. 1993. *Making Democracy Work: Civic Traditions in Modern Italy*. Princeton: Princeton University Press.

Rácsok, Gabriella. 2000. "A Critical Analysis of the Social-Ethical Positions of the Servant Church Theology of the Reformed Church of Hungary between 1948 and 1989." Master's of theology thesis, Calvin Theological Seminary.

Ragin, Charles C. and Howard S. Becker. 1992. *What Is A Case? Exploring the Foundations of Social Inquiry*. Cambridge: Cambridge University Press.

Rainer, János. 2002. "The New Course in Hungary in 1953." Woodrow Wilson International Center for Scholars, Working Paper No. 38. Washington, DC.

Rákosi, Mátyás. 1951. *A békéért és a szocializmus építéséért*. Budapest: Szikra.

Rákosi, Mátyás. 1952. *Wir bauen ein neues Land: Ausgewählte Reden und Aufsätze, 1948–1951*. Berlin: Dietz Verlag.

Rákosi, Mátyás. 1955. *Válogatott beszédek és cikkek*. 4th, enlarged ed. Budapest: Szikra.

Bibliography

Ramet, Pedro. 1987. *Cross and Commissar: The Politics of Religion in Eastern Europe and the USSR*. Bloomington and Indianapolis: Indiana University Press.

Ramet, Pedro, ed. 1990. *Catholicism and Politics in Communist Societies*. Durham and London: Duke University Press.

Ramet, Sabrina Petra, ed. 1992. *Protestantism and Politics in Eastern Europe and Russia: The Communist and Postcommunist Eras*. Durham and London: Duke University Press.

Ravasz, László. 1988. *Válogatott írások 1945–1968*. Bern: Az Európai Protestáns Magyar Szabadegyetem.

Remmer, Karen L. 1985. "Redemocratization and the Impact of Authoritarian Rule in Latin America." *Comparative Politics* 17:3, April, 253–75.

Roberts, Kenneth M. and Erik Wibbels, 1999 "Party Systems and Electoral Volatility in Latin America: A Test of Economic, Institutional, and Structural Explanations." *American Political Science Review* 93:3, 575–90.

Romsics, Ignác. 1999. *Hungary in the Twentieth Century*. Budapest: Corvina and Osiris.

Róna-Tas, Ákos. 1997. *The Great Surprise of the Small Transformation: The Demise of Communism and the Rise of the Private Sector in Hungary*. Ann Arbor: The University of Michigan Press.

Rose, Richard, ed. 1980. *Electoral Participation: A Comparative Analysis*. Beverly Hills, CA: Sage.

Rothschild, Joseph. 1993. *Return to Diversity*. New York: Oxford University Press. 2nd ed.

Ruszkai, Miklós. 1959. "Az 1945. előtti magyar választások statisztikája." *Történeti statisztikai közlemények* 2:1–2, 11–57.

Salacz, Gábor. 1988. *A magyar katolikus egyház tizenhét esztendeje (1948–1964)*. München: Görres Gesellschaft.

Sani, Giacomo. 1976. "Political Traditions as Contextual Variables." *American Journal of Political Science* 20:3, 375–405.

Sartori, Giovanni. 1976. *Parties and Party Systems: A Framework for Analysis*. Cambridge: Cambridge University Press.

Schmitt, Karl. 1989. *Konfession und Wahlverhalten in der Bundesrepublik Deutschland*. Berlin: Duncker & Humbolt.

Schöpflin, George. 1979. "Hungary: An Uneasy Stability." In Brown and Gray, *Political Culture and Political Change in Communist States*. London: Macmillan, 131–58.

Schöpflin, George. 1993. *Politics in Eastern Europe*. Oxford, England and Cambridge, MA: Blackwell.

Schuessler, Alexander A. 2000. *A Logic of Expressive Choice*. Princeton: Princeton University Press.

Scott, James C. 1985. *Weapons of the Weak: Everyday Forms of Peasant Resistance*. New Haven and London: Yale University Press.

Scott, James C. 1989. "Everyday Forms of Resistance." In Colburn, *Everyday Forms of Peasant Resistance*. Armonk, NY: ME Sharpe, 3–33.

Scott, James C. 1990. *Domination and the Arts of Resistance*. New Haven and London: Yale University Press.

Scott, James C. and Benjamin J. Tria Kervliet, ed. 1986. *Everyday Forms of Peasant Resistance in South-East Asia*. London: Frank Cass.

Shaffer, William R. and David A. Caputo. 1972. "Political Continuity in Indiana Presidential Elections: An Analysis Based on the Key-Munger Paradigm." *Midwest Journal of Political Science* 16:4, 700–11.

Shively, W. Phillips. 1972. "Party Identification, Party Choice, and Voting Stability: The Weimar Case." *American Political Science Review* 66:4, December, 1203–25.

Siavelis, Peter M. 1999. "Continuidad y Transformación del Sistema de Partidos en una Transición 'Modelo'." In Drake and Jaksic, *El modelo chileno: democracia y desarrollo en los Noventa*. Santiago: LOM ediciones, 223–59.

Siegel, Jacob S. 1958. *The Population of Hungary*. Washington, DC: US GPO.

Siegfried, André. 1913. *Tableau politique de la France De L'Ouest sous la IIIe République*. 2nd ed. Paris: Librairie Armand Colin, 1964.

Siegfried, André. 1949. *Géographie électoral de l'Ardèche sous la IIIème République*. Paris: Armand Colin.

Sivini, Giordano. 1967. "Il comportamento elettorale in Italia. Primi risultati di un'analisi ecologica (1945–1963)." *Rassegna Italiana di Sociologia* 1, March, 99–125.

Skilling, Gordon H. 1985. "Czechoslovak Political Culture: Pluralism in an International Context." In Brown, *Political Culture and Communist Studies*. Armonk, NY: ME Sharpe, 115–33.

Snyder, Richard. 2001. "Scaling Down: The Subnational Comparative Method." *Studies in Comparative International Development* 36:1, 93–110.

Soós, László, ed. 1997. *A Magyar Szocialista Munkáspárt Központi Bizottságának jegyzőkönyvei 1957–1989*. Budapest: Magyar Országos Levéltár.

Stettner, Andrea. 1988. "Katolikus Lánykörök Szövetsége: KALÁSZ." In Turányi, *Magyar Katolikus almanach II*. Budapest: Szent István Társulat, 313–22.

Stumpf, István. 1994. "Választói magatartás a generációs és vallási törésvonalak mentén." In Balogh, *Törésvonalak és értékválasztások*. Budapest: MTA Politikai Tudományok Intézete, 147–67.

Stumpf, István, ed. 1997. *Két választás félidejében*. Budapest: Századvég and Institute of Political Sciences.

Sukosd, Miklos. 1992. "Why History Doesn't Repeat Itself: The Saga of the Smallholders' Party." *East European Reporter* 5:4, July–August, 53.

Szabó, Csaba. 2000. *Egyházügyi hangulat–jelentések 1951, 1953*. Budapest: Osiris-Budapest Főváros Levéltára.

Szabó, István. 1989. "A Long Period of Inner Bleeding: The 'Theology of Service' as the Reflection of the Miseries of the Reformed Church in Hungary." *Kirchliche Zeitgeschichte* 2:1, 190–8.

Szántó, Konrád. 1990. *Az Egyházügyi Hivatal titkai*. Budapest: Mécses Kiadó.

Szántó, Konrád. 1992. *Az 1956-os forradalom és a katolikus egyház*. Miskolc: Szent Maximilian Lap- és Könyvkiadó

Szeghalmi, Elemér. 2000. *Keresztény küzdelmek és megtorpanások: Az Új Ember 1945–1956 között*. Budapest: Új Ember Kiadó.

Bibliography

Szelenyi, Ivan. 1988. *Socialist Entrepreneurs: Embourgeoisement in Rural Hungary*. Madison: University of Wisconsin Press.

Szelényi, Iván and Szonja Szelényi. 1991. "The Vacuum in Hungarian Politics: Classes and Parties." *New Left Review* 187, May/June, 121–37.

Szépfalusi, István. 1984. *Pótszigorlat 1955–1983*. München: Máté András Nyomdájában.

Szerencsés, Károly. 1992. *A kékcédulás hadművelet: (választások Magyarországon 1947)*. Budapest: IKVA.

Szoboszlai, György, ed. 1990. *Parlamenti választások 1990: politikai szociológiai körkép*. Budapest: Társadalomtudományi Intézet.

Takacs, Aurelia E. 1960. "A Christian Church in a Communist State: The Impact of the Communist Regime on the Theology and Life of the Reformed Church in Hungary." Th.D. diss., Union Theological Seminary.

Tarrow, Sidney G. 1988. "Old Movements in New Cycles of Protest: The Career of an Italian Religious Community." In Klandermans, Kriesi, and Tarrow, *From Structure to Action: Comparing Social Movements Across Cultures*. International Social Movement Research Series, vol. 1, Greenwich, CT: JAI Press, 281–304.

Tarrow, Sidney. 2004. "Bridging the Quantitative-Qualitative Divide." In Brady and Collier, *Rethinking Social Inquiry: Diverse Tools, Shared Standards*. Oxford: Roman & Littlefield, 171–9.

Terray, László G. 1997. *He Could Not Do Otherwise: Bishop Lajos Ordass, 1901–1978*. Grand Rapids, MI: William B. Eerdmans.

Tibori, János. 1996. *A tiszántúli református egyházkerület története 1957–1965*. Debrecen: Debreceni Református teológiai akadémia.

Tibori, János. 1998. *A tiszántúli református egyházkerület története 1966–1975*. Debrecen: Debreceni Református teológiai akadémia.

Tibori, János. 2000. *A tiszántúli református egyházkerület története 1975–1986*. Debrecen: Debreceni Református teológiai akadémia.

Tobias, Robert. 1956. *Communist-Christian Encounter in East Europe*. Indianapolis: School of Religion Press.

Tóka, Gábor. 1993. "The Impact of the Religion Issue on Electoral Preferences in Hungary, 1990–1991." In Gabriel and Troitzsch, *Wahlen in Zeiten des Umbruchs*. Frankfurt: Peter Lang, 331–77.

Tóka, Gábor. 1994. "Pártok és választóik 1990-ben és 1994-ben." In Andorka et al., *Társadalmi riport 1994*. Budapest: Tárki, 460–89.

Tóka, Gábor. 1995a. "Voting Behavior in 1990." In Tóka (1995c), *The 1990 Election to the Hungarian National Assembly: Analyses, Documents, and Data*. Berlin: Sigma, 84–123.

Tóka, Gábor. 1995b. "Seats and Votes: Consequences of the Hungarian Electoral Law." in Tóka (1995c), 41–66.

Tóka, Gábor, ed. 1995c. *The 1990 Election to the Hungarian National Assembly: Analyses, Documents, and Data*. Berlin: Sigma.

Tóka, Gábor. 1999. "Voting Behavior." In Kolosi et al., *Social Report 1998*. Budapest: Tárki, 389–408.

Tóka, Gábor and Zsolt Enyedi, eds. 1999. *Elections to the Hungarian National Assembly 1994: Analyses, Documents and Data*. Berlin: Sigma.

Tomka, Miklos. 1979a. "The Religious – Non-religious Dichotomy as a Social Problem." *The Annual Review of the Social Sciences of Religion* 3, 105–37.

Tomka, Miklós 1979b. "A szekularizáció mérlege." *Valóság* 22:7, 60–70.

Tomka, Miklós. 1988a. "Stages of Religious Change in Hungary." In Gannon, *World Catholicism in Transition*. New York: MacMillan, 169–83.

Tomka, Miklós. 1988b. "A magyarországi katolicizmus statisztikája és szociológiája." In Turányi, *Magyar katolikus almanach II*. Budapest: Szent István Társulat, 510–77.

Tomka, Miklós. 1991a. "Church and Religion in a Communist State, 1945–1990," *The New Hungarian Quarterly* XXXII:121, Spring, 59–69.

Tomka, Miklós. 1991b. *Magyar katolicizmus 1991*. Budapest: Országos Lelkipásztori Intézet, Katolikus Társadalomtudományi Akadémia.

Tomz, Michael, Joshua A. Tucker, and Jason Wittenberg. 2002. "An Easy and Accurate Regression Model for Multiparty Electoral Data." *Political Analysis* 10:1, Winter, 66–83.

Tomz, Michael, Jason Wittenberg, and Gary King. 2003. CLARIFY: Software for Interpreting and Presenting Statistical Results. Version 2.1. Stanford University, University of Wisconsin, and Harvard University. January 5. Available at http://gking.harvard.edu/.

Turányi, László, ed. 1988. *Magyar katolikus almanach II*. Budapest: Szent István Társulat.

Tworzecki, Hubert. 2003. *Learning to Choose: Electoral Politics in East-Central Europe*. Stanford: Stanford University Press.

Urbán, Károly, ed. 1991. *Mindszenty és a hatalom*. Budapest: Lex Kft.

Váli, Ferenc A. 1961. *Rift and Revolt in Hungary*. Cambridge, MA: Harvard University Press.

Valenzuela, Arturo and J. Samuel Valenzuela. 1986. "Party Oppositions under the Chilean Authoritarian Regime." In Valenzuela and Valenzuela, *Military Rule in Chile: Dictatorship and Opposition*. Baltimore: Johns Hopkins University Press, 184–229.

Valenzuela, Arturo and J. Samuel Valenzuela, ed. 1986. *Military Rule in Chile: Dictatorship and Opposition*. Baltimore: Johns Hopkins University Press.

Valenzuela, Samuel J. and Timothy R. Scully. 1997. "Electoral Choices and the Party System in Chile: Continuities and Changes at the Recovery of Democracy." *Comparative Political Studies* 29:4, July, 511–27.

Varga, Zsuzsanna. 2001. *Politika, paraszti érdekérvényesítés és szövetkezetek Magyarországon 1956–1967*. Budapest: Napvilág Kiadó.

Vasary, Ildiko. 1987. *Beyond the Plan: Social Change in a Hungarian Village*. Boulder, Co and London: Westview Press.

Vass, Henrik, ed. 1979. *A Magyar Szocialista Munkáspárt határozatai és dokumentumai 1956–1962*. 3rd ed. Budapest: Kossuth Könyvkiadó.

Vaughan, Diane. 1992. "Theory Elaboration: The Heuristics of Case Analysis." In Ragin and Becker, *What Is a Case? Explaing the Foundations of Social Inquiry*. Cambridge: Cambridge University Press, 173–202.

Bibliography

Vecsey, Josef and Johann Schwendemann. 1957. *Mindszenty Dokumentation*. vol. III. "Prozess gegen den Kardinal." St. Pölten: Verlag der Pressvereins-Druckerei.

Victor, János. 1950. "Theology in the Reformed Church after the Liberation." In Kádár, *Five Years of Hungarian Protestantism*. Budapest: Hungarian Church Press, 32–8.

Vida, István. 1986. *Koalíció és pártharcok, 1944–1948*. Budapest: Magvető Könyvkiadó.

Volgyes, Ivan, ed. 1975. *Political Socialization in Eastern Europe: A Comparative Framework*. New York: Praeger.

Wädekin, Karl-Eugen. 1982. *Agrarian Policies in Communist Europe: A Critical Introduction*. London: Allanheld Osmun.

Wald, Kenneth D. 1983. *Crosses on the Ballot: Patterns of British Voter Alignment Since 1885*. Princeton: Princeton University Press.

Wald, Kenneth D., Dennis E. Owen, and Samuel Hill, Jr., 1988. "Churches as Political Communities." *American Political Science Review* 82:2, June, 531–48.

Wald, Kenneth D., Dennis E. Owen, and Samuel S. Hill, Jr. 1990. "Political Cohesion in Churches." *Journal of Politics* 52:1, 197–215.

Waller, Michael. 1996. "Party Inheritances and Party Identities." In Pridham and Lewis, *Stabilising Fragile Democracies: Comparing New Party Systems in Southern and Eastern Europe*. London and New York: Routledge, 23–43.

Walsh, Katherine Cramer. 2004. *Talking Politics: Informal Groups and Social Identity in American Life*. Chicago: University of Chicago Press.

Welch, Stephen. 1993. *The Concept of Political Culture*. New York: St. Martin's Press.

Welsh, William A., ed. 1981. *Survey Research and Public Attitudes in Eastern Europe and the Soviet Union*. New York: Pergamon Press.

White, Anne. 1990. *Destalinization and the House of Culture: Declining State Control over Leisure in the USSR, Poland, and Hungary, 1953–1989*. London and New York: Routledge.

Wildmann, János. 1986. "Hungary: From the Ruling Church to the 'Church of the People'." *Religion in Communist Lands* 14:2, 160–71.

Wiener, György. 1997. "A választási magatartás történelmi meghatározottsága és dinamikája." In Stumpf, *Két választás félidejében*. Budapest: Századvég and Institute of Political Sciences, 145–82.

Wittenberg, Jason. 1999. "The 1994 Hungarian Election in Historical Perspective." In Tóka and Enyedi, *Elections to the Hungarian National Assembly 1994: Analyses, Documents and Data*. Berlin: Sigma, 139–67.

Wittner, Lawrence S. 1993. *One World or None: A History of the World Nuclear Disarmament Movement through 1953*. Stanford: Stanford University Press.

Woodrow, Alain. 1979. "Les croyants en Hongrie." *Le Monde* October 17, 6–7; October 18, 8–9.

Young, Glennys. 1997. *Power and the Sacred in Revolutionary Russia: Religious Activists in the Village*. University Park: Penn State University Press.

Zala Megyei Levéltár. 1999. *Dokumentumok Zala megye történetéből 1947–1956*. Zalaegerszeg: Zala Megyei Levéltár.

Primary Sources

This section makes use of the following abbreviations.

ZMB: Zala Megyei Bizottsága
ZML: Zala Megyei Levéltár MSZMP Zala megyei Bizottsága Archívuma
ZMT: Zala Megyei Tanács
HBMB: MSZMP Hajdú-Bihar Megyei Bizottság Archívuma
MOL: Magyar Országos Levéltár.

Note: Each primary source document has been assigned a unique code that reflects the archive from which it came and the date it was created. Spelling and style reflect modern Hungarian usage, which in some cases differs slightly from the title on the original document.

Zala County Archive

Z3/1949. "Nyilatkozat." ZML MDP ZMB 1949. 57. 30 őe.

Z5/1950. Untitled. ZML MDP ZMB (1948–1956). 57. 30 őe.

Z6/1951. "Tájékoztató a kultúrotthonhálózat továbbfejlesztéséről." ZML MDP ZMB 57.

Z8/1951. "Munkaterv. A kultúrotthon belső élete és a DISZ szervezet kulturális munkájához." ZML MDP ZMB 57.

Z12/1952. "Jelentés a hittanbeiratásról." ZML MDP ZMB 57. 31 őe. 57.

Z13/1953. "Jelentés a pót–hittanbeirással kapcsolatban." ZML MDP ZMB 57. 31 őe.

Z14/1953. "1953.I. negyedévi munkaterv." ZML MDP ZMB 57. 20 őe.

Z15/1953. "Értékelő jelentés." ZML MDP ZMB 57. 20 őe.

Z16/1954. "Havi jelentés." ZML MDP ZMB 57. 20 őe.

Z17/1955. "Tájékoztató az 1955. évi hittan-beiratkozásokkal kapcsolatban." ZML MDP ZMB 57. 31 őe.

Z18/1956. "Havi jelentés." ZML MDP ZMB 57. 20 őe.

Z19/1956. "Az ateista propaganda helyzete megyénkben." ZML MDP ZMB 57. 31 őe.

Z20/1956. "Jelentés az 1956–57. tanévi hittanbeiratásokról." ZML MDP ZMB 57. 31 őe.

Z21/1956. "Hittanbeiratásokkal kapcsolatos tájékoztató." [1956] ZML 58. 33 őe.

Z22/1958. "A klerikális reakció tevékenysége megyénk területén." ZML MSZMP ZMB 2 leltár 1958. 28 őe.

Z23/1958. "MSZMP Zala Megyei Végrehajtó Bizottságának felhívása." ZML MSZMP ZMB 2. leltár. 1958. 28 őe.

Z26/1960. "Értékelő jelentés a Zala megyei egyházpolitikai helyzetről." ZML MSZMP ZMB Agitációs és Prop. Osztály. Jelentések a megyei egyházpolitikai helyzetről. 30 őe.

Z29/1962. "Zalamegye egyházpolitikai helyzetének felméréséről jelentés." ZML MSZMP ZMB 1962 Agitációs és Propaganda Osztály Egyházügyi Hivatal jelentései. 29 őe.

Bibliography

Z29.5/1959 "A termelőszövetkezeti szervezés és megszilárdítás tapasztalatai." ZML MSZMP ZMB 2. leltár 1959. év 12 őe. (Termelőszövetkezeti mozgalom iratai. 1959. nov. 7.-1960 március 8.)

Z30/1962. "Hittanbeiratásokról jelentés." ZML MSZMP ZMB Agitációs és Prop. Osztály. ÁEH jelentései. 29 őe.

Z35/1964. "A vallásos ideológia elleni eszmei harc helyzete és eredményei." ZML MSZMP ZMB 1964 Prop. és Művelődési Osztály. Ateista propagandamunka megszervezésével és értékelésével kapcsolatos munkatervek, jelentések. 24 őe.

Z36/1964. "Ateista propaganda megszervezésével és értékelésével kapcsolatos munkatervek, jelentések." ZML MSZMP ZMB 1964 Propaganda és Művelődési Osztály. 24 őe.

Z38/1965. "Egyházügyi Hivatal jelentései." ZML MSZMP ZMB 1965. Propaganda és Művelődési Osztály Iratai. 29 őe.

Z48/1967. "Feljegyzés a Zala megyében lévő 22.tvr.-es papokról." ZML ZMT Egyházügyi Iratok. 1962-7. 1967. VI 20. 64/1967.

Z70/1975. "Az 1975/76. évi iskolai hitoktatással kapcsolatos feladatok." A megyei egyházügyi titkár jelentése az 1975/76. évi hittanbeiratásról. ZML MSZMP ZMB 1975. Apparátus Iratai. Propaganda és Művelődési Osztály 21 őe.

Z72/1976. "Az 1976/77. évi iskolai hitoktatással kapcsolatos feladatok." A megyei egyházügyi titkár jelentése az 1976/77. évi hitoktatásról, valamint feladatterve az egyházi reakció visszaszorítására. ZML MSZMP ZMB 1976. II/18 őe.

Z72.5/1976. "Feladatok az egyházi/papi/reakció visszaszorítására, befolyásának csökkentésére." Megyei Egyházügyi titkár jelentése az 1976/77. évi hitoktatásról, valamint feladatterve az egyházi reakció visszaszorítására. ZML MSZMP ZMB 1976. II/18 őe.

Z73/1964. "A vallásos ideológia befolyásának alakulása a járásban 1960. óta." ZML MSZMP ZMB 1964 Prop. és Művelődési Osztály 24 őe. Az ateista propagandamunka megszervezésével és értekelésével kapcsolatos munkatervek, jelentések.

Z74/1959. Untitled. ZML MSZMP ZMB 1959 Agitációs és Prop. Osztály 26 őe. Párt- és állami szervek jelentései egyházpolitikai kérdésekről, hittanbeiratásokról, a vallásos ideológia elleni harcról kapcsolatos iratok.

Z75/1962. "A hittanbeiratásokról összesítő jelentés." ZML ZMT Egyházügyi iratok 1962-7.

Z80/1962. "Hittanbeiratásokról jelentés. (Lenti, 1962)." ZML ZMT Egyházügyi iratok 1962-7. 1962. (95/1962.eln.)

Z81/1964. Untitled. Ateista propagandamunka megszervezésével és értékelésével kapcsolatos munkatervek, jelentések. ZML MSZMP ZMB 1964. Propaganda és Művelődési Osztály. 24 őe.

Z82/1962. "Hittanbeiratásról jelentés." ZML ZMT Egyházügyi iratok 1962-7. 7636-2/1962.

Z90/1960. "Feljegyzés a hittanbeiratások előkészületeiről a zalaszentgróti járásban." Jelentések a megye egyházpolitikai helyzetéről. ZML MSZMP ZMB 1960 Agitációs és Propaganda Osztály. 30 őe.

Z125/1953. "Hittanbeírásokról jelentés." ZML MDP Nagykanizsai Járás Bizottsága 59.

Z126/1958. "Kimutatás a hittanra beiratkozott tanulókról, iskolánként, szám szerint." ZML MSZMP ZMB Nagykanizsa Járási Bizottsága.

Z129/1958. "Pártszerv jelentése a hittanbeiratásokról és a klérus tevékenységéről." ZML MSZMP ZMB Lenti Járási Bizottsága és alapszervezetei fond 2. leltár 1958. 18 őe.

Z130/1951. "A letenyei járásban 1951/52. tanévre hittanoktatásra jelentkezett tanulókról községenkénti kimutatás." ZML MDP ZMB Letenyei Járási Bizottsága 61.

Z136/1959. "Jelentés a vallásos ideológiai elleni harcról." ZML MSZMP ZMB 4. f. Lenti Járási Bizottsága és alapszervezetei 2. leltár 21 őe.

Z137/1960. "Hittanbeiratási eredmények jelentése." ZML MSZMP Zalaegerszegi Járási Bizottsága 2. f. 1960. 12–25 őe.

Z138.5/1962. "Hittanbeiratási eredmények jelentése. (Zalaegerszegi, 1962)." ZML ZMT Egyházügyi Iratok 1962–1967. 1962.

Z139/1963. "Kimutatás az 1961/62. tanévi hittanbeiratásról." Párt-, állami- és társadalmi szervek jelentései és egyéb iratai az ateista propaganda helyzetéről. ZML MSZMP ZMB 1963. Propaganda és Művelődési Osztály. 23 őe.

Z141/1965. "Hittanbeiratási eredmények jelentése." ZML MSZMP Zalaegerszegi Járási Bizottsága 2. fond, 23 őe.

Z142/1969. "Jelentés a hittanbeiratásról és a húsvéti ünnepek megtartásáról." ZML MSZMP Zalaegerszegi Járási Bizottsága 2 fond. 1969. 21 őe.

Z150/1976. "Templomi hitoktatás tapasztalatai. 1976/1977.év." ZML Megyei Tanács iratai, Egyházügyi Iratok 144/1976.

Hajdú-Bihar County Archive

HB1/1950. "Kimutatás a ref. egyháznál tisztséget betöltő vezetőkről és presbiterekről." HBMB 43 f., 2 f. cs., 27 őe. Egyházi vezetőkről kimutatás.

HB4/1951. "Jelentés." HBMB 48 f., 2 f. cs., 23 őe. Jelentések egyházi vezetőkkel történt beszélgetésekről.

HB6/1952. "Jelentés az 1951-, 52-es oktatási évad hitoktatásra való beiratkozásról." HBMB 45 f., 2 f. cs., 27 őe. Egyházügyi iratok.

HB8/1950. "Kimutatás a Hajdu-Bihar megye területén működő egyházak és szekták lelkészeiről, hitoktatóiról, szerzeteseiről és predikátorairól. HBMB 41 f., 2 f. cs., 72 őe. Az egyházakról és egyházi vezetőiről.

HB10/1950. "Egyházak tevékenysége Hajdú vármegyében." HBMB 41 f., 2 f. cs., 72 őe. Az egyházak és egyházi vezető személyek munkájával kapcsolatos iratok, jelentések, levelek.

HB11/1953. "Megyénk területén a klerikális reakció munkájának kiértékelése és új munkamódszere." Hajdú-Bihar Megyei Tanács VB. egyházügyi előadójának iratai 1949–56. XXIII 24.1 d.

HB16/1955. "Munkaterv 1955. február 1-től április 30-ig." Hajdú-Bihar Megyei Tanács VB. egyházügyi előadójának iratai 1949–56 XXIII 24.1 d.

HB19/1959. "Jelentés Hajdú-Bihar megye egyházpolitikai helyzetéről." HBMB 1f. PMO 0010/39/1959.

Bibliography

HB21/1962. "Feljegyzés: a református egyház milyen módszerekkel és milyen koncepció alapján foglalkozik az ifjúsággal." Kelt Debrecen, április 12, 1962. HBMB 1f. 1960–1. Egyházügyi iratok.

HB22/1962. "1962. I. negyedévi eseményekről jelentés." HBMB 1f. 1960–1. Egyházügyi iratok Ag/68/1/62.

HB23/1962. "Az egyházak tevékenysége Hajdú-Bihar megyében a mezőgazdaság átszervezésének idején és után." HBMB 1f. 1960–1. Egyházügyi iratok 0076/1962.

HB26/1962. "Reakciós papokkal való beszélgetésről jelentés." HBMB 1f. 1960–1 Egyházügyi iratok 0046/1962.

HB31/1961. "Elsőáldozásról, bérmálásról, úrnapi körmenetről és konfirmációról jelentés." HBMB 1f. 1960–1. Egyházügyi iratok 203/1961.

HB37/1961. Untitled report on religious instruction in the schools. HBMB 1f. 1960–1. Egyházügyi iratok Ag/220/1/61.

HB39/1960. "Melléklet az 1959/60. tanévvégi jelentéshez." HBMB 1f. 1960–1. Egyházügyi iratok Ag/208/1/60.

HB43/1959. "Feljegyzés az 1959. június 26-,27-én tartott hittanbeírással kapcsolatos hangulatról." HBMB 1f. 1960–1. Egyházügyi iratok Agit/141/1.

HB44/1959. "Az 1959. évi június 26,-27-én megtartott hittanbeírásról összefoglaló jelentés." HBMB 1f. 1960–1. Egyházügyi iratok 0010/20/TÜK.

HB45/1959. "1958/59.-es tanév hittanoktatásának értékelő, valamint az 1959/60-as tanév hittanbeiratásának jelentése." HBMB 1f. 1960–1. Egyházügyi iratok.

HB46/1959. "Javaslat a megyei ateista propaganda munka megszervezésére." HBMB 1f. 1960–1. Egyházügyi iratok Agit/176/1.

HB49/1959. "Határozati javaslat a vallásos világnézet elleni harc feladatairól Hajdú-Bihar megyében." HBMB 1f. 1960–1. Egyházügyi iratok /AgitProp/.

HB64/1964. "Jelentés az 1964-75. évi hittanbeiratásokról." HBMB 1.f. 2.fcs. 30 őe. Egyházügyi főelőadó jelentései. Ag/103/1/64.

HB89/1965. "Jelentés az 1965-66. évi hittanbeiratásokról." HBMB 1.f. 2. fcs. 29 őe, 1965. Egyházügyi főelőadó jelentései.

HB116/1970. "Jelentés az 1970-71. évi hittanbeiratásokról." IV/30. 1.f. 10. fcs. Egyházügyi ügyek.

HB134/1975. "Az 1975/76. tanévi hittanbeiratások adatainak összesítő táblázata." 1.f. IV. f.cs. Egyházpolitika 29 őe. PMO/182/1/75.

Hungarian National Archive

M05/1959. "Jelentés és javaslat a Hazafias Népfront Bizottságok pap tagjainak tevékenységéről." XIX A-21-e-0012-4/1959. (18.d.)

M39/1958. "Tájékoztató az 1957/58. évi hittanbeiratásról, a hitoktatás néhány tapasztalatáról." MOL XIX-A-21-e-25-1/1958. (16.d.)

M40/1958. "Jelentés az általános iskolában folyó vallásoktatás helyzetéről, problémáiról." MOL XIX-A-21-e-25-3/1958. (16.d.)

M43/1958. "Az 1958/59. tanévi hittanbeiratások lefolyása." MOL XIX-A-21-c-25-6/a/1958. (16.d.)

M45/1958. "Jelentés az 1958/59. tanévi hittanbeiratásokról." XIX-A-21-e-25-7/1958. (16.d.)

M46/1958. "Az elmúlt év tapasztalatai a vallásoktatásról." MOL XIX-A-21-e-25-6/b/1958. (16.d.)

M47/1958. "Hittanbeiratásról jelentés." MOL XIX-A-21-e-25-6/d/1958. (16.d.)

M48/1959. "Hitoktató értekezlet anyagának felterjesztése." MOL XIX-A-21-e-25-1/1959. (16.d.)

M50/1962. "Hittanbeiratásokról jelentés." XIX-A-21-e-25-7/e/1962. (16.d.)

M61/1964. "A hittanbeiratásokról jelentés." XIX-A-21-e-25-7/c/1964. (16.d.)

M63/1964. "Jelentés az 1964-65. évi hittanbeiratásokról." XIX-A-21-e-25-7/g/1964. (16.d.)

Reformed Church Archive, Debrecen

Ref32/1951. Untitled. TtRel I.1.C. 523 d.

Ref34/1951. "Kivonat a békési református egyházmegye 1951. okt. 19.–én Békéscsabán tartott közgyűlésének jegyzőkönyvéből." TtRel I.1.C. 526 d.

Ref36/1951. "Esperesi jelentés. Felolvastatott a Bihar-Érmelléki egyházmegye Debrecenben, 1951. október 24-én tartott közgyűlésén." TtRel I.1.C. 526 d.

Ref92/1949. "Jelentés a vallásoktatás megindulásáról és mostani állapotáról 1949.-50. iskolai év." TtRel. I.31.h.42.

Ref96/1949. "Jelentés a vallásoktatásban a legutóbbi két hét alatt történt zavaró változásokról." TtRel. I.31.h.42.

Ref97/1950. "Jelentés a vallásoktatás állapotáról 1950. januártól május hó 15-ig." TtRel. I.31.h.42.

Ref104/1951. Untitled. TtRel I. 27.c.37.4 d.

Ref115/1952. "Körlevél valamennyi gyülekezet lelkipásztorához." Kelt június 26. TtRel I.28.j.18.

Ref116/1952. "Körlevél valamennyi gyülekezet lelkipásztorához." Kelt március 25. TtRel I.28.j.18.

Ref117/1952. "Körlevél valamennyi gyülekezet lelkipásztorához." Kelt március 17. TtRel I.28.j.18.

Ref123/1953. "Körlevél valamennyi esperesi hivatalnak." Kelt június 8. TtRel I.28.j.18.

Ref124/1953. "Körlevél valamennyi gyülekezet lelkipásztorához." Kelt március 27. TtRel I.28.j.18.

Ref138/1957. "Körlevél valamennyi egyházközség lelkipásztorához az 1957/58. tanévi vallásoktatási beiratás tárgyában." TtRel I. 28.j.18.

Ref140/1958. "Előadás a Nagykunsági egyházmegye 1958. október 9-én, Szolnokon tartott gyűlésén." TtRel I.27.c.35.

Ref186/1982. "A szocializmus programja megfelel az emberszeretet követelményeinek." TtRel I.2.33.

Bibliography

Szabolcs-Szatmár-Bereg County Archive

Sz6/1964. Untitled. 1964 Report on religious instruction, with a table. MSZMP Baktalórántházai Bizottsága és alapszervezetei iratai XXVII 402. 2. VII. 1956–70, 6 őe.

Sz7/1964. Untitled. Report on the development of religious ideology. MSZMP Baktalórántházai Bizottsága és alapszervezetei iratai XXVII 402. 2. VII. 1956–70, 6 őe.

Sz9/1966. "Jelentés az 1966/67.-es tanév hittanbeiratásáról." MSZMP Baktalórántházai Bizottsága és alapszervezetei iratai XXVII 402. 2. VII. 1956–70, 6 őe.

Sz10/1969. "Kimutatás az 1969/70-es tanév hittanbeiratásáról a baktalórántházi járásban." MSZMP Baktalórántházai Bizottsága és alapszervezetei iratai XXVII 402. 2. VII. 1956–70, 6 őe.

Sz37/1955. "Kimutatás párttag szülőkről, akik hittanra iratták gyermeküket, az 1955/56 tanévre." MDP Fehérgyarmati Bizottsága iratai XXVII 323 39.2, 1948–56, 42 őe.

Sz38/1956. "Jelentés azokról a pártvezetőségi és párttagokról, akik karácsonyi szentmisén voltak." MDP Fehérgyarmati Bizottsága iratai XXVII 323 39.2, 1948–56, 42 őe.

Sz39/1956. "Az egyházi szertartásokon résztvett párttagokról jelentés." MDP Fehérgyarmati Bizottsága iratai XXVII 323 39.2, 1948–56, 42 őe.

Sz63/1952. "Hittanbeiratás." MDP Nyíregyháza Városi Bizottsága XXVII 312 43.2 1948–56 34 őe.

Sz66/1954. "Jelentés a hittanbeiratásokról." MDP Nyíregyháza Városi Bizottsága XXVII 312 43.2 1948–56 34 őe.

Sz67/1954. Untitled. MDP Nyíregyháza Városi Bizottsága XXVII 312 43.2 1948–56 34 őe.

Sz69/1955. "Jelentés az úrnapi körmenetről és a hittanbeiratásokkal kapcsolatos előkészületekről." MDP Nyíregyháza Városi Bizottsága XXVII 312 43.2 1948–56 34 őe.

Veszprém Archepiscopal Archive

Veszprém Érseki Levéltár Egyházmegyei Iktató 1957, 1958, and 1959.

Ve4/1957. "Marcaltői plébános jelentése hitoktatói ügyében." Veszprém Érseki Levéltár. Egyházügyi akták. 5401.3/1957.

Ve13/1959. "A csurgói Szentlélek Plébánia hivataltól." Veszprém Érseki Levéltár. Egyházügyi akták. 5401.57/1959.

Ve25/1959. Untitled letter from Szilárd Bakos Szabó. 121/1959. Originating in Pacsa, June 28, 1959. Veszprém Érseki Levéltár. Egyházügyi akták. 5401.49/1959.

Ve27/1959. Untitled minutes of clerical meeting. Created in Tapolca, October 15, 1959. Veszprém Érseki Levéltár. Egyházügyi akták. 2801.40/1959.

Ve28/1959. "A Füredi Esperesi kerületnek Balatonakaliban 1959. okt. 1-én tartott őszi tanácskozásról felvett jegyzőkönyve." Veszprém Érseki Levéltár. Egyházügyi akták. 2801.44/1959.

Ve29/1959. Untitled minutes of clerical meeting from the Keszthely and Zalaszentgrót clerical districts. Veszprém Érseki Levéltár. Egyházügyi akták. 2801.52/1959.

Index

Adenauer, Konrad, 34
ÁEH. *See* State Office for Church
  Affairs
agricultural collectivization in Hungary
  Communist Party (Hungary) and,
    173–7, 183
  Greek Catholic Church and, 177
  incentives, 174
  local elites and, 175
  propaganda, 174
  Reformed Church and, 175, 176
  religious instruction in Hungarian
    public schools and, 183–6
  religious life and, 186–8
  Roman Catholic Church and, 175,
    176–7
Alliance of Free Democrats (SZDSZ),
  31, 60, 61, 62, 63, 64, 65
Alliance of Young Democrats (Fidesz),
  60, 61, 62, 63, 64, 233. *See also*
  Alliance of Young Democrats-
  Hungarian Civic Party
  (Fidesz-MPP)
Alliance of Young Democrats-
  Hungarian Civic Party
  (Fidesz-MPP), 62, 64–5, 212.
  See also Alliance of Young
  Democrats (Fidesz)
Antall, József, 6, 30

Bács-Kiskun, 7, 68–70, 150–1, 251
Baranya, 7, 68–70, 251

Bartha, Bishop Tibor, 180
BBWR. *See* Non-Party Bloc for the
  Support of Reforms
Békés, 7, 68–70, 251
Bereczky, Bishop Albert, 86, 103, 105,
  133, 180
Beresztóczy, Miklós, 121
Bethlen, István, 30
Bihar. *See* Hajdú-Bihar
Borsod-Abaúj. *See* Borsod-Abaúj-
  Zemplén
Borsod-Abaúj-Zemplén, 7, 68–70, 121,
  177, 251
Budapest, 67, 161, 194
Bulányi, György, 182

Calvinist Church in Hungary. *See*
  Reformed Church in Hungary
Casaroli, Monsignor Agostino, 178
Catholic Bench of Bishops, 107–8,
  109–10, 136, 154, 155–6, 157,
  176–7
Catholic Center Party (Germany), 34
Catholic Church in Hungary. *See*
  Roman Catholic Church in
  Hungary
Chile, 4–5
Christian Democratic People's Party
  (KDNP), 31, 60, 61–2, 63, 64,
  65, 212, 226–8, 233
Christian Democratic Union
  (Germany), 34

Index